PEACE AND WAR IN THE MODERN AGE

PEACE AND WAR IN THE MODERN AGE

Premises, Myths, and Realities

Editors

FRANK R. BARNETT

WILLIAM C. MOTT

JOHN C. NEFF

ANCHOR BOOKS
DOUBLEDAY & COMPANY, INC.
GARDEN CITY, NEW YORK

The Anchor Books edition is the first publication of
*Peace and War in the Modern Age: Premises, Myths,
and Realities*

Anchor Books edition: 1965

FRANK R. BARNETT is President of the National Strategy Information Center, Inc., and Consulting Program Manager for the American Bar Association Standing Committee on Education Against Communism. He is a native of Illinois and a graduate of Wabash College. As an internationally known expert on Communist strategy, he has lectured to U. S. Armed Forces Staff and War colleges, and the NATO Defense College in Paris. He has also addressed many national conventions of civic and professional organizations, including the Chamber of Commerce of the United States, the National Association of Manufacturers, and the Reserve Officers Association. During World War II he became a Russian interpreter for the 69th Infantry Division, which met the Red Army on the Elbe River in April 1945. Before the war he was a student of geopolitics, Russian language, and history at Syracuse University. After serving as a Military Government official in Berlin, he won a Rhodes Scholarship from Indiana and read philosophy, politics, and economics at Oxford University. Mr. Barnett helped to initiate the first National Strategy Seminar for Reserve Officers held in the summer of 1959 at the National War College in Washington, D.C., and has served on the faculty of each subsequent seminar held there.

WILLIAM C. MOTT, Rear Admiral, U.S.N. (Ret.), was the Judge Advocate General of the Navy at the time of his retirement April 1, 1964. A native of New Jersey, he graduated from the United States Naval Academy in 1933, and subsequently received his law degree from the George Washington University Law School. After practicing law for a number of years, he returned to the Navy and during World War II participated in several combat operations in the Pacific, including the Marianas, Iwo Jima, and Okinawa. For exceptionally meritorious service he was awarded the Legion of Merit with Combat Citation. Admiral Mott gained experience in negotiating with the Communists while representing the U.S. at many international conferences. He served as an aide to President Roosevelt and did special work for succeeding Presidents. He also served as aide to two Chairmen of the Joint Chiefs of Staff. He is a Fellow of the American Bar Association, a member of the American Society of International Law, and a member of the American Bar Association Standing Committee on Education Against Communism. He has been a professional writer and speaker for many years. Admiral Mott is now Executive Vice President of the United States Independent Telephone Association in Washington.

JOHN C. NEFF, Colonel, U.S.A.R. (Ret.), is co-editor of *American Strategy for the Nuclear Age,* a Doubleday Anchor Book published in 1960. Since retiring as Chief of Staff of the 77th Infantry Division of the Army Reserve in 1962, he has devoted much of his time to preparing research studies of Communism. He attended the first National Strategy Seminar for Reserve Officers at the National War College in 1959 and served there as a staff assistant during the seminar in 1960. During World War II he served in the Intelligence Section of the 83d Infantry Division in the European Theater and for his services was awarded the Bronze Star with Cluster, the Croix de Guerre, and the Legion of Honor. A native of Ohio, he graduated from Kenyon College in 1936, and has published articles, book reviews, and stories in several national magazines including the *Army Information Digest, Collier's,* and the Sunday New York *Times* Book Review. In recent years Colonel Neff served on the staff of The Richardson Foundation in New York City, and is now Vice President of the National Strategy Information Center, Inc.

TABLE OF CONTENTS

EDITORS' NOTE   XV

PREFACE   1

PROLOGUE: Unilateral Disarmament:
A Case History, *by Donald Armstrong*   5

PART ONE—THE HISTORICAL SETTING   15

Introduction   15

1. Power and Peace, *by Arleigh Burke*   17

Power Processes among Nations—The Essential
Elements of Peace—Collapse of the Concert of
Europe—Power Alone Is Not Enough—The Con-
frontation Is Absolute—The Struggle for Men's
Minds—The Myth of "World Opinion"—Power
and Peace: An Opportunity for the West

2. The Cold War: Origins and Development,
by Paul C. Davis   36

The Beginnings—The Continuing Revolution—
Soviet Expansionism—American Countermoves—
Communist Threat to Western Europe: Ameri-
can Reaction—The Strategy of Peaceful Coex-
istence—Piecemeal Reaction by the U.S.—Guer-
rilla Warfare—Changes in Soviet Strategy and
Tactics—Subversion of Peoples and Political
Structures—A Challenge for the Sixties

3. The Mainsprings of Soviet Secrecy,
    by Walter F. Hahn   50

    Ethnic, Historical, and Cultural Factors—Rus-
    sian Historical Experience—The "Peasant Men-
    tality"—Secrecy and the Russian Authoritarian
    Tradition—The Communist Contribution to the
    Secrecy Complex—The Conspiratorial Nature of
    the Party—Prevention of Invidious Comparison
    —Maintenance of Ideological Conformity—The
    Dogma of Progress and the "Conniving So-
    ciety"—Retention of the Image of a Hostile
    World—Some Implications for U.S. Policy—Con-
    clusion

PART TWO—THE WORLD IN FLUX   73

Introduction   73

4. Withdrawal from Europe? An Illusion,
    by Dean Acheson   75

    Three Centuries of Involvement—The Need for
    European and North American Cooperation—
    Soviet Countermoves—Germany's Role Defined
    —The Development of Atlantic and European
    Unity—NATO's Army—The French Nuclear
    Program—German-American Collaboration—In-
    ternational Monetary Arrangements

5. The United Nations Reconsidered,
    by Raymond A. Moore, Jr.   87

    The Crisis of Confidence—Is the UN Living Up
    to Its Charter?—A Mirror of World Politics—
    Domination by the Afro-Asian Bloc?—Changes
    in the Secretariat—Soviet Espionage and the UN
    —The Problem of Finances—The UN: Corner-
    stone of U.S. Foreign Policy?—Improving the

UN—Positive Achievements—Regional Security
Arrangements—Conclusion

6. Perspectives for Eastern Europe,
   by *Richard V. Burks*   107

   Ideology and National Interest—Increased Contacts with the West—Emergence of Public Opinion—Development of Mixed Economies—Coun-
   terforces and Countertrends—Conclusion

7. How Monolithic Was the Monolith?,
   by *Robert V. Daniels*   125

   Early Schisms in Marxism—The Romantics and
   the Pragmatists—Establishment of the Monolith
   —The Stalin Revolution—The World Movement
   Unharnessed—Conclusion

PART THREE—COMMUNIST IDEOLOGY, STRATEGY, AND
      TACTICS   141

Introduction   141

8. The Strategy of Peaceful Coexistence,
   by *Richard V. Allen*   143

   What Is Peaceful Coexistence?—Strategy or
   Tactic?—A Form of Class Struggle—Agreements
   with the Enemy—Communist "Humaneness"—
   A Strategic Doctrine—What Does Peaceful Co-
   existence Accomplish?—The Challenge to the
   West—End of the Cold War?

9. Cuba: Thoughts Prompted by the Crisis,
   by *Charles Burton Marshall*   161

   Why the Russians Are There—Afterthoughts on
   the Blockade—A Game of One-Upmanship—Is
   the Charter Obsolete?—Hide and Seek: Dour

Thoughts on Inspection—Natural Law and In-
spected Truth—Intrusion and Inspection

10. Communists in Coalition Governments,
    by Gerhart Niemeyer   179

The Five Elements of Coalition Agreements—
Communist Orientation toward the Future—
Occupation of Positions of Power—Legitimiza-
tion of Power—Elimination of Rival Parties—
Control of the Masses—The Use of Terror—Fatal
Illusions about Coalitions—Conclusion

11. Communist Pre-Insurgency Techniques,
    by Franklin M. Osanka   196

Insurgents' Operational Environment—The Insurgent Organizers—Identification Phase—Propagation Phase—Organization Phase—Insurgency
Population Control—Conclusion

12. The Role of Intelligence in the Cold War,
    by Allen W. Dulles   205

The Secret Penetration of Free States—The Soviet Blueprint for World Domination—U.S. Reactions—The Soviet Apparatus for Subversion—
Communist Front Organizations—Infiltration of
Target Governments—The Scope of Soviet Propaganda—What the U.S. Can Do—Vulnerabilities
of Communist Subversion—The Choices We
Must Make

PART FOUR—ALTERNATE STRATEGIES: THE CONTINU-
ING DEBATE   223

Introduction   223

13. Strategic Goals in Soviet Policy,
    by Robert D. Crane   225

    The Goal of Economic Growth—The Goal of
    Equal Strategic Power—The Goal of Strategic
    Supremacy—Conclusion

14. How Strong, How Weak Is the Soviet Union,
    by Robert Strausz-Hupé   244

    Some Weaknesses of Russian-Based Commu-
    nism—A Despotic Bureaucracy Topped by an
    Autocracy—Often Repeated Promises of an Im-
    proved Economy—Changes in the Commu-
    nist World—Stresses and Strains Within the
    Communist Bloc—Communist Mastery at Psy-
    chological Strategy—The Myth about "Opening
    Up" Communist Society—The Soviets' Greatest
    Vulnerability—The West's Greatest Weakness

15. Shifts in Soviet Strategic Thought,
    by Thomas W. Wolfe   257

    Soviet Strategy by Marshal Sokolovskii—A Try-
    ing Period for Soviet Leaders—The Main Ele-
    ment of Soviet Military Power—Local and
    Limited Wars—The Balance of Military Power

16. Soviet Education for Scientific and Technical
    Supremacy, *by Nicholas DeWitt*   271

    The Soviet Commitment to Functional Educa-
    tion—Education in the U.S. and U.S.S.R.: Basic
    Differences—Educational Trends in the U.S.S.R.
    —Two Central Problems—Educational Reform—
    Science Education: "The Light and Hope of Hu-
    manity"—Conclusions

17. Peace in Our Time?, *by Hans J. Morgenthau*   283

    The Lesson of Neville Chamberlain Unlearned

—The Myth of "Relaxations of Tensions"—Origin and Nature of the Cold War—The Substance and Modalities of the Cold War—The Soviet Union Faces a Triple Crisis—The Folly of the Commercial Approach—Soviet Alternatives—Conflicting Views of Trade

PART FIVE—THE ROLE OF THE MILITARY   295

Introduction   295

18. Military-Civilian Partnership in Educating to the
     Communist Threat, *by Dwight D. Eisenhower*   297

     Need for Non-Partisan Education on the Nature of the Communist Threat—The Appropriate Military Role in Helping to Inform the Non-Military in Respect to the Tactics, Strategy and Concepts of Communism—The Singular Qualifications of Senior Officers—The National War College Seminar for Reserve Officers—The Lesson of Korea—Military and Non-Military Strategy Closely Related—Informing the Public: The Rule of Reason—Communism Profits from Rigid Restrictions on U.S. Military—Absurdity of Charges that American Military Is Extremist or Politically Partisan—No Iron Curtain for American Military—Voluntary Cooperation Better than Censorship

19. The Challenge to Military Professionalism,
     by Robert N. Ginsburgh   306

     The Military's Sense of Corporateness—The Erosion of Authority—Military Expertise—The Scientist, Engineer, and Industrialist—The Growing Influence of the Lay Strategist—The Development of Greater Expertise—Solutions to the Problem

20. Security Is Too Important to Be Left to Computers, *by Colonel Francis X. Kane, U.S.A.F.* 323

The Marriage of Theory and Machine—"How Many Nuclear Wars Have You Fought?"—The Role of Intuition—The Key Role of Decision-making—A Search for Insights—Calling All Philosophers

PART SIX—WHAT FORWARD STRATEGY FOR AMERICA? 337

Introduction 337

21. Why We Treat Different Communist Countries Differently, *by Dean Rusk* 341

Communist Designs—Our First Objective—Working for Peaceful Progress—Trying to Reduce the Risk of War—Our View of Communism—Economic Shortcomings of Communism—Policy toward Various Communist States—The Threat of Communist China—The Castro Regime in Cuba—Our Goal Remains Constant

22. Exploiting Communist Vulnerabilities, *by Richard L. Walker* 353

The Nature of the Opponent—Our Own Condition—Communist Weaknesses—Our Experiences to Date—Developing a Winning Strategy

23. The Cold War of Words, *by John Richardson, Jr.* 371

The Communist Compulsion to Control Thinking—Opportunities for the West—Radio Free Europe—The Impact of RFE Broadcasts—Communist Attacks against RFE—Benefits to the West—Conclusions

24. Planning in Foreign Affairs: The Missing Ele-
     ment, *by Franklin A. Lindsay*   386

     Program Planning—Examples of Inadequate
     Planning and Research—Why the Lack of Pro-
     gram Planning?—The Need for Greater Institu-
     tionalization—An Illustration of Planning Needed
     —Summary

25. Public Opinion, the Private Sector and National
     Defense, *by Frank R. Barnett*   401

     Political Warfare Defined—Other Forms of Non-
     military Warfare—A Lesson from Cuba—The
     Question of Public Opinion—Assumption #1:
     The Profile of Future Conflict—Assumption #2:
     Changing Nature of the Threat—Assumption #3:
     No Stalemate in the 20th Century—Assumption
     #4: The Importance of Public Opinion and the
     Private Sector—The American Bar Association:
     A Case Study of Action by a Professional So-
     ciety—Trade and Professional Association Semi-
     nars—Action Programs—Propaganda Analysis Is
     Everybody's Business—Appendix

EDITORS' NOTE

This book is published under the auspices of two organizations: the National Strategy Information Center, Inc., 130 East 67th Street, New York, New York 10021; and The Institute of Fiscal and Political Education, 225 East 46th Street, New York, New York 10017. The National Strategy Information Center is a tax-exempt, educational corporation organized to broaden public understanding of the meaningful differences between the major competing social systems and of the methods and aims of their historic rivalry. The Center provides speakers, educational materials, and consulting services to national associations and societies as well as to university workshops for high school teachers studying totalitarianism versus freedom. The Center is nonprofit and nonpartisan. Its President and Chief Executive Officer is Frank R. Barnett.

The Institute of Fiscal and Political Education, also a nonprofit and tax-exempt corporation, is chartered by the Board of Regents of the University of the State of New York. Its purpose is to promote the broadest possible understanding in the areas of fiscal and political education by publication of pamphlets, textbooks, and other teaching materials and by collaboration with institutions of higher learning and secondary education. John Marshall is President of the Institute; Donald Armstrong, Vice President; and Harry G. Marquis, Secretary and Treasurer.

This volume could not have been prepared without the permission of copyright owners to use their materials. For their generous cooperation the editors are indebted. The editors also wish to thank the many individuals in government, universities, research centers, the publishing profession, and private life who made valuable comments and recommendations regarding the contents of this book. The editors are especially grateful for the assistance of these people in the tasks of preparing typescripts and proofreading: Frank O'Regan, Marjorie Barnett, Dorothy E. Nicolosi, and Robert E. Maxwell.

FRANK R. BARNETT

New York City   WILLIAM C. MOTT
September 30, 1964   JOHN C. NEFF

The articles in this book were written before the deposing of Khrushchev, the subsequent changes in the Kremlin, and the shifting power relationships of the various Communist parties of Russia, China, and Eastern Europe. Does this mean that these analyses are obsolete? Will not new men bring new brooms to Red Square? Inevitably, this question is debated in London, Paris, and Washington, since "politics" in the Western arena is so intimately based on personality and individual style. In the West, a wealthy, Catholic liberal (intellectual, aristocratic, detached) views the world and the shape of the future from a perspective quite different from the *Weltanschauung* of a middle class, Baptist conservative (shrewd, folksy, devout). The presuppositions, life experiences, and touchstones for decision-making of such men can differ sharply—and hence their choice of political objectives, priorities, and policy advisers.

While all men are different, the hierarchical chiefs of a Communist church militant, steeped in the same dogma for nearly fifty years, are not likely to entertain premises or develop outlooks that diverge in any pronounced degree from established Party tenets. Tactical differences, yes; heresies, most improbable; disavowal, no! Moreover, while the President of the United States or the Prime Minister of Great Britain is subject to all the diverse pressures of a pluralistic society, the harassment of the Loyal Opposition, and the surveillance of a free press, Russian dictators, especially in time of transition, need bid for the support of three groups only: Party, military, and secret police. Since these three have an enormous vested interest in the maintenance of a paramilitary State governed by an ideological elite, the "personality" of a

Communist boss is not likely to alter substantially the main direction of events.

To change the analogy, however good or bad the actors, *Hamlet* is always a tragedy. The cast of players may change; the structure of the drama remains the same. At the end, almost everyone of consequence lies dead on stage. Give *Hamlet* a happy ending, turn it into musical comedy, and it is no longer *Hamlet* or Shakespeare. On the world stage of the twentieth century, the name of the drama is Communist Imperialism. The playwright is still Lenin. (All of the competing factions in Russia, China, and Eastern Europe pledge their adherence to his script and, indeed, assail their rivals for departing from Leninist lines.) We must not become so bemused with the performance of understudies that we forget the purpose and mighty intellect of him who fashioned a global drama, whose first two acts presage universal tragedy for free men if they do not address themselves more intelligently to the theater of conflict. As an illustration of the persistent influence of Lenin, here is a quote from Leonid Brezhnev's maiden speech, welcoming the three Soviet cosmonauts to the celebrations in Red Square immediately following Khrushchev's fall from power:

> The general line of our party worked out by its 20th, 21st and 22d congresses is a Leninist line. It was, is and will be the only immutable line in the entire domestic and foreign policy of the Communist party and the Soviet state.
>
> The party sees its supreme duty in serving the people, in strengthening the might of our Socialist country, adding to its glory and prestige, consistently and unswervingly implementing the great ideas of Marxism-Leninism. . . .
>
> The Central Committee of the C.P.S.U. and all our party, aware of their high responsibility for the destinies of the country, are determined to carry into life undeviatingly the Leninist principles of guiding the life of the party and state, and follow consistently the Leninist path.

It is not without significance that, in 1964, forty years after Lenin's death, three American publishers brought forth the biography of that dramatist whose works predetermine the behavior of Mao and Stalin, Khrushchev and Che Guevara,

Ho Chi-minh and Suslov, Brezhnev and all the other chief actors on the Communist stage. It is not amiss to quote from the Preface to one of those biographies;* for, whatever voice is heard temporarily in the perpetual clamor of the rival factions, the hand is the hand of Lenin.

The reign of Lenin, the first revolutionary tsar of Russia, lasted from November, 1917, to January, 1924. During these seventy-five months he was incapacitated for almost twenty of them, and he operated at reduced efficiency for about ten more. In all, his effective rule lasted less than four years; yet in this short span of time he influenced the course of world history more profoundly than any other ruler of the twentieth century.

Lenin was a thinker, a political boss and a strategist. As a thinker, he combined Marx with the Russian revolutionary tradition and integrated the new amalgam with Machiavelli and Clausewitz. As a political boss, Lenin invented new political techniques and organizations and put in motion a world-wide totalitarian movement. As a strategist, he introduced novel combinations of violent and non-violent combat, conquered a great empire, and conceived the multi-dimensional war of the modern age.

Lenin started communism—or Russia—on the road to world domination. He begot the victories which Stalin, his successor, won twenty years after his death. By way of historical parallel, Lenin may well be compared to Philip of Macedon, who prepared for the victories of Alexander the Great; but Lenin's role also resembled that of Aristotle, who functioned as Alexander's intellectual guide.

The great world struggle between freedom and totalitarianism which Lenin initiated has lasted for more than four decades. Presumably it will continue for several more generations, and it may terminate in nuclear war. The outcome of the conflict which Lenin bequeathed to mankind will probably for several centuries determine the fate of the human race.

* Stefan T. Possony, *Lenin: The Compulsive Revolutionary* (Chicago: Henry Regnery Co., 1964).

PROLOGUE:
UNILATERAL DISARMAMENT:
A CASE HISTORY

by Donald Armstrong

> *Commissioned a Second Lieutenant, Coast Artillery Corps in 1910, Brigadier General Donald Armstrong, U.S.A. (Ret.), has had distinguished careers in the Army, industry, the Foreign Service, and education. He graduated from many U.S. and French military schools and was former Commandant of both the Industrial College of the Armed Forces and the National Strategy Seminars for Reserve Officers at the National War College. While on duty in the War Department he was also for two years Professorial Lecturer in the Classics Department of George Washington University.*

This article, based on material in the author's recently completed manuscript, tentatively entitled *Cold War in a Toga, Its Roots and Consequences in the Fall of Carthage,* was originally published in 1963 as a *World Affairs* pamphlet by the American Peace Society. Reprinted by permission.

Twenty-one centuries ago, a certain nation so loved peace that no price to keep the peace was too exorbitant. It faced a ruthless enemy, but it abandoned war as an instrument of policy. It tied its hands by giving three hundred young noblemen as hostages to prove its peaceful intentions. It surrendered unconditionally when the enemy declared war. Finally, on the enemy's demand, it disarmed unilaterally. Appeasement could go no further.

We might suppose the millennium had arrived. Surely now

the lion and the lamb would lie down together in peace and harmony. But there was more agony to come, and that is the theme of this story of the death of a nation. War or peace is a two-sided thing. Wanting peace is no insurance against brutal and militaristic imperialism.

This is a tale of two cities and of the ultimate violence and fraud of one of them in destroying the other. To begin with, the origins of both were insignificant. Tradition records the birth of Carthage in 814 B.C. and of Rome sixty-one years later. Exploration and maritime trade eventually made Carthage the queen of the Mediterranean. Rome grew by military conquest of its neighbors in the Italian peninsula. But when Carthage had become a glittering metropolis, lording it over a loosely knit empire stretching for hundreds of miles along the North African and Spanish coasts, parts of Sicily, and the other Mediterranean islands, Rome was still a collection of mud huts on its seven hills by the Tiber. For centuries there was no conflict between Carthage and Rome. But in 264 B.C. Roman expansion reached the Straits of Messina and crossed to Sicily. The epic conflict commenced.

In the First Punic War, lasting from 264 to 241 B.C., Carthage lost her navy and her command of the sea. She also lost Sicily. A fearful mutiny of her army of mercenaries joined by the ill-treated native Africans nearly destroyed Carthage in a war of three years. At its end, Rome declared the unnumbered, unfought Punic War. Carthage, unable to resist, surrendered with the loss of all her island colonies and a heavy indemnity. In 218 B.C. Hannibal led his army from Spain across the Alps. He destroyed many Roman armies, and occupied Italy for sixteen years; but unsupported from home, he was ordered to return and suffered defeat at Zama in 202 B.C. Thus ended what is called the Second Punic War; Carthage, deprived of all her possessions, except the territory contiguous to her city (roughly modern Tunisia) settled down to a life of foreign commerce which prospered and quickly restored her wealth.

But Rome had strengthened the kingdom of Numidia lying between Carthage and the former Carthaginian possessions in Spain. It was originally a buffer state. In time it became much more—Rome's proxy power to weaken Carthage as Roman imperialism and lust for power grew by what it fed on. Eventually Numidia under its remarkable king, Masinissa, so weakened its neighbor by the salami tactics of slicing off, bit by bit, half of the territory and resources of Carthage that, when we reach the last stage of the protracted cold war, Carthage was a shadow of its former self.

Rome used all the tools of modern cold war against Carthage; we can only emphasize here that fraud and deceit, blackmail by terror, subversion, psychological warfare, and a proxy power figured prominently in her unorthodox warfare. The greatest of these by far were Masinissa's depredations—Rome's proxy power. For Rome's peace treaty of 201 B.C., severe as the Treaty of Versailles after the First World War, kept Carthage under close control. For nearly fifty years, in successive Roman arbitrations of the border dispute between Carthage and Masinissa, Roman envoys decided the issues, always in favor of Numidia, with one exception—in 152 B.C. In that year, in my opinion to delude the Carthaginians by a shift from a hard to a soft line so familiar to us in our own cold war, and to enable Rome to arm Masinissa for a major campaign against Carthage in 151 B.C., Rome gave Carthage the decision.

But in 153 B.C. a new commission had reached Carthage. At its head was Rome's most famous citizen, Marcus Cato. This octogenarian observed Carthage closely. His fear and hatred and jealousy of Carthage hurried him back to report to the Roman Senate; *"Carthago delenda est"* was his urgent message. "Carthage must be destroyed." Alongside these well-known words from antiquity demanding war we, in our day, hear a *prediction*, not a plea, for action—Khrushchev's "We shall bury you."

The Roman Senate decided on war, then and there in 153 B.C. But they were not yet ready to fight. Their cold war accelerated and at last when Roman agents had bribed or influenced Utica, the second Carthaginian city, to secede and become a Roman satellite, Rome declared war on Carthage. Utica, only twenty miles from Carthage, provided a perfect base for a Roman expeditionary force which, eighty-four thousand men and fifty triremes strong, invaded North Africa in the spring of 149 B.C.

Two old men, Masinissa and Cato had become the two chief gravediggers of Carthage. Appian, the Greek historian and friend of Rome, writes with some exaggeration that Masinissa "was a cause of the destruction of Carthage, having left it a prey to the Romans, completely deprived of strength." Plutarch reports that "it was largely in consequence of the advice and counsel of Cato that the Romans undertook the Third Punic War."

But the Romans were too wily and wise to fight a war if they could so weaken an enemy by blackmail of terror that it would surrender. Carthage in 149 B.C. sent successive delegations to Rome to ward off a war. Appeasement was stepped up. Nevertheless Rome had mobilized and sent its armed forces to threaten and blackmail Carthage. When Rome promised to maintain the autonomy of Carthage and allow business as usual, the plenipotentiaries agreed to unconditional surrender and, trusting in Roman good faith, to send three hundred hostages, sons of senators and of other distinguished citizens, to Rome.

The two Roman counsuls near Utica then called on the enemy to send a delegation to the Roman camp. The Carthaginian envoys were led to the counsuls through the long lines of the fully armed Roman legions. The counsul Censorinus spoke:

"If you are sincerely desirous of peace why do you need any arms? Come, surrender to us all your weapons and engines of war, both public and private."

The Carthaginians objected, but the objections were overruled. According to Appian, when Rome's disarmament commission finished its work Carthage delivered two hundred thousand sets of military equipment consisting of helmet, shield, breastplate, metal shinguards, swords, and spears and two thousand catapults, the artillery of those times. He adds that "it was a remarkable and unparalleled spectacle to behold the vast number of loaded wagons which the enemy themselves brought in."

Unilateral disarmament was the climax of the peace-at-any-price appeasement of Rome. Now, of course, Rome would call off its legions. Now all would be well with the world.

For Rome the cold war had reached its last act. It had succeeded beyond any conceivable hopes. The onetime rival of Rome in the western Mediterranean was now ready for the kill.

The Roman counsuls, after hearing the report of the armistice commission, which had returned to Utica when all armament had been delivered, summoned the envoys to learn the final condition for a peace treaty. This time Carthage had sent with the usual negotiators, "leading senators and citizens, priests and other distinguished persons, who hoped to inspire the counsuls with respect or pity for them." Now they stood with bowed heads before the counsuls.

Censorinus rose. With a frown on his face, he gazed on the Carthaginians. After a long silence, he spoke. This is what he said:

"Your ready obedience up to this point, Carthaginians, in the matter of the hostages and the arms, is worthy of all praise. But in cases of necessity, we must not multiply words. Bear bravely the remaining command of the Senate. Yield Carthage to us, and betake yourselves where you like within your own territory at a distance of at least ten miles from the sea, for we are resolved to raze your city to the ground."

Thunderstruck by Rome's cruel sentence, the cringing Carthaginians were changed instantaneously into wrathful men of infinite courage. They had no choice, however, but to carry the news to their senate. The folly of appeasement, of unilateral disarmament, of unconditional surrender had lost them their freedom. Rome had sentenced Carthage to a lingering death.

Obedience to Rome's command meant the loss of their homes and occupations, their commercial and naval harbors, their maritime commerce and their industries, their temples and public buildings. To build a new city would take years. Without their city walls, how could they defend themselves against Masinissa and Utica? Certainly, economic and political reasons moved these delegates to overt defiance.

Without hesitation, the Carthaginian senate, on hearing Rome's death sentence, declared war on the ruthless enemy.

In spite of their military impotence of their own creation, they preferred to fight for freedom. Peace at any price was forgotten. Zero will to resist was raised to a crescendo of indomitable will to die if necessary in defense of their country. It was a people's war from beginning to end. For three years they never faltered. For the first two years they won every fight—on the walls, in the streets, in the field. They had every reason to feel Rome would give up its costly siege and allow Carthage to survive. But starvation finally won for Rome what the Roman sword could not win. Carthage fell amid the flames of a burning city.

One last word on the marvelous transformation of these people. In the only record of an industrial mobilization I have ever discovered in extensive reading of most all Greek and Roman military history by ancient writers, Appian tells us that:

"All the sacred places, the temples, and every other wide and open space, were turned into workshops, where men and women worked together day and night, on a fixed schedule, without pause, eating by turns. Each day they made one hundred shields, three hundred swords, one thousand missiles for catapults, five hundred javelins and spears, and as many catapults as they could. For the torsion ropes to fire them, the women cut off their hair for want of other fibers."

The city's furnaces and forges by the hundreds, each small in size with only a few employees, worked hard to produce the metal parts of weapons and shields and helmets. The wood workers made the shafts for spears and the frames and other wooden parts for catapults. There was ample skilled labor, judging by the large production figures, usually employed in the arsenal and ship-building plants, to turn out daily this amazing quantity of weapons when aided by the eager volunteers—men, women, and children—and by the new manufacturing facilities hastily set up in the city.

At all events, this industrial mobilization met the needs of a growing army with sufficient weapons to win in the first two years of the war.

Alas, for Carthage, the amazing will to resist Rome's aggression came too late. The enemy's creeping advances, the deterioration of Carthaginian will during the cold war, their modest hope to maintain the status quo, combined to ensure the death of an empire.

Let us bear in mind the advice of Polybius and Santayana. The Greek historian and friend of Rome, who personally observed the last months of the Carthaginian struggle for survival, tells us that "we should regard as the best discipline for actual life the experience that accrues from serious history; for this alone makes us, without inflicting any harm on us, the most competent judges of what is best at every time and in every circumstance." (Polybius, *The Histories*, I, 35, 9–10).

And two millennia later, Santayana added: "Those who cannot remember the past are doomed to repeat it."

The Sources

Except for its topography, little trace of ancient Carthage has survived the destruction of 146 B.C. But historical sources have fared even worse. Not a single history of Carthage written by a Carthaginian, not one sample of its literature has escaped total loss. We know about Carthage and the Phoenicians in general only from books written by authors of nations known for their hostility to Carthage, i.e., the Hebrew writers of the Old Testament and the Greek and Roman historians. What is amazing, however, is the evidence we find in these histories of the Punic Wars, the 120-year conflict between Rome and Carthage, of Roman injustice and deception, especially in the latter years of that period.

What can be expected when a militaristic imperialism bent on world domination determines to bury a wealthy, peace-loving mercantile and industrialized rival? Polybius does not hesitate to state the issue. He writes, as he describes the beginnings of the Battle of Zama where Hannibal was defeated in 202 B.C.: "The Carthaginians [were] fighting for their own safety and the domination of Africa, and the Romans for the empire of the world." (Polybius, *The Histories*, XV, 9, 2). It is only from these sources that we learn to what depths of injustice and fraud and deception such an imperialism can descend.

Polybius (203–120 B.C.) was a native of a Greek city-state in the Peloponnese who reached Rome as one of a thousand Greek hostages after the Roman defeat of the Greek army at the Battle of Pydna, in 167 B.C. He was a well-educated, highly cultured man with much military and political experience. Polybius became an honored member of an aristocratic Roman intellectual group who loved and admired Greek civilization. In time he was made the tutor of the young Roman who would destroy Carthage in 146 B.C.—Scipio Africanus the Younger. His history of Rome sought to explain how it conquered and dominated the world in the years from 264 B.C. to 146 B.C.

Although Polybius admired Rome's constitution and her rise to empire, he did not hesitate to write that the war Rome declared against Carthage in 238 B.C., which I call "the unnumbered, unfought Punic War," was without "any reasonable pretext or cause" and the loss of Sardinia after Carthaginian surrender was "contrary to all justice." Other evidence of his objectivity can be cited, also observable in later historians who depended on him for the events of the Punic Wars.

Polybius wrote a history of forty books of which only the first five are intact. Fragments and excerpts of other books have reached us, but for the period of the last half century of Carthage very little has been salvaged. This is unfortunate because Polybius accompanied Scipio in 146 B.C., and witnessed the agony and fall of Carthage.

Certainly later historians followed Polybius's account of the Third Punic War. Internal evidence supports the view that Appian, a Greek historian and Roman official who flourished about A.D. 150, adheres closely to Polybius. At any rate his description of the so-called Third Punic War is the only fairly complete account of that war and fortunately it is the best book of his Roman history. Appian is neither a distinguished nor always a reliable historian, but there is less reason to question the accuracy of his Punic Wars than other portions of his work.

Other sources of value are Livy (59 B.C.–A.D. 17), whose

voluminous history of Rome was written to glorify his native
land and is frequently prejudiced and sometimes even false.
His books on the Third Punic War are also lost and only summaries survive. In Plutarch, in Diodorus Siculus (about 40
B.C.), and in Strabo (63 B.C.–A.D. 21) we find additional information relevant to the final fifty years of Carthaginian
history. The authors cited are all available in the Loeb Clas-
sical Library, which publishes the Greek or Latin text facing
the English translation.

The principal data on Carthaginian disarmament are as
follows:

Polybius (via Suidas) XXXVI, 6, 7
Appian, *The Punic Wars,* Chap. XII, 80
Livy, Vol. XIV, *Summaries,* p. 25
Strabo, *The Geography,* Vol. VIII, pp. 185–87

PART ONE

THE HISTORICAL SETTING

INTRODUCTION

They [the Russians] wish to rule the world by conquest; they mean to seize by armed force the countries accessible to them, and thence to oppress the rest of the world by terror. The extension of power they dream of is in no way either intelligent or moral; and if God grants it to them, it will be for the woe of the world.

The Marquis de Custine (1839)

The great issue of our time is which of these two concepts of a world order will prevail: freedom or coercion. And here let me say again something I have said on several occasions: The Communist goal, proclaimed in doctrine and supported in action, is world domination. Both of the main branches of the Communist movement have the same goal—even though they may differ over tactics. They have made it clear that by "peaceful coexistence," they mean a continuing attempt to spread their system over the earth by all means short of the great war which would be self-defeating. No one has to convince us the contest between freedom and Communist imperialism is for keeps. For this struggle is our first order of business in the State Department. And it must never cease to be our first order of business until a world-wide victory for peace and for freedom has been secured.

Dean Rusk (August 2, 1964)

The opinion also prevails, that ministers are constantly subjected to a system of espionage, and that even their Russian servants are made to disclose what passes in their household, their convictions, associates, and so forth. If therefore I do not write as often as may be desired, that is my apology. And if I do not furnish matter of more interest it must be attributed in part at least, to the great difficulty of obtaining correct information. No courtesy or liberality whatever, is shown in this particular by this Government. Secrecy and mystery characterize everything. Nothing is made public that is worth knowing unless it is for propaganda purposes . . .

> From a composite dispatch sent to the U. S. Department of State by Neil S. Brown and Thomas Seymore, American Ministers to the Court of Czar Nicholas I, 1850–54

Today it is the world socialist system and the forces fighting against imperialism for a socialist transformation of society that determine the main content, main trend, and main features of the historical development of society. Whatever efforts imperialism makes, it cannot stop the advance of history. A reliable basis has been provided for further decisive victories for socialism. The complete triumph of socialism is inevitable.

> Statement of the 81 Communist and Workers Parties in Moscow, December 1960

POWER AND PEACE

by Arleigh Burke

Arleigh Burke is Director of the Center for Strategic Studies, Georgetown University. During the Korean War he was a member of the United Nations Truce Delegation to negotiate a military armistice in Korea. In 1952 he became Director of the Strategic Plans Division of the Office of the Chief of Naval Operations. In 1955 he was named Chief of Naval Operations and served in that post until 1961. He is recipient of the James V. Forrestal Award, a member of the Atlantic Council, and a member of the Board of Visitors of the Fletcher School of Law and Diplomacy.

Based on a condensation of the Walter E. Edge lectures delivered by the author in the spring of 1962 at Princeton University, this selection originally appeared in the Summer 1962 issue of *Orbis*. Reprinted by permission.

The major problem confronting the world today is how to maintain order and peace. A general nuclear war threatens civilization with destruction. Thus we are faced with a terrible dilemma: Is it possible to preserve both peace and the freedom which makes peace worthwhile? In our day, a new form of struggle has been introduced in international relations which threatens liberty, without which man has only a physical existence.

The present struggle is more than a struggle for real estate. Indeed, it springs from a crisis at the very roots of our souls. Two roads to peace lead in opposite directions. The Communists, waging total class conflict, would destroy the old order—our order—and rebuild the world in the image of Communism. The outcome of this process, the Communists tell us, is predetermined, and dialectical materialism supplies the laws of history.

To the Communists, the ultimate good is the ruthless process of history itself. Hence, Communist morality is whatever advances their cause.

The contemporary struggle, therefore, is not a conventional struggle based solely, or even principally, on military force. It is a total effort at annihilation of our way of life. This urge for destruction is nourished by a belief in the skillful and ruthless use of total power. Exercising this total power, the Communists expect to control events and rewrite history.

Against this total power, we have pitted, thus far, only partial power and partial objectives. We have not yet confronted Communism with all our might. We fight on only a few fronts, and on these only defensively. We are fighting the wrong war, the war that exists only in our imagination. Consequently, Communism moves forward while the West stands handicapped by its own misunderstanding. The true enemy is not the Russian or Chinese people, but the Communist power elite. Beyond territorial conquest, the Sino-Soviet Communist leaders aim at conquering men's minds and souls and bending them to a new faith.

What should be the policy of this country which promises peace with freedom and the maintenance and extension of our own social order without catastrophic general nuclear war?

The American approach to the problem of peace—to the problem of maintaining order in the world—has become hesitant and inconclusive. At the root of our troubles lies the confusion over the relations between reason and power. Unfortunately, we tend to think of reason and power as opposites and to identify all force with military force in war.

Reason and power are not only compatible, but reason itself is a form of power. While itself a source of power, reason accomplishes nothing in practical affairs unless it is supported by additional forms of power. Reason establishes the purposes and objectives of all means of power. Reason and power are compatible with each other; both are necessary in determining national courses of action. The Communists' reasoning, although completely different from our reasoning, is made effective because it harnesses power to the achievement of political ends.

The difference between "power" and "force" requires emphasis. A nation can exercise its power without ever exercising actual force. Force is only one application of power. Force applied by a nation does not necessarily signify the actual waging of war. Particularly, it does not signify only the waging of a general nuclear war. There are various types and degrees of force just as there are various types and degrees of power.

Power Processes among Nations

Power might be said to be the capacity to induce others to behave according to patterns in one's own mind. A state has power when it has the ability to compel other states to pattern their behavior after its own ideas.

The power process among nations operates through the transfer of ideas from the minds of the leaders of one nation to the minds of the leaders of another nation. Not all exercises of power occur in the same manner. The modes of power extend from pure force to pure persuasion. In the case of pure force, the direct physical application of violence by one nation—or the threat of force in circumstances that give credibility to the threat—causes another nation to act according to patterns communicated by the former.

What is the nature of this process? A state may yield to coercion while its people reject the rationale of this surrender. Neither the people nor its leaders agree with the policy that another power imposes upon them. Nonetheless, they comply because they are forced to do so. In the case of pure persuasion, a nation acts according to ideas which, although originated by some other nation, it has accepted freely. The power of persuasion lies in the ability to present ideas so attractively that they not only seem valid intellectually but also induce a desired type of response.

Pure and unrestricted choice seldom occurs in real life; pure persuasion is very infrequent. All decision involves the choice between, and the consequent rejection of, alternative modes of action. Consequently, persuasion usually results from an analysis of the relative gains and sacrifices involved in any course of action. Thus persuasion depends just as much on the prospect of loss as on the prospect of gain. Indeed, the most persuasive argument for any course of action is that it both maximizes gain and minimizes loss.

The term "influence" connotes the forms of power between pure force and pure persuasion. Behavior is neither "forced," nor is it determined by dispassionate persuasion. Rather, the power that exercises influence obtains the desired behavior by controlling the choices available to the "influenced." Such control can be either artificial or natural. That is, the possessor of power can add a further advantage to the type of behavior desired. He can also impose additional sanctions upon types of undesirable behavior. The principle can be illustrated in the homey example of the boy who receives a lollipop for taking his castor oil, or who will be sent to bed if he misbehaves at the table. The certainty of reward and punishment has been the most enduring way of influencing behavior. It should not be confused with force. For in every case the choice is left to the "influenced" party. Only the conditions of choice are controlled. In this particular case they are artificially controlled, since the advantages or disadvantages are not inherent in the choice.

Control simply insures awareness of the consequences of any decision. A nation possessing power, for instance, may refuse to rescue another from the consequences of a foolish policy. Thus, for example, if a nation is impoverishing itself by nationalization of foreign investment, we could suspend our program of foreign aid to let the full impact of nationalist folly be felt.

This is by far the most sophisticated mode of power. Its forms are numerous. It is equally clear that the exercise of this mode of power depends upon the ability to produce results in a wide range of human concerns. In the last analysis, a truly great power possesses and exercises this power to "influence" behavior in the entire spectrum of human concerns. A nation with only military power could use force to achieve some results, and through the threat of force could coerce a degree of conformity in others. Any power, no matter how weak, can attempt to persuade others to alter their behavior. Only a great power has those attributes of economic, political, moral and spiritual, military, and psychological superiority that permit it to determine the course of events apart from either pure force or pure persuasion.

It is not difficult to determine at any moment of history who are the wielders of power. A strong nation can exercise influence simply by existing. It stimulates imitation; it sets the fashions in thought and behavior; it becomes the teacher of peoples. But when weakness appears, the respect it previously enjoyed is replaced by envy and scorn. The first outward sign of this inward weakness is a loss of control over the course of events. Active leadership is replaced by defensive thought. Confidence yields to anxiety. The positive pursuit of just interests is displaced by fear-inspired measures intended to protect accumulated possessions. With fear comes indecision and vacillation. Of course, even weak nations exercise a type of power proper to the weak: the power of dissent. They threaten to misbehave unless they get what they want from the powerful ones. The root of such truculence on the part of the weak is the knowledge that the strong power is afraid or uncertain, that to protect itself from harm it will put up with irresponsible demands, even from the weak.

The Essential Elements of Peace

Let us now apply this analysis to the problem of peace among peoples by reviewing the characteristics of the Roman and English empires. Each established a peaceful order, the *Pax Romana* and the *Pax Britannica*. Rome established and preserved peace among the civilized peoples of the Mediterranean world. That peace was established and preserved by Roman policy. Moreover, the Roman Peace was ultimately accepted by the peoples who shared in it. And for a moment, however brief in the history of man, from Hadrian's wall in

England to the Bosporus, people lived with one another without war.

The essential elements of the *Pax Romana* are easily discernible. First, there was a power center based in the politically stable Italian peninsula. From this core of power, Roman legions gradually conquered and Roman administration integrated the Mediterranean world. The period of Roman expansion was characterized by the drive to pacify borders, to make the Mediterranean safe for trade, and the world safe for Rome. But it was not simply an operation of military conquest. Trade, persuasion, statesmanlike perceptions of diverse interests, all played their part in this expansion. The Roman Empire, like the British Empire, to use a famous description of the latter, was acquired in "a fit of absent-mindedness."

When Rome awoke to the realization that she *was* an empire, her policy then centered on the problem of maintaining it by a combination of justice, interest, advantage, penalties, pressure, persuasion, and, at the margin, force. The entire structure became dependent on the Romans' will to use the power available to them—military power if necessary, economic or psychological power if that sufficed. Those who accepted the leadership of Rome became prosperous. Those who did not were penalized economically, politically, socially. By the standards of the times, Roman law and rule were just. But fundamentally, the Empire depended on Roman power and the will to use that power.

The second characteristic of the *Pax Romana* can be found in the limited extent to which Roman power affected the internal life of the peoples in the Empire. Incorporation in the Empire did not involve change by coercion of the culture and customs of subjected peoples. Of course, the cosmopolitan segments of the Empire imitated the Roman way of life. But the life of the people was left untouched. Taxes and, to some extent, military levies were the sole burden. The Empire was in fact a centrally directed system of international law and relations backed up by Roman power. In personal affairs, the citizens of the Empire lived their own lives. It was only in the final period of confusion that the Empire, in its attempt to hold its possessions together, extended its power to the private lives of all the citizens.

In more recent times, England maintained international stability for nearly a century. The conditions of the *Pax Britannica* and the *Pax Romana* serve to illustrate the underlying similarity of basic principles on which both rested.

After a thousand years of internal development, Europe entered, in the fifteenth century, upon a period of world expansion. The movement outward was spontaneous, unplanned, dominated by the desire for trade, personal achievement, national interest, and all the other motives, grand and not so grand, that stimulate men to action. The immediate consequences of that expansion were chaotic. European rivalries, dynastic, national, and religious, were exported to the coastal regions of most of the world. A vital, aggressive, imaginative, and venturesome civilization began filling a new world and awakening an old one from a centuries-old lethargy. For three hundred years the history of the world was, in all significant aspects, a function of the history of Europe. When the center of power from which this dynamism sprang lapsed into disorder, so did the rest of the world.

The Napoleonic Wars afforded the occasion for Europe to achieve its own unique coordination of power. The Concert of Europe brought peace not only to Europe but to the world. Two basic elements were involved: First, from 1815 on, the Concert of Europe developed a unique system of integration, consisting not of a single dominant power, but of a core of states dominating the Continent. Lacking a central government, the system was not as cohesive as an empire; nonetheless, it provided stability. Secondly, Britain was both part of, and on the periphery of, the continental system. Under the *Pax Romana*, the Roman legions provided the basis for the effective use of the other forms of power; under the *Pax Britannica*, the order of the world depended on the Royal Navy. Over the years, that navy had developed into a flexible instrument of power, and the English possessed both the skill and the willingness to use it effectively. Its very presence was the guarantee of peace and the condition for the operation of the multiple forms of influence available to the Euro-British complex.

The preservation of peace depended as much on the controlling of conflict in the colonial dependencies as on the preservation of interstate understandings in Europe. On this delicate balance hinged the *Pax Britannica.* The system functioned efficiently, despite its seemingly complicated structure. Vigorous activity was necessary to maintain the balance. Trade was the heart of the system. The British Navy kept the trade routes open. In fact, if not in name, the pound sterling served as the world currency.

The *Pax Britannica,* then, just as the *Pax Romana,* rested on a core of power and a will to use it. Yet it differed significantly in the constitution of this core of power. Instead of a centralized state with overwhelming predominance, we have an amazing integration of independent powers into one great power complex whose balance wheel was Europe and whose cutting edge, in the rest of the world, was England. Upon a foundation of universal order, diplomats wove with consummate skill a pattern of wise and moderate agreements governing international relations. These agreements in turn were enforced by a complex balance of power, military and non-military. The European balance was dynamic. On the Continent, power shifted constantly. Yet the system retained its coherence. Colonial expansion reflected the shifting balance in Europe. At the margin, England controlled the course of events. By trade preferences, by persuasion and cajoling, by the sheer power of prestige, and by shrewd manipulation of the ambitions and desires of leaders and peoples, England was able to convince the world that what England wanted was beneficial, not only for England, but for everyone else as well.

Collapse of the Concert of Europe

The European-British system for maintaining order broke up with the collapse of the Concert of Europe. Under the impetus of the German power challenge, the European system collapsed in the tragedy of World War I. Afterward, both Europe and England, due to the economic dislocations of the

Great Depression, lost their dominant position in the world. This loss manifested itself in two basic changes: (1) a quantitative reduction in the amount of absolute power of all kinds available to the European system; and (2) an emotional exhaustion that resulted in a general unwillingness to intervene actively in world developments.

A major manifestation of this deficiency of will is to be found in the series of disarmament conferences between the First and the Second World War. The major nations were unwilling to bear the burden of power, and Europe attempted to achieve peace through abdication of power. The search for peace revolved around the assumption that arms were the cause of war. The Western publics embraced the idea that relative peace would be assured if armaments were reduced relatively, and absolute peace if they were reduced absolutely. The West nourished the illusion of international law bereft of the power of enforcement. Gradually, the Western nations lost their willingness to exercise power either for the good of the world or in their own interests.

From this power vacuum emerged total dictatorships. The Fascist pretensions of Mussolini, however pitiable in their lack of realism, did not meet with swift chastisement. But a more serious threat to world order arose from Nazism. Its emergence was made possible by the power vacuum and the moral listlessness of Western civilization.

If the Nazi movement is considered as a power phenomenon, its dream of world rule was not as foolish as it might seem at first glance. For the Nazis began by consolidating a strong power center in one area. From this, they launched their expansionist campaign. Trade and psychological pressures, and the attractiveness of firm purposes in an aimless world contributed to Nazi power. The Nazis understood power in all its forms. Moreover, they were buoyed by a deep faith that the good of the Aryan race was the good of the human race. By offering direction—any direction—the Nazi party was able to become a power center of vast magnitude.

Thus, World War II was caused by the failure of the Allies to use their power responsibly. Consequently, a small group of men used the lesser power available to them so effectively that it took the combined resources of the world to defeat them. "When reason dreams, monsters are born."

Power Alone Is Not Enough

These cases illustrate our basic point: international peace is a consequence of the rational use of national power by a dominant and dominating power center. But the possession of power alone is not enough. In addition to a will to use it, there must be skill, and even a "feel," in the use of its various forms. The organ furnishes an analogy. The forms of power resemble the great tiers ranging from the bass of war to the soprano of rhetoric. The various forms of power are used in well-integrated chords: economic influence is joined with persuasion, backed up by personal influence, threaded with overtones of threat and reward, combined with whatever other forms of influence and control an inventive diplomacy can develop. Finally, none of the multiple forms of power will avail without a known willingness to appeal to the ultimate form of force in matters of grave concern. Peace is dependent upon the rational use of the various forms of power.

Yet there are those who believe that the human race has moved to a new capacity for peace based solely on the power of persuasion, or more popularly, on the power of discussion. From 1914 till today, the major orientation of policy in the West has been toward discussion and persuasion rather than the deliberate "influencing" of behavior. For almost fifty years during which more human beings than ever before have been killed in war, starved, tortured, imprisoned, transported, subjugated, and, in general, dehumanized, we have consistently tried to solve our problems by persuasion only. It is not at all surprising that, when these policies fail, the public mood oscillates widely between the extremes of massive force and the hope for peace through disarmament. If this grisly circle of disarmament, discussion, and disaster is to be broken, it must be by the deliberate introduction of a new solution to the problem of peace. This solution can be found only in the conscious use of national power in all its forms. We must be willing to face the possibility of war, for there are values greater than peace, greater than life itself.

On the globe today one major power considers strife to be the birth pains of the final world social order. Another group of nations, the West, formerly the sole power center of the world, is now discovering the key to a new order in integration. As the European powers withdraw more and more from their former colonies, new nations born in the wake of their withdrawal begin to grope for their place in the sun. These new nations are weak, infected with hypernationalism, hostile toward one another, and inexperienced. They are exposed to Soviet influence and, ultimately, to Communist occupation. Careless of consequences, they play the chancy game of trading the Soviet Union against the United States and the West.

In this tense, hostile, and contradictory situation only one thing is certain: peace and order will return only when a dominating center of power takes up the burden and duty of power.

The United Nations cannot bring peace to the international scene for one simple reason: It has no power of its own. Whatever power it exercises, be it economic, political, or military, is *ad hoc* power loaned to it by member states. It can levy neither troops nor taxes. It cannot even discipline its own members, apart from an act of war or internationally organized sanctions. Tragically, the United Nations, whose principal function is the resolution of conflict by rational discussion, is condemned to irrationality in the exercise of power. At best, it epitomizes world conditions. It cannot be a government, for it has no citizens to govern. The United Nations can act only when the conditions of order have already been met.

Is empire a solution to the problem of peace? If the traditional conditions of empire obtained, that solution might be applicable. But our age is not characterized by the presence of a great power in the midst of barbaric or apathetic peoples. There are no peoples so remote from the influence of world civilization that they could be deprived justly or even successfully in the name of peace of the management of their domestic affairs. Moreover, the modern world is divided between two power centers, the United States and the U.S.S.R. One is already launched upon a course of conquest and domination. To commit the United States to the same kind of territorial and ideological expansion would make certain the ultimate conflict that would bring peace through exhaustion.

For the United States, the problem of peace in the bipolar world is interlaced with the problem of freedom. Domination is not possible for us. But direction is. The problem cannot be solved by the renunciation of all forms of power except discussion and persuasion. Such a renunciation would give a free field to the irresponsible use of the power of dissent by weak states and leave the entire world defenseless against Communist aggression.

The Communist objective is a new kind of empire over the minds and souls of men. Against this movement all the forms of power must be used. Within the Free World, influence and persuasion backed by a firmness in our capacity to resort to force when necessary can establish order and secure peace.

Peace is the product of power great enough and wise enough to give events direction and purpose. Power is nihilistic in the absence of purpose. Power is destructive when it serves totalitarian purposes. But the exercise of power, when it is motivated by a desire for peace among free, responsible nations, is beneficial.

The Confrontation Is Absolute

The national power of the United States is massive and varied enough to be capable of establishing a just and peaceful order among nations. Our root failure has not been in tactics but rather in strategy. Our strategy is faulty because it is based on a misconception of the nature of real peace in our day. We need to explore the conditions for the rational use of our immense power. Between the free West and the Communist movement, there can be no reconciliation, no real coexistence. The confrontation is absolute. For the two centers of power hold fundamentally different views of the process whereby order is established and preserved.

The United States seeks to establish order by reducing conflict, obviating tensions, and resolving differences of viewpoint. The Soviets conceive of order as the last stage of the dialectic of negation. The Communist Party is the crucible of this process. It does not need to ponder the problems of order and peace, for its task is to destroy whatever order exists.

Let us be clear about the nature of the enemy and the terms of the struggle. Hitherto we have been confused about both. Therefore, we have been fighting the wrong battles and gradually losing the protracted struggle. Our enemy is not Russia or China. Our enemy is the Communist movement. We properly speak of the captive nations of East-Central Europe. But are not Russia and China equally the captives of the movement? The Russian and Chinese peoples are manipulated by the Communist power elite as tools of the movement. The defense of civilization is tantamount to the destruction of the Communist movement throughout the world.

The threat of Communism is twofold. The first is domestic subversion by the Communist movement. The second is the growing power of the Soviet Union and Red China. Our foreign policy must be ordered to the ultimate removal of this threat.

Our habit of thinking in terms of national boundaries has resulted in disastrous losses. We have been unwilling to intervene in the domestic affairs of foreign countries upon which the Communists seek to impose their power. Wherever Communists fight non-Communists, conflict ceases to be domestic. The wars in Laos, Vietnam, Korea, were and are not civil wars. These lands have truly been victims of foreign aggression. It matters little that the Communist armies were not composed of Russian and Chinese, but of indigenous peoples. For these natives were Communists, hence members of an international movement. Moreover, these wars were waged not so much for the purpose of seizing territory as for capturing people. At this level of the struggle, therefore, military force constitutes the basic form of power.

The wars in Laos and Vietnam are "limited." What is the

place of "limited" war in our strategy? One school of thought conceives of limited war as a war in which the enemy sets weapons or territorial limitations. In such a war we forfeit the initiative and the advantage of our superior power; we reduce the risk posed to the aggressor, and hence weaken our capability of deterrence. The other school of thought conceives of a limited war as one in which we, not our enemies, dictate the degree and type of force to be used, and employ the most efficient means to make aggression unprofitable.

We must aim to destroy the sources of Communist power in any country where the Communists have provoked so-called "wars of national liberation," and impose upon ourselves no other limitation than the decision not to apply means more violent than necessary. This is a policy we must make clear to the enemy. But in order not to be forced to use means more violent than necessary, our military power must range from specially trained guerrilla forces to strategic nuclear power. We abdicate our power to limit war if we are not willing to employ, when necessary, additional forms of military power and if our resolution to do so is not made plain to our opponent.

The Struggle for Men's Minds

Another aspect of the conflict with Communism in the former colonial countries is the ideological struggle, often called the "struggle for men's minds." This struggle is primarily intellectual; its forms of power are education and propaganda. But here we should avoid a basic error: We should not try to force an American ideology on other peoples. The cultures of the Oriental and Arabic worlds are religious and inherently anti-Communist. By helping the new states to be themselves, we help them to build a sure defense against Communism. In these areas, cultural renewal is essential. Our objective should not be to compete with Communism for the absorption of these peoples' cultural identities, but rather to ensure that they resist Communism and develop free institutions in keeping with indigenous cultural patterns.

Intellectual resistance to Communism can be reinforced by exposing the fallacies in Communist thought and the deceptions in Communist propaganda. Many of the developing nations have two basic and interrelated characteristics: anti-imperialism, envenomed by suspicion and envy of the Western nations, and an impatient urge for speedy economic development that turns their eyes hopefully toward the Soviet Union.

The prestige of the Soviet Union is enhanced, first, by the supposed rationality of socialism in the eyes of some intellectuals; and second, by popular hopes for a redistribution of wealth in areas where the differences between wealth and poverty are glaring. Many of the underdeveloped nations, however, are struggling to reconcile rapid economic development with anti-imperialistic nationalism. Their dilemma is acute: On the one hand, they have been led to believe the importation of foreign capital is the most obnoxious form of imperialism. On the other hand, rapid development seems impossible without foreign investments. The Soviet system, viewed with eyes blinded by Communist propaganda, offers a way out because first, it is supposed to be rational, and second, it promises to redistribute wealth.

No major problem in these non-Communist areas has a short-range solution. But groundwork can be laid for a gradual improvement: first, by increasing stability throughout these areas, and secondly, by the basing of the domestic policies of these countries on realistic economic and political calculations. These objectives are contingent upon the cooperation of the former colonial areas with the European and Pacific areas.

To achieve this objective, we must stop treating neutrals as a third force. This current attitude is rooted in the balance-of-power approach of nineteenth-century Europe when nations were only too willing to avoid a one-to-one power situation. But the sum of the neutrals does not add up to a power center. They constitute a power vacuum. This vacuum continues to exist because the United States does not seek to fill it, while the Communist powers are held back from doing so by fear of the United States.

The situation, however, cannot be mistaken for one of mutual non-intervention on the part of the great powers. The Communists have already intervened in many countries and are waging a vast ideological war. More importantly, these new nations are plunged into the currents of world affairs by their very desires for rapid development and complete independence. The issue is not whether to intervene. We *have* intervened. The issue is the manner of intervention.

Today, the academic conceptions of intervention and neutrality are no longer meaningful—if they ever were. The new nations claim that they are neutral or, more descriptively, non-aligned. Yet, in the midst of the ideological struggle, non-alignment is a meaningless posture. The Communist movement intervenes in ways unknown to traditional international law. Against this challenge, U.S. policy has responded with countermoves carefully measured to the whimsies of the new nations. As a consequence, our policy encourages non-alignment as a most profitable venture for new nations. At the same time, the innate instability of the new nations invites a Communist takeover.

The policy of non-alignment is, given the current attitude of the United States, an effective power policy in the exercise of dissent. The neutral states decry the use of any power, economic or military. Their vocal censoriousness of American policy is matched by discreet silence about Soviet behavior. While the Communists nibble at their territories, they condemn a Western imperialism that no longer exists. The mere power of dissent, as long as it commands prestige and American economic aid, will delay rational solutions to the growing economic and social problems of the neutral nations.

The Myth of "World Opinion"

The United States, haunted by the myth of "world opinion," fritters away its power on projects of questionable value. Two and a half billion dollars worth of American aid have not solved India's problem. The twenty billion dollars we propose to give to South America are unlikely to prime the expansion of Latin American productivity. The industrialization of Latin America will depend upon the inflow of massive foreign investment and national self-discipline. Our policy of economic aid should not confirm for our Latin American neighbors the illusion that industrialization can be achieved by fiat. It will require many years of hard work.

We are constantly amazed that our policies win so few friends, insure so little support, and often increase the sullen resentment excited by our wealth. But this melancholy result should have been expected. For economic aid by itself solves no problems, and can even intervene with constructive developments.

The principle of a nation's responsibility for its actions must be invoked, and, if necessary, enforced. Wherever American interests are violated, wherever the peace is broken, and wherever Communists are courted deliberately in order to threaten or blackmail America, the United States must impose penalties. Conversely, cooperation and a realistic search for economic stability must be rewarded.

Such a policy, let it be understood, is not a policy of direct intervention. It is simply an insistence that no one shall escape the logical consequences of his choice. The new states must face the fact that no one is absolutely sovereign, that cooperation is the price of responsible independence. We must make it clear that U.S. power will be used to control the course of events by limiting the range of decisions and by rewarding those we approve. This dangerous world is not a kindergarten where children are protected from their own thoughtlessness. It is a hard and demanding place where mature judgment and careful decision are the minimum conditions for peace. The young states, for the first time bestriding the dangerous stage of world politics, must learn this truth—the hard way if necessary.

Power and Peace: An Opportunity for the West

The most important area of strategic importance to the United States and the employment of its power is Europe. Here our policy should be directed toward the solidification of the North Atlantic Community.

Fortunately, the postwar developments in Europe are unfolding in such a manner as to give hope for a renewal of European power, both military and economic. Faced with the prospect of a united Atlantic Community, the Kremlin will redouble its efforts to detach West Germany from NATO. Nuclear blackmail will remain a primary weapon. Another equally important weapon to split European unity is the exploitation of conflicting Western interests in the colonial and formerly colonial areas.

To avoid aiding unwittingly Moscow's strategy, the United States must throw its diplomatic, political, and economic weight onto the side of Western unity. Confidence in the alliance with Europe should not lead the United States to opportunistic demands for immediate evacuation of colonial areas. The problem is one of timing. And the neutral world should not be made more unstable by the precipitate creation of additional political units that are not viable.

The policy here proposed constitutes a sharp break with our previous policies. The essence of the change lies not in the area of specific tactics, but in our approach to the question of peace and order. Our earlier policies envisaged two major territorial powers facing each other in the traditional way. From this basic error derived such territory-centered policy proposals as containment, rollback, and withdrawal. Moreover, our earlier policies were vitiated by a guilt-ridden conception of power. Hypnotized by the atom bomb, our thinking stopped at massive retaliation and deterrence, both last-ditch policies, so to speak. Such policies have their place, but they are negative and defensive, and do not offer ultimate solutions to the problem of order.

The American policy proposed here envisages the destruction of an ideological movement. This policy depends, not on any particular form of power, but on all forms of power. It is oriented to a world order guaranteed by the power of the United States in cooperation with the wider base of power of the North Atlantic Community. With the North Atlantic Community as its core, the Free World can defeat Communism and bring peace and order to the whole world.

This positive policy should not be mistaken for an attempt

at creating by force an enclave of ordered freedom in a despotic world. Such an aim would be absurd. It should be our purpose to defeat despotism by a vigorous use of our power. The use of our power should be guided by a policy of confrontation:

Confrontation of Communism with the challenge of a vigorous freedom;

Confrontation of dissident and diffident neutrals with responsibility for their choice;

Confrontation of the West, in general, and America, in particular, with the responsibility of the effective use of power.

This essay cannot furnish a tactical blueprint for ending the cold war. It is concerned with an assessment of the realities that confront us in today's anxious world. If we face up to these realities, then we become new men and, collectively, a nation reborn.

So far, the history of our century has been that of a search for a peaceful world order based neither on reality nor responsibility. After two world wars we forgot the lesson which the history of all ages teaches: a just peace is the fruit of the responsible use of power. Now we have crossed the threshold into the nuclear age. This time, abdication of our responsibility will blight humanity for generations.

THE COLD WAR:
ORIGINS AND DEVELOPMENT

by Paul C. Davis

Dr. Paul C. Davis graduated from the U. S. Military Academy and received Masters and Doctoral degrees in International Relations from Yale University. He has taught at the Army War College and the School of International Affairs of Columbia University; he has been a Research Associate in Columbia's Institute of War and Peace Studies, a Visiting Associate Professor in the Department of International Studies of the University of South Carolina, and the Associate Director of the Institute of International Studies. Among his numerous assignments as a professional Army officer were Battalion Commander during World War II and Chief of Psychological Warfare, U. S. European Command 1952–55. Since September 1964, Dr. Davis has been a Senior Staff Member of the Institute of Naval Studies, a component of the Center for Naval Analyses, Cambridge, Massachusetts.

It is common to ascribe the beginning of the cold war to the series of diplomatic crises which took place between mid-1945 and mid-1947 involving Soviet and American differences over the organization of the peace in Turkey, Eastern Europe, and Germany, since it was these differences which alerted the United States to the real underlying attitudes of the Soviet leadership and caused us to acknowledge our position of world leadership in the task of opposing the intentions of the Soviet Union.

The Beginnings

The outbreak of the cold war arose from Soviet actions which stemmed directly from their revolutionary world outlook. Indeed, some have advanced the almost inescapable thesis that the cold war actually began when Lenin and his cohorts first seized power in Russia and established an operating base for the conduct of the world revolution. The Russian Bolsheviks did not coin the term "cold war," but this pales beside the fact that they invented the concepts which give it meaning. If we think of the cold war as the consequence of permanent hostility of one nation or system of nations toward others, of the notion that there are but two possible viewpoints as to the way the world shall be organized; that all nations and all peoples must not only share one or the other, but take up arms until the "wrong" view is smashed, until the struggle to establish the supremacy of Communism is decided; if we think of the cold war as representing an intense and continuous struggle, deliberately conducted with the idea of exacerbating the differences between two sets of nations, then the prescription for the cold war was, of course, laid out in the theories of Marxism-Leninism. Typical of these ideas is the statement by Lenin at the end of World War I, frequently quoted by his followers:

> We are living not merely in a state, but in a system of states, and the existence of the Soviet Republic side by side with imperialist states for a long time is unthinkable. One or the other must triumph in the end. And before that end supervenes, a series of frightful collisions between the Soviet Republic and the bourgeois states will be inevitable. (Report of Central Committee at Eighth Party Congress, 1919).

Or again, Lenin's 1920 statement:

> As long as capitalism and socialism exist, we cannot live in peace; in the end, one or the other will triumph—a funeral dirge will be sung over the Soviet Republic or over world capitalism.

Such statements indicate that the Soviet leadership posits a permanent hostility toward all capitalist nations—indeed, all non-Soviet nations—that it demands continuous struggle and that the object of the struggle is the triumph of Communism under Soviet leadership over all other states.

The Continuing Revolution

These are not simply antiquated postulations which have lost reality. They have guided Soviet practice ever since. Soviet leadership conceived the idea of continuing revolution; it formulated the proposition that all who are not friends of the Soviet Union are its enemies; it invented the concept of the "front" group; and it created the idea that all wars should be used as steppingstones toward the ultimate destruction of the non-Communist world.

If the United States was not conscious that a cold war was going on in the period of the 1920's and 1930's, it was because we were not active participants in the world community and played only a minor role in the settlement of conflicts. Some voices of warning had been raised earlier, such as the Committee for Cultural Freedom. But by and large, American leaders first became fully conscious of Soviet intransigence in World War II.

During that war the basic Soviet distrust and suspicion for the West became evident to several American leaders stationed in the U.S.S.R. Major General John R. Deane, Chief of the United States Military Mission in the Soviet Union, for example, in a letter to General Marshall on December 2, 1944, had this to say:

> The truth is that they want to have as little to do with foreigners, Americans included, as possible. We never make a request or proposal to the Soviets that is not viewed with suspicion. They simply cannot understand giving without taking, and as a result even our giving is viewed with suspicion. Gratitude cannot be banked in the Soviet Union. Each transaction is complete in itself without regard to past favors. The party of the second part is either a shrewd trader to be admired or a sucker to be despised.

During the war the Soviet Union engaged in political activities contrary to the interests of her allies, including the subversion and takeover of the governments of Allied states on her Western border. Ambassador W. Averell Harriman, reporting from Moscow as early as January 1945, accurately described the Russian arsenal of subversion, sabotage, and political pressure used to dominate the countries of Eastern Europe:

> The relative lull in military activities on the Eastern Front has in effect given the Soviet Union a chance to pursue its political objectives in areas liberated by the Russian Army. . . . the pattern of Soviet tactics in Eastern Europe and the Balkans has taken shape and the nature of Soviet aims has been clarified. It has become apparent that the Soviets, while eschewing direct attempts to incorporate into the Soviet Union alien peoples who were not embraced within the frontiers of June 21, 1941, are nevertheless employing the wide variety of means at their disposal—occupation troops, pathetic leftist organizations, sponsored cultural societies, and economic pressure—to assure the establishment of regimes which, while maintaining an outward appearance of independence and of broad popular support, actually depend for their existence on groups responsive to all suggestions emanating from the Kremlin. The tactics are endless in their variety and are selected to meet the situation in each particular country, dependent largely on the extent and strength of the resistance to Soviet penetration. It is particularly noteworthy that no practical distinction seems to be made in this connection between members of the United Nations whose territory is liberated by Soviet troops and ex-enemy countries which have been occupied.

Soviet Expansionism

The ruthlessness of the Soviet Union in these operations was typified by its betrayal of the Warsaw Underground. As the Soviet forces approached the gates of Warsaw in the summer of 1944, its leaders lured the Warsaw Underground into rising

against the Nazi occupation forces with the spurious promise
of Red Army assistance. The army was brought to a halt, per-
mitting the Nazi occupation forces to destroy the Underground
forces of General Bohr, after which the Soviet forces took
over the city. This action, in addition to the Soviet massacre
of the elite of the Polish officer corps in the Katyn Forest, can
only have been carried out with the purpose of eliminating
the non-Communist postwar Polish leadership in order to substitute for it the Polish leadership trained in Moscow.

Such actions generally failed to alert the Allies to the probability that the Soviet Union would continue its expansionist
efforts into the heart of Europe. The deceptive blandishments
of Stalin and Molotov, together with the euphoria which resulted from victory and from the cooperation of the Soviet
Union in the establishment of the United Nations, delayed the
realization by many Western leaders that the maintenance of
peace on the basis of genuine cooperation between the Soviet
Union and the West was impossible.

Again, one month after the Soviets signed an agreement at
Yalta in February 1945 to establish governments broadly representative of all democratic elements, Soviet Minister Vy-
shinsky arrived in Bucharest and compelled King Michael, by
an ultimatum, to eliminate the Radescu government and to
substitute one led by the Communist Petru Groza. This violation of the agreement took place fifteen months before Secretary of State Byrnes confirmed America's assumption of responsibility for defending Europe in his Stuttgart speech. Only
three weeks after the close of the Yalta Conference the Soviet
government had also contradicted its agreement with respect
to the composition of the Polish provisional government.

From early 1945 until July 1946 the United States and
Britain used diplomatic measures to attempt to deal with the
more flagrant Russian violations of wartime agreements. At
that time the United States had not made a major readjustment
of its wartime policies toward Russia. American acceptance
of the challenge of the cold war might at the earliest be dated
from the speech of Secretary of State James F. Byrnes in Stuttgart in July 1946, in which he pledged that the United States
would maintain its position in Europe for a period of twenty-

five to forty years to prevent the recurrence of a new threat to the peace. This speech had bipartisan support. American assumption of a role in the cold war occurred only after the demobilization of the very American military forces which were needed to guarantee the effective performance of that role.

American Countermoves

American diplomatic countermoves of 1945–46 were not accompanied by the creation or use of force. With the exception of the British-American veiled threat which persuaded the Soviet Union to withdraw its troops from Iran in March 1946, the United States accepted no military responsibilities in the cold war until the spring of 1947. In that year President Truman decided to provide military assistance to Greece and to Turkey; in the one case, to suppress the Communist guerrilla warfare on the Greek border and, in the other, to strengthen Turkey's hand against Russian attempts to claim territory in the eastern area of Turkey and bases in the Straits area. Until then Russia had been thought difficult on certain specific issues only. Now American leaders recognized that the Soviet Union saw its relationship with the West as one of innate and continuing antagonism. We moved toward a fundamentally new policy of active leadership in an effort to contain the Soviet drive at all points, with the expressed hope that ultimately the frustration of Soviet expansion would result in a transformation of its internal structure and of its aspirations. Americans had finally faced the reality of the permanent cold war struggle which was to follow into our time.

Communist Threat to Western Europe: American Reaction

The broad lines of the development of the cold war in terms of Soviet shifts in strategy and the revision of American counterstrategy to meet it are fairly clear. In the period 1947–50 the Soviet Union sought to consolidate its control of Eastern and Central Europe and then to threaten the capture of Western Europe. The scope of this plan became evident with the Communist coup in Czechoslovakia in 1948. Western Europe lay open to both ideological and organizational tactics of subversion and to the possibility of overt invasion by Soviet military forces. Europe was in economic chaos and lacked the means to create a military force to oppose the possibility of Soviet attack. The United States, in an imaginative and ingenious economic proposal, the Marshall Plan, was able between 1948 and 1951 to help restore Western Europe to its prewar economic stability and set it on the path to rapid economic growth. This counterstrategy had much to do with the decline in Communist Party strength in France and Italy, which had reached its high-water mark in 1947. The threat of Soviet military might which hung like a cloud over Europe became particularly dark and ominous with the Communist attack in Korea. The ratification of the Western European Union in 1948 and the formation of the North Atlantic Treaty Organization in 1949 created anew the sense of unity and will necessary to oppose Soviet power in Europe; and in the 1950's it enabled the construction of much of the military power needed to give Europe's will meaning. The one Russian attempt to maintain the initiative in Europe, the blockade of Berlin, having been brought to failure by the American airlift, the Soviet Union found itself blocked in its European strategy and indeed compelled to construct the Warsaw Treaty forces.

Encouraged by the Communist takeover of mainland China in 1949, Soviet strategy then made a rapid shift to Asia. An attack upon South Korea in June 1950 probably had as its larger purpose the attempt to draw Japan into the Communist sphere of influence. This, again, was frustrated by a quick United States response.

The Strategy of Peaceful Coexistence

After the death of Stalin, and recognizing that overt military pressure had become counterproductive, the Soviets shifted cold war policy. The new strategy, brought to fruition under Khrushchev, was a shift to "peaceful coexistence." "Peaceful coexistence" had early been defined by Lenin to include temporary cooperation with bourgeois groups and institutions as a means to penetrate them and subvert non-Communist countries by guile. In Asia the new "peaceful co-existence" took several forms. First was an effort to deceive the weakened neutralist nations into believing that the Communist bloc would respect the independence and internal affairs of neutralist countries. Second, the strategy called for exploitation of anti-imperialism among many nations there. Third, since the United States had now become the leader of the Free World, and therefore Communist enemy Number One, it took the form of an attack upon United States "imperialism," which sought to link United States behavior with the older colonialism of the European powers. Finally, it exploited the growing industrial and military power of the Soviet Union by holding out promises of assistance to leaders of new nations who aspired toward industrialization and an end to dependence upon European export markets.

Piecemeal Reaction by the U.S.

This strategy, which has developed gradually from 1954 to the present, has gained in flexibility and subtlety and has become the most complicated challenge of the cold war yet posed for the West. American counterstrategy has developed in piecemeal fashion, in part because of our slow realization of the scope and integral character of the Soviet strategy. Initially the United States undertook a series of military assistance obligations to strengthen the South Asian and Middle Eastern countries on the borders of Communist China and the Soviet Union against the possible repetition of limited wars in the "Korean style." Simultaneously the United States undertook a piecemeal economic development-aid program. The effort reflected a growing but initially ill-understood recognition of the importance of economic and political development for the in-between nations.

Guerrilla Warfare

Meanwhile, the Communist bloc had, beginning early in the postwar period, undertaken an increasingly threatening series

of guerrilla warfare actions to capture power on the model of
the Chinese Communist performance. In 1954, after many
years of fighting against the French, Ho Chi-minh succeeded
in capturing North Vietnam by this means. Similar tactics
failed in British Malaya and in the Philippines, where effective
countertactics were devised. The Communists have also
sought to capture the leaders of guerrilla warfare operations
who, while perhaps sympathetic to the Communist regime,
were essentially nationalists.

The Soviet sponsorship of guerrilla warfare and of peaceful
coexistence has been somewhat ambiguous since the dispute
between the Soviet Union and Communist China over the
proper cold war strategy. The essential public difference
has been this: Communist China advocates the dogmatic
purity of Communist action within foreign countries, emphasizing extreme militancy as well as the use of military force,
particularly guerrilla warfare or "wars of national liberation"
(any war to overthrow a capitalist regime), while Russia follows a basic strategy which de-emphasizes this means of
takeover, and instead claims to seek victory through more
subtle combinations of tactics in the guise of "peaceful coexistence." How clearly Russia is adhering to the announced
strategy is not clear, since there is evidence that Russian arms
still flow freely to guerrillas in Southeast Asia.

Paralleling both the period of Sino-Soviet strategic cooperation and the later period of separate strategies was a basic
military strategy designed to exploit the rapid growth of Soviet
military power. Particularly since the Soviet acquisition of the
thermonuclear bomb and the intercontinental ballistic missile,
the Soviet Union has shifted its propaganda strategy once
again to Europe. It has sought to weaken the will of the
Western European countries and the unity of NATO by blackmail threats, exploiting both the supposed missile superiority
of the Soviet Union over the United States (in the late 1950's)
and the danger of fallout.

Changes in Soviet Strategy and Tactics

With the public realization after 1961 that the United States
had, after all, retained thermonuclear missile superiority and

still had the will to use its military superiority when blatantly challenged (as over Cuba in October 1962), Soviet strategy seems to have undergone another modification. Since October 1962 the U.S.S.R. has apparently decided to maintain a soft approach for a significant period of time in the hope of inducing a general softening of the Western stance which might then be exploited for further victories. In this period, public fears both in the West and in neutral nations about the costs of a future war have served to set limits to the risks which Western leaders are willing to take in opposing the Communist bloc. While it is theoretically possible that Moscow's present soft tactics mark a fundamental change in Soviet attitudes, there is little in past performance to substantiate this view. Given the long record of Soviet intransigence, deceit, and hostility, discretion requires the continuing assumption that the present pattern of Soviet behavior marks simply one more in a series of strategic shifts in the cold war which are likely to continue into the foreseeable future.

Strategies in the cold war have been consistent on two general aspects: the first is to shift the kind of pressure used, so as to take advantage of Western limitations in meeting new forms of action; the second is to shift expansionist pressures from one geographic area of the world to another. In each case, the Soviet cold war strategy and tactics seem to have been aimed at exploiting gaps in either Western ideology, Western organizational means of struggle, or Western influence in particular regions. In many areas the reality of Communist practice is too remote to be widely understood, and Communist leaders have been able to exploit strongly rooted animosity toward one or another Western power frequently linked to conditions of political instability, to attitudes formed in the recently ended colonial past, and to frustrated demands and aspirations for a better shake in life.

Subversion of Peoples and Political Structures

While the Soviet strategy has in numerous instances been frustrated, for example in Western Europe, in Korea, and in its effort to establish a missile base in the Western Hemisphere, there has since the onset of the cold war been a tremendous expansion of the area of Communist control as well as a tremendous growth in the political and military skills with which the Communists conduct the cold war. Of all forms of Communist threat, the United States has seemed most capable of handling the military; for our military capability lies within our cultural and industrial capacity. A most difficult challenge of the cold war probably lies in the subversion of the peoples and political structures of the underdeveloped areas of the world. Not only are the conditions in these areas the most propitious for Communist success, it is in the organization of these societies and in assistance to their social and political development that the United States is the least experienced. The United States will have to develop the most sophisticated understanding of these tasks and in a painfully short time. American impatience, lack of understanding of the cultures of other areas, and inadequacies in grasping their organizational, ideological, and political needs pose extreme difficulties in the further conduct of the cold war. Only the education of a sufficiently large and well-qualified leadership at all levels, sufficient to carry out United States policies throughout the world, is likely to enable us to meet these pressing tasks.

A Challenge for the Sixties

The United States now possesses a wide array of policy means. Doctrines for their use vary considerably in clarity and fullness of development, and their further elaboration constitutes a most challenging task for the sixties. There is a wide network of collective security pacts and bilateral agreements to which the United States is a party, bringing it into military alliance with forty-four nations.

Complementing our collective security arrangements, the United States has constructed a large, powerful, and highly integrated military structure based upon strong air, naval, and ground units designed to do two things: to deter the Soviet Union from a major attack upon the United States or Western Europe and also to prevent Communist-bloc countries from obtaining victories in limited wars in peripheral areas of the world.

The United States has also conducted a sizable foreign aid program costing between $2.5 and $3.5 billion a year. This has two main purposes: (a) facilitating the modernization of the economies of underdeveloped countries to relieve the tensions and societal maladjustments which produce the seedground for Communist takeovers; and (b) forestalling the immediate political collapse of weaker nations through short-range stopgap forms of aid.

The United States now operates a propaganda program of significant size under the United States Information Agency. It has as its purposes explaining American foreign policies and the American application of the basic principles of a free society and, secondly, unmasking the spurious claims of Soviet Communism. Our governmental propaganda operations are supplemented by those of certain private propaganda organizations, of which the most important are Radio Free Europe, which broadcasts to five of the satellite countries of Eastern Europe; Radio Liberty, which broadcasts to Russia both in Russian and in a variety of minority-group languages; and the Free Asia Committee, which conducts similar operations in the Far East, particularly toward Communist China.

The Central Intelligence Agency (CIA), established in 1947, has become an arm of American operations of considerable size and importance. Performing originally almost entirely in the field of intelligence collection and interpretation, it has now developed a capability for and a role in the conduct of unacknowledged political operations abroad. It can be particularly useful in countries where a hostile or reactionary leadership is challenged by a liberal but suppressed opposition. The value of CIA operations outside the field of intelligence is a matter of considerable controversy; CIA nonetheless has to its credit significant successes of great importance to the United States. It is generally believed to have had a role in the overthrow of the Communist regime in Guatemala, for example. Its failures are better known, such as the debacle of the Bay of Pigs landing.

More recently the United States has begun developing new tools of policy for which doctrine remains undeveloped, although considerable activity is taking place in these fields. One

of these is *counterinsurgency*. This consists of the training by
American military personnel of the government and armed
forces of countries threatened by Communist guerrilla warfare in the techniques for defeating such warfare. Counterinsurgency embraces not only military techniques but those political and economic reform measures and internal security
provisions necessary to create environments in which guerrilla
warfare movements find it difficult to thrive. Another new instrument of American foreign policy is *military civic action*.
This consists of the training of military personnel of other
countries in civilian-type activities which contribute to the
modernization and the political stability of their countries.

Yet another new American approach is the Peace Corps.
Its basic policy requires that Peace Corps operations remain
independent of American foreign policies, and they even continue in some countries where American diplomatic recognition has been withdrawn. The connection of Peace Corps operations to American foreign policy is also remote because
its services are performed at the grass roots. Nonetheless, it
is clear that such operations can serve the more enduring purposes of the United States.

The Communist challenge has called for emphasis on still
another type of policy action. Communist organizational tactics have brought the threat, particularly in Latin America, of
capture of local political power through subversion of the left-
wing reformist parties. The United States has been seeking to
develop a new capacity to counter these tactics. Its performance in this field is, so far, very limited, most of it being conducted by private American groups. Typical are the activities
of the Latin-American affiliate of the AFL-CIO, known as
ORIT (in English, the Regional International Labor Organization). Operating through this affiliate as well as by means of
a school located in Washington, D.C., the AFL-CIO seeks to
train Latin-American labor leaders in the principles of democracy, the principles of organization and means for defeating
Communist efforts at penetration and subversion of the labor
movement.

Such instrumentalities are the raw material of effective foreign policy. The warp and woof of the Western response to

the Soviet cold war challenge consists of an effective understanding, not only of what each of these instruments can contribute to the basic Western policies for defeating the Communist challenge, but also of how one must coordinate the use of each of these instruments in order to bring their full weight to bear in the service of policy.

THE MAINSPRINGS
OF SOVIET SECRECY

by *Walter F. Hahn*

Walter F. Hahn is a staff member of the Institute for Defense Analyses, where he specializes in international relations and military affairs. Prior to assuming his present post he was a Research Fellow with the Foreign Policy Research Institute's quarterly journal, Orbis. *A graduate of Temple University, where he also received an M.A. degree, Mr. Hahn is co-editor with John C. Neff of* American Strategy for the Nuclear Age *(Doubleday, 1960) and a frequent contributor to various journals, magazines, and compendia.*

A longer version of this selection, based on a paper prepared under the auspices of the Institute for Defense Analyses, originally appeared in *Orbis,* Winter 1964. Reprinted by permission.

Much has been said and written in recent years about the baffling phenomenon of Soviet secrecy—the welter of inordinate sensitivities and suspicions which warp the Soviet Union's image of the world at large. The fear, real or alleged, of foreign espionage restrains the Soviet Union from paying the price of territorial inspection for any meaningful agreement on arms control. In this context, the discussion has centered largely on what are deemed the "legitimate military motives" underlying the Soviet secrecy complex. Yet, the uniqueness of the Soviet phenomenon lies perhaps not so much in external requirements and objectives as it does in the peculiarities of a complex social organism. If, tomorrow, the cold war were miraculously ended and the armies of all nations were disbanded and their weapons destroyed, the likelihood is that secrecy would still shroud Soviet society. Between the Soviet citizen and his meaningful interaction with the world at large would still stand two major barriers: (1) an ethnic-historical-cultural tradition, and (2) the imperatives of the Communist system.

Ethnic, Historical, and Cultural Factors

Russian Historical Experience. Few historians can agree on the ethnological composition of today's Russian. They can point only to the major transmigrations which left discernible marks on Russia's ethnography: the Scythians, the Sarmatians, the Goths who descended from the north in the third century, and the Huns, the most predatory of the nomadic invaders who swept eastward from the Mongolian desert in the fourth century, inundating a large part of Europe. Let us briefly review the major invasions which, during the thousand years following the collapse of the Hun empire, overwhelmed Russia:

1. In the tenth century, the Pechenegs, a people of Turkish stock, swept over almost all of what is today South Russia, penetrating as far north as Kiev.
2. The Pechenegs were replaced, in the eleventh century, by the Cuman Turks (or Polovtsi), surging up from the southern steppes. Their raids far into Russian territory (the first major thrust occurred in 1061) continued intermittently for 150 years, right up to the Mongol invasion.
3. The Mongols, or Tatars, occupied Russia at the beginning of the thirteenth century under Genghis Khan's grandson Batu. In all, the Mongol yoke endured for two and a half centuries.
4. In the middle of the thirteenth century an invasion by the Knights of the Teutonic Order was repelled by Alexander Nevsky at Lake Peipus.
5. The Teutonic Knights were followed, in the early part of the fourteenth century, by Lithuanian armies, and later by the combined forces of Lithuania and Poland, which had

merged their dynasties. Between the early fifteenth and seventeenth centuries, Poland occupied most of Russia west of Moscow and down to the Caspian Sea.

6. In the seventeenth century, the Swedes raided deep into northern Russia. The conflict was climaxed by Charles XII's defeat at Poltava in 1709.

7. A little more than a century later, Napoleon's army traveled the road to Moscow, only to meet the fate that befell its predecessor.

8. The German invasion of Russia in World War I was more successful. By 1917, the Emperor's armies had occupied the entire Ukraine, most of White Russia and the Baltic area, and in the following year imposed the Treaty of Brest-Litovsk upon the Soviets.

9. The peace with Germany was followed, in 1918, by the Allied interventions and the Allied-supported "White Russian" forces commanded by Denikin, Wrangel, Kolchak, and Semenov. These interventionist efforts were not defeated until the spring of 1920.

10. In that same spring, Polish forces under General Pilsudski drove into the Ukraine, reaching the Dnieper and capturing Kiev by early May 1920, to be driven back finally by Red Army forces under Budenny and Tukachevsky.

11. In 1941, Adolf Hitler took the well-traveled road to Moscow.

A thousand years of almost unremitting struggle have left their scars on the Russian psyche. The following speech made by Stalin, on February 4, 1931, illustrated the national paranoia lurking behind Communist ideology:

One feature of the history of old Russia was the continual beatings she suffered because of her backwardness. She was beaten by the Mongol khans. She was beaten by the Turkish beys. She was beaten by the Swedish feudal lords. She was beaten by the Polish and Lithuanian gentry. She was beaten by the British and French capitalists. She was beaten by the Japanese barons. All beat her—because of her backwardness, because of her military backwardness, cultural backwardness, political backwardness, industrial backwardness, agricultural backwardness. They beat her because to do so was profitable and could be done with impunity. You remember the words of the pre-revolutionary poet: "You are poor and abundant, mighty and impotent, Mother Russia." Those gentlemen were quite familiar with the verses of the old poet. They beat her, saying:

"You are abundant," so one can enrich oneself at your expense. They beat her, saying: "You are poor and impotent," so you can be beaten and plundered with impunity. Such is the law of the exploiters—to beat the backward and the weak. It is the jungle law of capitalism. You are backward, you are weak—therefore you are wrong; hence you can be beaten and enslaved. You are mighty—therefore you are right; hence, we must be wary of you.[1]

The "Peasant Mentality." Sociological generalizations are at best hazardous, but some have stood the test of history. One of these is that predominantly agricultural societies have tended to be more "atomized" in structure, and more introverted in their relations with other societies, than their urbanized, commerce-oriented neighbors.

The reasons for this contrast are fairly obvious. One is isolation—the physical remoteness from other pockets of the society which engenders, on the one hand, a tight interlocking of the particular community itself and, on the other, a wariness vis-à-vis all intruders into the community domain. This attitude is bolstered by the conservatism of people who are tethered to their plot of land and to an unchanging routine imposed by nature. It is reinforced by suspicion, tinged with a mixture of contempt and envy, of the "city slicker" common to rural societies.

Historically feudalism in Russia endured longer than elsewhere in Europe. Serfdom was not legalized until the early part of the seventeenth century; but as a practical condition of life it dates back to the fifteenth century or even before. The plight of the Russian peasantry was symbolized by two institutions: serfdom, by which the peasant was bound in perpetuity to the soil and to the master he served; and the village commune, or *Mir.*

Narrowly defined, the *Mir* was the village assembly. Functionally, however, it was much more than that. The word in Russian has no plural forms; historically it is the same as the word for "world." The *Mir* was the peasant's world—the world which regulated his life, governed his interactions with the fellow inhabitants of this world, and impersonally linked him with the "outside world." The collectivism inherent in the institution emerges clearly in the following description:

> That a mystical-religious sanction was given to the decisions of the *Mir* is indicated in such common folk sayings as "The *Mir* is like a wave; one man's thought is everybody's thought," and "The *Mir's* conclusion is God's decision." These expressions of feeling about the *Mir* had a direct parallel in the religious concept of *sobornost:* congregational or collective equality and responsibility in the eyes of God. The fact that the communal unit and not the individual made the decision permitted the individual to slough off his responsibility and assign it to the group. Life and personality were thus given to the group. Things sanctioned by the *Mir* inevitably were "right."[2]

Serfdom was abolished in Russia in 1861 by Tsar Alexander II, long after the last vestiges of feudalism had crumbled in Western Europe, but the embracing mystique of the *Mir* has lingered. Wright W. Miller points out that, although peasants now form less than half the Russian population (as compared with 80 per cent before the Revolution), most of the Russians who are today forty or more years old must have been raised in the atmosphere of the *Mir*, while persons under that age were born into communities where the *"Mir* spirit" was still strong. The collectivization of 1930–33 decimated the peasantry through deportation, killing, or starvation. It converted the old patchwork of *Mir* lands into collective farms. But in this drive, as well as the second collectivization of 1951, the villages were preserved as basic units. Miller concludes that, if anything, the *"Mir* spirit" in rural areas of Russia has been strengthened: "An inevitable result of so many years of interference [by the Communist regime] has been to drive the country people more compactly together, in a reaction which anyone in town clothes can feel as he attempts to make contact with suspicious villagers."[3]

When we speak of a "peasant mentality" in the Soviet Union, we allude, therefore, to environmental factors which have conditioned the great majority of the Soviet population —by virtue of either present status or formative childhood experience. They are starkly reflected in the traits of a man like Khrushchev: joviality combined with crudely articulated anger; acute sensitivity to criticism and fierce pride in accomplishments; and an expansive attitude toward kindred spirits, contrasted with distrust toward the forces of exploitation in the "outside world."

Secrecy and the Russian Authoritarian Tradition. In Russia, secrecy has historically been a uniting link between the values of the society and those of its government. As an attitude toward the outside world on the part of the rulers, it was the reflection of the various historical and cultural factors sketched above, and shared by the people as a whole. At the same time, as a policy, it served the needs of the ruling class in its effort to maintain itself in power. The motive of the Tsars was essentially the same one which has animated their Communist successors—namely, to protect a hierarchic society against what they deemed the debilitating ingress of the outside world.

In more modern times, secrecy served as the moat between the autocratic system of the Tsars and the Industrial Revolution. Secrecy became a self-perpetuating force. In order to safeguard their power, the Russian rulers deliberately preserved the backwardness of the country. The wider grew the gap between Russia and her industrializing Western neighbors, the greater became the imperative of secrecy. The Russian masses had to be prevented from comparing their abject lot with that of their more fortunate neighbors, and they had to be protected against contamination by the "dangerous" ideas which in Western Europe traveled in the wake of the industrial upheaval. At the same time, backwardness had to be barred to the inquisitive eyes of foreigners, lest they employ knowledge of the intrinsic weakness of Russia in planning military adventures.

Even during the stirrings of cultural life in the nineteenth century, when the Tsars began their losing battle against a swelling flood of internal intellectual and artistic activity, the barriers to the outside world were maintained with dogged tenacity. Some of the observations noted by the Marquis de Custine in his famous book, *La Russie en 1839,* could easily have been made by more recent visitors to the Soviet Union. The following is a sample.

> In Russia secrecy presides over everything: secrecy—administrative, political, social; discretion—useful and useless; silence—superfluous for assuring necessary security; such are the inevitable consequences of the primitive character of this people, corroborated by the influence of its government. Every traveler is indiscreet; so it is necessary, as politely as possible, to keep track of the always too inquisitive foreigner lest he see things as they are—which would be the greatest of inconveniences.[4]

The external and internal functions of secrecy—its role as a defense against attack and its use as an instrument of social control—thus tended to reinforce each other. Given the structure of Russian society and the motivations of its upper strata, however, the internal function became by far the more important one. The contrast between Tsarist autocracy and Soviet totalitarianism can perhaps be best summarized as follows: The Tsars saw the sharp division between ruling class and people as the basic prerequisite of the maintenance of power. The Soviets, by contrast, seek to bridge the gulf between rulers and ruled by harnessing the entire society to a common ideal. Despite sporadic reforms, the Tsars viewed national progress as inimical to the preservation of the old order. The Soviets regard progress as a motivating and unifying social force.

The Communist Contribution to the Secrecy Complex

While there is continuity in the Russian-Soviet experience, there has also been a significant break with the past. To determine how much of Soviet Russia is "Russian" and how much "Soviet" is as fruitless an effort as arguing over the relative influence of heredity and environment in the shaping of individual personality. Nevertheless, it is clear that the objectives of "statism" in Russia have undergone significant changes in the transition from the old to the Bolshevik order, and that, along with these objectives, there has been a change in the rationale of power. While the principle of social control—and secrecy as part of that control—has remained fairly intact, the relative importance attached to the various tools through which control is exercised has varied since 1917. The unique Communist inputs into the old secrecy complex might be sketched as follows:

The Conspiratorial Nature of the Party. The hallmark of Leninism was the concept of the role of the Communist Party as a disciplined, highly selective "vanguard of revolution," and the driving force of the "dictatorship of the proletariat" which would guide the revolution from its first, "bourgeois" phase to the ultimate condition of Communism. Disdaining the revolutionary consciousness of the masses—"workers have to go to work in the factory as if on a chain gang, and neither time nor possibility remains for them to become socialists"[5]—Lenin regarded the role of the Party as that of the teacher, the manipulator, the propagandist, and the agitator.

Thus, superimposed upon chicanery and deception as the traditional tools of the Russian leadership was a conception which elevated conspiracy to the level of an operational dogma—a dogma embraced by men who had spent the better part of their lives in the darkness of the conspiratorial underground. Inexorably, this dogma entered into the official ideology and thus passed on to the new generation which did not itself take part in the initial Bolshevik experience. Frederick C. Barghoorn lists among the irrational factors in Soviet thinking "those generated by the long underground struggle of the Bolsheviks against heavy odds." These factors, he asserts, "have been incorporated into Soviet thinking in the form of political maxims strewn throughout key works of Lenin and Stalin which Soviet leaders study in school and then restudy in special Party educational institutions. Thus, they become steeped in them."[6]

By its very nature, the system which evolved in the Soviet

Union after the Revolution placed a premium on conspiracy. In the absence of any clearly defined stepladder to political power—and in Stalin's world in which political survival tended to be synonymous with physical survival—the political process became a game of wits, deception, and ruthlessness. The present Soviet elite not only inherits the older tradition of scheming and conspiratorial technique, but now has behind it a generation of specifically Soviet experience. The members of this elite, although they have cut the Stalinist umbilical cord, are in positions of power because they proved to be the most successful disciples of the wily dictator: "They draw upon a whole bag of tested tricks."[7]

Prevention of Invidious Comparison. As was pointed out in the discussion of the historical-cultural bases of Soviet secrecy, one of the abiding objectives of Tsarist rule was to prevent the masses from obtaining a clear picture of their abject lot compared with that of their neighbors. Under the Soviets, this tendency has been strengthened by the need of maintaining the fiction of Communist progress as contrasted with the decay of capitalist society riven by "contradictions."

To preserve the contrasting image of Communist economic justice and capitalist inequities, the Soviet leadership has been forced constantly to belittle the prosperity in the West, or at least to ridicule it as a cheap veneer which camouflages the widespread misery and poverty of the masses. Consider, for example, the following warning by Otto V. Kuusinen, a member of the Presidium, to the select corps of Soviet citizens privileged to travel abroad:

> Among Soviet people there sometimes appear nearsighted Philistines who, going abroad in happy tourist groups, take the magnificent show windows of stores as signs of abundance of goods and products. Actually, in many stores [in the West] the shelves are bursting with goods, but in no show window is written how many millions of people in such a country suffer poverty and cannot buy these goods.[8]

"Comparison prevention" presents one of the most persistent motifs in Soviet domestic propaganda. Observers find that this propaganda effort has been fairly effective—that the great mass of Soviet citizens is thoroughly indoctrinated with the idea that the standard of living of the rank-and-file citizen of Western countries is lower than in the Soviet Union. Despite the respect generally held for American productive capacity as reflected in the avowed goal to "surpass the United States" in various fields of the economy the regime maintains that the bulk of production does not benefit the ordinary American citizen. "Many, though probably not a majority of Soviet Russians accept this contention even though their own standard of living is low."[9]

Maintenance of Ideological Conformity. Whatever may be the decline—if any—of Communist ideology as a determinant of Soviet external policy, there is little question that, as a secular religion practiced with more or less ritualistic dedication, it continues to constitute one of the most significant cohesives of Soviet society. Ideology serves as a means of communication: the Soviet leaders were trained in a Marxist vocabulary, and they continue to couch their views of the world in its language. The esoteric nature of that vocabulary enables them to dissimulate the real nature of the strains and contradictions within the complex system to others while continuing to communicate among themselves: "Communist theory supplies a ritual language through which the Soviet rulers communicate their intentions, define the razor's edge which divides loyalty from rebellion, distinguish friend from foe, and convey to the initiated an official interpretation of current situations and forces."[10]

Second, ideology serves to cushion the impact of the accelerating process of socio-economic change in the Soviet Union. In this respect, it fulfills roles analogous to those of religious movements in the transformation of internal values. "Changes in the structure of the society are . . . 'justified' in terms of a system of beliefs which are held with high emotional intensity and are indeed, in their sociological characteristics and functions, far removed from 'technical' considerations of economic efficiency and political effectiveness."[11]

In addition to explaining away the contradictions within Communist society, Communist doctrine is essential to the

ruling elite for another, and perhaps compelling, reason: it
provides the sole basis of legitimacy for the maintenance of
their rule. A Soviet defector describes succinctly the crucial
place of ideology in the structure of Communist power:

> . . . there is one thing which the Party professional
> would resist to the bitter end: the loosening of the Party's
> grip on the people. He himself may be disdainful of Com-
> munist doctrine, but he will allow no one else to question
> it, since all his claims to a privileged position in Soviet
> society, as well as his Party's sole claim to power, are
> based on doctrine. Whatever the citizens may think in the
> solitude of their minds, they must conform outwardly. The
> Party will maintain its monopoly on the means of com-
> munication for no other reason than to check the spread
> of "heresy." Criticism of Marxism, the Party, or the
> policies of the leadership will remain a punishable crime.
> Soviet citizens will continue to be denied any but official
> sources of information and forced to accept the official
> interpretation of events.[12]

Ideology remains an extremely important rationale of the
Soviet socio-political structure and of its inner workings. The
Soviets' fear of "contamination" is understandable, especially in an age of far-reaching socio-economic change—an
age, moreover, in which ideology is challenged from other
parts of the world Communist system.

The Dogma of Progress and the "Conniving Society"

In the curious secular religion that is Communism, there
is a sharp distinction between Man and The System. Man,
no matter how lofty his position in the hierarchy, is fallible:
he makes errors, he is selfishly motivated, he may even commit
crimes against the State. The System, on the other hand, can
do no wrong. Man and The System eventually will merge
with the advent of Communism, when the "New Soviet Man"
will be perfected—selfless, principled, and in perfect harmony
with his environment: "For all their diversity, the requirements of people will express the sound, reasonable require-

ments of perfectly developed persons."[13] Meanwhile, however, man continues to fall prey to the "remnants of the bourgeoisie"—to enticements to corruption and self-aggrandizement—and to outside forces hostile to the construction of Communism.

This division between Man and The System provides the rationale for the ever-changing power relationships in a socio-political structure which lacks anything resembling the orderly, constitutional processes of Western society. Since the system is infallible, the blame for any dislocations in the system *must* be traced to human hands. The "scapegoat" technique is universal; but in the Soviet Union it has the full backing of the ideology. Thus, the factory manager whose future hinges on meeting an arbitrarily imposed production quota, but who knows that the resources are not available for meeting the task, faces an acute dilemma. In the words of an expert in Soviet economics and recent visitor to the Soviet Union:

> The Russian manager works within a fine mesh of rules, procedures and detailed targets for all aspects of his operations. If he breaks these rules, he is not simply violating company policy. He is committing a criminal offense under Soviet law; for it is sacred Soviet dogma that "The Plan is law!"[14]

The obvious exit from the dilemma is dishonesty. Books are juggled, figures are falsified, and superior officials are "persuaded" to close their eyes at the appropriate moment. Alternatively, the needed resources which are unavailable through legitimate channels are obtained through illicit means. The factory manager is by no means the only offender. The Soviets have a word for their whole system of "wheels within wheels"—the word *blat*. According to Edward Crankshaw: "*Blat* in its classic form stands for an extremely elaborate and all-pervading 'old-boy' network: the granting of favors in the hope, the expectation, of favors to come. Everyone, including the most ardent Party members, deals in it—everyone, that is to say, who has anything to offer."[15]

In short, the very nature of the Soviet system and its ideological-political mainsprings tends to encourage secretiveness. The distinction between the infallibility of The System, on the one hand, and man's frailty, on the other, strongly influences disclosure of policies at the official level. It stands to reason that large-scale dislocations cannot be attributed to the machinations of "bourgeois remnants" or hostile foreign forces; they reflect upon The System. Since The System is infallible, the logical tendency is to deny these setbacks by hiding the facts and diverting attention.

Retention of the Image of a Hostile World. Anyone who reads the Soviet press tends to find himself in a shadowy "never-never land" in which the imagery seldom changes: the peaceful, selfless "socialist camp" beleaguered by the dark, aggressive forces of imperialism. In order to maintain this image, facts are distorted beyond recognition or they are not mentioned at all. For example, the Soviet public was informed only weeks after the fact, and then only tersely, about the Soviet resumption of nuclear testing. By contrast, a propaganda barrage depicted the "inhumanity" of the U.S. test series in the Pacific. The reader of *Pravda* and *Izvestia* is told in florid detail about the presence of "imperialist gangsters" in South Vietnam who are intent upon placing that country in bondage, yet he knows nothing about Soviet material help to the rebel forces in Laos.

He is firmly convinced that the purpose of the Wall in Berlin is to protect the "peaceful" inhabitants of the German Democratic Republic from the incursions of fascist agents and provocateurs; never has he seen any mention of East Germans being shot while attempting to escape to the West.

It could be argued that Soviet censorship is a wasteful exercise: the screening of domestic affairs is relatively ineffective because most Soviet citizens get fairly complete information on the over-all state of the domestic economy through the "grapevine," and the screening of foreign news is superfluous because most persons either care little about foreign affairs, or—to the extent that they do care—are generally ready to support the regime. Nevertheless, the regime continues to devote huge resources to censorship. This extravagant behavior is prompted by several reasons: one is leadership conservatism. The "average" Soviet citizen may not be unduly shaken by the revelation that Soviet practice abroad does not conform always to the lofty platitudes mouthed by the regime. The members of the higher Party echelons, too, may not be shocked by such revelations, having a personal stake in the preservation and smooth functioning of the system. But, between these two layers of society is another, burgeoning stratum: the privileged class of technicians, managers, and scientists whose loyalty is essential to the regime and its commitment to progress. Although many members of this rising class have been absorbed by the Party machinery, and thus share more or less of the "preservation of power" anxiety, many others have not. They represent the only real basis for a "thinking minority" in the Soviet Union which, though committed to the regime's broad policy, conceivably might grow strong enough to exert significant pressure upon its day-to-day decisions. This is a danger which the higher strata of the Party, jealous of their prerogatives, cannot contemplate blithely. It is much easier to suppress the facts than to cope with the possible consequences of their revelation.

Beyond this practical and specific consideration, however, there is another, broader one which bears upon the functioning of the system as a whole. Totalitarianism is obsessed with self-justification of absolute power, a psychological trait which Richard Lowenthal terms the "collective paranoia":

> The two-camp doctrine is the Communist version of what we have called the element of "collective paranoia" in totalitarian ideology—its need for a single, all-embracing enemy who is assumed to pull the wires of every resistance to the Party's power. The term "paranoia" is used here not to infer that the phenomenon in question is due to psychotic processes in either the leaders or the mass following of totalitarian parties, but merely to describe, through a convenient psychological analogy, the ideological mechanism of projection that ascribes the regime's drive for unlimited power to an imagined all-enemy. The essential point is that in the nature of totalitarianism, any inde-

pendent force—either inside or outside the state—is regarded as ultimately hostile; the concept of "two camps" and that of "unlimited aims" are two sides of the same phenomenon.[16]

This trait obviously ties in with other factors that we discussed above. The Soviet regime fitted easily the image of "capitalist encirclement" into the traditional Russian sense of insecurity. After more than four decades in power, it has become ludicrous to attribute dislocations in Communist society to "bourgeois remnants."

Much more plausible is the tactic of blaming them on the nefarious work of outside forces: either directly on the activities of "imperialist agents" against whom the Soviet populace must practice constant vigilance, or more broadly on the need to funnel national resources into the defense against the unrelentingly aggressive designs of capitalism.

Some Implications for U.S. Policy

Is Soviet secrecy predominantly a cultural reflex or does it reflect the attitudes of the Soviet leadership? We might attempt an answer to this question by citing another passage from the travelogue of the Frenchman, the Marquis de Custine, who observed Russia firsthand in the early part of the nineteenth century. He notes the following:

I observed from the beginning that any Russians of the lower classes, suspicious by nature, detest foreigners through ignorance and national prejudice; I have since found that any Russian of the upper classes, equally suspicious, fears foreigners because he believes them hostile; he says: "The French, the English, are convinced of their superiority over all peoples." This is sufficient motive for the Russian to hate the foreigner. A barbaric jealousy, an envy—childish but impossible to allay, governs most Russians in their relations with people of other countries; and as you sense this unsociable tendency everywhere you finish, while feeling sorry for yourself, by showing the distrust that you inspire. You conclude that a confidence which never becomes reciprocal is fraudulent; hence you remain cold and reserved.[17]

De Custine thus drew a rough division between Russian elite and popular attitudes pertaining to secrecy. The Tsars and the aristocracy were motivated largely by envy and superiority and the imperative of preserving the Russian power structure. The Russian intelligentsia, to the extent that it accepted Russia's relative isolation, did so because it shared the aristocracy's envy of the more progressive and opulent world beyond Russia's borders, and attempted to compensate for its sense of inferiority with Slavophile beliefs regarding the inherent superiority of Russian institutions. By contrast, the xenophobia of the broad masses fed upon ignorance and backwardness. Linking these three attitudes was the submissiveness in the Russian character, born of a long authoritarian tradition—a tradition which was in turn reinforced by the very policies of secrecy which it helped to implement and sustain.

Contrast now de Custine's observation of more than a century ago with the following impression of an experienced observer after a recent visit to the Soviet Union:

> What particularly strikes an observer is the naïve enthusiasm and thirst for knowledge of every kind displayed by these gifted people who have only quite recently learned to read and write. They apply themselves with a discoverer's zest to the tasks confronting them . . .
>
> A primitive curiosity is at work in this historically young nation. It manifests itself in a thirst for knowledge, a desire to understand the world—surely one of the most fruitful of human characteristics. Soviet man would, indeed, be fundamentally different from his fellow men if he were not inquisitive and accepted unchallenged everything his rulers set before him. Fortunately, he has not lost his desire to get at the bottom of things; on the contrary, he inquires into everything, and he does not stop at national boundaries.[18]

Klaus Mehnert's description bespeaks an impression which nearly every recent visitor has brought back from the Soviet

Union. There is little doubt that the revolution in education —which in the span of four decades has transformed a nation of earthbound peasants into a formidable challenger of the U.S. in the space age—is also in the process of transforming Soviet society and confronting its leadership with a host of problems of social and ideological control. Whatever may be the ultimate implications of an enlightened populace and a burgeoning "new class" of technicians and specialists for the structure of Soviet society, popular xenophobia (such as that reflected in the *"Mir* spirit") is apparently weakening as a pillar of the Soviet secrecy complex.

This does not mean that these trends will remove the secrecy barriers or the regime's hold on the society. The Russian people remain submissive to their masters. Western observers who have spent protracted periods of time in the Soviet Union report fairly drastic ups and downs in their access to Soviet people at unofficial levels. They attribute these fluctuations to an almost uncanny ability of the individual Soviet citizen to sense changes in official policy and pattern his conduct accordingly. For example, U.S. diplomats who were able to foster cordial social relations with individual Russians during the halcyon "Camp David" period of Soviet-American relations suddenly found the same contacts barred following the U-2 incident in the spring of 1960. Of late, a barrage of "vigilance campaigns" in the Soviet press, punctuated by a series of spy trials, has further tended to isolate the visitor from the populace at large. In short, however aroused may be the curiosity of the new Soviet generation, it has thus far tended generally to accept the regime's limitations upon that curiosity, especially as it concerns relations with the outside world.

Moreover, the conclusion that Soviet secrecy is primarily a policy-elite phenomenon does not necessarily render it a more rational one. Although Soviet material progress may gradually allay those acute feelings of inferiority which have nourished distrust and resentment toward the outside world, envy and suspicion of the West probably will continue to color heavily the outlook of Russia's present rulers. Even to the extent that secrecy policies mirror the regime's concern for preserving the levers of internal control, this concern may not be a rational one—in the sense of being susceptible to reasoned persuasion. Thus, the regime may well underestimate the extant level of popular support for its policies. It may overestimate the need for secrecy as an instrument of internal control.

Yet, the recognition that secrecy is primarily a policy problem—and perhaps in conflict with popular desires—does modify the pessimistic notion that the entire phenomenon is beyond our reach, and suggests at least that a concerted policy of penetrating Soviet secrecy at the sub-official level could reap results. It may not be possible in the foreseeable future to make rapid headway against the regime's abidingly rigorous lines of internal authority, let alone to exert direct pressures against the regime and its apparatus. At best, any hope of success must be a long-range one. Americans must temper their thirst for quick and lasting results and live with the realization that vast social change does not occur overnight. At the same time, they must dampen their ingrained optimism and recognize that such change is not preordained by any laws of social evolution or industrial progress—that, in order to capitalize on some of the forces now stirring in the Soviet system, we must attempt to encourage them.

Perhaps even more promising in terms of short-range results is direct pressure against the regime itself. The very sensitivity to outside criticism which constitutes an important prop of Soviet secrecy policies is exacerbated by these policies themselves. Put differently, the Iron Curtain serves not only to shield from the Soviet people the extent of their backwardness relative to the rest of the world, but it is intended also to hide the weaknesses and shortcomings of the society from gloating foreign observers. At the same time, however, the Soviets have betrayed their sensitivity to the charge that a great, powerful, technologically advanced nation, living in "Socialist harmony," should not have to stoop to petty measures of surveillance and censorship characteristic of more primitive and oppressed societies. It seems quite plausible that this sensitivity has already accounted for some otherwise inexplicable modifications of Soviet secrecy practices in the past: e.g., the abolition of direct censorship of the dispatches of foreign correspondents in the Soviet Union and the relaxation of efforts to jam Western broadcasts. Again, U.S. propaganda has sought to exploit Soviet vulnerability. The contrast between the open and closed society, for example, has been a consistent theme accompanying U.S. man-in-space efforts. Yet the U.S. can, and should, stress this theme more loudly and consistently.

Conclusion

Soviet secrecy confronts the United States at two principal levels. At the military-strategic level, it obstructs our insight into Soviet capabilities and intentions, thus keeping alive a variety of "destabilizing" elements in the thermonuclear environment, particularly the perils of war triggered by surprise attack, pre-emption, or miscalculation. At the level of Soviet domestic society, secrecy helps to perpetuate the arbitrariness of the Communist system and the regime's irresponsibility in its conduct of external Soviet policy. It tends to block outside attempts at penetrating the system, spurring popular pressures against the leadership's freedom of action and thus helping to transform the Soviet regime into a more responsible government and the Soviet Union into a more mellow member of the international community.

These two dimensions of Soviet secrecy as a United States policy problem suggest two objectives for breaching secrecy barriers: the short-range objective of lifting the military Iron Curtain, and the longer-range aim of influencing change in Soviet society. The urgency of the first objective has waned conspicuously during the past half decade. The march of technology, which has placed fantastic new weapons at the service of military planners, at the same time has yielded equally fantastic means of detecting and appraising these weapons in the arsenal of the opponent. Our policymakers seem reasonably assured that the "intelligence gap," which in the past bestowed considerable advantages to Communist conflict management, has dwindled substantially in important strategic sectors. They are confident that their knowledge of

Soviet strategic capabilities-in-being (as distinct from weapons in the research and development stages) is increasingly comprehensive and incisive.

If the military side of the Iron Curtain is thus becoming progressively porous, however, there still remains the longer-range task of what might be described in shorthand fashion as "social penetration." The urgency of this task has not receded, despite the breakthrough in strategic intelligence and despite the current climate of U.S.-Soviet détente. The most accurate and up-to-date knowledge of the opponent's capabilities cannot yield an accurate gauge of his intentions, especially so long as these intentions are not circumscribed by internal restraints. By the same token, no détente can be considered permanent so long as a small and ideologically oriented leadership elite continues to function without having to bend to popular pressures, thus remaining in a position to change course overnight.

But on this "social-systemic" level of the secrecy problem, too, opportunities are beckoning. Forces are stirring in the Soviet Union which, although still largely inarticulate and not addressed to an "opening" to the outside world as such, certainly seem to be pointed in that direction—or, at least, can be pointed in that direction. As we suggested earlier, however, we can neither assume that these forces will become irrepressible in their own rights, nor can we blithely hold to the hope that the Soviet regime will substantially lower secrecy barriers either as a reward to a thirsting intelligentsia or as a sacrifice to a détente with the West. The Soviet leadership, in its theoretical pronouncements as well as its actions, has made it clear that "liberalization" stops at the point of a meaningful intercourse between the Soviet citizen and the outside world. This is one of the implicit meanings of the "continuing ideological struggle," as Khrushchev defined this qualifying dogma within his "peaceful coexistence" concept. This is also the message of recurring spy trials and harassment of Western visitors, such as the recent arrest of Professor Barghoorn.

In short, the forces at work in the Soviet Union require encouragement—or, more crassly, "manipulation." Any strategy of exploitation, however, must be a comprehensive one in which success is not measured merely by such superficial yardsticks as the volume of Western tourists traveling the prescribed Soviet routes or the number of American athletes competing in Moscow's stadium. And to be comprehensive, the attack must be carried out with as much coordination as the United States policy apparatus can muster.

NOTES

1. J. V. Stalin, "The Tasks of Business Executives," in *Works: July 1930–January 1934,* Vol. 13 (Moscow: Foreign Languages Publishing House, 1955), pp. 40–41.

2. Thomas Fitzsimmons, Peter Malof, John C. Fiske, *USSR: Its People, Its Society, Its Culture* (New Haven, Conn.: Human Relations Area Files Press, 1960), p. 409.

3. Wright W. Miller, *Russians as People* (New York: E. P. Dutton & Co., 1961), p. 82.

4. Phyllis Penn Kohler, ed., *The Journals of the Marquis de Custine; Journey for Our Time* (New York: Pellegrini & Cudahy, 1951), p. 190.

5. Lenin, *Sochineniia,* Vol. 23, p. 82, cited in Alfred G. Meyer, *Leninism* (Cambridge, Mass.: Harvard University Press, 1957), p. 30.

6. Frederick C. Barghoorn, *Soviet Russian Nationalism* (New York: Oxford University Press, 1956), p. 167.

7. Raymond A. Bauer, Alex Inkeles, and Clyde Kluckhohn, *How the Soviet System Works: Cultural, Psychological, and Social Themes,* Harvard University Russian Research Center Studies, No. 24 (New York: Vintage Books, 1960), p. 168.

8. Quoted in Robert Strausz-Hupé, "The Sino-Soviet Tangle and U.S. Policy," *Orbis,* Spring 1962, p. 29.

9. Bauer, *et al.,* op. cit., p. 127.

10. Gerhart Niemeyer and John S. Reshetar, Jr., *An Inquiry into Soviet Mentality* (New York: Frederick A. Praeger, for the Foreign Policy Research Institute, 1956), p. 43.

11. Talcott Parsons, "Some Principal Characteristics of Industrial Societies," in Cyril E. Black, ed., *The Transformation of Russian Society* (Cambridge, Mass.: Harvard University Press, 1960), p. 21.

12. Vladimir Petrov, "Whither Soviet Evolution?" *Orbis,* Fall 1959, p. 293.

13. Draft of the Twenty-Year Plan, New York *Times,* August 1, 1961, p. 16.

14. David Granick, *The Red Executive: A Study of the Organization Man in Russian Industry* (Garden City, N.Y.: Doubleday & Company, 1960), p. 43.
15. *Russia without Stalin: The Emerging Pattern* (New York: The Viking Press, 1956), pp. 60–61.
16. "The Logic of One-Party Rule," in Abraham Brumberg, ed., *Russia under Khrushchev: An Anthology from Problems of Communism* (New York: Frederick A. Praeger, 1962), p. 33.
17. Kohler, ed., op. cit., p. 191.
18. Klaus Mehnert, *Soviet Man and His World,* translated by Maurice Rosenbaum (New York: Frederick A. Praeger, 1962), pp. 139–40.

PART TWO

THE WORLD IN FLUX

INTRODUCTION

It is high time to put aside all myths and face the realities confronting our country. The strongest and most aggressive military power in Europe is a Communist power—the U.S.S.R. This is no myth. The strongest and most aggressive military power in Asia is a Communist power—Mao's China. This is a reality. The strongest and most aggressive military force in Latin America is a Communist power—that "distasteful nuisance," Castro's Cuba. The divisions in the Communist camp will serve to strengthen the free world only if we exploit them in the cause of peace and freedom. On the other hand, the divisions and illusions in the Western camp, if continued, will invite new Communist aggressions. At this moment in history, the paramount task of the free world is to assure superior strength and restore its unity of policy and action.

George Meany (May 1964)

When the whole East awakes, as it will sooner or later; when it realizes its mighty power and determines to speak its mind, then threats, violence, and superficial victories will not remedy the internal discord. This is why it is Russia's part to grow in power unobserved amidst the wastes and deserts of the North in expectation of the conflict between two worlds, in which the decision will depend on neither of them.

E. Ukhtomskii, "Travels in the East of Nicholas II Emperor of Russia when Cesarewitch 1890–1891" (1896)

The Soviet Union's "Achilles' heel" remains Eastern Europe, where—despite the Soviets' elaborate attempts to forge its people into a homogeneous Communist society—the forces of history, in the shape of powerful nationalisms, continue to run counter to the Kremlin. The Communists must invest large resources in Eastern Europe to maintain their fortuitously established position. Communism could not have come to power in Eastern Europe had it not been for the presence of the Red Army; nor could the Communist regimes, such as those, for example, in East Germany or Hungary, retain control without the support of massive Soviet military forces.

Robert Strausz-Hupé, *et al., Protracted Conflict* (1959)

The truth is, though we have not often spoken of it in recent years, that the best hope for peace with justice does not lie in the United Nations. Indeed, the truth is almost exactly the reverse. The best hope for the United Nations lies in the maintenance of peace. In our deeply divided world, peace depends on the power and unity of the Atlantic Community and on the skill of our direct diplomacy.

Senator Henry M. Jackson, March 20, 1962

WITHDRAWAL FROM EUROPE?
AN ILLUSION

by Dean Acheson

Mr. Acheson, Secretary of State from 1949 to 1953, has frequently served as an adviser on foreign policy to the White House since 1961. He has been Undersecretary of the Treasury and Assistant Secretary and Undersecretary of State. He has devoted much of his life to the service of his country in the military, economic, legal, and diplomatic fields. He received his A.B. degree from Yale University and his LL.D. degree from Harvard University.

This selection, which originally appeared in the New York *Times* Magazine, December 15, 1963, is adapted from an address the author delivered as the Brien McMahon Lecture at the University of Connecticut on November 18, 1963. Copyright 1963, by The New York Times Company. Reprinted by permission.

Unhappily, amity is not the inevitable result of close relations between either people or peoples. Marriage and war lock both into close embrace. Sometimes the parties live happily ever after; sometimes they don't. So it is with allies. It is not surprising, then, that periodically we have a great debate in this country on the issue of reversing this or that major tenet of our foreign policy.

The debate of the coming winter seems likely to be a repetition of the so-called "Great Debate" of the winter of 1950–51. In each case, a Republican ex-President led off the debate— Mr. Hoover in 1950, General Eisenhower in 1963, though in 1950 General Eisenhower was on the opposite side of the argument. Each debate concerns the strength of American forces in Europe, but the implications of each are—and were—political, in no pejorative sense of the word.

". . . The mood which prevailed in many quarters at the time," said the Council on Foreign Relations in its review of world affairs in 1951, "found typical expression in an address by ex-President Herbert Hoover (Dec. 20, 1950) decrying the nonsupport of American policy by hitherto friendly nations, recommending a virtual halt in American aid to Europe, and suggesting an alternative world policy based on withdrawal from the Eurasian Continent and, if necessary, to the Western Hemisphere."

This same longing to return to the womb is discernible in the recrudescence of the same debate. "We lived for more than a hundred years," says Mr. George Kennan, "on principles of withdrawal from the mainstream, and maybe this should be done again."

The conclusion of the debate in 1951 was a reaffirmation by the United States Senate on April 4, 1951, that "the security of the United States and its citizens is involved with the security of its partners under the North Atlantic Treaty, and the commitments of that treaty are therefore an essential part of the foreign policy of the United States," combined with a decision to maintain in Europe the ground, air, and naval forces which are still there today. This time, too, the conclusion of the matter will doubtless be the same reaffirmation and decision.

If we examine the realities of our position, no other conclusion is tenable. Internal political pressures or lures may lead political figures to talk as though we had a choice between continuing or reducing our involvement in European affairs (for, at the moment, we are speaking of Europe). But that is an illusion, and a dangerous one. To withdraw military forces from Europe will not reduce our involvement in European affairs. It may actually increase it. We can no more extricate ourselves from involvement in Europe than Germany can. This is nothing new.

Three Centuries of Involvement

We Americans, all North Americans, have been caught up in European affairs for more than three hundred years—with European successes and failures, brilliant discoveries (including the hemisphere we live in) and (to us) senseless quarrels; with all, to use General Washington's phrase, the combinations and collisions of Europe's friendships and enmities.

Almost continuously from 1689 to 1815 enmities between European nations involved North Americans in bitter fighting on our shores. Then for a century, from 1815 to 1914, we succeeded in staying clear of European collisions, until the civil wars of 1914–45 once again drew us in.

The old Europe-oriented world order of the nineteenth century crashed amid the wreckage of the great empires and their colonial dependencies upon which it rested. The United States reluctantly emerged from isolated absorption in its own, and hemispheric, affairs and, equally reluctantly and at first almost unaided, accepted responsibility for preserving an environment in which free societies could exist and flourish.

The Soviet Union had suffered tremendous losses of population and property during the wars. With unbelieved power of recuperation and under Stalin's ruthless drive, within a decade it had greatly exceeded its prewar power and the combined power of all the rest of Europe.

Europe, without this self-regenerative capacity to recover, needed and received massive outside help. Its economic recovery has been phenomenal; but it has not been translated, as in the case of the Soviet Union, into the military constituent of power. For eighteen years Americans have stood guard in Europe to prevent another attempt by one European power to achieve by force of arms hegemony over the others.

The Need for European and North American Cooperation

The idea that there are national, or European, or North American interests which can be safely pursued in disregard of a common interest belongs to that past which has brought us all such loss and suffering. The truth is that the task of preserving, nourishing, and enlarging the environment for freedom is too great for either North America or Europe alone. It requires their combined and jointly managed efforts. If they should drift or be driven apart, the problems of both would become unmanageable.

The new leaders in Europe charted the course of European unity by insisting upon the common consideration of concrete common problems to reach solutions in the common interest. Their innovations of political ideas and methods were as startling as those taking place in physics. They saw that a unified Europe created in this way would be different from, and greater than, the sum of its parts. With its enlarged vision, problems presented to Europe and to North America could be seen as requiring joint action to reach solution in a still larger community of interest.

The fallacy of the quest for national hegemony has been recognized since the end of the European civil war. Former Premier Michel Debré in his recent book repeatedly exclaims, "If we were only a hundred million Frenchmen." We in America know that 190 million Americans must find community of interests with societies beyond our own to meet the dangers and the opportunities, the challenges and the hopes, of a world which we share with so many others—some well disposed, some ill disposed. Since this is true for us, a nation of fifty million people is courting disappointment, if nothing worse, in setting out to establish an independent power base.

France's effort to do so constitutes an erosion on one side of the grand alliance. Present French policy increases the difficulty of action within the alliance by opposition to joint and integrated measures designed to advance common interests and solve common problems.

Soviet Countermoves

The Soviet Union attempts erosion from the other side. Twice since the war we have experienced the Soviet tactic of alternating the relaxation of a peace offensive with the tension of cold or hot war—once, through the Stockholm peace proposals and, again, through the spirit of Camp David. Neither heralded the dawn of the millennium, or even a change in Soviet aims.

We are now undergoing a third application of the same treatment. The present is said to be a period of détente, of relaxation of tensions. The test ban treaty—wholly desirable in its strictly limited way—is cited as a "first step" to broader agreement. Even before the Russian harassment of our convoys to Berlin, this view was wholly unsupported by evidence. The Russians would obviously gain a great deal by getting others to believe that they could safely relax.

Europeans are now hearing urged, as desirable United States policy, the very withdrawal of forces from Europe which, for more than a decade, has been denounced as "unthinkable" when the possibility was whispered by Europeans.

It all goes to show that to think the unthinkable is not so hard as we thought. Furthermore, as the current and the 1951 discussions both show, it is easier when we get the impression that our allies are not doing their share, have regained their critical faculties, and have so lost their sense of propriety and interallied etiquette as to impose a duty on our chickens.

At the very time our European friends hear talk of a Europe denuded of all but token formations of American and British troops and of Germany neutralized and degraded, they hear or read Mr. Khrushchev. He is always clear and intelligible. Asked not long ago why Soviet troops are in East Germany, he told why:

"The reasons are entirely political. . . . I can say that if the Socialist revolution should win in West Germany—and I cannot say when that will happen—then I would have considerable hopes that Germany could be reunited.

"But . . . until that time the question probably will not be solved."

Mr. Khrushchev's answer is brutally frank. Soviet troops are in Europe for a political purpose. So are ours. Never more than today and never more than with the Soviet Union, the correlation of military power is a major factor in the resolution of political issues. The Soviet purpose is to undermine the Bonn Government, detach the Federal Republic from the Western alliance, and attach a new all-German regime to the Soviet bloc.

To prevent such an outcome is essential. But it is no less important to preserve and carry on all the progress which has been made toward a countersolution. This progress has been toward a strong and united Europe with immense power of attraction; a Europe stable and at peace, by having within it a united Germany; a Europe which, closely linked with North America, can make possible a vibrant, healthy, and secure environment for free societies. This progress has been checked. The checks may be largely temporary but they are critical.

Germany's Role Defined

Because of this crisis, my thesis is that in making political and military judgments affecting Europe a major—often *the* major—consideration should be their effect on the German people and the German Government. It follows from this that the closest liaison and consultation with the German Government is an absolute necessity. (Such practice would not imply any change or diminution of our other allied consultations.) Unexpected or unexplained action nearly always causes consternation in Germany. Sensible decision after careful consultation, even when there has been some difference of view, rarely does.

The reasons for urging this priority can be stated briefly.

Germany is the point of contact between the Atlantic alliance and the Soviet bloc. The division of Germany and the continued occupation of Eastern Germany by Soviet troops, as Mr. Khrushchev brutally pointed out, is for the purpose of bringing all Germany under Soviet influence. Such a result would destroy the Atlantic alliance and make Russian will dominant in Europe.

Germany's division and its occupation threaten the stability and peace of Europe and the security of the United States.

Germany's geographical position and strength make that country indispensable to the existence of both a united Europe and a European defense.

Germany has surpassed all other large European countries in steadfast support of the principles and institutions of a united Europe and of the defense forces and system of NATO. In this course, all of her major parties are united and clear.

Germany is the most sensitive and responsive of all European countries to American action, whether or not we wish it, and for good or ill. This reaction, of course, is the natural concomitant of Germany's exposed position and the use made —or not made—of America's great power.

Germany not only is the most sensitive of the large countries and reacts most vigorously to American action, but German reactions are important, far-reaching, and possibly decisive. The other large countries either do not react, or react less, or their reactions have less effect than Germany's.

The Development of Atlantic and European Unity

A few simple "don'ts" and "dos" might serve as guides for acting on the policy suggested.

First, don't decrease our fighting strength in Europe; and don't talk about doing so in the mistaken belief that talk will move our allies to greater efforts. Talk does only a little less harm than actual withdrawal itself.

I shall not discuss whether we can "afford" the cost of our forces abroad or, stating it differently, whether any supposed necessity of balancing our foreign accounts requires bringing them home. No such necessity exists. Many other ways of dealing with balance-of-payments problems make it possible to state categorically that payments considerations need not affect decision on any major defense requirement.

General Eisenhower has written: "One American division in Europe can 'show the flag' as definitely as can several." But the purpose of the American forces in Europe is very different from that of T.R. when he sent the "Great White Fleet" to "show the flag" (and itself) around the world.

NATO's Army

The NATO army, of which the American contingent is, and should be, a substantial part, has a military mission of the greatest importance to the political purposes of NATO, as important to us in North America as to our friends in Europe. We cannot disentangle our fate or our security from theirs. Our troops are in Europe not as a favor to Europeans. They are there to furnish to NATO forces that stiffening and strength from across the Atlantic which leaves Moscow in no doubt that to engage them will and must bring into action this country's colossal nuclear power.

This deterrent against major attack is by no means the whole mission. For, alone, it would not be enough to prevent a more gradual erosion of the alliance and the imposition on Europe of Russian will. Consider the recent Russian interference with access to Berlin and the earlier threats of it. Can such interference be met more favorably or less favorably to the NATO allies if five of our divisions are withdrawn? Would it be met more favorably if NATO succeeded in its plan for increasing NATO power, including the six American divisions, to the level of Russian power on its Western front?

The answers are plain. Weakness is not strength, and equal power is better than unequal power. It is also true that different kinds of power may not be equally useful and usable in certain situations.

We have many examples of the truth that nuclear power is too great, too destructive, too catastrophic to be used in any but the most serious contingencies. Hence, if one side has a considerable superiority in what is called conventional power and the other in nuclear power, it is foreseeable that the greater nuclear power will deter the lesser power from major aggressions. But it is also foreseeable that the greater nuclear power is not usable, will not be used, and hence will not deter aggressions which the superior conventional power judges correctly will be below the point of provoking nuclear retaliation.

For this reason our great nuclear superiority did not deter

the building of the wall in Berlin. This was a very considerable shock to the Germans, not only those in the West, but to our friends in East Germany as well. They and all our friends and allies began to reappraise the *usable* strength of the United States in the struggle which has been going on for fifteen years in Central Europe.

Their calculation will be profoundly affected, as will the outcome of the struggle, if we persevere in our fixed design to increase NATO forces and deprive Russia of her conventional advantage on her Western front and her tactic of slicing the baloney thin. But our friends will stop calculating, for the outcome will be clear, if we forget the magnitude of our own interest and, out of pique with our allies, take our soldiers and go home, leaving the flag as a symbol of our inability to persevere.

Second, don't continue the British-American-Soviet talks about Germany. The uneasiness and suspicion they cause in Germany far outweigh the massed clichés about keeping contact, doors open, and avenues explored. Suppose a hundred years ago, the British, French (Napoleon III), and Russians had kept talks going on "the Confederate question" in America. Need I go further?

The French Nuclear Program

Third, don't help the French nuclear program. To help will not cause General de Gaulle to deviate in the slightest from any of his policies which are now eroding the unity of Europe and the alliance with America. But to support separate and, supposedly, independent British and French nuclear programs, while offering Germany a different—though intrinsically better—multilateral one, both denigrates the offer to Germany and gives ground for a charge of discriminatory treatment. This puts another obstacle in the way of moderate government in Germany.

It also plays against the excellent possibility that after further experience with their own programs and with the factor of obsolescence in them, the multilateral proposal may be regarded more favorably in both London and Paris. In Paris recently 160 members of the Gaullist-dominated National Assembly voted against funds for the French program.

German-American Collaboration

In four fields essential for the development of both European and Atlantic unity only the closest joint collaboration between the German and American Governments can produce any progress in this period of deep freeze. Lack of progress means retrogression.

All four are equally important and should be tackled at once. Military progress is stymied until something is done about allied association in the nuclear arm. The most helpful road to this end, both militarily and politically, is the multilateral force, where all willing to come in are to man the ships and join in the planning and command.

The German Government is eager to get on with the job, willing to pay its share of the expense and to provide its share of the crews. Others have showed interest and entered the talks.

The greatest incitement to interest is to get the project under way, if only on a trial basis. To do this, we would be wise to work closest with the most enthusiastic, those most eager to have the plan succeed.

Then there is agricultural policy, where problems can arise —and have arisen—certain to cause grave trouble, both among the six members of the Common Market and between the Common Market and the rest of the world, including the United States. If the Common Market follows French policy, it will become a closed, self-sufficient, agricultural unit.

"It is not worth talking of the European Community," said General de Gaulle in July [1963], "if it must be understood that Europe does not obtain its food essentially thanks to its own agricultural products, which can be largely sufficient." This point of view runs counter to the interests of Europe's suppliers of agricultural commodities, and also of Germany, which must buy abroad in order to sell abroad. There is sufficient mutual interest here to make possible an understanding on purposes between Germany and the United States which could shape policy within and with the Common Market.

The same is true of the broad tariff negotiations soon coming up at Geneva. Here again the issue will be whether the Common Market will follow France into a policy which is autarchical and self-absorbed, or will accept its responsibility for a system of international trade in the free world which will not divide and weaken allies and will permit the participation of the developing nations.

Both German and American interests lead to support of the broader view. The great preponderance of German foreign trade is with nations outside the Common Market. Here again, it is of utmost importance that the two governments concert their strategy and tactics.

International Monetary Arrangements

There remains agreement between us on speed and method in modernizing international monetary arrangements. Vast changes have occurred in the past twenty years in the volume of international payments and in the time required for great industrial nations to adjust their economies to changes affecting their balance of payments. The arrangements of Bretton Woods are no longer adequate.

The present Washington fashion is to worry about our balance of payments, usually for the wrong reason. Because we have been losing gold (though our reserves are still large), a lot of otherwise sensible people are urging reversal of most of the wise policies which have brought prosperity and security to the West. A recent Brookings Institution publication shows how this situation will in adequate time correct itself if the nations, largely our allies, which have been acquiring our gold and dollars, will be willing to accept an end to the inflow and a beginning to the compensating outflow.

The chance of their being willing to do this—which begins a drain upon their monetary reserves—is small, unless international monetary arrangements are improved to supplement gold and American dollars as international reserves. This is not difficult to do. The so-called Group of Ten has already agreed to get on with the task. But it is very hard to get technicians and bureaucrats started—and especially monetary technicians and bureaucrats.

To be done, the job needs an infusion of vigorous statesmen. The Germans have the same interest in finding a solution as we have, and Chancellor Erhard has an unequaled reputation for getting things done.

Here is a program of action which calls for a beginning. If a lead is given, others will follow and opposition will have to buck a tide instead of using inertia as an ally. Both the present state of affairs and similarity of interest have cast the United States and Germany in the role of partners to get the Atlantic community moving again.

THE UNITED NATIONS RECONSIDERED

by Raymond A. Moore, Jr.

> *Dr. Moore, an Associate Professor in the Department of International Studies and a member of the Institute of International Studies at the University of South Carolina, received a B.A. from The New School for Social Research and M.A. and Ph.D. degrees from Columbia University. He has taught at Columbia, Adelphi College, and Upsala College, and in 1963–64 was a Fulbright Lecturer in History at Punjab University in Lahore, West Pakistan. During World War II he served with the Fifteenth Air Force in Italy. Dr. Moore is working on a study of "The Modernizing Role of the Army in Pakistan."*

This selection is adapted from the Introduction to *The United Nations Reconsidered*, Studies in International Affairs No. 2, Institute of International Studies, University of South Carolina. Copyright 1963, by University of South Carolina Press. Reprinted by permission.

The current national debate about the place of the UN in U.S. foreign policy is the culmination of strong intellectual currents which have been stirring in the scholarly community and the decision-making elites for a number of years, especially since the Suez crisis of 1956 split the United States from its traditional European allies, Britain and France.

Let it be said at the outset that the United Nations is not served best by those who regard it as above criticism. It is admittedly a fragile instrument for facilitating the conduct of international relations in the enormously complicated world of the mid-twentieth century. Its goals and aspirations deserve the support of intelligent men, but its performance ought to be measured by critical evaluation. A reconsideration of the UN by informed people can aid markedly in throwing light on the problems of the organization which, if not solved, can only jeopardize its future development.

In recent years it has become increasingly clear that the United Nations is undergoing an ordeal which, to paraphrase Lincoln, tests whether this organization, conceived in victory and dedicated to the proposition that all nations are sovereign equals, can long endure. As the UN approaches its first score years of existence it is beset with difficulties from all directions. The Soviets have tried to run it down with the *troika* and tie it up with the veto. The Afro-Asians seek to neutralize it to amorality, and convert it into a stick with which to beat the colonial powers. The colonialists either fight it or ignore it, the chauvinists are eager to desert it, and the one worlders seek to reform it past reality. And on top of all else, the UN is threatened with bankruptcy.

The Crisis of Confidence

The problem had become so severe that Secretary General U Thant, in his first annual report of September 3, 1962, referred to the "crisis of confidence" that the UN is passing through and remarked, "I have faith that the United Nations will survive this 'crisis' and emerge stronger than before as a force of peace."[1]

Unfortunately, the trials and tribulations of the UN have been used by many to condemn the organization out of hand or to advocate U.S. withdrawal from what is labeled a "supranational threat to our sovereignty." But the problem of how to steer a sensible middle course between those who believe the UN can solve all of our problems and those who believe it can solve none of them is not new. It originated with the birth of the UN in 1945 and has been continuous ever since. Lincoln Bloomfield observes:

The postwar years effectively dissipated many of the

extravagant and utopian ideas which the American people and some of their leaders earlier entertained about the United Nations. But the process of disillusionment, as so often happens, left a void. So long as the earlier notions were not replaced with more serviceable attitudes, the American view of the United Nations in succeeding years has tended to become increasingly mechanical. We have gone through the motions of pledging support, making speeches, and voting on resolutions. At crucial moments —Korea, Suez, the Congo—the United Nations suddenly seemed to dominate American policy making. The remainder of the time it existed in a backwater of policy. But in neither case did American performance reflect an entirely rational view of the place of international political organization in world affairs.[2]

The search for a "rational view" of the proper place of the UN in world affairs, while hardly a new venture, is attracting more attention each year.

That able, experienced, and thoughtful men, sympathetic to the aims and aspirations of the UN, have raised questions about the organization in the "Great Debate" indicates that the "vital center," to use Arthur Schlesinger, Jr.'s apt phrase, need not be neglected. In fact, it is imperative that it should not be.

Is the UN Living Up to Its Charter?

One of the basic criticisms is that the UN is not achieving its purposes—it is not doing its primary job of maintaining international peace and security. In Chapter I of the Charter, the Purposes and Principles of the organization are set forth. Article I, Paragraph 1, says that the maintenance of international peace and security is the chief, although not the only, purpose of the United Nations. This purpose is to be realized by collective measures which (1) prevent and remove threats to the peace, (2) suppress acts of aggression or other breaches of the peace, and (3) settle international disputes or situations which might lead to a breach of the peace.

Another point made by critics is that the UN is not living up to its Charter because it bears so little resemblance to its original form. Beginning as an organ run by the Great Powers in the Security Council with the General Assembly having consultative functions, it has now become an organization in which the role of the Great Powers has declined and the Assembly has taken over the functions of the Council. Charles de Gaulle has been particularly disturbed on this count. He also has stressed that the UN was originally created by the victors in World War II, but that it is now controlled by nations which never experienced the war and do not appreciate the problems of those who did. Instead they frequently use the UN to attack the very powers which created it. The decline of the Council and the growth of the Assembly, however, are recognized by some to be the by-product of a situation which in large measure is no fault of the UN as such. It is the result of the breakup of the Great Power unanimity which was supposed to be the keystone of postwar security.

A Mirror of World Politics

The UN, to the extent that it is a mirror of world politics (although Bloomfield prefers to think of it as a "prism"), has reflected the split between the U.S.S.R. and the West. It does not function today according to its original plan because in the postwar world the Grand Alliance of World War II did not turn out to be either very grand or very much of an alliance.

Certainly, the Soviet veto, exercised a hundred times since the United Nations' founding, has been a key cause of the decline of the Council and the gradual shift of power to the Assembly which has grown rapidly since the Uniting for Peace Resolution of November 3, 1950. This resolution enables the Assembly to convene emergency sessions when the Security Council becomes hamstrung by the veto and authorizes the Assembly to recommend collective measures, including the use of force if necessary.

Domination by the Afro-Asian Bloc?

The result of this shift of power has been paradoxical. Some critics believe the UN does too much and others believe it does too little. Many feel that in passing resolutions against the colonial or ex-colonial powers it is overstepping its bounds, thus letting ambition outrun capability. Senator Mike Mansfield, majority leader of the Senate, has pointed out that "It is not the finances which are at the heart of the United Nations problems. It is the procedural distortion between the power to make decisions and the power, the will and the responsibility to carry out decisions which has produced these difficulties in the United Nations." When such issues arise as India's attack on Goa and the Indonesia-Netherlands dispute over New Guinea there is criticism that the UN does not act forcefully enough—that the failure to act condones aggression or rewards those who threaten it. These two apparently contradictory views actually have in common the same basic apprehension—the domination of the Assembly by the new Afro-Asian nations.

It is necessary to appreciate that the UN is not a sovereign body. It is not an alliance. It is not infallible. In fact, it is hardly more than an association of nations with the faults and qualities of all the members. Ambassador Stevenson has said:

> The United Nations has few of the real attributes of government: it has full sovereignty over no territory, it has no citizens, it cannot tax individuals or draft soldiers. Except in certain cases of threats to the peace, breaches of the peace or acts of aggression, it lacks even the legal power, let alone the actual capacity to enter a country against the will of that country's government. Its motive force must be provided by its members.[3]

However, the domination of this association has clearly shifted from the Western powers to the constellation of nations known as the Afro-Asian Bloc. In the growth of the United Nations from fifty-one members in 1945 to 110 in 1962, fifty of the new members have come from the recently independent countries in Asia and Africa. In toto, the fifty-three Afro-Asian powers comprise almost one-half of the membership of the UN. While this newly emergent bloc is hardly monolithic, it is in a position to hold the balance of power in the Assembly if its members agree on any given issue—and on many colonial issues they are united. As a result, they need add only a few members to their side to constitute the simple majority needed to carry procedural questions in the Assembly. Since a two-thirds vote is required to carry substantive issues, they can exercise a veto over the proceedings if their unity is preserved.

The day of "escalating membership" in the United Nations is not yet over. Six new members were admitted in the Seventeenth Session in 1962 alone. There is a strong likelihood that another six new members will be added in the next few years and that eventually the membership of the international organization will reach 124 or 125.

The preoccupation of this restructured General Assembly with colonial problems is no doubt understandable in the light of the postwar anti-colonial revolution, but it has nonetheless been subjected to much criticism. Particularly objectionable to some critics has been the tendency of the Assembly to pass resolutions calling for immediate independence for the remaining colonial territories, irrespective of existing conditions. UN Resolution 1514 of December 14, 1960, states, "Immediate steps shall be taken in Trust and Non-Self-governing Territories, as in other Territories which have not yet attained independence, to transfer all powers to the people of these territories without any conditions whatever. Inadequacy of political, economic, social or educational preparedness should never serve as a pretext for delaying Independence."

Senator Henry M. Jackson of Washington has noted that the UN has been passing all sorts of resolutions that are intellectually dishonest.[4] Some of these have touched on another matter which is of great concern to those reconsidering the UN, that is, the issue of the domestic jurisdiction of member states. The Charter states in Chapter I, Article 2, Paragraph 7, "Nothing contained in the present Charter shall authorize the United Nations to intervene in matters which are essentially within the domestic jurisdiction of any state or shall require the Members to submit such matters to settlement under the present Charter." The only exception to this is that enforcement measures under Chapter VII may be applied when authorized under the duly constituted organs of the United Nations.

In sum then, the shift of power away from the Council, the emergence of the Afro-Asian bloc, "escalating membership," rampant nationalism, fuzzy and irresponsible resolutions, and the violation of domestic jurisdiction comprise the bill of particulars that critics have drawn up against the General Assembly. It results in the indictment that the Assembly has assumed power in the UN without assuming responsibility; that the "one nation, one vote" formula distorts the true facts of mid-twentieth-century life and promotes an unhealthy gap between those who have voting power and those who have actual power. The result is a United Nations which increasingly confronts the United States and the Western nations with a choice between supporting UN resolutions with which they disagree or following policies which they believe to be for their best interests but which undermine the authority of the UN.

Changes in the Secretariat

Structural difficulties in the UN, however, are not confined solely to the Council and the Assembly. They extend to the Secretariat as well. When the Soviets began their general assault on the organization at the General Assembly meeting in the fall of 1960, it was in response to the efforts of the late Secretary General Dag Hammarskjold to carry out the Assembly's resolutions on the Congo. At this time Khrushchev presented his so-called *troika* plan, providing for a three-man body to replace the Secretary General. The three major blocs —the Communists, the Western, and the neutrals—would be represented. It also allowed a veto power for any one of the three members over the other two. Combined with the Soviet veto in the Security Council and the alliance with the Afro-Asians in the Assembly, it held the possibility that the UN might be turned, as Senator Thomas J. Dodd of Connecticut suggested, "into a captive instrument of Soviet foreign policy."

Although sufficient opposition developed to thwart the Soviet proposal for a *troika,* concessions were made which weakened the power of the Secretary General. The Soviets extracted their pound of flesh. The concept of an "inner cabinet" was accepted. This was to be a small but representative group of advisers who would counsel the Secretary General on political and other matters.

Initially, the United States pressed for a five-member cabinet to be made up of representatives from the U.S., U.S.S.R., Western Europe, Latin America, and Africa. The Soviets then suggested a nine-member body with three representatives each from the Western, the Communist, and the neutral blocs. After a considerable harangue, it was finally decided to let Hammarskjold's successor, U Thant of Burma, determine the number of the membership of the new "inner" group.

It is worth pointing out here that U Thant's selection as Hammarskjold's successor represented a triumph for the Afro-Asians and for a type of neutralism which, on other than the colonialism issue, treats all parties to a dispute as equal, regardless of the merits or the demerits of their cases.

On December 30, 1961, U Thant announced the selection of an eight-man cabinet composed of three Western, two Communist, and three neutral representatives. While these so-called "principal advisers" do not have veto power over the Secretary General's actions, their mere existence constitutes a dilution of the powers of the Secretary General. The composition of the cabinet also comes closer to the view of the Soviets than that of the U.S. As U Thant himself is from one of the neutral nations the composition of the cabinet is actually three, two, and four. Senator Dodd remarked of this development, "Once again the Soviets have demanded the moon, settled for half the moon—and persuaded the free world that they were being generous in compromising on their original stand." That the Soviets still have hopes of obtaining the other half of the moon was clear in their renewed demands on October 11, 1962 for the *troika*—this time to be applied wholesale to the entire UN administrative machinery.[5]

The actual composition of the Secretariat itself is of course one of the most sensitive problems of the organization. Its employees are chosen by an agreed-on ratio and are supposed to become international civil servants once they join the United Nations. However, both of these conditions are easier to fulfill in theory than in practice. In the early days of the UN United States representation was heavy because of the location of the organization in New York City. Of late, the Soviets and the new members have been demanding that the employment ratios be more closely observed and, as we have seen in the case of the Soviets above, even changed to conform to the *troika* principle. Insofar as the present arrangements are concerned, there is no question that Communist and Afro-Asian quotas have been undersubscribed in the past. This condition has now begun to be remedied. As Lawrence Malkin pointed out, "during the past year [1962], special job recruiters have gone out to Africa and the Communist countries. The number of Communist bloc staff members has risen from 122 to 132 in one year. The total of Africans went up from forty to fifty-two staff members. The Americans adjusted downward to 368 (or three less than a year before) and Western Europeans to 383 (or four less).[6]

Soviet Espionage and the UN

Of even more significance in the long run may be the undermining of the principle that members of the Secretariat are international civil servants serving the UN, not their own countries. The record of Soviet espionage indicates clearly that it has utilized both its nationals abroad and local Communists to commit illegal acts in its behalf. In the FBI "Exposé of Soviet Espionage," dated May 1960, ten Soviet nationals were listed who had been forced to leave the United States when their activities were uncovered. Non-Soviet nations were not included in this report which stated:

Attention is called to the fact that many of the incidents and cases previously cited involved Soviet employees of the

United Nations. They are guests of the United States and are supposedly dedicated to the cause of international peace but they are, in fact, carefully selected envoys of the international Communist conspiracy, trained in trickery and deceit and dedicated to the concept of fully exploiting the freedoms of the countries they seek to destroy. It is too much to expect that they would not prostitute the United Nations.[7]

The Soviets are also increasingly using their appointees to advance their own UN political interests and, when the occasion calls for it, they are not above using their influence to force the removal of an official who refuses to disclose information gathered from unfriendly sources. What happened to the Danish diplomat and onetime assistant secretary of the United Nations Committee on Hungary, Povl Bang-Jensen, is a case in point. Bang-Jensen was suspended by Secretary General Hammarskjold in December 1957 because he refused to turn over the names of witnesses who testified before the Special Committee on Hungary on condition that their names would not be made public. On January 24, 1958, the list of the twenty-one witnesses' names was burned on the roof of the UN with Bang-Jensen, his lawyer, and a representative of the Secretary General standing by. In July 1958, the Secretary General dismissed Bang-Jensen from his UN position. An appeal to the Administrative Tribunal was turned down in December 1958. Less than a year later, on Thanksgiving Day, November 26, 1959, the Dane was found dead in Queens, New York, with a bullet through his head. The circumstances of his death remain shrouded in mystery. It was this case that Norman Thomas described as "A black and everlasting blot on the escutcheon of the United Nations."

The Problem of Finances

Yet another major point in the reconsideration of the UN involves finances. The UN has been continually threatened with bankruptcy since it undertook such "peacekeeping" operations as those in the Gaza Strip in 1956 and the Congo in 1960. Debts have run in excess of $200 million and at one time the UN was incurring an additional $10 million a month in the Congo operation and $1,625,000 a month in the Gaza Strip. France, the U.S.S.R., and numerous Afro-Asian countries have refused to pay special assessments on the Congo, and the Soviets along with a number of Arab states have withheld funds to pay for the policing of the Gaza Strip area.

As Senator George Aiken stated on March 5, 1962, "only thirty-two states paid their 1960 Congo assessments in full and only nineteen paid their 1961 assessments, while sixty-four states have never paid a single dime toward the cost of the Congo operation." By 1962, sixty-six members were in arrears on their Congo assessments and fifty-six on the Gaza Strip assessments. The entire Soviet bloc was behind in payments. In addition, many states have been delinquent in their regular budget payments. The situation became so desperate on one occasion that Secretary General U Thant made an internal loan of $12 million from the UN's Childrens' Emergency Fund. The legality of such a procedure under the Charter was challenged in some quarters. The U.S., besides paying 32.02% of the UN's regular bills, 47% of the Congo cost, and 46.9% of the Middle East cost, has made voluntary contributions of approximately $65 million since 1958 to help the UN meet its obligations.

To help tide the UN over until some more permanent steps could be taken to settle the problem, the Secretary General on December 20, 1961 proposed a $200 million international bond issue which would pay 2% over a twenty-five-year period. In the meantime, the International Court was asked for an advisory opinion on whether or not expenses incurred by the UN in emergency operations, such as the Middle East and the Congo, could be charged to the regular budget, where failure to pay assessments can mean withdrawal of the right to vote. Article 19 of the Charter states:

> A member of the United Nations which is in arrears in the payment of its financial contributions to the Organization shall have no vote in the General Assembly if the amount of its arrears equals or exceeds the amount of the

contributions due from it for the preceding two full years. The General Assembly may, nevertheless, permit such a member to vote if it is satisfied that the failure to pay is due to conditions beyond the control of the Member.

In the spring of 1962 the United States was asked to purchase one-half or $100 million worth of the UN bonds. President Kennedy quickly requested Congress to authorize this purchase. The matter of the UN's financial crisis then became a public concern and was debated vigorously in the Congress and the press. Inevitably the debate quickly spread from the narrow issue of authorizing the purchase of the bonds to a general review of the United Nations. Yet, on April 5, 1962, the Senate passed the bill authorizing the purchase of the bonds. The House followed suit on September 14 and the final authorization was sent to the White House following a Senate-House Conference Committee agreement containing the proviso that the U.S. could only match dollar for dollar the total purchases by other members. The UN bond sale was, however, more of a palliative than a cure. It hardly ended criticism of the UN over its financial arrangements. There may never be a cure if member nations continue to renege on their budgetary obligations and refuse to abide by majority decisions of which they disapprove—as many members did in the Congo and Gaza operations. Nevertheless, a great step toward finding a solution was taken July 20, 1962, when the International Court of Justice, by a 9–5 vote, handed down an advisory (non-binding) opinion which held that all members of the UN were legally obligated to pay for the emergency operations of the United Nations. These costs, according to the Court, were "expenses of the organization within the meaning of Article 17, Paragraph 2 of the Charter of the United Nations." In other words, the emergency expenses were included under the regular outlays which are obligatory on the members.

This decision, the first of an international judicial body dealing directly with the ability of the UN to incur expenses for "peacekeeping" activities, gave sanction to the UN's power to tax its membership for its many and varied activities.

Although the decision is advisory only and does not require members to pay their bills, it could represent a substantial step toward both legalizing and stabilizing the financial operations of the international body.

A final major point of criticism directly involves the relationship of the United States to the United Nations. Some critics have drawn attention to what they believe is an over-reliance by the U.S. on the advice of the U. S. Mission to the UN and the UN Ambassador when matters of vital interest to the nation's security are involved. Both Henry Cabot Lodge and Adlai Stevenson, the two most recent UN Ambassadors, have played prominent roles in their respective Administrations and exercised considerable leverage on the decision-making process. Under Lodge and Stevenson the influence of the U. S. Mission to the UN has increased—so much so that in a speech to the National Press Club on March 20, 1962, Senator Jackson asked, "Should our delegation to the United Nations play a larger role in the policy-making process than our representatives to NATO or to major world capitals?" His answer, which has ignited a warm and wide discussion of the issue, is, "I think the answer is 'no,' and the burden of proof should be with those who advocate a unique role for our embassy in New York."

The UN: Cornerstone of U.S. Foreign Policy?

From a previous underreliance on the UN, the U.S. has in recent years moved to a position where it seems to have taken seriously the injunction that the UN should be "the cornerstone of American foreign policy." President Kennedy, in his September 25, 1961 speech to the UN General Assembly, declared ". . . in the development of this organization rests the only true alternative to war—and war appeals no longer as a rational alternative."[8] This assumption, that the UN plays the central role in preserving peace and avoiding war, is thought by some critics not only to reflect an exaggerated view of the UN's influence, but actually to weaken the UN by burdening it with responsibilities it cannot carry.

In assessing criticism leveled against the UN, it is well to keep in mind that much of it is prompted by some specific action of the UN of which a senator, editor, statesman, or scholar disapproves sufficiently to speak or write about. Perhaps it is the Goa invasion, the Congo affair, the fighting in Katanga, the bond issue, a resolution by the Assembly, the death of Hammarskjold, or an adverse vote by the alliance of the Communists and the Afro-Asians. This implies, of course, that the UN is indeed acting, not just lying dormant.

Some criticism, it is true, has taken cognizance of long-run trends in the UN or has viewed trends running outside it, as in NATO, for example. What has been characteristic of all these points of view, however, is that they have been advanced by men who have for many years demonstrated their interest in, and knowledge of, international affairs. Moreover, these men are not blind opponents of the United Nations. Few, if any of them, want the UN to fail. What they are concerned with is the health of the organization and safeguarding the security of their country and the free world.

Improving the UN

What suggestions for improving the UN—implicit as well as explicit—can be found in criticism by responsible leaders? The following, while by no means exhaustive, are the most significant:

1. The UN must put its own financial house in order. It must compel nations in arrears to pay their bills. It must take steps to secure a firm financial base for the body.
2. Member nations of the UN must resist any further attempts to weaken the authority of the Secretary General's office; moreover, the Secretary General's office and the Secretariat must not become "politicized." In fact, both must be strengthened. As Assistant Secretary of State Harlan Cleveland has said, "in order to develop the United Nations' capacity to act there is one priceless and essential ingredient—the United Nations executive must be run by a single, competent, and independent-minded official, heading a Secretariat dedicated to serving the Char-

ter, a Secretariat whose staff members are international civil servants and do not report daily to the foreign offices of the countries from which they come."[9]

3. The Afro-Asian nations must begin to grow up politically in the United Nations. Instead of having two sets of standards—one that is rigid for the colonial or ex-colonial powers and another which is loose and flexible for themselves and the Communists—they should follow the old rule of "What's sauce for the goose is sauce for the gander." The AFL-CIO puts the matter bluntly in its *Free Trade Union News* when it says, "Actually, the admittance of the Afro-Asian countries to the world organization was welcomed and sponsored by the West, including the former colonial powers which gave these countries their independence. If there is some Western dissatisfaction with the United Nations, it is not because half of the Members call themselves 'non-aligned,' but rather because many of these new countries do not pursue a true policy of non-alignment."[10]

4. Weighted voting should be considered in the General Assembly. The U.S.S.R already has three votes (The Byelorussian Soviet Socialist Republic, The Ukrainian Soviet Socialist Republic, and the Union of Soviet Socialist Republics) to one for the United States. Since the principle has already been accepted, even if under wartime conditions, some criterion is needed, such as percentage of contributions to the budget, per capita income, population, etc. Some such reform is necessary to offset a situation whereby Gabon, with fewer than five hundred thousand people, 90% of whom live in primitive rural areas, has the same vote as India or the United States.

5. There must be recognition that the future of the UN depends, in large part, on the climate of diplomacy outside the United Nations. It depends especially on the relations of the Communist and Western blocs. As former Prime Minister Macmillan told the House of Commons on February 5, 1962, "The United Nations can never be made to work unless political conditions can be created in a world which allows the Security Council to operate, not for per-

petual propaganda purposes, not as a body permanently divided, but gradually as a team." Therefore, emphasis must be given to creating those conditions under which the UN can function as it was designed.

6. In the very likely event, however, that conditions conducive to reactivating the Security Council cannot be created, at least in the near future, more attention must be paid to building what Senator Fulbright calls, "a cohesive community of free nations." This may require the strengthening of NATO—expanding it from a military to a political union —or creating what Herbert Hoover has called a "Council of Free Nations," to be modeled on the nineteenth-century Concert of Europe. Senator Fulbright himself has argued for a "Concert of Free Nations" and has endorsed Hoover's suggestion that such a Council be ready to act if Communist obstruction prevents the UN from responding to an emergency. Hoover felt that such a "Council" or "Concert" is "the remaining hope for peace in the world" and Fulbright believes it would only serve to strengthen the UN in the long run because, "Constitutions of and by themselves mean little; the history of both the League of Nations and the United Nations demonstrated that. But a powerful sense of community, even with little or no machinery, means a great deal."

7. Member nations, especially the Great Powers, must not shift the onus of responsibility for national decisions involving their vital interests to the United Nations. Such abrogation of authority merely weakens the UN by burdening it with tasks which it is not equipped to perform. The UN then must not be "the cornerstone" of the foreign policies of the Great Powers, especially the United States, but a valuable and indispensable supplement to their traditional diplomacy, alliances, and regional organizations.

Positive Achievements

The positive achievements of the United Nations deserve mention here. It is certainly true that in many trouble spots—

Iran, Greece, Palestine, Korea, and Suez—the UN's "peace-keeping" functions have been important. Its programs in the World Health Organization, International Telecommunication Union, technical assistance, and regional agencies are almost universally commended.[11] In addition, there are undeniably many advantages accruing to the U.S. by membership in the United Nations. It serves as a worldwide town meeting where we can proclaim our ideological convictions before the largest audience in existence. It provides a day-by-day example of our respect for and cooperation with other states and international organizations. It is an arena for the pursuit of our traditional national interest policies. It frequently provides a welcome sanction for our policies, softening what would otherwise be blunt unilateralism. It is a contact point for U.S.-U.S.S.R. relations and U.S.-Afro-Asian relations. By performing its role as the "Honest Broker," the UN can also immunize areas from the politics of the cold war and thereby reduce the risks of thermonuclear confrontation.

Another subject which deserves mention concerns the complex of overlapping institutional memberships which the United States has constructed by virtue of its activities in various regional and functional organizations. Ambassador Stevenson, for instance, has rebutted charges of U.S. overdependence on the UN by saying:

> As a world power the United States must defend its interests and pursue its goals through a variety of institutions which serve quite different national purposes. NATO, for example, was formed not to preserve colonies but to defend Europe and the Atlantic Community against aggression by the Soviet Union. We look to it, not to the UN, to perform that vital function. Conversely, we look to the United Nations, not NATO, to shield small and weak nations in Africa and the Middle East and Asia, and to provide a community in which they can feel a measure of security and equality and of comity with their former rulers. . . .
>
> Sometimes we hear the suggestion that the United States should give less emphasis to the United Nations because—so the argument runs—the UN is not a dependable basis for

our security against hostile forces. This argument misses the point. This country does not rely on the United Nations to do anything which some other instrumentality can do better. The greatest achievements of the United Nations for peace and security—Suez, Lebanon, the Congo, and all the rest—have been achievements for which no really valid alternative means existed.[12]

Regional Security Arrangements

Mr. Stevenson can in turn be criticized for thinking the UN can really defend the small countries around the world, especially against Communist aggression, better than a regional security pact or a bilateral treaty with the United States. Moreover, it is the view of others that a good deal of the trouble with the UN is that it *has* tried to do things which other instrumentalities can do better. As for multiple memberships in international institutions in pursuit of a variety of goals, one could say that not all memberships and goals are equally important. The problem is how the nation allocates its scarce resources of time, money, materials, and energy to maximize a given end—that of preserving a peace which includes the security and the independence of the U.S. and its allies. What is good for the U.S. may or may not be good for the United Nations. And what is good for the UN may or may not be good for the United States.

The dilemma of how to reconcile the need for protection of a nation's vital interests with the demands of participation in an international organization such as the UN is a very real one. After all, it is more than possible that the strength of the U.S. and the Western nations is just as vital to "maintain international peace and security" as the strength of the UN itself. To maintain that peace and security in a world where, as the Preamble to the Charter states, "faith in fundamental human rights, in the dignity and worth of the human person, in the equal rights of men and women and of nations large and small" is upheld, it is not only possible but also probable that the strength of the United States and the Western nations is just as important—and perhaps more so—than the strength of the United Nations.

As President Kennedy once remarked, "For the next ten or twenty years the burden will be placed completely upon our country for the preservation of freedom."[13] To the extent that this is true the U.S. must carefully assess its relationship to and dependence on the United Nations. The power, composition, and policies of the UN deserve continual scrutiny. If the UN is no cure-all for the problems of the world, it is not necessarily an albatross around the neck of the U.S. either. It certainly is not a superstate, nor a world government. It is not a Communist conspiracy nor the simple tool of the Afro-Asians. Can it be called the lapdog of the U.S. or of the Western nations? Hardly. More than a debating society, but less than a true collective security organization, it depends on its members for what it can do.

Conclusion

Because the UN is essentially so weak an organization in international affairs, because the Communist members obstruct its purposes and thwart its ambitions, because the membership has changed so radically, and because the Assembly has assumed such complete control, the United States should not, for moralistic and legalistic reasons, avoid the hard task of conducting an "agonizing reappraisal" of the international body and the relationship of the U.S. to it. One would have to search far to find a better guideline for such a reappraisal than these wise and measured words of Senator Henry M. Jackson: "The United Nations is, and should continue to be, an important avenue of American foreign policy. But we need to revise our attitude in the direction of a more realistic appreciation of its limitations, more modest hopes for its accomplishments and a more mature sense of the burdens of responsible leadership."

NOTES

1. From *Annual Report of the Secretary General,* General Assembly Official Record, 17th Session, Supplement No. 1, A-5201, pp. 1–182.
2. Lincoln P. Bloomfield, *The United Nations and U.S. Foreign Policy* (Boston: Little, Brown & Co., 1960), Preface, p. v.
3. *Hearings* before the Committee on Foreign Affairs, House of Representatives, 87th Congress, 2nd Session, on S.2768, "A Bill to Promote the Foreign Policy of the United States by Authorizing the Purchase of United Nations Bonds and the Appropriation of Funds Therefor," p. 4.
4. New York *Times,* July 9, 1962.
5. New York *Times,* October 12, 1962.
6. Lawrence Malkin, "The Battle For the Independence of the U.N. Secretariat," *The Reporter,* September 27, 1962. See also Leland M. Goodrich, "Geographical Distribution of the Staff of the U.N. Secretariat," *International Organization,* Summer 1962, Vol. 16, No. 3, pp. 465–82.
7. "Exposé of Soviet Espionage," Federal Bureau of Investigation, U. S. Department of Justice, May 1960, p. 14.
8. New York *Times,* September 26, 1961. Reprinted in *Department of State Bulletin,* Vol. XLV, No. 1164, October 16, 1961, pp. 619–25.
9. "Four Popular Canards about the United Nations," *The Department of State Bulletin,* Vol. XLV, No. 1168, November 13, 1961, p. 801.
10. AFL-CIO, *Free Trade Union News,* Vol. 18, No. 1, January 1963, p. 2.
11. For a convenient summary of information on the Specialized Agencies and other UN Committees, see Appendix IV of Inis L. Claude's *Swords into Plowshares: The Problems and Progress of International Organization,* 2nd edition, revised and enlarged (New York: Random House, 1959).
12. *Hearings* before the Committee on Foreign Affairs, House of Representatives, 87th Congress, 2nd Session, op. cit., pp. 6–7.
13. New York *Times,* August 29, 1962.

PERSPECTIVES FOR EASTERN EUROPE

by Richard V. Burks

A specialist in Byzantine history and East European Affairs, Mr. Burks joined Radio Free Europe in July 1961 and is now Policy Director of RFE in Munich. As a Professor of History at Wayne State University in Detroit, he founded that university's graduate studies program in East European Studies. He graduated from Miami University, Oxford, Ohio, and received his Ph.D. degree from the University of Chicago. His book The Dynamics of Communism in Eastern Europe *was published in 1961.*

This selection originally appeared in the March-April 1964 issue of the U. S. Information Agency's bimonthly publication *Problems of Communism*.

There is little doubt that the Sino-Soviet dispute came as a greater surprise to Eastern Europe than to any other part of the world. Indeed, the extent and nature of this conflict are still not generally understood there, and this fact will most probably delay the full impact of the break. Nonetheless, the conflict is already introducing a totally new element into East European politics.

The contention between Moscow and Peking is much more than a passing quarrel; it is rather in the nature of a schism in a worldwide movement, comparable to the separation of the Orthodox and Catholic churches in the eleventh century, or to the breakdown of Western religious unity in the sixteenth. It is an expression of deep-going cultural differences between

Europe and Asia as well as an outgrowth of clashing Soviet and Chinese national interests. The doctrinal disputes which remain at the focus of international attention only reflect these underlying differences, and it is unlikely that a genuine reconciliation can take place within the foreseeable future.

The schism leads in two directions. For one thing, it promotes the division of the Communist world into two camps: one with its capital in Peking and its main support among the colored peoples of the developing countries: the other with its center in Moscow and its following among the more advanced industrial countries of preponderantly white population. But the schism has also produced a marked intensification of factional conflict within existing Communist parties and the splinter parties. The long-range consequences of these developments for the inherently unstable Communist regimes of Eastern Europe should be far-reaching.

Ideology and National Interest

It is, first of all, important to remember in this connection that in the doctrinal aspects of the Moscow-Peking conflict, it is the Soviets who are the innovators, particularly as far as the twin doctrines "peaceful coexistence" and "peaceful transition," or such concepts as the "all-people's state" are concerned.[1] In the pursuit of their struggle to maintain the leadership of the Communist movement, the Soviets will therefore feel compelled to insist on the orthodoxy and acceptance of their "revisionist" views, and this will be an additional reason for their dependents, particularly in Eastern Europe, to adopt a similar posture. In this respect, Moscow's official position will reinforce the latent political tendencies in the area.

On the other hand, however, Soviet capacity to ensure political conformity in the bloc has been weakened by the fact that the world Communist movement no longer possesses a single center of undisputed authority. In such a situation, the individual parties find more room for maneuver, and the risks of deviation are smaller.

The most recent case in point is the estrangement between Moscow and Bucharest. The issue that has clouded Soviet-

Rumanian relations over the past two years is the question of the kind of industrial development Rumania should pursue: should capital investment be limited to the fields of petrochemicals, synthetic fertilizer, and food processing, as Moscow has proposed through Comecon, or should the industrialization of the country proceed along more traditional Stalinist lines, i.e., by concentrating on the development of a heavy-industrial base, as the Rumanian leadership desires? What Moscow has proposed is perhaps more reasonable, especially when viewed from the standpoint of the interests of the bloc as a whole, but what Bucharest insists on is more orthodox and, at the same time, more in consonance with its conception of Rumanian national interests.

Rumania's resistance to Soviet pressure first became evident in the winter of 1961–62, after the Twenty-second CPSU Congress and Khrushchev's open denunciation of the Albanian leadership. The proportion of Rumanian trade with non-Communist countries, which began growing even before the congress, continues to increase; it has risen from 22 per cent of the total foreign trade amounting to 5.7 billion lei in 1958 to 33 per cent of 10.6 billion in 1962.[2] Thus in exchange for such hard-currency-earning products as oil and oil drilling and refining equipment, and through the sale of emigration visas to citizens who have wealthy relatives in the West, the Bucharest regime appears to be importing much of the advanced machinery and hiring most of the technicians required for the construction, now just beginning, of a major iron and steel works at Galati. There are apparently no Soviet experts at Galati, and since June of 1960 there has been no public reference by any Soviet leader to this project.

In the spring of 1962, furthermore, the regime completed the collectivization of agriculture, which at the Rumanian party congress of 1960 had been foreseen as a gradual process ending only in 1965. Since collectivization of agriculture had been the key to Soviet industrialization, providing both the necessary (forced) savings and the necessary labor, it seems reasonable to conclude that the hasty final collectivization drive in Rumania was intended to provide additional resources for an independent policy of all-round industrialization.

It is worth recalling at this point that Gheorghe Gheorghiu-Dej, the Rumanian party leader, defied Khrushchev on yet another issue, that of de-Stalinization. At the Central Committee plenum convoked in Bucharest shortly after the Twenty-second CPSU Congress, Gheorghiu-Dej and his colleagues undertook a public reinterpretation of Rumanian party history. According to the view that emerged from this presentation, the evils of Stalinism in Rumania had been perpetrated by foreign and pro-Soviet elements in the party leadership. Since these had been removed from power with the purge of Pauker, Luca, and Georgescu in 1952, and of Chisinevschi and Constantinescu in 1957, nothing further needed to be done along the line of de-Stalinization. It is true that police controls have been relaxed somewhat in the interim, since the new policy has earned for Dej a certain amount of popular support, but surely it is not without significance that in traveling through the country by road citizens still must pass an inspection point every fifty kilometers!

Rumanian party historians have also revised the official interpretation of the events of August 23, 1944, when Rumania deserted the Axis. The advance of the Soviet Army across the Rumanian border is now minimized or even ignored altogether, and the changeover is presented as the result of a broad national movement, under Communist leadership to be sure, but including the traditional bourgeois parties and even the King. This shift in historiography was followed by such events as the closing of the Maxim Gorky Institute, the chief Rumanian center for the spread of Soviet culture, the dropping of Russian as a required language in secondary schools, the discontinuation of the Rumanian edition of the Soviet political journal *Novoe vremia,* and the favorable re-evaluation of the works of leading pre-Communist Rumanian authors. The new policy of the regime thus combines Stalinist orthodoxy with an assertive nationalism.

The Rumanian determination to pursue a policy of all-round industrialization has severely hampered Soviet plans for a closer integration of East European economies, including common planning institutions and procedures, as well as common investment allocation. The Rumanians have insisted on their right not to participate in economic planning they deemed against their national interest, and they seem to have gotten their way.

There are two points to be made in connection with this rather startling development. One concerns the successful Rumanian use of blackmail. In January 1963, Rumania, the first and only Soviet-bloc country to do so, sent its ambassador back to Albania. The following June, the Bucharest press published extensive excerpts from the now notorious Chinese letter of the fourteenth of that month denouncing the Soviet leaders and their policies[3]—and this in spite of the explicit warning from Moscow that any propagation of the document prior to a Soviet formal reply would be regarded as an unfriendly act. No other satellite regime even mentioned the existence of the letter. Later that same June, Gheorghiu-Dej ostentatiously refused to go to East Berlin, where all Soviet-bloc leaders had been summoned by Khrushchev. Finally, in November 1963, the Rumanian delegation at the United Nations voted with the Yugoslavs in support of an atom-free zone in Latin America, even though the U.S.S.R. and the other members of the Soviet bloc abstained.[4] All these moves indicated the Rumanians' willingness to deal with Peking if Moscow were not sufficiently amenable, and Khrushchev, who was already facing a host of troubles, apparently decided he could not afford to risk the defection of another, and major satellite.

Secondly, it should be borne in mind that the Rumanian deviation could constitute an important precedent. What Rumania has done, any other European satellite, with the notable exception of East Germany, can also attempt. In other words, the Rumanian action has introduced into Eastern Europe a potential for some degree of independence in foreign policy —this in addition to the greater autonomy in internal affairs which the satellites have acquired since Khrushchev's rise to power.

The opening of West German trade missions in Warsaw, Bucharest, and Budapest, a significant increase in Western tourism, and new access to non-Soviet sources of iron ore and grain are all recent developments that complement the loosening of Soviet controls in Eastern Europe and make for greater diversity and a freer play of national interests. The current Soviet rapprochement with Yugoslavia adds further to this atmosphere of permissiveness.

Increased Contacts with the West

Reinforcing certain tendencies that have been discernible in satellite politics for some time, the Sino-Soviet schism has thus strengthened in Eastern Europe the forces of revisionism, while contributing to a decline in Moscow's authority. It may be expected that in the longer run this trend is likely to express itself in the following developments: (1) greater contact with and dependence upon the West; (2) the emergence of at least an embryonic public opinion; and (3) the development of mixed economies.

Increased traffic with the West may soon become apparent, especially in the sphere of trade. Within the next three to five years, satellite trade with the West is likely to rise in absolute terms and also as a proportion of the total foreign trade of the area. Almost all the members of the bloc are already planning to import sizable quantities of grain. Bulgaria signed a long-term wheat contract with Canada in October 1963,[5] and the Soviet Union and Hungary have now made their purchases in the United States.[6] More and larger agreements are expected in the future. The grain shortage which has been chronic in Eastern Europe since World War II became critical in 1963 because of crop failure in the U.S.S.R., which has limited the Soviets' supply ability, and because of the poor harvest in the satellite countries themselves. Remedial measures are now being taken in the Soviet Union—mainly in the form of increased investment in the production of synthetic fertilizers—but it will be some years before this can have an effect on average per-hectare outputs, and even fertilizers will not help soils that suffer from want of moisture.

But grain shortages are only one element in the painful economic condition of Eastern Europe. There is also the difficulty of securing up-to-date machinery from bloc sources. The Rumanians have therefore been buying increasingly large quantities of equipment in the West, and they have made it known to their bloc partners that deliveries from the West arrive on schedule and are of higher quality and cheaper.[7] The Yugoslavs, whose economy is by and large functioning better than that of any other country in Communist Eastern Europe, now receive some 75–80 per cent of their imports from the non-Communist world.[8] Czechoslovakia, too, would like to draw on Western industrial technology; the country is plagued, among other things, by a labor shortage and outmoded productive facilities, and it could alleviate its economic crisis by importation of modern equipment from the West. The regime in Prague, just as the Bulgarian Government, has therefore indicated an interest in exchanging trade missions with West Germany—and presumably at the same political price the Poles, the Rumanians, and the Hungarians have already paid for the same purpose: surrender of the demand for diplomatic relations with Bonn and *de facto* recognition of West Berlin as a part of the West German economy.

However, if they are to increase their trade with the West the regimes in Eastern Europe will have to find new sources of hard currency, for the availability of long-term credit is limited. Something along this line could be achieved by a readaptation of some of the East European manufactures to Western market requirements. Another quick, though shortrun, solution is tourism. The Yugoslavs have already made a major national enterprise of the tourist trade and they now issue visitor's visas at the frontier with few questions asked. Bulgaria has built a major resort area at Varna, on the Black Sea, and has relaxed visa and currency requirements. Hungary has experimented with free entry for attendance at the music festival at Sopron, and visitors are no longer limited to Budapest and Lake Balaton. Czechoslovakia has opened her border with Austria to three-day visitors, and a similar practice is soon to be established along her West German frontier. Entry and exit requirements along the Czechoslovak-Hungarian border have been substantially eased.

It is true that quick foreign-exchange gains could be made in the tourist field, but the longer run limitations of this approach are clearly visible. For one thing, Varna and Prague

and Sopron will have to be able to compete with Corsica and
Madrid and Salzburg. It is as difficult for state-owned enterprises to provide personal service as it is troublesome for
totalitarian regimes to tolerate the freedom of individual
movement and contact which tourism involves. To take a
single instance, at Varna only Communist Western newspapers have been available in hotel lobbies. But why should
a German-speaking businessman do without his *Frankfurter
Allgemeine* or his *Neue Zürcher?* And if such papers should
be distributed in the hotels, how can they then be denied to
the local citizenry? Furthermore, if foreigners in great numbers are let in, how can the regimes in the long run refuse to
let their own "middle" class out? That this kind of pressure
makes itself felt is shown by the example of Hungary, which
in 1962 granted 45,000 passports for travel to Western Europe. In the first eleven months of 1963, more than 120,000
Hungarians visited the West as private tourists.[9]

An increase in trade with the West will most likely be
accompanied by stepped-up cultural contacts. Even though the
Communist regimes are interested mainly in scientific and
technological information, East European intellectuals are
hungry for contact with their Western counterparts. Recently,
for example, Slovak writers have put forward the demand
that they should be granted access to Western writings in order
to know better the enemy they are called upon to combat.
It is a good argument, if somewhat disingenuous.

One sign of the Communists' willingness to increase cultural
contact with the West is the decline in the jamming of Western
radio broadcasts. The Soviets have set the example here; in
June 1963 they ceased jamming official Western radios such
as the Voice of America. The following month all jamming
of Western broadcasts in the Rumanian language ceased, and
seven months later, in February 1964, an end was put to
all jamming of Western broadcasts in Hungarian.[10]

Jamming has always been a costly operation, costly in
electricity (which is in short supply) and costly in lost prestige.
Furthermore, it makes little sense to spend money on cultural
exchanges and at the same time reduce contact through expensive jamming operations. It is also hard to pretend having

the ultimate in the way of a social order and, at the same time, blot out broadcasts coming from the "older" centers of civilization.

One effect of the decline in jamming should be an improvement in Communist news media. They will have to reduce the amount of time or space devoted to propaganda and increase the attention given sports, human interest stories, and news. Such changes should in turn improve the political atmosphere.

Emergence of Public Opinion

Increased contact with the West should also assist East European writers and artists in their struggle for freedom of expression. Of late this fight is being fought more and more in the open. Recently the Hungarian writer Peter Veres announced to an assembly of Hungarian, Rumanian, and Czechoslovak authors that in Hungary the writers themselves determine the "what" and the "how" of the new socialist literature.[11] In Czechoslovakia, confronted with a Party admonition to mind their own business, the writers have publicly reasserted that they represent the "conscience of the nation," a slogan they first advanced in 1956.[12] Interestingly enough —and much to the dismay of the East Germans—the Prague regime has now officially rehabilitated the works of Franz Kafka, an author whose art is deeply rooted in the Bohemian capital but is hardly reconcilable with the canons of socialist realism. In Bulgaria, similar pressures against the political strait jacketing of the arts have been felt. There First Secretary Todor Zhivkov has called in the writers for a private showdown, while a major poet has published rhymes obviously meant to criticize the personal foibles of the Bulgarian leader.

In other spheres of public life, signs of a growing concern for non-Party opinion are also becoming apparent. Significantly, opinion polls have been tolerated in Poland for some time now and recently they have made their appearance in Hungary too. In the latter country, a year ago, the Communist Party conducted national elections as if there were any doubt about the outcome; Party leaders took to the hustings, mass meetings were held throughout the country, and there was a strong pretense of currying public favor. Furthermore, both Hungary and Bulgaria have shown signs of reviving, in guarded fashion, the parliamentary practice of interpellation. In Poland, recently, the regime even permitted the Sejm (parliament) to write substantial modifications into a bill on the organization of the bar which it had submitted for that body's approval.[13]

Increased cultural exchange, the decline of jamming, greater use of parliamentary institutions, and, above all, the ever more insistent demands of writers for freedom of self-expression will all contribute to the formation of an embryonic public opinion in Eastern Europe.

The most promising development in this direction would be the emergence of the writers and artists as a second source of authority and ideas alongside the Party. If writers and artists are allowed to debate public issues in their work—as they are already beginning to do—the Party's monopoly of ideas and information will not have been broken, but it will have been seriously infringed upon. The substance of dictatorship will not have changed, of course, but its totalitarian character will have been diluted. As long as the regimes continue to seek the active cooperation of their subjects at home and a measure of respect for themselves and their policies abroad, they will have to manifest concern for non-Party opinion.

Development of Mixed Economies

Apart from a certain relaxation of ideological control, we have witnessed in Eastern Europe during the past five years increased emphasis on improving the living standards of the people. The stick of police terror has been much less in use throughout the area and the carrot of consumer goods much more in evidence. Where industry is increasingly characterized by complex machinery and complicated processes, the positive cooperation of the mass of workers is more and more required; and whenever governments feel politically dependent

on a measure of public support, their commitment to a betterment of living conditions is even more important.

In Eastern Europe a major obstacle to improved standards
has been the low productivity of collectivized agriculture
which has been unable to feed the increasingly urbanized
population of the area. As a result, except for Rumania, the
East European regimes are partially dependent on imports of
bread grains. Probably a good deal could be achieved with
heavier inputs of mineral fertilizer, insecticides, hybrid seeds,
and machinery, but all the countries concerned are characterized by capital shortages; and the fact that throughout the
bloc the favored state farms operate in the red is by no means
encouraging. On the other hand, the astonishing contribution
of the miniscule private plots to national income suggests that
in conditions of capital scarcity the short route to improved
yields lies in the area of personal incentive. This road is also
indicated by the success the Poles and the Yugoslavs have
had with their state-managed private agricultures.

In the development of personal incentive the Hungarians
have without fanfare taken a commanding lead. The variety of
"material incentives" now offered the Hungarian peasant is
impressive. To take but one example, hay is now farmed
throughout Hungary on a crop-sharing basis (one-third goes
to the farmer), and in some collectives common fields have
been turned over to individual peasant families to farm on
shares. (While sharecropping may represent a retrograde
practice in the American South, in Eastern Europe it has the
great advantage of liberating the *kolkhoznik* from his status
of residual claimant at harvest time which makes him bear
the risks of nature.) The number and variety of officially
sponsored "material incentives" is so great that the government recently got out a pamphlet cataloguing and characteriz-
ing them all. In the course of 1963 most collective farms in
Hungary adopted one or another system of personal incentives,
combining it with the traditional *trudoden*. Hungarian agriculture thus appears to be in the process of fumbling toward a
system which will be collective in form but something else in
fact.

While the other East European countries with collectivized

agricultures have so far done little in this respect, a few concessions to the private sector have recently become known.
Czechoslovakia has restored the free market for goods produced on private plots, and Bulgaria has begun to double the
size of such plots. (There have been meat lines of late in
Czechoslovakia, while Bulgaria has introduced *de facto* bread
rationing.) It seems likely that in the next several years we
shall witness in Eastern Europe a retreat from collectivization,
either in the form of greatly increased material incentives or
even, perhaps, in a turn to state-managed private agriculture.

The situation in East European industry is not much better
than that prevailing in agriculture. Real wages throughout the
area, except again for Rumania, either remained static in
1962, or declined.[14] The Polish, Czechoslovak, and Bulgarian
regimes are in fact faced with economic problems of a critical
nature. The situation is worse in Czechoslovakia, where the
regime had to abandon long-range planning and accept for
1963 an absolute decline in industrial production.[15] Except
for Rumania and Yugoslavia, the short-term outlook for industrial growth is poor.

One of the causes of this predicament is the gap between
Communist dogma and economic reality. It is no surprise,
therefore, that in the industrial sector Communist doctrine has
already begun to erode. As usual, the Yugoslavs were the first
to grapple with reality. Under cover of their workers' councils
they began experimenting with a semi-market economy approximately a decade ago. Their success has been only moderate, but they were the first Communists to put factories on a
profit-and-loss basis, to reintroduce the concept of an
economic rent in private housing, and to accept the notion
that a modicum of unemployment may be the lesser of several
evils. Their reversion to a modified market economy greatly
facilitated their commercial connections with the West.

More recently, the satellite regimes have begun to experiment along somewhat similar lines. As early as 1955 such
Polish economists as Lange and Bobrowski were talking about
a "new-model" economy by which they meant something
approximating the Yugoslav experiment. In the last few years
the Poles have actually set aside fifty-two factories to work

experimentally on a profit-and-loss basis. The Hungarians in November 1963 quietly decreed the introduction (as of January 1964) of an annual levy of 5 per cent on all equipment and stock, to be deducted from the net income of industrial enterprises; in other words, the equivalent of an interest rate. That same month, *Hospodarske noviny,* the official economic organ of the Czechoslovak Party Central Committee, published proposals involving the decollectivization of the service industries and greater over-all reliance on market mechanisms. At the same time, *Novo vreme,* the theoretical organ of the Bulgarian Party Central Committee, carried an article proposing the introduction of something equivalent to the Yugoslav variety of workers' councils and suggesting much greater reliance on private property as a source of worker and peasant motivation. Even in East Germany there has been serious consideration of introducing interest rates and enterprise autonomy.

The drift of all these experiments and proposals is in the direction of mixed economies in which industry remains nationalized but certain market forces are set in operation. Under such a system, central planning of over-all goals would continue, but not central management. Instead of receiving allocations of productive resources at a centrally determined price, enterprises would have to compete for them in the market. Instead of being rewarded for overfulfillment of a gross output target, enterprises would be rewarded for a given assortment mix of products at reduced cost. Thus state interference with price formation would become more indirect and the price structure more flexible. It is quite possible that in the next several years one or two of the satellites may refashion their economies along these lines.

Counterforces and Countertrends

In the preceding pages attention has been concentrated on the forces making for change in Eastern Europe. Little has been said, however, about the forces that run counter to the trends described. In most countries in Eastern Europe, the greatest single obstacle to the drift toward more enlightened and humane government is the Party apparatus.

In the U.S.S.R., evidence of a divergence of views between the apparatus and the central leadership has been accumulating for a number of years, and Khrushchev's successive de-Stalinization campaigns have been directed in part against recalcitrant elements in the Party bureaucracy. They were meant to be a warning that the apparatus, selected and trained under Stalin, must change its ways and learn the arts of persuasion and leadership. The Party statutes were revised to require rotation in Party office, and a continuing effort has been made to better educate the cadres for their tasks. It has even been argued, and quite persuasively, that Khrushchev's Party-state reform of November 1962–February 1963 was designed to downgrade the apparatus.[16] Certainly one effect of the reform was to replace the First Party Secretary, hitherto the kingpin in the system, with two competing First Party Secretaries in most oblasts.

One country where the apparatus has so far put up a stubborn and successful struggle against de-Stalinization is Bulgaria. The present Zhivkov leadership—apparently imposed on the Party in November 1962 by Soviet intervention—has been unable until now to subdue successfully the Stalinist elements among the bureaucracy. Zhivkov did put into effect an amnesty for political prisoners, but a new set of rules of order aimed toward a revival of parliamentary activity proved stillborn. He seemed also unable to enforce existing legislation providing for an equitable distribution of fodder to the holders of private plots. And while he did succeed in enlarging the size of the private plots in some provinces, he evidently thought it wiser to keep this from public knowledge for many months. His effort to improve relations with the West, and notably with the United States, was offset in December 1963 by the mounting in Sofia of an anti-American spy trial and a controlled riot in front of the American Embassy.

In Hungary, to take a converse case, the regime has moved slowly but steadily toward liberalization. The stiff opposition of the provincial apparatus was offset by Janos Kadar's skillful leadership and by the shadow of the 1956 revolutionary upheaval. Kadar's principal weapon has been the policy of rehabilitation of the non-Party expert. Many, if not most, of these experts are in fact anti-Communist, but Kadar ruled that the past should be forgotten and that non-Party experts could hold any office in the land, except Party office. By assigning them to positions as factory managers, *kolkhoz* chairmen, and bureau chiefs, Kadar in effect began developing a second non-Party hierarchy of public officials.

The Bulgarian and Hungarian examples suggest something of the dimensions of the problem. What Lenin called the "party of the new type" is pre-eminently designed to seize and hold power, but evidence suggests that it cannot successfully govern an advanced industrial country. In part this is a problem of personnel, particularly in the younger regimes of Eastern Europe where the great bulk of the *apparatchiki* are men without university training, and a sizable minority has only completed elementary school. While it is true that considerable numbers of people of education and culture in these countries have joined the Party in order to continue the practice of their professions, few of these have joined the apparatus. The Polish so-called Partisans—a faction in the PUWP whose members are bound by common service in the Armia Ludowa of 1944–45—are more typical of the East European *apparatchiki* than many might think. Most of these prewar Party members are men who have only finished elementary school, who both hate and fear intellectuals, who are nationalist in their sentiments and anti-Semitic, and whose idea of government, in the main, is the discipline of the knout.

However, the poor quality of Party personnel is by no means the whole story. The Soviets have had forty years in which to educate the apparatus—great strides have been taken in this direction under Khrushchev—and yet, the Party is having great difficulty in governing a modern state.

Conclusion

To sum up then, we can expect that the East European governments, with the notable exception of East Germany, will continue their erratic evolution toward greater diversity and a less totalitarian form of despotism. As a result of the deep split in the world Communist movement, they may feel compelled to look more and more inward, and less outward; in other words, the ruling parties are likely to become more national and less universal in character, more established and less sectarian, more concerned with the accumulation of worldly goods and less with the propagation of the faith. Furthermore, declining Soviet authority in the bloc, in conjunction with Moscow's need to establish revisionism as the new Communist orthodoxy, is likely to encourage continuing differentiation through local adaptation. The extent of the already existing diversity gives us some measure of what the future may bring: there are now in Eastern Europe two countries with essentially private agriculture, one operating a qualified market economy, two that have been receiving Western economic assistance, four where the jamming of Western broadcasts is either nonexistent or substantially reduced, one that has set out on an independent course of industrialization based in good part on trade with the West, and one that has become the protégé of an Asian power.

The question arises once again whether or not the Communist Party dictatorship, as we know it today in Eastern Europe, is a suitable way of governing relatively modern and increasingly industrialized societies. When Khrushchev rose to power in the Soviet Union, he supplanted Stalin's antiquated counterproductive personal despotism by reviving the Party apparatus as the main organ of control and by introducing material incentives as the principal stimulus to productivity. This pattern was followed with more or less alacrity elsewhere in Eastern Europe, and yet, today, as grain shortages, planning deficiencies, and falling rates of economic growth plague the bloc, Khrushchev's response appears insufficient. As a result, the search for solutions may now lead even farther along the path toward a system that would be less revolutionary and totalitarian than the present one, but more rational and cognizant of the virtues of bureaucratic efficiency. More specifically, as there come to the fore in each country increasingly numerous and autonomous groups of scientists, technicians, and industrial managers—not to speak of the newly articulate writers and artists who are beginning to infringe upon the Party's monopoly of ideas and information—one may legitimately wonder whether the swift flow of social development has not already bypassed the Party apparatus as a useful instrument of government. There are thus in Eastern Europe important social and economic forces pressing for basic political change. Whether the change comes, and whether it will be timely in coming and peaceful, will depend in large part on the means and tenacity with which the *apparatchiki* are ready to defend their system of absolute rule.

NOTES

1. The doctrine of "peaceful coexistence" holds that because of the present strength of the "socialist camp" war is no longer inevitable, even under conditions of "imperialism." The doctrine of "peaceful transition" asserts that under present conditions the seizure of power by the proletariat led by the Communist Party through parliamentary process is possible, thus reinforcing the proposition that the ultimate world triumph of Communism need no longer be preceded by a military holocaust. The doctrine was extensively formulated by a Czech Communist writer, Jan Kozak, in a pamphlet entitled *How Parliament Can Play a Revolutionary Part in the Transition to Socialism* (London, Independent Information Centre, 1961; published in Czech in 1957). The "all-peoples'" state was officially proclaimed in the Soviet Union at the Twenty-second CPSU Congress (October 1961) as having succeeded the "dictatorship of the proletariat." Since the latter concept was based on the notion of the class struggle which in Stalin's time justified terror, the new formulation signified the formal abandonment of arbitrary force in the conduct of domestic affairs.

2. *Rebista de statistica* (Bucharest), October 1963, pp. 54, 56. For the citations in East European languages I have to thank my colleagues in the research departments of Radio Free Europe.

3. *Scinteia* (Bucharest), July 18, 1963, p. 3.

4. Ibid., November 21, 1963, p. 4; *Borba* (Belgrade), November 22, 1963, p. 3.

5. BTA (official Bulgarian news agency), October 9, 1963, as monitored by Radio Free Europe.

6. *Pravda* (Moscow), October 2, 1963, p. 2; Carl Zoerb, "Bloc grain imports: A Box Score," Radio Free Europe Budget Item

F–1730; *Wall Street Journal,* February 3, 1964; *Nepszabadsag* (Budapest), December 10, 1963, p. 4.

7. *Scinteia,* May 24, 1963, p. 3 and May 31, 1963, p. 5.

8. *Ekonomska politika* (Belgrade), January 25, 1964, p. 152.

9. *Magyar nemzet* (Budapest), February 1, 1964, p. 1.

10. Polish ground-wave jammers were destroyed by the mob in 1956 and never rebuilt, but Western broadcasts in Polish are jammed by sky-wave installations located outside the country. Bloc sky-wave jamming of Western broadcasts in Albanian stopped simultaneously with sky-wave interference with Western broadcasts in Rumanian. There have never been ground-wave jammers in Albania.

11. "Vita a szocialista irodalomrol," *Elet es irodalom* (Budapest), October 5, 1963, pp. 3–4.

12. Speech of Vojtech Mihalik at the Third Congress of the Union of Czechoslovak Writers as reported in *Kulturny zivot,* May 25, 1963, pp. 1–9.

13. Aleksandra Stypulkowska, "Czyzby koniec niezaleznej adwokatury?", *Na antenie* (London), September 22, 1963, p. 2; *Dziennik ustaw,* No. 57, December 21, 1963, item 309, pp. 596–604.

14. *Economic Survey of Europe, Part I:* European Economy in 1962 (New York: United Nations, 1963), pp. 26–30; *Neue Zürcher Zeitung,* November 24, 1963. Regime 1963 plan fulfillment reports indicate a continuance of the stagnation in real wages.

15. *Rude pravo* (Prague), January 25, 1964, p. 1.

16. See Richard Lowenthal, "The World Scene Transformed," *Encounter* (London), October 1963, pp. 3–10.

HOW MONOLITHIC WAS THE MONOLITH?

by Robert V. Daniels

After receiving his Ph.D. degree from Harvard University, Dr. Daniels spent a year as Research Associate at MIT's Center for International Studies and two years as Assistant Professor of Slavic Studies at Indiana University. He has been Professor of History at the University of Vermont since 1956. His books include The Nature of Communism *(New York: Random House, 1962) and* The Conscience of the Revolution: The Communist Opposition in Soviet Russia *(Cambridge, Mass.: Harvard University Press, 1960).*

This selection originally appeared in the March-April 1964 issue of the U. S. Information Agency's bimonthly publication *Problems of Communism*.

The deteriorating relationship between the Soviet Union and Communist China is one of the most misunderstood phenomena of the current international scene. This misunderstanding can usually be traced to the common, if inaccurate, assumption that Communism, thanks to its presumably binding and guiding ideology, has always been distinguished by monolithic international unity and discipline.

The picture of a tightly unified and blindly disciplined Communist movement is, to be sure, historically true for a certain phase of the movement—the period of Stalin's domination of Russia and of Soviet domination of the international movement from the late 1920's until 1948. A point of doctrine established in this period was the insistence that the

Communist movement *ought* to be tightly disciplined in this manner, and that no national or factional variation in doctrinal interpretation was permissible.

In line with these doctrinal claims of Stalinism, all disagreements or deviations from the Moscow line of theory or practice had to be condemned as heretical. The previous Soviet history of factional splits and debates was therefore rejected as the work of counterrevolutionaries trying to undermine the "general line of the Party." A more objective appraisal of the early history of the movement shows to the contrary that the many diverse schools of Communist thought were equally grounded in the ambiguities and inconsistencies of Russian Marxism. Theory in the absence of authority was never a force for unity, but a fertile source of controversy.

It can be shown, viewing the history of Communism as a whole, that theory has never served to unify and discipline the movement except when it could be made the instrument of one dominant institution of power. Given a plurality of power centers—whether resulting from a split in the Party or the rise of Peking as a rival national center in the international movement—the effect of Communist theoretical commitment is to compel controversy rather than enforce unity.

Early Schisms in Marxism

The Communist movement originated, as a matter of fact, in a schism among Marxists, if we may trace its existence back to the Bolshevik-Menshevik split of 1903. The two groups had started out with a more or less common ideology. They split mainly because of differences in tactics and temperament and the personal ambitions and assumptions of one strong-minded man—Lenin—whom other strong-minded Russian Marxists could not stomach. Clear doctrinal differences came considerably later, though it may be said that as early as 1902 Lenin was implicitly changing the philosophy of Marxism by his stress on the vital role of the Party organization in revolutionary activity. He was, in effect, propounding a new doctrine with his contention that the Russian proletariat should take the lead in the "bourgeois" revolution—though it was characteristically Lenin's pose to claim that not he but his rivals were the ones who were changing, and hence "betraying," Marxism.

Differences of temperament analogous to the Bolshevik-Menshevik antithesis were present to some degree in all the major Marxist parties of Europe prior to World War I and the Russian Revolution. The war and the Bolshevik seizure of power in Russia had the effect of extending the Bolshevik-Menshevik break to all the parties of the Second International, as the more radical wing in each country took its stand against the war and in sympathy with the October Revolution. From 1919 on into the 1920's, acrimonious battles were fought in many a Socialist party between the factions favoring and opposing affiliation with the new Communist International. In most places the outcome was a complete rupture, with the left-wing, pro-Soviet minorities seceding to form separate Communist parties belonging to a distinctly new international movement.

If the splits of 1903–5 in Russia and 1919–21 in the International are used as a model for assessing the Sino-Soviet schism, certain parallels immediately suggest themselves. Like the cleavage between Social Democracy and Communism, the Sino-Soviet disagreement has proceeded from what was initially a common ideological ground. Continuing the parallel, it appears to have been differences of temperament, tactics, and national circumstances, and the underlying issue of who is to command the movement, that have divided Moscow and Peking, rather than any initially clear differences of philosophy and program. The Russians now, like the Mensheviks and Social Democrats of earlier days, are prone to rest on their laurels, avoid risky violence, and trust to the presumably natural work of history to bring them new successes. The Chinese show much more of the old Bolshevik fervor, the impatience with compromise and gradualism, the emphasis on willful action to promote the fortunes of revolution. Chinese criticisms of Moscow recall Lenin's harping on the sins of "spontaneity" and "tail-endism," i.e., following behind the social forces of history instead of leading them.

At this point it may well be objected that the Bolshevik-

Menshevik split is a false parallel because it was only as a result of this split that the modern Communist movement came into being—that the discipline, unity, and doctrinal rigor of the Communist movement embracing both Russia and China are traceable only to the Bolshevik side of the 1903–17 cleavage. This, of course, is quite true, and it therefore behooves us to direct more detailed attention to the history of schisms and disagreements within the Communist movement itself, after it became established in Russia and coordinated around the world by the Third International.

The Romantics and the Pragmatists

Lenin never tired of stressing unity and discipline as the essential conditions of success in a revolutionary party (an attitude sustained by his successors), and he condoned challenges to the leadership of the movement only when there were rivals at the helm whom he could not control, as was the case until 1912 while the Bolsheviks and Mensheviks remained formally within one party. (Lenin's qualified endorsement of "splitting" tactics in this situation was recalled by the Chinese last fall [1963] and again in February as justification for their encouragement of anti-Moscow splinter movements in many Communist parties.) But even within Lenin's own movement, unity was more wish than reality until nearly the time of his death. The image of totally monolithic, mindless, and submissive unity in the international Communist ranks dates only from the time of Stalin. This kind of unity was itself the product of a tumultuous history of controversy, schism, and purge both in the Soviet Communist Party and in the Communist International.

Even before the 1917 Revolution, as well as for years afterward, Lenin's Bolshevik movement was troubled by discord between the pragmatic authoritarianism represented by Lenin himself and the revolutionary romanticism that animated many of his adherents. As early as 1909 this cleavage came to a head over the question whether or not to boycott the Tsarist Duma. Lenin thought the boycott politically inexpedient, while the hotheads considered participation in the elections a betrayal of revolutionary principle. The upshot was a Party purge with the expulsion of Alexander Bogdanov and the other left-wing romantics from the Bolshevik ranks. This did not, however, prevent renewed dissension over purist and adventurist tendencies in the movement, particularly among the ultra-internationalists led by Nikolai Bukharin and Yuri Piatakov between 1914 and 1917.

In 1917, following the fall of Tsar Nicholas and the establishment of the Provisional Government, Lenin himself took the adventurist line by calling for immediate proletarian revolution. Most of the support for this view came from romantics of the Bukharin type, together with numerous ultra-leftists from the Menshevik party who came over to Lenin between 1914 and 1917—people such as Alexandra Kollontai, Gregory Sokolnikov, Karl Radek, and finally, Leon Trotsky —all, incidentally, emigrés. Among the Bolsheviks from the underground in Russia there was only a small faction in Petrograd, headed by Alexander Shliapnikov and, of all people, Viacheslav Molotov, who took the insurrectionist line immediately after the February Revolution. The main body under Lev Kamenev and Joseph Stalin came out for support of the Provisional Government and a defensive war. When Lenin returned to Russia in April 1917, Stalin hastened to switch to the leader's radical line, while Kamenev with Gregori Zinoviev and Alexei Rykov led an anti-insurrectionist minority who dragged their feet until the October Revolution was an accomplished fact.

However, Lenin's tie with the romantics—exemplified by his oft-quoted but untypical book of 1917, *State and Revolution* —was shortlived. Within three or four months after the October Revolution Lenin abandoned the utopian view as to the foreign policy of revolutionary war and the domestic policy of democratic workers' control. Despite a bitter political struggle with the representatives of the ultra-revolutionary line led by Nikolai Bukharin, Lenin insisted successfully on the Treaty of Brest-Litovsk with Germany, which was, of course, based on considerations of power politics. Domestically, he began to push for a structure of bureaucratic authoritarianism for the industry, government, and army of the new Soviet society. One of the few Bolshevik leaders, incidentally, who followed every shift of Lenin's was Joseph Stalin (apart from his brief period of "defensism" in March and April 1917, which has been perhaps overemphasized in the Khrushchevite campaign against the "cult of personality").

Idealist criticism of Lenin's arrangements was strongly voiced between 1919 and 1921 by the "Democratic Centralist" faction of Valerian Osinski and Timofei Sapronov and by the "Workers' Opposition" led by Shliapnikov and Kollontai. These purists tried to insist on democratic "collegiality" in government, army, and industry, such as Marx had envisioned and as the Yugoslav Communists revived in part after 1948. But in Lenin's Russia the idealists were easily overcome by the Party organizers, and by 1921 the regime's course toward totalitarian national power was definitely set.

The foreign sympathizers with the Russian Revolution, who made up the Communist International, continued making trouble for a number of years. These people were mostly the revolutionary romantics who had split off from the Socialist parties and naturally expected the Communist movement to take an uncompromising and purist stand in every instance. As a result, most of the Russian effort in the Communist International, from the time of its founding in 1919 to the date of its formal dissolution in 1943, was devoted not to promoting foreign revolution but to restraining it, and to the imposition of firm Soviet control over the foreigners.

Lenin spelled out his answer to the romantics as early as April 1920, when he wrote in *Left-Wing Communism—an Infantile Disorder*:

> There are compromises and compromises. . . . To refuse beforehand to maneuver, to utilize the conflict of interest (even though temporary) among one's enemies, to refuse to temporize and compromise with possible (even though temporary, unstable, vacillating and conditional) allies—is this not ridiculous in the extreme?[1]

His problem was to keep the foreign purists under Russian tactical control, and to this end he applied his Russian doctrine of the Party:

Repudiation of the Party principle and of Party discipline —such is the net result of the opposition. And this is tantamount to completely disarming the proletariat in the interest of the bourgeoisie.[2]

It did not take long before the Russians brought the foreign Communists under effective control. The move was taken at the Second Congress of the International (the first real one), held in August 1920, where all member parties of the Comintern were required to subscribe to the "Twenty-One Conditions" drafted by Lenin. The document specified the principles of international Communist discipline under a centralized leadership—located in the Russian Communist Party headquarters in Moscow. Under Lenin's direction, the movement was thus firmly set on a course of militant discipline and Machiavellian pragmatism in the service of the Soviet state.

Establishment of the Monolith

A crucial step toward the implementation of this Leninist pattern within Soviet Russia came in 1921 with the introduction of the moderate New Economic Policy (NEP), the suppression of the Russian utopians who could not accept this retreat, and a shakeup of the Party's organizational staff that put the Trotskyists out and the Stalinists in. Scarcely more than a year later Lenin was afflicted with his first in a series of strokes, and the leadership fell to a team of his pragmatic heirs—Zinoviev, Kamenev, Stalin, and Bukharin (a utopian-turned-pragmatist after 1921). Impelled by personal emotions as well as reasons of principle, the more theoretically minded has-beens clustered around Trotsky, and in the fall of 1923 they launched their attack on the successor leadership over the issues of economic development, favoritism to the workers, and intraparty democracy.

The Trotskyist opposition of 1923 was cut down in a bitter, open political battle in the Communist Party organizations. In January 1924, just before Lenin finally died, the opposition was condemned as a "petty bourgeois," un-Leninist and un-Marxist deviation, and the leadership firmly established the principle that any factional challenge to the unity of the party was *ipso facto* counterrevolutionary. This did not, however, prevent the opposition from struggling on to condemn the NEP as a betrayal of the workers and a step toward "state capitalism." In 1925–26, when Zinoviev and Kamenev broke with Stalin and Bukharin and went over to Trotsky, the opposition got a temporary boost, but Stalin's organization held firm. In fact, ever since 1923, the efforts of the opposition seem to have been foredoomed to failure, and it was only as a belated anticlimax that in 1927 the Trotskyists and Zinovievists were expelled from the Party, with Trotsky's exile from the country following in 1929.

A major theoretical development during Stalin's contest with Trotsky was the former's theory of "Socialism in One Country." This doctrine has often been misunderstood as a shift to nationalism, in opposition to the "world revolution" which Trotsky presumably represented. In line with this picture the parallel has sometimes been drawn (even by the Russians in 1963) between the Chinese Communists and Trotsky as ardent exponents of the revolutionary offensive on the one hand, and Khrushchev and Stalin or Lenin as representatives of political caution on the other. Actually, both the Stalin and Trotsky factions endorsed the goal of world revolution in theory and recognized the need for a defensive line in practice. Theory was not the source of the argument between the two sides, but a political football. The Trotskyists tried to argue that the Stalin-Bukharin regime was becoming un-Socialist because it was in fact confined to one country, and Stalin tried to counter by falsifying Lenin's doctrine and claiming that the national isolation of Communism made no difference to its internal prospects in Russia. The main significance of the entire question lay in the manner in which Stalin was able to start treating theory—revising its meaning and imposing the twisted revision on the Communist movement as though it had always been the official truth. From this time on, the Soviet dictatorship would never be compelled to follow abstract doctrine where it did not wish to tread.

Apart from the fainthearted who dragged their feet in 1917, all the intraparty opposition to Lenin and to Stalin up to 1928 came from the left, utopian, theoretically committed elements of the Bolshevik-Communist movement. As old-style, unadjusted, romantic revolutionaries who emotionally rejected compromise efforts to live with the status quo, these protestants resembled today's Chinese leaders. However, they differed from Mao Tse-tung's party in having no separate seat of power from which they could defy the pragmatist centralizers, and their theoretical perspective was also very different. The early oppositions—above all the Trotskyists—were genuinely operating in the expectation of a world proletarian revolution and the establishment of a workers' state in the true Marxist meaning of the term. Communist China has totally departed from any meaningful Marxist framework of social evolution and working class rule, in favor of an ultra-Stalinist bureaucratic regime that rules by imposition on workers and peasants and everybody else alike.

The Stalin Revolution

The more exact analogue of Chinese Communist thinking is to be found in the policy and propaganda undertaken by Stalin in 1928. For reasons which probably were mainly political, Stalin broke with the Bukharin group at that time and initiated the program of violent collectivization which the Bukharinists were bound to oppose. They honestly thought it would mean disaster, as well as an unacceptable abandonment of the aims of the revolution. "Military-feudal exploitation of the peasantry" is what Bukharin and Rykov called Stalin's collectivization program when it took shape in 1929. This reaction, interestingly, differs only in degree from the view that the Soviet leaders took of the Chinese communes of 1958.

The "Stalin revolution" from 1928 to the mid-1930's meant a profound change in the Communist system in a number of respects. It was a fundamental readjustment from the goal of working class socialism in an industrialized country, to the pursuit of bureaucratic socialism in a developing country. Secondly, by eliminating all dissent within the Party and imposing strict Party control on all non-political aspects of life, the Stalin revolution perfected totalitarianism in the U.S.S.R. (China and Russia are both still profoundly totalitarian in this respect.) Thirdly, the Stalin revolution represented a shift from Leninist pragmatism to a compulsively self-justifying fanaticism, culminating in the Great Purge. China has exhibited a markedly similar fanaticism since 1958, while Russia under Khrushchev has returned to the more pragmatic dictatorship of Lenin and Bukharin. Bukharin still gets no credit, though his rehabilitation at the present time would be logical. It is noteworthy that the two Communist countries which have shown the most dislike of Chinese Communist policies—Yugoslavia and Poland—are the two with distinctively Bukharin-type economies relying much more than the Soviet Union on market mechanisms and individual peasant initiative.

Stalin's victory in the late 1920's was the victory of the truly monolithic, military-style Party organization that he had built up from his position as General Secretary of the Party. The actual disgrace of the Trotskyists in 1927 and of the Bukharinists in 1929 was anticlimactic, following the quiet consolidation of power by Stalin, and in the case of the Bukharinists, the almost entirely secret, behind-the-scenes defeat of the opposition in 1928. Here is another point of reference to the Sino-Soviet controversy, i.e., the tendency of the Communist movement to keep its power struggles veiled under the cloak of ideological identity until dissension has reached the point where one or both sides are ready to make an open break on the theoretical plane.

The outcome in Stalin's case was total victory for his personal cause. The result was to cast the whole of Soviet society and the international Communist movement in the same monolithic mold. The Great Purge destroyed the possibility of future opposition in Russia—of actual opposition there was already none—and even the memory of opposition was expunged or defaced in the subsequent propaganda of latter-day Stalinism.

The World Movement Unharnessed

Stalin paralleled his consolidation of dictatorial power in Russia with the elimination of all independent-minded elements from the Comintern. His tactic was to intervene in the factional disputes within the various Communist parties—most notably in Germany—and by political and financial favor to give the nod to the more subservient candidates for the local leadership. He worked with Zinoviev to oust the moderate-leaning German Communist leadership in 1923 and 1924 and install the compliant Center; then ousted the Bukharinists as a "right deviation" in 1928. By 1927 the entire Comintern was shaken by the Stalin-Trotsky controversy, and the pro-Trotsky factions began to quit or suffer expulsion from the movement. This softened up the Communist parties for an equally sweeping purge of the pro-Bukharin groups in 1928 and 1929, after the Sixth Comintern and the adoption of the radical "Third Period" line. After 1930 there was scarcely a single Communist Party where most of the original native leaders had not been ousted under Soviet pressure.

Thanks partly to the stimulating presence of their leader in exile, the supporters of Trotsky outside the U.S.S.R. fought back by organizing their own movement. Trotskyist parties were formed with programs of uncompromising revolutionary internationalism that condemned Stalinism as a bureaucratic betrayal of the workers' cause. In 1934 the formation of the "Fourth International" was proclaimed by the Trotskyists, and the movement still survives under this banner as a splinter tendency in many countries.

The crucial weakness that has prevented Trotskyism from achieving the impact that Titoism has had since 1948 is the fact that no government has ever been controlled by the forces of the Fourth International. It is in this respect that the Chinese-led radical tendency in the Communist movement today differs decisively from the Trotskyist movement. On the other hand, judging from the Trotskyist experience, there is every reason to expect that the Chinese leadership can, if they want, create a new international of formidable proportions by promoting splits in the Communist parties around the world and organizing the pro-Peking factions into a mono-lithic revolutionary movement of their own. This would be no more than the Russians did in the Socialist International in 1919.

The perfection of the Stalinist monolith inside the U.S.S.R. during the purges of the 1930's did not suffice to uproot the potential for further dissension in the international Commu-nist movement. When the results of World War II brought the movement opportunities for power or enhanced strength in countries outside the U.S.S.R., deviations of both the ro-mantic and pragmatic type appeared. In the closing months of the war it was once again the insurrectionary romantics—guerrilla fighters in Southeast Europe and the underground resistance movements in the West—who gave Moscow the most difficulty with their premature urge to strike for power in disregard of the appearances of inter-Allied unity, which Stalin still seemed to prize. On the other hand, with the Soviet occupation of Eastern Europe and the telescoped Staliniza-tion which Moscow undertook to impose on the satellite gov-ernments, the local opposition took the direction of right-wing caution and pragmatism exemplified by Wladislaw Gomulka.

Both kinds of Communist dissent, whether impelled by theoretical purism or local opportunism, unavoidably raised the issue of "national Communist" autonomy versus absolute subservience to Moscow. Tito's defiance of the Kremlin was the only successful act of its kind in Stalin's time, partly for reasons of Yugoslavia's geography and wartime history, partly because Tito was the first to have tried it openly. Independ-ence of the national power center has been the consistent denominator of Yugoslav policy through a striking shift of doctrinal stance from the ultra-Stalinist fanaticism of 1945–48 through the Djilas idealism of 1949–50 (which created the workers' councils) and the pragmatic market socialism of today. Tito's would-be emulators in East Europe came from either end of the doctrinal spectrum, but whether it was the doctrinaire fanaticism of a Laszlo Rajk or the gradualism of a Gomulka, the result was national resistance to Soviet influence, which Stalin was determined to smash by any means at his disposal.

Similar developments could be observed within the major Communist parties in the West, where each Moscow policy move has enlisted the inflexible loyalty of a particular Communist faction. In many cases, purges—such as the ouster of Earl Browder from the U. S. Communist Party for his softness on capitalism in 1945—became a necessary means to accomplish tactical shifts. A notable instance on the other—romantic—side was the 1952 ouster of André Marty and Charles Tillon from the French Communist leadership because they could not shift from the internationalist revolutionary line to that of a nationalist appeal against American influence. In such a situation a most ardent internationalist in the movement can find himself forced into the position of a national resistant against Moscow.[3]

The case of the deepest national resistance to Moscow—sometimes with a pragmatic inspiration and sometimes a utopian one—is that of Chinese Communism. Ever since 1930 China has been a notable exception to the rule of Soviet dictation in the selection of native Communist leaders. To be sure, Chen Tu-hsiu, founder and leader of the Chinese Communist Party from 1921 to 1928, was blamed for the Comintern's 1927 debacle in China, and expelled from the movement on charges of Trotskyism. Moscow did not, however, succeed in imposing its own candidates for the succession, all of whom had met with failures because of the Comintern's ultra-proletarian line in China at that time.

Instead, as the world well knows, success went to Mao Tse-tung with his totally unorthodox strategy of working through the peasants to win power by guerrilla warfare. The crucial point of the story is that while Mao was for the time being ardently loyal to the Moscow line ideologically, he was independent organizationally. This independence must be attributed in the last analysis to the territorial political base which Mao established in Shensi Province in the mid-1930's, a base the like of which no other Communist Party had enjoyed until World War II brought some of them the opportunity to emulate the Chinese strategy of guerrilla warfare.

If the Chinese Party was never part of the Stalinist mono-lith, the other Communist movements that succeeded through guerrilla warfare all sooner or later proved to be thorns in the Soviet side. In Europe this has been the case with both the Yugoslav and Albanian parties, the one breaking with Stalin to maintain its national integrity a scant three years after the war ended, and the other managing an incredible record of defiance with Chinese encouragement as the Com-munist bloc entered the 1960's. In sum, the record of unity among Communist governments is highly negative wherever the country concerned has not been directly occupied or threatened by the Soviet Army.

Tito's break with Stalin in 1948 is actually the closest ana-logue to the Sino-Soviet schism. Apart from the relative weak-ness of Yugoslavia and its dependence on outside (i.e., West-ern) support, Tito's break paralleled Mao's in that it arose, under conditions of ideological unity, as a result of unsolved questions concerning the power relationships between Com-munist governments. Both Tito and Mao took a stand when their independence or stature within the movement seemed threatened, and then began to conjure up ideological reasons to justify resistance to Moscow. It was perhaps only an ac-cident of time and place that Yugoslavia, in defying Stalin, turned ideologically toward the pragmatic, lower-pressure Communism of Lenin and (without credit) Bukharin, while Mao saw his best political opportunity in rejecting the decom-pression of Khrushchev and reaffirming the uncompromising stance of Stalinism.

Conclusion

The history of modern Communism does not show any durable ideological bond between Communist power centers, but rather a natural tendency to split over ideological inter-pretations wherever the existence of separate factions or in-dependent Communist governments permits this. Inherent in the movement are two types of deviation—the romantic or fanatic ("dogmatist" or "sectarian") rejecting compromise or delay, and the cautious or practical ("revisionist" or "opportunist") that opposes great risks or unnecessary antagonizing of a target nation. Secondly, it now seems a well-established rule that separate national power bases in the Communist world, such as were created in the guerrilla campaigns of World War II, establish a ready potential for deviation in either the romantic or the pragmatic direction. Thirdly, in the disputes between Communist states, theory figures not as a unifying or inhibiting force but as a major weapon of controversy. Contemporary events are making it clear that a dogmatic movement such as Communism, when it spreads to encompass more than one independent country, is likely to have far more trouble maintaining a semblance of unity and cooperation than an old-fashioned alliance of non-dogmatic powers based on common interest.

NOTES

1. Lenin, *Selected Works* (1952), Vol. II, Part 2, pp. 360, 395–96.
2. Ibid., p. 366.
3. See Marshall Shulman, *Stalin's Foreign Policy Reappraised* (Cambridge, Mass.: Harvard University Press, 1963), pp. 233–37.

PART THREE

COMMUNIST IDEOLOGY, STRATEGY, AND TACTICS

INTRODUCTION

He is skillful in attack whose opponent does not know what to defend; and he is skillful in defense whose opponent does not know what to attack. . . . The spot where we intend to fight must not be made known; for then the enemy will have to prepare against an attack at several different points. . . .

Sun Tzu, *The Art of War* (ca. 500 B.C.)

The Marxist-Leninists do not understand the policy of peaceful coexistence as a tactical maneuver designed for some limited span of time, but as the strategic line designed for the whole period of the transition from capitalism to socialism on a world scale.

Pravda (December 6, 1963)

In human history, the forces of the new always defeat the forces of decay. New, emergent forces, though seemingly weak, always prevail over the old, moribund forces which are still seemingly strong. What is decaying will inevitably be replaced by the newborn—such is the law of development and in society.

Yu Choa-li, in *Red Flag*
(August 16, 1958)

My deep belief is that the time will come when all people, all nations will have one and the same ideology. Then a reign

of peace and labor will set in. This will happen when there
are neither exploiters nor exploited, when there are no opposing classes. Then there will be no opposing ideologies and
all people will be friends and brothers, all will strive to live
in peace and friendship. This time will come. When? It will
come when communism triumphs on earth!

N. S. Khrushchev, *Pravda*
(June 21, 1964)

But the gravest difference between the two worlds is that the
Communist world has a set aim while we have none. This may
seem a hard saying, but it is the only one which describes the
facts. It has been said that the only aim common to the whole
liberal world is self-defense, i.e., survival. But survival is not
an aim, save perhaps for rats or for tigers.

Salvador de Madariaga, *The Blowing
Up of the Parthenon* (1960)

THE STRATEGY OF
PEACEFUL COEXISTENCE

by Richard V. Allen

Mr. Allen is a Research Principal of the Center for Strategic Studies, Georgetown University, and is a specialist in Communist ideology. He has taught with the University of Maryland Overseas Division and at Georgia Tech, and has been awarded a Congressional Fellowship by the American Political Science Association. A Consultant to the American Bar Association Standing Committee on Education Against Communism, he is also co-editor with David M. Abshire of National Security: Political, Military, and Economic Strategies in the Decade Ahead *(New York: Frederick A. Praeger, 1963). He received his B.A. and M.A. degrees from the University of Notre Dame, and studied at the Universities of Freiburg and Munich in Germany.*

This selection is adapted from Mr. Allen's recent study *Peaceful Coexistence: A Communist Blueprint for Victory,* published by the Standing Committee on Education Against Communism of the American Bar Association, August 1964.

What Is Peaceful Coexistence?

Traditionally, Communists have always given the greatest care to defining carefully the strategic course of action to be followed over a given period of time. Tactics may vary within the period of time in which the strategy operates, but the latter will remain constant until officially changed and until that change has been proclaimed to the world movement.

Hence, as stated by *Fundamentals of Marxism-Leninism,* an authoritative manual for Communists everywhere, a careful distinction is made between strategy and tactics:

> The term tactics often implies a political line for a relatively short period of time determined by particular concrete conditions, whereas strategy refers to the line for a whole historical stage.[1]

The manual goes on to point out that

> When elaborating the strategic line of the Party under capitalist conditions, it is important, in the first place, to determine correctly the *main aim* of the working class at the given stage and the *chief class enemy* against whom it is necessary to concentrate at the given stage the class hatred and the shock force of all the working people in order to overcome this enemy's resistance.[2]

Despite what has appeared on the surface to be a substantially complete "break" with the past of "Stalinism," these definitions bear a remarkable similarity to those laid down by Stalin in 1924:

> Strategy deals with the main forces of the revolution and their reserves. It changes with the passing of the revolution from one stage to another, but remains essentially unchanged throughout a given stage.

> While the object of strategy is to win the war . . . against the bourgeoisie . . . tactics pursue less important objectives, for the object of tactics is not the winning of the war as a whole, but the winning of some particular engagements or some particular battles.[3]

From this it is clear that Communists set themselves certain well-defined priorities to be accomplished by the concentration of "class hatred" and the "shock force of all the working people" under the guidance of the "strategic line of the Party." In individual cases the details may vary, but at heart it is always a question of assuming political power through the overthrow of the "enemy."

It is important to understand, then, what the Communists

themselves understand as the "strategic line" to be followed for an entire "historical stage."

Strategy or Tactic?

Is "peaceful coexistence" a strategy or a tactic?

The Marxist-Leninists do not understand the policy of peaceful coexistence as a tactical maneuver designed for some limited span of time, but as the strategic line designed for the whole period of the transition from capitalism to socialism on a world scale.[4]

Peaceful coexistence is therefore the strategy which will carry forth the Communist revolution to the final overthrow of the free world and the establishment of worldwide Communist rule.[5] To take it as something less important than the "strategic line," or to dismiss it as a "semantic phrase" would be to ignore the fundamental statement of the plan to accomplish the final phase of the attack against the non-Communist world.

As the principal "strategic line" of the majority of the Communist movement, peaceful coexistence is quite young. It received its initial, cautious formulation and blessing by Khrushchev at the Twentieth Party Congress in 1956, but escaped widespread attention in the West because of the sensational nature of the "de-Stalinization" pronouncements made at that time. It was Stalin, however, who first affirmed that "coexistence" was a temporary possibility designed to buy time. Speaking at the Fifteenth Congress of the Communist Party of the Soviet Union in 1927, he said that

> The period of "peaceful coexistence" is receding into the past, giving way to a period of imperialist attacks. . . . Hence our task is to pay attention to contradictions in the capitalist camp, to delay war by "buying off" the capitalists and to take all measures to maintain peaceful relations. . . . Our relations with the capitalist countries are based on the assumption that the coexistence of the two opposing systems is possible. Practice has fully confirmed this.[6]

Still earlier references to coexistence may be found in Trotsky and Lenin, but until recent years it has been a descriptive slogan; i.e., it described a condition to which, however unfortunate for the Communists, they had to adapt.

Under conditions of obvious inferiority to the "capitalist world," until 1956 the Communists described their position as one of "capitalist encirclement." The major task under those conditions, according to Stalin, was to strike incessantly at the "weakest link" of the capitalist chain in an effort to break out of the "encirclement." At the Twentieth Party Congress the declaration was made that the chain had been broken, and that the worldwide revolution had begun to enter the final phase of human history, the "transition from capitalism to socialism on a worldwide scale." It is in this phase that the Communists relinquish the defensive position assumed under the previous conditions of peaceful coexistence, and go over to the strategic offensive under a new and enriched kind of peaceful coexistence.

While the phraseology has undergone no change—i.e., "peaceful coexistence" is still used to describe Communist policy objectives—the content of the slogan has changed radically to accommodate the new period of the offensive. Thus it is that the period of peaceful coexistence contains such nonpeaceful events as the construction of the Berlin Wall and the Cuban missile buildup.

A Form of Class Struggle

As to its specific content Nikita Khrushchev has said that the policy of peaceful coexistence, as regards its social content, is a form of intense economic, political, and ideological struggle of the proletariat against the aggressive forces of imperialism in the international arena.[7]

From this definition, it would appear that peaceful coexistence, inasmuch as it prescribes "intense struggle," does not accord with the meaning of the word "peaceful." But the *Statement of the 81 Communist and Workers Parties* of December 1960, a major policy declaration, goes into greater detail:

> The policy of peaceful coexistence is a policy of mobilizing the masses and launching vigorous action against the enemies of peace. Peaceful coexistence of states does not imply renuciation of the class struggle. . . . The coexistence of states with different social systems is a form of class struggle between socialism and capitalism. In conditions of peaceful coexistence favorable opportunities are provided for the development of the class struggle in the capitalist countries and the national-liberation movement of the peoples of the colonial and dependent countries. In their turn, the successes of the revolutionary class and national-liberation struggle promote peaceful coexistence. The Communists consider it their duty to fortify the faith of the people in the possibility of furthering peaceful coexistence, their determination to prevent world war. They will do their utmost for the people to weaken imperialism and limit its sphere of action by an active struggle for peace, democracy, and national liberation.[8]

It should be noted that Communists consider peaceful coexistence and the "national liberation movement," the revolutionary movement in the underdeveloped countries, to be mutually reinforcing. The principal impact of this mutual reinforcement is the ability to "limit the sphere of action" of "imperialism." Accurately translated, this means that the successes of the Communists can be turned into an advantage by restricting the freedom of action of the Western countries, chiefly the United States.

The *Statement* notes that the Communists will do everything possible "to prevent world war." It has been said that peaceful coexistence implies that, as far as the Communists are concerned, war has become an "impossibility." Khrushchev has stated that

> Our foreign policy is peaceful coexistence, not war. It is the Communists who in general want to exclude war between states from the life of human society.[9]

But such general statements rarely go uninterpreted in the Communist camp, and the theme has been repeated and elaborated in dozens of ways. In such elaborations one is apt to find a more complete candor than is present in the public pronouncements of the leaders. From the following recent statements one can gain an appreciation of the real meaning attached to the relationship of war to peaceful coexistence:

Some try to reduce the notion of peaceful coexistence to the renunciation of war. *But peace and peaceful coexistence are not one and the same thing.* Peaceful coexistence does not mean a temporary and unstable armistice between two wars, but something more complex.[10]

Peaceful coexistence, which is the general line of the foreign policy of the Soviet Union and the other Socialist countries *does not imply a temporary absence of war, or a breathing space between clashes.* Not at all. Peaceful coexistence is the only positive, constructive policy which promotes economic, social, and cultural progress all over the world.[11]

It is fairly safe to assume that the Communists do not desire a general war at this time. They fully realize that whatever benefits would accrue to them as the result of a war would be outweighed by the damage which they would suffer. Khrushchev, speaking on August 19, 1963, stressed that "we Communists want to win this struggle with the least losses."

However, it is quite a different matter to assume that, because the Communists do not view war as a realistic instrument of policy at the present time, they will never employ it. It is also necessary to point out that the Communists have differentiated between the various types of wars, and have clearly delineated those which *are* acceptable and are to be *encouraged and assisted.*

Agreements with the Enemy

Even when certain measures can be agreed upon with the "enemy," allegedly to reduce the chances of a nuclear war, as was the case with the signing of the Partial Nuclear Test Ban Treaty, the Communists find it necessary to underscore the value of such agreements by reiterating their view of peaceful coexistence. Immediately in the wake of the Treaty, Khrushchev said:

> The essence of the policy of peaceful coexistence of countries with different social systems lies precisely in *compelling* the big Western powers to renounce war as an instrument of their policy and to adhere to peaceful, not military, methods of settling international problems *through the superiority of the peace-loving nations over the forces of militarism and aggression.*[12]

And a later article on the Treaty by an Estonian Communist pointed out that

> In the view of the Communists, peaceful coexistence between the two systems is certainly not a passive process in which there is some sort of parallel development of capitalism and socialism, no freezing of social relationships, *or strengthening of any status quo* in the relationship between the forces of socialism and capitalism . . . *but an active and intense struggle, in the course of which socialism irresistibly attacks, while capitalism suffers one defeat after another.*[13]

While such agreements may be of limited value to the "capitalists," by this view they will redound infinitely more to the benefit of the Communists. Note that Khrushchev stresses that peaceful coexistence *"compels"* the West to submit to the policies of the "superior" forces, i.e., the Communists, and that the latter statement emphasizes that such agreements by no means imply a status quo between Communists and non-Communists, but that "socialism" attacks and deals "capitalism" successive defeats.

The "competition" which Communists profess to pursue with the West in the name of "peaceful coexistence" likewise smacks of the language of total victory over a thoroughly vanquished enemy:

Comrades, when we speak of victory in economic competition, the point in question is not only cement or metal, but policy as well—the power of our ideas, the power of Marxist-Leninist theory . . . the superiority of the socialist system over the capitalist system.

The capitalists know the cruel laws of competition: if one firm outstrips another, the stronger one swallows the weaker one. The competition of the two systems in the economic field strikes even greater fear into the hearts of the imperialists: they see that the rapid growth of socialism is increasingly *shaking the foundations of capitalism, bringing nearer the end of this system, which is doomed by history.*[14]

Since Communism takes an active role in "shaking the foundations of capitalism," Khrushchev certainly does not intend to operate on the "live-and-let-live" principle which dominates the Western concept of peaceful coexistence.

If it were merely a matter of a straight competition between the two powers, with the winner's only prize the satisfaction that he had won and had demonstrated that his system performed in a manner superior to the loser's, then the West would have little to fear from the bumbling and centralized economy of the Communist states. The conditions of totalitarian rule have endowed the Communist countries with an inability to compete successfully with the free world in general, and with the United States in particular.

But it is not a case of "straight competition." The stakes in this novel form of "competition" are simply the freedoms which we have fought so hard and so long to defend; and like it or not, it is the Communists, not we, who have determined that the stakes should be set so high.

It is essential to note here that while the principle of peaceful coexistence serves as an operating code for Communist behavior in the realm of relations among nations, it has never been stated that peaceful coexistence applies *within* the boundaries of the capitalist countries. The struggle which is to take place under the conditions of peaceful coexistence can utilize *any form of opposition,* and can be waged with *every* instrument, including violence. Thus in colonial or newly independent countries as well as in the advanced industrial countries "everything goes," and no holds are barred:

> If the class struggle within the capitalist states has internal and only internal roots, it is clear that the principle of peaceful coexistence is not applied to the relations between classes within the bourgeois countries. The class struggle of the exploited against the exploiters and the struggle of the people against reactionary regimes *cannot be dissolved by international agreement. For this struggle to cease, the causes eliciting it must be eliminated, i.e., capitalism must be liquidated.*[15]

In sum, this statement declares that subversion, class warfare, and the general attempt to overthrow non-Communist societies will not come to a halt until "capitalism" has been destroyed. Since capitalism actually *causes* the Communists to wage a struggle against it, capitalism must be destroyed in order to stop the struggle. This is akin to a robber telling his victim that because the latter has earned the money which he carries in his billfold, he has forced the robber to take it from him. It is because of such perverted reasoning that non-Communists so often feel at a loss either to understand or explain the "logic" which Communism employs.

Communist "Humaneness"

Similar confusion is often experienced when coping with the Communist claim to universal representation of the "downtrodden masses of working people," and when, in spite of the terror and inhumanity which millions have suffered at the hands of the Communists, the claim is made that the "humane" movement of Communism employs only true humanitarian methods. It taxes the imagination when claims such as this are made:

> The Communist morality is the morality of the revolutionaries who are fulfilling their historic mission of saving all people from social inequality, from all forms of perse-

cution and exploitation, and from the horrors of war, and
who are establishing a system of the greatest justice and
humaneness on earth.[16]

Peaceful coexistence is the *specifically proletarian* form
of the class struggle conducted on an international scale.
Being specifically proletarian, peaceful coexistence is at the
same time also the *most humane* and the most rational
form.[17]

Note that peaceful coexistence is reserved exclusively to
the *proletariat;* that is to say, to the Communists themselves.
It is because the Communists alone may implement this
principle that it is automatically elevated to the level of "the
most humane" form of struggle.

A Strategic Doctrine

If only the Communists have title to peaceful coexistence,
then it should be clear that what the West professes to practice, i.e., its own form of "coexisting peacefully," cannot
serve as a medium for improving relations with Communists
or for alleviating the internal "class struggle." And herein lies
the most important point: one does not "practice" peaceful
coexistence, one *wages* it. Peaceful coexistence is to the Communists a *unilateral strategic doctrine which is imposed upon
the "inevitably doomed" adversary through the combined inherent "moral" and physical "superiority" of the Communist
system, and to which the adversary may only "respond" because he is denied a creative and participating role in determining its essence and application.*

From the conclusion that Communism determines both
the form and content of peaceful coexistence has arisen the
most brazen and extensive claim yet to be made: specifically,
that *peaceful coexistence* and *international law* are identical:

> Without exaggeration one can designate all contempo-
> rary generally recognized international law, as it exists to-
> day, as a code of peaceful coexistence. From this it follows
> that everything which is incompatible with the principle of

peaceful coexistence does not exist juridically in international relations. Conversely, all the old and new principles which contribute to the development and consolidation of peaceful coexistence can with complete justification lay claim to legal validity.[18]

It is as much to say that all which is incompatible with peaceful coexistence is *illegal.* Therefore, if the task of peaceful coexistence is to insure that Communism triumphs over capitalism as quickly and as efficiently as possible, the resistance which the non-Communist world may put up is basically contradictory to "law," and hence is "not legal." That such is the task of this new form of "international law" is made clear by the following statement by the dean of Soviet international lawyers, Korovin:

> One of the consequences of Socialism's transformation into the decisive factor of international relations is that peaceful coexistence has gradually become an accepted principle of international law. Initially it was the expression of a peaceful "breathing space," but being a specific form of class struggle between Socialism and capitalism on an international scale, peaceful coexistence was filled with new content as the relation of world forces changed. Its ultimate objective at the present time is to ensure the most favorable conditions for the victory of Socialism in its peaceful competition with capitalism.[19]

While it has become fashionable in the West to speak of "victory" in the cold war as "meaningless," the Communists persist in employing it as an official goal. Needless to say, they have a very real appreciation that "victory" by means of nuclear war would very probably be a victory in the true sense for no one; but to exclude a single method of achieving victory as an unrealistic instrument of policy does not signify that the entire concept of victory has been relinquished.

What Does Peaceful Coexistence Accomplish?

That Communists envision a genuine "victory" is demonstrated by the remarks of Khrushchev in July 1963 following the signing of the Nuclear Test Ban Treaty:

> Today the imperialists pretend to be brave, but only in words, whereas in reality they tremble before the world of growing and strengthening socialism. And let them tremble. So much the better for us.

> If everyone acted and thought in the Communist way then there would be no antagonistic classes and Communism would already be victorious everywhere. However, while there are still two systems, socialist and capitalist, each system has its own policy, its own course, and we cannot but take into account the fact that two systems exist. *A fight is in progress between these two systems, a life and death combat. But we Communists want to win this struggle with the least losses and there is no doubt whatsoever that we shall win.*[20]

The recognition that two systems do *in fact* exist in the same world is given only grudgingly; and because there does exist in the world an alternative system to that of the Communists, the contest between them assumes, in Khrushchev's own words, the form of "a life and death combat." Peaceful coexistence fulfills the Communist objectives in this mortal combat by "insuring" that victory is accomplished with minimal losses.

It follows from this statement that the Communists are prepared to accept some losses in propelling the revolution forward, but nowhere is it made clear just what these losses could entail. Despite the possibility of such setbacks, however, Khrushchev emphasizes the certainty of triumph.

The specific function of peaceful coexistence is not, as we have found, the establishment of a mere period of relative calm on a worldwide scale. Rather, it is to provide conditions favorable for waging a many-pronged offensive at and within the non-Communist world. Above all, it creates a degree of flexibility hitherto unknown to the Communist movement, inasmuch as it allows for harnessing and utilizing the most disparate forces to the revolutionary cause:

> The successes of our movement and the possibilities opening up before it, together with the responsibility devolving on our movement, all demand that Communists pursue a well-thought-out and well-founded policy, a policy designed to bring us victory over imperialism in the conditions of peaceful coexistence.[21]

Among these "possibilities" is the fact that

> Peaceful coexistence creates the most favorable conditions for the fight of the oppressed nations against their imperialist oppressors. *Peaceful coexistence means the maximum support to the oppressed nations including arms.*[22]

Hence, wherever the Communists declare an "oppressed nation" or an "oppressed area" to exist, there weapons will be supplied to forces which serve to undermine peace and stability, and which seek to establish either a Communist regime or, at minimum, a regime favorably disposed to existing Communist states. It is remarkable that the Communists, by unilateral proclamation, have reserved the right to themselves to determine "war zones" and "peace zones," and have repeatedly emphasized the "morality," "legality," and "necessity" for universal recognition of the "inherent justice" contained in such proclamations.

Confident that the initiative in dictating the essence of the tasks which peaceful coexistence will accomplish belongs to them, Communist leaders have labored to create the impression that time is on their side:

> The policy of peaceful coexistence meets the basic interests of all peoples, of all who want no new cruel wars and seek durable peace. This policy strengthens the positions of socialism, enhances the prestige and influence of the Communist Parties in the capitalist countries. Peace is a loyal ally of socialism, for time is working for socialism against capitalism.[23]

And again:

> Peace and socialism are indivisible—this Marxist formula has a profound meaning. In an atmosphere of peaceful coexistence, time works on the side of socialism, which is why the imperialist ideologists have such a dread of the very concept of peaceful coexistence.[24]

In providing conditions favorable to the diverse forms of "struggle," peaceful coexistence acts as an accelerator of the "world revolutionary process." By not concentrating all the resources of the movement in any one direction for the support of any single objective, the Communists seek to implement the entire spectrum of techniques designed to overthrow established governments by allowing a maximum degree of "leeway" in selecting the weapons of struggle to be used at a given place and time.

The Challenge to the West

Faced with such a real and formidable opponent, the West must clarify and reaffirm the goals which it has so long sought to achieve. And if a just and lasting peace is foremost among those goals, then it will have to keep sight of that goal while steeling itself to meet even greater threats than those experienced in the past.

There can be little doubt about the goals which the Communists have set for themselves; they have been forthrightly stated on these pages by the Communists themselves, and were summarized by Khrushchev:

> Capitalism . . . wants to bury the Socialist system and we want—not only want but have dug—quite a deep hole, and shall exert efforts to dig this hole deeper and bury the capitalist system forever.[25]

Whether there will continue to be room on the earth for the opposing systems of capitalism and Communism is a question which history alone will answer. For our part, we are willing to examine serious proposals for peace at any time; but "peace" on the basis of the Communist doctrine of "peaceful coexistence" is clearly an impossibility.

There is, however, a very real danger to the free world should it fail to judge accurately the intentions of the Communists. After some eight years of peaceful coexistence as the principal strategic line of the international Communist movement, we have no evidence that it seeks genuine peace with the rest of the world. Above all, it is clear that the Communists have not given up their long-range goal of world domination, and in the final analysis we must judge their motivations according to that goal. An intervening period of "peace" and relaxation, regardless of how inviting it may seem, must not be allowed to lower the guard of the free world.

End of the Cold War?

It is clear that when Communists employ the language of "peace," they do so to mask their true strategic purpose: the isolation, encirclement, weakening, and final destruction of the free world and its way of life. The cold war has not concluded, but has entered a new and still more complex phase in which the spectrum of psychological, political, economic, and class warfare will be radically expanded. Such classic techniques as subversion, espionage, propaganda, sabotage, terrorism, deceit, and incited disorder will remain and be refined; but the new techniques of nuclear blackmail are also to be employed whenever feasible. It would be totally unrealistic to hold, as some do, that nuclear weapons have only a military purpose. Long ago the Soviet Union appreciated fully the political purposes of these enormously destructive modern weapons, and their early decisions to invest huge sums of money and manpower into their development indicates their willingness to attain real supremacy over the West.

During the period of peaceful coexistence, the Communists also hope to reap the benefits of a worldwide "détente," i.e., a relaxation of tensions. Under such conditions they would hope not only to gain through an American and Western slowdown in armaments, but also to subvert and paralyze hostile governments in the hope that at the critical moment such governments will capitulate or will be incapable of offering effective resistance.

The great paradox of our time may well turn out to be our inability to recognize that the cold war has in reality become more intense despite the increasing appearances of peace. It need not be emphasized that the overwhelming sentiment of the free world is to live in peace. But to mistake the illusion of peace for genuine peace would be a profoundly dangerous, perhaps fatal mistake.

Our purpose in this great struggle imposed upon us by the Communist world is, as our Presidents and statesmen have repeatedly stressed, the victory of our way of life. If the clash between the two systems is, as the Communists never tire of stating, irreconcilable, then our victory will not be achieved until freedom and justice prevail everywhere in the world.

NOTES

1. Otto V. Kuusinen, ed., *Fundamentals of Marxism-Leninism* (Moscow: Foreign Languages Publishing House), 1961, p. 424. Second, revised edition 1963, p. 345.
2. Ibid., p. 425; 2nd ed., p. 346 (italics in original).
3. Josef Stalin, "The Foundations of Leninism," in *Problems of Leninism* (Moscow: Foreign Languages Publishing House), 1953, pp. 83–84.
4. "For the Unity and Solidarity of the International Communist Movement," *Pravda*, December 6, 1963.
5. It has been pointed out, however, that "What is strategy on one level is a tactic on another. The merging of the one into the other gives rise to the possibility of differing interpretations of what actually is 'strategy.' "
6. Josef Stalin, *Political Report of the Central Committee to the 15th Congress of the CPSU (B), December 3, 1927* (Moscow: Foreign Languages Publishing House), 1950, pp. 26–27.
7. Nikita Khrushchev, "For New Victories of the World Communist Movement," *Kommunist*, No. 1, January 1961. This is the famous speech delivered on January 6, 1961 which has

become a major document of the Communist movement. In January 1962 *Time* Magazine reported that President Kennedy had directed the nation's top policymakers to read the speech. The most comprehensive analysis of the speech has been made for the Senate Internal Security Subcommittee by Dr. Stefan T. Possony of the Hoover Institution on War, Revolution, and Peace, Stanford University.

8. *Statement of the 81 Communist and Workers Parties Meeting in Moscow, USSR,* December 1960, p. 16.

9. Nikita Khrushchev, radio-television speech, August 6, 1961.

10. H. Dona, *Peaceful Coexistence: A Basic Principle of the Foreign Policy of the Rumanian People's Republic* (Bucharest: State Publishing House), 1963, p. 2. Italics added.

11. I. Glagolev and V. Larionov, "Soviet Defense Might and Peaceful Coexistence," *International Affairs* (Moscow), November 1963, p. 33. Italics added.

12. N. S. Khrushchev's message to the 9th International Conference in Hiroshima for the banning of atomic and hydrogen weapons, August 19, 1963. Italics added.

13. N. Shishlin, "Nuclear Test Ban Agreement: A Leninist Coexistence Principle in Action," *Sovetskaya Estoniya,* October 23, 1963. Italics added.

14. N. S. Khrushchev, Speech at the Plenary Meeting of the Central Committee of the Communist Party of the Soviet Union, June 21, 1963. Italics added.

15. Dona, op. cit., p. 31. Italics added.

16. I. Kuz'minkov, "Communist Morality and General Moral Standards," *Kommunist,* No. 1, January 1964.

17. Ibid., p. 32. Italics in original.

18. Yevgeniy A. Korovin, "The Declaration of the Conference of Representatives of Communist and Workers Parties and the Tasks of the Science of International Law," *Vestnik Moskovskogo Universiteta,* August 1961, p. 66. Needless to say, the Communists use the conventional meaning of international law when it suits their purposes.

19. Yevgeniy A. Korovin, "An Old and Futile Demand," *International Affairs,* April 1963, p. 100.

20. N. S. Khrushchev, "Speech at the Soviet-Hungarian Meeting, August 19, 1963," *Current Soviet Documents,* August 19, 1963. Italics added.

21. L. Sharkey, "Creative Marxism Is the Basis for Revolutionary Practice," *World Marxist Review,* October 1963, p. 10. Sharkey is General Secretary of the Communist Party of Australia.

22. Kjeld Oesterling and Norman Freed, *Peace, Freedom and You* (Prague: Peace and Socialism Publishers), 1963, p. 15. Italics added.

23. *Statement of the 81 Communist and Workers Parties,* op. cit., p. 16.

24. V. P. Kalugin, "The Magnetic Force of the Leninist Ideas of Peaceful Coexistence," *International Affairs*, (No. 8), August 1963, p. 24.
25. N. S. Khrushchev, Speech at the Plenary Meeting, op. cit.

CUBA:
THOUGHTS PROMPTED BY THE CRISIS

by Charles Burton Marshall

Charles Burton Marshall is Research Associate at the Washington Center of Foreign Policy Research. A graduate of the University of Texas, he received his Ph.D. from Harvard University, and was an instructor at Harvard and Radcliffe. He served as an officer in the U. S. Army from 1942–46. Mr. Marshall was Staff Consultant on the House of Representatives Committee on Foreign Affairs from 1947–50; a member of the Policy Planning Staff of the Department of State, 1950–53; and Visiting Scholar at the Carnegie Endowment for International Peace, 1958–59. A contributor to numerous publications, he is the author of The Limits of Foreign Policy, *1954, and* Two Communist Manifestoes, *1961.*

Reprinted from *The New Republic*. This selection appeared in *The New Republic* as a series of three articles on October 1, November 10 and 24, 1962. Copyright Harrison-Blaine, Inc.

Why the Russians Are There

The versions of self-enthrallment are many. One, well liked at the Capitol, combines the best elements of mutually exclusive notions. It proposes a peaceable blockade[1] on Cuba, awarding us prerogatives of belligerency without its pains and responsibilities. Other governments would acquiesce in our wish to have matters both ways. Ships would be submitted to our visits and searches and their destinations changed at

our demand. We could enjoy the benefits of war without
being forced to fire a shot—a beautiful dream.

A columnist discerns in events a pattern of historic reci-
procity: Cuba is turn-about for Greece and Turkey. We are
to watch the contest like disinterested spectators high in the
stands. Never mind if the ones in red jerseys make some
touchdowns now, for our team had the ball in their part of
the field, too. It's all good sport to be viewed from Olympian
eminence.

The Administration also invokes a broad view. Berlin—
not Cuba—is the danger spot, as if there couldn't be two. It
takes a cue from *The King and I*:

> . . . I hold my head erect
> And whistle a happy tune
> So no one will suspect
> I'm afraid.

The happy tune emphasizes the defensive character of the
military preparations and the technician status of the Soviet
forces in Cuba.

Technician is a handy sort of Milltown word—a euphemism
covering fighting men sent abroad as tactical instructors and
weapons specialists to act on the military environment in
another land. Such an undertaking is deep and pervasive
under conditions imposed by modern weapons systems. This
Russian training mission has the look of a permanent fix.
Presumably it will mold the thirteen thousand or so men
from Castro's original insurgent force and the quarter million
or so of the peasant militia into a cogent military force with
a unity based on a common discipline and doctrine.

A defensive undertaking? One could call it that. The specu-
latively hopeful term does not tell us much. No attack on
New York, New Orleans, Cape Canaveral, Miami, the Canal,
or probably even Guantanamo is foreseeable. That is not
the point. Such a force will foreclose the possibility of a
domestic rising against Castro. The lingering active resistance
to the regime will presumably be snuffed out. The political
import of civil discontent will diminish. The underpinnings
of the regime can be prepared in such depth as to rule out

selective assassination as a means of redress and reform. One can suppose the Russians are there to make Communism stick, with or without Castro or any other particular personage.

Castro and Cuba are finally and fully stuck with a label and an association hostile to the environment. The Russians can scarcely renounce the undertaking now without acknowledging a failure of enormous magnitude.

For the first time the Soviets have formed a common military front with a Communist state overseas and sitting next to the United States. Khrushchev and Castro must have approached the project with trepidation, studied it with caution, and then undertaken it finally with a sense of assurance of getting away with it—notwithstanding our President's pledge, in the immediate sequel to the boggle at the Bay of Pigs, that the United States would never abandon Cuba to Communism.

The events have negligible military significance and involve only our prestige, a bishop assured me. Why *only?* Prestige is the faculty enabling a great power to avoid final, miserable choices between surrender and war. Prestige is the ingredient of authority in international affairs. One may point up its meaning by an account of a geneticist who crossed a tiger with a parrot. When asked about the results of the experiment, he replied: "When it talks, I listen." The quality which demands being listened to is prestige—and a nation suffers loss of it at great peril.

These Cuban developments are a big thing. We should acknowledge them as such with the public candor of General Joe Stilwell after a debacle in Burma: "I claim we got a hell of a beating. . . . It's humiliating as hell. . . ." Only thus can we make a start on seeing our way clearly to next steps.

All too likely is that our attention will be diverted by other and happier tunes. There is always room for solace in some marginal event. One is reminded of the case of a man who dropped dead at Brighton after two weeks of a rest cure on the beach. "He got a wonderful suntan," said the man's brother viewing him at the mortuary. "Yes," the widow concurred, "that last fortnight did him a world of good."

Policy goes on pledging a stand at some deferred barricade.

What inhibits policy in such matters as Cuba—and this shows in reluctance to draw issues and in dreams of drawing them without risk—is consciousness of perils inherent in the hitting power and range of contemporary weapons, linked with an outlook once described by Ortega y Gasset: "Modern morality has cultivated a sentimental standard by which anything becomes preferable to the thought of dying. Life is thus prolonged in proportion as it is not used. It gains extension at the cost of vitality."

We assure ourselves of the adversary's similar basic preference for peace. This gives us comfort but no purchase. Our position is like that of a peaceable character in a TV Western facing an opponent disposed to wear his guns ostentatiously, to boast of his draw and marksmanship, and to interpose and to push weight in all manner of issues. One can reassure himself of the adversary's preference for not shooting up the town—for prevailing without violence. This gains nothing if in every difference the adversary makes persuasive his willingness to draw in extremity and the peaceable hero abides by his civilized reluctance. We shall have to face up also to the effects on policy of this contrast if Cuba is not to prove the first of a series of such developments.

Afterthoughts on the Blockade

That crucial October fortnight, with the issue of Soviet missiles in Cuba arising and having to be met, provided simple but profound lessons about the nature of policy and decision. Four aspects, widely misunderstood and misinterpreted, seem to deserve particular attention: namely, the justification and necessity of the President's not confronting Soviet Foreign Minister Andrei Gromyko with "preliminary hard information" concerning emplacement of missiles when the two conferred on October 18; this Government's omission of consultation with its allies before announcing a blockade and bringing to bear threats of further measures on October 22; the status of the actions under international law; and finally the question of how our side came out on balance.

To begin, one has to be clear as to the nature of negotiating relationships between governments involved in a basic conflict of interests and purposes, as the United States and the Soviet Union are. The relevant points are so elementary as to seem banal.

Such relationships differ fundamentally from those between governments with compatible outlooks and aims. Diplomatic interchange between the U.S. and the U.S.S.R. is only a way of registering the wills and capabilities brought to bear by the opposing sides. It is a mode of conducting the power contest —not an alternative to it. This reciprocal process is exacting and risky. It calls for hardy wills and fine discernments. It is susceptible of getting out of hand and eventuating in war when one party overcommits itself to a proposition which underestimates the adversary's will to prevail or resist.

Any agreement on terms of peace negotiated by adversary powers must be conditioned on their fear of the consequences of not agreeing.

In this perspective, President Kennedy's favored and oft-repeated apothegm about never negotiating in fear and never fearing to negotiate is quite misleading, even contradictory. Adversary powers have to negotiate in fear of what may happen in the sequel to a failure to settle on terms. A power must rationally fear having to negotiate under unfavorably disproportionate compulsion.

Whatever its precise effect on relevant military factors, the Soviet Union's deployment of missiles to Cuba constituted a clear attempt to redress factors of compulsion in its own favor so as to render the United States amenable to terms more to the Soviet Union's advantage. The President's response was an initiative designed to be countervailing.

Whether there was some misunderstanding regarding meanings and facts, especially with respect to content of the elusive word "defensive" applied to the Soviet armament of Cuba, is a niggling point. One can only wonder at the import attributed to the point in supposedly serious criticisms of the President's conduct of the meeting with Gromyko.

On a basis of cold words contained in snippets from the key conversation, no outsider can competently judge the state of understanding between the President and the Soviet regime. It was a matter for intuitive judgment—not a matter susceptible of being tested under the rigors of judicial evidence. As Commander-in-Chief, as primary agent of our foreign policy, and as the specific executor of the Congressional resolution of intent regarding Cuba, only the President was in constitutional position to make the judgment. Only he, as our chief participant in the interchanges, was able to take into account all relevant nuances.

For the President to have taken further pains to notify and to warn the adversary regarding our knowledge of what the adversary must have known we knew could have gained nothing. To have made the prospect and thrust of our counterinitiatives a topic of diplomatic interchange would in high probability have lost much. It would have deprived the contemplated actions of whatever cogency they might have, dulled the impressions of resolution we wanted to convey, and afforded the adversary opportunity to forestall or to nullify our initiatives with some more of his own.

A Game of One-Upmanship

Should our man in the White House have given warning and disclosure of our next move—have told the opposing fellows that in fairness we owed them advance word of plans to get one-up on them in turn? Absurd is the word for the idea.

Mere words would not serve. Too much of a past had to be overcome. We had bespoken determination over Laos, only to settle for the troika there. We had flinched on following through at the Bay of Pigs. The pattern of the call-up of reserves in mid-1961 had prefigured an addition of five or six divisions to our Army. After words of rage privately conveyed from Khrushchev, the plan had petered out. We had huffed and dawdled as a wall rose in Berlin.

Admittedly, the problem of discoursing both to give pause to adversaries and to humor the timorous and uncommitted is not easy, but we had long overdone the latter aspect with maxims about no alternative to negotiation and about willingness ever to traverse another last mile in parleying—this last an invitation to adversaries to go on setting up mileposts along an interminable course.

Only a few days earlier the President himself had ferociously assailed an Indiana Senator for proposing, with respect to Cuba, a course involving exposure of other people's sons to risk. A prerogative to expose other people's sons to risk underlies state authority as distinguished from that of a tribe, whose powers are circumscribed by kinship. State authority endangers other people's sons when it quenches a fire, quells a riot, or defends a homeland. With respect to Cuba, the President had gone so far as implicity to derogate from his power to perform constitutional duties.

With so much in the record to be offset, immediate and unequivocal action was called for to re-establish credit. This was not abandonment of diplomacy. It was a step necessary for reconstituting an acceptable basis for it. To have gone off consulting far and wide on next steps with three dozen allies would have vitiated the whole idea. What was to be done had to be done without regard to contingencies of support or assent from other quarters. United States determination to act thus alone in sovereign discretion had to be manifested to friends as well as opponents as a fact requiring to be taken into account in their relations with us. Advance consultation could only have obscured the fact.

A further circumstance militated against consultation. The great ranges of lands and peoples in the world are the Northern and the Western Hemispheres. Cuba interacted within and between them both. The United States, besides being custodian of a nuclear shield integral to the security of either hemisphere, is the only great power located in both hemispheres. It is the sole nation involved in both relevant security structures—the North Atlantic Treaty Organization and the Organization of American States. Its Government alone among the American allies had appreciation of the interaction between Cuba and, say, the Berlin situation. Among the Atlantic allies it alone was intimately knowledgeable of Cuba's implications through the Americas. To have gone off now on exploratory talks could scarcely have added anything to what was required for us to resolve our will.

The cavil about consultation misses an essential of alliances. I can perhaps make my point clear by an analogy to something I observed when in the Army. When a man was not up to the mark, the practice was to assign him a helper also not up to the mark. I learned to call this faulty premise the half-wit fallacy because it involved a notion of combining half-wits to form whole wits. Actually the relationship was not additive but multiplicative, producing quarter-wit results. Deficiency does not compound into sufficiency. The lesson applies to factors of heart as well as mind. Half-heartedness does not combine into courage. An alliance can be strong only as its leading elements have and show moral capacity to act alone in exigency. In potential, if not in accomplished fact, our alliances are stronger now because the United States seized a sole initiative.

Is the Charter Obsolete?

The legality of our actions can best be left to international law classrooms. Blockade is a belligerent prerogative. If parties affected choose not to acknowledge its belligerent character, it gets by as a peaceable act. Our resort to such action and hints of worse to come were probably not countenanced by the letter of Article 51 of the United Nations Charter, for no attack to justify invocation of force in our own behalf had as yet occurred. By a purist's argument, we should have cleared our plans with the veto-bound Security Council before acting at all. The point lies with equal relevance to our post facto clearance with the Council of the OAS, whose warrant to authorize forcible remedial actions is subordinated to Security Council approval under Article 53 of the UN Charter.

Capacity to bring about drastic shifts in force factors by sudden, stealthy, massive weapon deployments in a nuclear age simply renders obsolete the precondition of attack to the licensing of self-defense under Article 51. Facts have outgrown a concept.

It is beyond law to provide a signal for transgression against one's vital interests. A Government must make up its own mind on that. Goethe provides a proper answer on the legalities: "In the long run, over-great goodness, mildness, and moral delicacy will not do, while underneath there is a mixed and sometimes vicious world to manage and hold in respect."

Yet, finally, to what avail? The results could have been worse. They provide that small measure of comfort. The Government at least desisted from retracting missiles from Turkey to balance withdrawal of missiles from Cuba—a course urged by commentators and bishops out of what seemed an aesthetic hankering for symmetry. Perhaps, indeed, the outcome was the best achievable in view of the lag in drawing an issue. No one will ever know for sure.

The paeans occasioned by Soviet agreement to dismantle baffle me. Only by focusing narrowly on the issue of missile deployment can one call this a retraction on the part of the Soviet Union. Our President's avowal, on April 20 last year, of resolve never to abandon Cuba to Communism has been publicly put aside—no mean feat of word-swallowing. By contrast, the Soviet pledge to shelter the Cuban regime is now redeemed. Cuba is now unmistakably a Soviet protectorate. We have negotiated on this basis with the Soviet Union. Communist power is ensconced in this hemisphere. We have in effect legitimized this. We have joined in invoking UN blessings on the arrangement.

One must await what events may disclose as to the power of precedent in the pattern—what other positions may go in a sequence of seeing a Communist regime put into power by whatever means, having the stakes raised, then guaranteeing the position in return for having the stakes lowered. As a gain, Cuba is somewhat akin to that victory at Ausculum: a few more such could be our undoing.

A disposition to view the developments as giving promise for negotiating a general détente seems borrowed from fantasy. It reminds me of an occasion when the Duke of Wellington was approached by a man saying, "Mr. Peabody, I believe!" The Duke replied: "If you believe that, you can believe anything."

Hide and Seek: Dour Thoughts on Inspection

Some key terms relevant to arms control and disarmament —a field of endeavor overburdened with ambiguities—have been mauled about by government spokesmen, news analysts, and editorial writers since the onset of our troubles over missiles in Cuba. I feel prompted to offer, on behalf of rigor, some simple definitions. I begin with the generic term, *verification*.

One kind of verification can be carried out without the acquiescence or cooperation of the government subject to check. Certain information is explicit in, or inferable from, open sources within the country, from covert operations within or over the domain concerned, and from observations from adjacent territory. An appropriate term for this kind of verification is *monitoring*.

A second kind of verification requires grant of access by a government whose actions or capabilities are assessed. The operations divide into two classes.

One sort of access is that conceded by a government for a specific limited occasion. Outside authority is permitted to enter an area to confirm that the inviting government has done what it claims to have done (e.g., dismantled a missile pad). The visitors have no warrant to ferret out unreported matters. In effect the government is host, the outside authority is guest. An appropriate term here is *authentication*.

A contrasting sort of access is exercised when a government vests an outside authority with power not merely to check matters admitted by the subject government but also and essentially to determine, within limits of relevance, what may have been left undone or done covertly. The correct term here is *inspection*. Such is its sense in official parlance generally—in banking, postal operations, military outfits, and so on. An inspector comes around, welcome or not, with warrant to poke and to raise issues—not merely to nod through a prearranged checklist.

The general concept, *verification*, is what was alluded to in Chairman Khrushchev's offer to take his missiles out of

Cuba—concurred in at once by President Kennedy, subject
to a proviso for continuing U.S. monitoring in an interim.
U.S. spokesmen immediately began calling the prospective
operation inspection. But by any feat of imagination, the essential attributes of inspection were lacking. Nevertheless,
U.S. officials, having espoused inspection through drudging
years of talks on test bans and arms limitation, appeared
anxious to nudge arrangements toward at least nominal or
symbolic conformity to this standard. With equal alertness
to record and precedent, the Soviets set out to attribute an
invitational and *pro forma* character to whatever, if anything,
had been agreed to.

For an outsider, an analysis of the ensuing exercise in
tactical diplomacy revolving around these opposed themes is
highly difficult—much like trying to comprehend a merry-go-
round by glimpsing it in motion through a fence crack, or
a score of counterpoint by hearing gust-borne sounds of a
distant orchestra. Who and what prompted U Thant to the
pilgrimage that resulted in establishing a UN absence in
Havana? On the basis of what estimates did the U.S.S.R.
propose and did the U.S. hasten to accept the impeccably
humanitarian International Committee of the Red Cross as
a verifying agent on matters of war technology outside its
familiarity? Were Castro's dissents at the instance, by leave,
or in defiance of Moscow? Perhaps the explanations of these
and many other mysteries will never be known.

One matter seems fairly evident, however: both sides have
been doing their cagey utmost to avoid precedents and to
minimize compromising basic positions on verification. As an
augury for the eighteen-nation disarmament conference, this
maneuvering is probably much more significant than the
fervent pieties about disarmament exchanged between Chairman Khrushchev and President Kennedy at the peak of the
crisis.

Here, at risk of elaborating what is evident, I want to
emphasize that the main parties to negotiation at Geneva are
the governing groups in the U.S. and the U.S.S.R. Their
views do not necessarily coincide—and in some aspects are
not at all likely to coincide—with the views found in literature

on arms control. This literature is written by psychiatrists and sociologists intent upon resolving policy conflicts by dismissing them as aberrant, by physicists disposed to evaluate an adversary government's aims from sentimentalities uttered over cocktails at a Pugwash meeting, by psychologists seeking clues to the weapons riddle by analyzing chit-chat of train attendants and of concierges met during a Russian tour, and by various other sorts of imaginative but nonresponsible authors.

The governing groups in the U.S. and the U.S.S.R. are aware of the chances for calamity. A shared desire to get armaments under control may be assumed without arguing, for on any other premise the negotiations consist of subterfuge and fall beyond rational analysis. Arms control and disarmament, however, are not absolute and discrete aims. They overlap and interact with a great range of other considerations. The rub is—or at least has been up to now—with respect to these other matters.

A bargain, if and when arrived at, must be a *political* one, in the broadest sense. Each party is under constraint to ensure terms which will preserve the order of values basic to its polity. As a test of their providence, the terms must have convincing marks of being provident—convincing to constituents and allies whose concurrence is necessary as a condition to giving the terms effect. While still in position to give or to withhold consent, each party is constrained to seek terms consistent with other purposes reflecting its relevant order of values.

This gets close to the heart of the inspection issue. Each side—with reason—attributes to the other ultimate desires and preferences incompatible with its own. Each side—again with cause—suspects that the other, given opportunity, would bring its more remote desires and preferences into its pattern of immediate actions. This reciprocal anxiety is nothing to puzzle about. Authentic spokesmen for the U.S.S.R. articulate international goals entirely incompatible with the U.S. order of values. Spokesmen on our side articulate world goals which could be realized only after a frustration of the U.S.S.R. amounting to historic defeat. That the articulated goals of both parties may lie beyond reach is beside the point. Each side makes plain enough what preferences it would establish as purposes of policy if it could.

In analyzing the interplay between inspection and the basic conflict of purposes, it is important to recognize that individuals may accept, draw upon, and apply orders of values prevalent within their culture even while ignoring or renouncing beliefs underlying them. One may act on monotheistic postulates while professing agnosticism. In this respect, hopes for a détente between the U.S. and the U.S.S.R. founded on Khrushchev's indifference or even cynicism—often alleged but never demonstrated—regarding Marxist-Leninist tenets are probably like fantasies that a Borgia Pope, because inconstant on finer points of practice, might have been flexible on matters in controversy with Luther.

Natural Law and Inspected Truth

The mode of thought underlying the U.S. approach, whether or not recognized and acknowledged, rests on ideas of natural law. A unified Creation, with a pattern of right reason inherent, is postulated. Good is identified with it. Principles are held as reflections of this good. What opposes good is ascribed to aberrant free will. Interests are seen as colored with such aberrant imperfections associated with misguided free will. Principles thus transcend interests. Social good inheres in upholding principles impartially. The concept of authority—which is to say, power to bind in conscience—is based on devotion to principles unswayed by interests, impartially applied. Facts are items of information developed impartially by authority and are an objective basis on which to apply principles. Such are the justifying, if not always reigning, concepts in state life.

In the U.S. view, an inspectorate in connection with arms control comprises institutional arrangements for projecting onto the world scene, and especially onto the U.S.S.R., a fact-finding function based on the conception of authority described above. It must be above interests, impartial in endeavor—its authority acknowledged, permitted scope, facilitated in operations, submitted to without cavil or hindrance. Its existence and functions, thus serving as both a substantive and symbolic substitute for trust between the great adversaries, would gradually evolve a basis for confidence. It would serve to assemble and to verify facts to bolster assurance or to confirm doubt. In extremity—that is, in event of the need to abrogate an agreement in face of unacceptable violations by others—the system would provide warrant and vindication. In sum, the U.S. plan for a disarming or disarmed world is congenial to the U.S. view of legitimacy.

The U.S.S.R. view is different. The U.S.S.R. asserts a total claim on the future, based on its dialectic concepts of history. An essential aspect of this claim is that history progresses by inherent momentum toward a final perfection perceivable only through Communist doctrine. Concepts of legitimacy are derived from the law of history which ordains eventual universal triumph for Communist interests and purposes. All other interests and purposes are deemed deviant and devoid of legitimacy. The ruling Communist Party is considered sole interpreter and custodian of legitimacy. Bearers of Party authority are constrained not to concede legitimacy to any authority beyond their control.

Intrusion and Inspection

No thread, I contend, has been more consistent in Communist conduct than this sensitivity to making any concessions to external authority—manifested in the World War II period by the Soviet's obduracy against the scheduling by the Western allies of chain bombing out of Russian airfields, stiffness over timing of lend-lease convoys, and impingements on UNRRA operations. The instances often cited as countervailing turn out to be unconvincing under examination. Russia's acceptance of inspection in post-World War II occupation agreements, for example, pertained to domains not yet brought to heel. Soviet agreement to inspection in Antarctica involved no Communist area. Communist accession to inspection in North Korea under armistice terms has proved nugatory in real effect. According to a notion persistent within the so-called disarmament community, the U.S.S.R. did once offer concessions on inspection in test-ban discussions. But should we construe a martini recipe as an offer of a drink?

An index to this attitude is the Soviet practice of linking inspection with the term *intrusion*. All too often, Americans echo the linkage, using "intrusive inspection" for inspection proper and "nonintrusive inspection" for monitoring. A standard definition of *intrusion* is "forcing of oneself into a place without right of welcome, the act of wrongfully entering onto property of another." *Inspection* is defined in lexicons as "the act of examining officially"—and *officially* means "with authority, with sanction." "Intrusive inspection" is a contradiction in terms and "nonintrusive inspection" a tautology. Both expressions should be banned from U.S. discourse.

Soviet willingness to invite in an authenticating agency on occasion is quite conceivable but has no bearing on submitting to inspection. The U.S.S.R. persistently says inspection is out—a stand consistent with Communist dogma. In face of this, it is difficult to explain lingering U.S. hopes that the U.S.S.R. really does not mean it, and that obduracy can some day be overcome by adjusting details. The U.S. may indeed exaggerate the efficacy of inspection. In this connection, the notion that inspection has a potential for guiding the U.S.S.R. toward becoming an open society may be laid aside as inherently too marginal and speculative for serious consideration. The point of inquiry is whether inspection could do the job for which designed. I am not in a position to state definitive views. I can only raise questions.

One question pertains to inspection as a way of ensuring compliance with any agreement. For the moment, and for argument, formal acceptance of inspection terms by the U.S.S.R. and other Communist regimes may be assumed. But formal acceptance does not necessarily mean cooperation. The Korean armistice pattern might well be repeated —continuous frustration, postponement, avoidance, and administered ambiguity. The level and quality of information afforded might well be less than attainable through monitoring—that is, verification by means available to the U.S. irrespective of Soviet cooperation. The international inspectorate would probably provide small, if any, assurance of compliance.

A second question concerns the qualities of an international inspectorate. To gain necessary respect and credit even under favorable conditions, such an inspectorate would have to have high motivation and technical competence. Yet presumably an inspectorate would have to draw heavily on people from uncommitted countries. Most of these countries are—and will remain for a long time—short on technicians. They will need to keep their best men at home.

Third, a question is in order concerning the integrity of findings by an international inspectorate. U.S. expectations are based on the assumptions that everyone can divorce "truth" from its consequences. The U.S. envisages an international inspectorate disciplined and constrained to rigorous, exacting attitudes toward empirical data, irrespective of preconceptions and preferences. Yet the U.S. doubts the detachment of Communists in an inspectorate, in the event neutrals may prove equally self-interested.

U.S. expectations overlook a disposition, basic in the cultures of many of the neutralist countries, to view magisterial functions as intended not so much to forward the triumph of good over evil as to keep contention between them from getting out of hand. This calls for temporizing, mitigating, hoping always to work out arrangements to save something all around, but in a pinch favoring concessions to the more intransigent. F. S. C. Northrop's *Philosophical Anthropology and Practical Politics* reflects good insights into this attitude.

I recall an illustrative instance. Representing the Government of the United States at an International Red Cross Conference during 1952 I was forced to the limit of my patience in trying both to avoid a donnybrook and to preserve national prestige in the face of outrageous attacks from Chinese Communist delegates. At intermission, a delegate from a leading neutralist country, after praising me for reasonable forbearance, added, "These men are mad dogs. You should have let them have their way"—a *non sequitur* to me but obviously plausible to him.

To expect unequivocal findings by an international inspectorate which has neutrals in the swing position—especially with respect to crucial considerations likely to precipitate renewed competition on armament—is probably too much. Should the U.S. ever find itself constrained to abrogate a disarmament treaty, it would probably have to do so, and to face consequences, on its own sole sovereign discretion—without any international certificate.

It could be—who can say for sure?—that inspection would not raise the level of technical surety over that achievable by monitoring. Some experts say this. Perhaps also the U.S. has not realistically appraised factors of feasibility in regard to plans for an inspectorate. These negative considerations, however valid, do not dispose of the matter. It is necessary also to take account of the political acceptability of an agreement within the U.S.—an aspect bearing on the juridical character of an agreement.

So systematic and far-reaching a venture as a formal agreement on arms control and disarmament should be an act of state of a most solemn character—to be undertaken only on a basis of firm and demonstrated concurrence between the Executive and the coordinate political branch. It should commit the nation beyond the term of the Administration launching it, with a status above party contention. It should contract other parties to obligations equally durable and deep. A treaty seems appropriate, even indispensable, as an instrument for any such formal agreement.

In this perspective, limits, difficulties, and doubts regarding inspection recede to academic import. Questions of confidence and dependability are not merely technical. They never were. They might conceivably have become so if at some juncture relationships between the U.S. and the Communist imperium had turned onto a basically better course. Then armaments might conceivably have been tethered without all the paraphernalia of inspection. But this hypothesis is based on fantastic rather than realistic imagination. Whatever the theoretical possibilities under dreamt-up conditions, one now must take account of the autumn missile crisis. I have heard hopeful speculations regarding its effect, as if fellowship might grow out of a shared crisis, as if wrestling a bear to the brink were a mutually endearing experience. I am skeptical. I see little in recent events to nourish the mystique of trust. An uninspected arms control compact seems out for the calculable future. The outlook is dour—indefinite impasse on formal terms, with abatement of the problems restricted to unilateral steps and to informal and tacit agreements, with or without more such crises as the one over Cuba.

NOTE

1. Author's note: Blockade pertains to general interdiction of commerce as distinguished from the highly selective restraint, termed a quarantine, applied against offensive weapons.

COMMUNISTS IN
COALITION GOVERNMENTS

by Gerhart Niemeyer

Dr. Niemeyer is a widely recognized authority on the history and nature of Communism. He is the author of several books and a frequent contributor to scholarly journals. A native of Germany, he studied at the universities of Cambridge and Munich, and received his doctorate from Kiel University. He has taught at the universities of Frankfurt, Madrid, and Munich, and at Princeton, Oglethorpe, Yale, and Columbia universities. From 1950 to 1953 he was planning adviser in the U. S. Department of State. Since 1955 he has been Professor of Political Science at the University of Notre Dame.

This selection is adapted from a booklet with the same title published by the American Enterprise Institute for Public Research in June 1963. Reprinted by permission.

Coalition governments as such do not constitute a problem that requires much special analysis. They are more the rule than the exception in modern parliamentary democracy. Most Western countries have been governed by coalitions in one form or another. Some countries have been under stable coalition governments, as, for instance, Austria, for very long periods. In other countries, the pattern of coalition has persisted while coalitions of various component elements succeeded one another, as in France and Italy. In all these cases, however, one finds the same parties, now in power, now out of power, now participating in a coalition, and now in opposition. When a coalition collapses, the participating parties go their separate ways but do not exclude an eventual return to a new coalition. In these fluctuations, there may be problems on how to achieve or continue a particular combination of parties in a given country at a given time, but the institution of coalition as such does not present serious problems for the social analyst.

It is altogether different with coalitions combining non-Communist parties with Communists. As soon as Communists enter as political partners, the coalition ceases to be one of a continuing series and turns into something final, a one-way road to some definitive end. Coalitions including Communists have invariably ended either in Communist dictatorship or in a complete rupture between the non-Communist and Communist members of the coalition. The rupture has sometimes taken the form of an armed conflict, at other times that of the exclusion of Communists from any further participation in the country's government. There is no case of Communist cooperation in a coalition within the limits of the traditional parliamentary pattern in which parties accept and expect alternations between participation in power and opposition. In spite of this fact of experience, both Communist and non-Communist parties have again and again sought to enter into coalitions with each other. Coalitions with Communists thus present a problem that does indeed require analysis. They follow a law of their own that lifts them out of the ordinary. They seem to be unworkable in the fashion of other coalition governments and yet they are resorted to, time after time. Why is this so? What are the expectations of the partners in coalitions with Communists? How are these coalitions used by Communists for ends that depart from those of normal coalitions? Why are these coalitions so final?

Coalitions including Communists fall into a pattern that is repeated in country after country, allowing for certain differences of time and circumstances. The first thing that strikes the observer is the strong Communist urge to come to power within the framework and the legitimacy of a coalition. Even where, as in Rumania, the order of Vishinsky, backed by naked armed force, instituted a Communist gov-

ernment by fiat, the appearances of a coalition still meant
a great deal to the Communists. Again and again they urge,
nay even compel non-Communist parties to participate in
elections, to agree to a joint ticket, or to send their leaders
as ministers into a government. The need for the blessing
of non-Communists seems to be axiomatic in Communist
strategies.

The Five Elements of Coalition Agreements

If one analyzes the basis of coalition agreements, one finds
in practically all cases five elements: (1) agreement that
there is a "common cause" in which Communists and non-
Communists share alike; (2) agreement on the value of unity
as such; (3) agreement on the goals of national policies to
be jointly pursued; (4) agreement on non-toleration of certain parties, ideas, and individuals in the political theater; and
(5) agreement on the distribution of power positions among
the coalition partners.

The "common cause" serves as the rationale for the coalition; the "value of unity" enjoins loyalty to the coalition as a
moral obligation; the "national policy goals" provide the coalition with a practical purpose; "non-toleration" is directed
against elements that play the role of the devil in the design;
and the "sharing of political power" is the *modus operandi*.

All this presupposes certain situations in which such agreements are possible because they seem to make sense to non-
Communists. The postwar period offered opportunities because of the Fascist and Nazi danger against which the Allied
powers had just won a victory. Fascism was easily coupled
with "reaction," so that all postwar coalition agreements
stress the "common cause" of a fight against "Fascism and
reaction." The vagueness of the definition lends itself readily
to Communist manipulation. "Imperialism," "war," "milita-
rism," and other devil-notions of our time provide similarly
suitable contents for agreements on a "common cause." The
"value of unity" has powerful appeal to all Marxists, because of their fixed idea that the workers' revolution would
have inevitably triumphed if it had not been for the split of

workers' parties into Socialists and Communists, not to mention the anarchists. "Disunity" among workers has been considered tantamount to a betrayal of the workers' movement. The "value of unity" has an equally strong appeal in any country where national calamities can be ascribed to a lack of unity, particularly among the democratic parties. Furthermore, "unity" is strongly desired in any difficult situation, particularly a period of national reconstruction. All this makes for minds to which "unity" as such seems to be more important than the principle or end for the sake of which unity is desired, so that political ends, values, and principles are then used as bargaining points in order to achieve and maintain unity. Agreement on "national policy goals" can thus usually be slanted toward the Left, because the non-Communist parties feel that, in moving toward the Left, they can obtain the cooperation of the Communists while they themselves have no strong objections in principle to a certain measure of socialism.

Having established agreement on both basic points and practical things to be done, it seems only natural that the available power positions should be shared proportionally among the partners, and that Communists should participate in many key government agencies.

There is a significant difference in the assumptions of non-Communists and Communists regarding the basic coalition agreements. Non-Communists think essentially in terms of the status quo, that is, the present. For them coalition is a matter of mutual concessions entered into in order to safeguard the basic elements of the status quo while sacrificing certain unessential aspects. One can almost say categorically that for all non-Communist democratic parties, the continuation of their own functioning as political units is the essence of the status quo. This would not apply to the Kuomintang, which was designed by its creator, Sun Yat-sen, as a party which would exercise a temporary revolutionary dictatorship leading to a new China. If self-preservation motivates the democratic parties entering into a coalition with Communists, no such assumption can be entertained by Communists, for Communists regard the present not as a status quo to be preserved, but as a period of transition in the revolutionary struggle for a Socialist future. The destruction of the status quo, including the parliamentary multi-party system, must therefore be the Communist design regardless of what Communists tell their coalition partners. One cannot accuse the Communists of insincerity when they say that they are interested in democracy, elections, civil liberties, and coalition governments. They are, indeed, interested in having these advantages which greatly facilitate their operations. Unlike others, however, they do not look upon these things as elements of an enduring order, but only as means of power in a passing phase of history which must be "liquidated" with all possible speed.

Communist Orientation toward the Future

The Communists are oriented toward a future which in no wise resembles that of present-day democratic politics, whereas their coalition partners are oriented toward the democratic order of the present as something desirable in itself. Their orientation toward the future causes the Communists to think not in terms of desirable solutions for present-day living, but rather in terms of an endless accumulation of power for the Party which "holds the future in its hands." In *Das Kapital,* Karl Marx used the formula $M-C-M'$ to describe the process of the circulation of capital from money (M) through commodity (C) and to increased money (M'). Using the same device, one may say that the normal process of politics is one in which parties start from a certain legal situation, seek power in order to introduce certain changes, and end up with a new legal situation. Using L for legal situation and P for power, one can schematize the process as $L-P-L'$, which describes the subordination of power to the order of daily life. In Communist thinking the road to the future counts for everything, and that road is one of spiraling power accumulation. Thus the political process, for Communists, is best described by the formula $P-L-P'$, so that any legal achievement serves above all the purpose of accumulating increased power for the Communist onward movement.

It is this basic difference in orientation which causes Communists to manipulate other parties by means of agreements on "common causes," "value of unity," "national policy goals," and so on. Taken by themselves, many of these causes are good causes, and the joining of several political parties for a common pursuit of such causes is a good thing. Since the Communists are essentially oriented toward a future world that by design has nothing in common with the present, they cannot feel loyal to any cause that is conceived in terms of the present, including the fight against present evils. In any apparent common cause the Communists can only see opportunities to further a struggle that, according to them, cannot come to an end until the world has been completely transformed into the opposite of what it is now. Communists feel obligated to nothing but their vision of the future. In the present world, everything must be either an obstacle to, or a tool for, Communist power. When Communists enter an agreement with non-Communists, there is therefore an absence of that essential ingredient of political arrangements which Edmund Burke called "the public faith." What seems to be a "common cause" uniting Communists with non-Communists is but an illusion.

The creation of this illusion with respect to ends and means is the most important element in the Communist design. Wherever Communists succeed in creating the impression that they have entered with others into a basic agreement on common ends, and on means appropriate to these ends, they succeed in being accepted as friends and partners, which enables them to move in circles previously closed to them and to manipulate institutions to which otherwise they would have no access. Once this kind of *entrée* has been obtained, the Communists begin the operations which are important to them. In these operations one can distinguish the following: (1) occupation of positions of power, (2) legitimization of Communist power, (3) the elimination and destruction of rival parties and political forces, (4) organized control of the masses, and (5) terrorization of the opposition.

Occupation of Positions of Power

The "occupation of positions of power" aims at getting Communists into two kinds of agencies: those having the authority and the means to arrest, punish, and ultimately terrorize, and those having authority and means to change the basic order of society. In most countries of the world, such agencies are the ministries of the Interior, Justice, Industrial Production, and Agriculture. Occasionally, an Institute of Agrarian Reform will do in lieu of the latter. The Communists also are interested in getting their hands on the official means of propaganda, but may content themselves with staffing these agencies rather than directing them, or even merely with controlling their supplies, such as paper for the press.

Legitimization of Power

"Legitimization of Communist power" is something that Communists seem to crave almost with the strength of passion. They are profoundly aware of their being rejected by the public opinion of the world, and of the impossibility of legitimizing their rule in terms of their own ideology which is not shared by the people. Precisely because they define themselves as strangers in the present world and enemies of all that now exists, they know that they cannot count on the consent of the masses if they appeal to the masses mainly as Communists. Thus they know that the legitimization of power can be conferred upon them only by political processes and elements that have standing in the present world, above all by those of democracy. They are extremely anxious to have their own power sanctioned by democratic parties, leaders, procedures, and, above all, to base their "mandate" on popular elections. Coalition governments therefore have the important purpose of obtaining for Communists the official endorsement of what Karl Marx called the "overwhelming majority" of the people. In addition, Communists treasure the legitimacy that comes from joint manifestoes and declarations, the approval and partnership of acknowledged demo-

cratic leaders, the authority of democratic constitutions, and
the title conferred by elections. In order to obtain the desired
electoral support, the Communists exploit the "national policy
goals" to which the coalition has committed itself. They push
policies that appeal to this or that part of the population,
upset the entire society, destroy social and political elements
opposed to their rule, and profit again from a public indictment of these elements. Socialization, agrarian reforms, "mil-
lionaires' levies," wage raises, and even constitutional reforms
are thus tactical devices by which the Communists hope above
all to increase their electoral support. In the eyes of the people, they give themselves the appearance of advocates of the
downtrodden, champions of reform, initiators of innovation,
leaders of all meaningful action. Such policies, once enacted,
often supply the Communists with further means to secure
the adherence of the masses, particularly in the case of land
reform or land confiscation. For all this, they need the cooperation of democratic parties, but only for as long as it
takes to establish a "legitimate" basis for the rule of Communists.

Elimination of Rival Parties

Ultimately, the Communists are determined not to share
power with anybody. While using the coalition with democratic partners for the purpose of legitimization, they proceed
simultaneously with "the elimination and destruction of rival
parties," their partners in the coalition. In this process, they
exploit to the hilt the possibilities created by the "basic agreements," above all the "common cause," and the "non-toleration of certain parties, ideas, and individuals in the political
theater." The "common cause" includes the fight "against
reaction." When certain parties, ideas, and individuals are
barred from political activities because of their "reactionary"
character, it is not difficult to throw suspicion of complicity
with "reactionaries" on leaders of bourgeois parties that are
members of the coalition. Discrediting leaders on political
and personal grounds, the Communists find it possible to undermine the people's support of democratic parties. In an

atmosphere of high political pressure, it is always possible to find evidence of "plots" and to pass off such "plots" as attempts to destroy the coalition and to endanger the "unity" that has been declared of supreme value. The very existence of several parties can be made to appear as a threat to "unity." With this kind of public argument, the Communists manage to maneuver their partners into consenting to joint tickets for the entire coalition. A joint ticket is the first step to the termination of autonomous parties. The next step is the absorption of other parties into a "Marxist Bloc," or into a "Government Bloc," in either of which the Communists alone call the tune. "Unity" can be pleaded in various terms which appeal to different groups. Workers' parties can be induced to merge with the Communists in the name of "proletarian unity," left-wing bourgeois parties in the name of "socialist unity," and other democratic parties in the name of "patriotic unity." Once the Communists have persuaded other party leaders to agree to a merger, these leaders all too often become willing and permanent tools of Communist leadership. While there have been many defections from the ranks of the Communists themselves, former liberal or democratic leaders who have passed into the camp of a "unity party" seem incapable of reversing themselves.

Control of the Masses

The "organized control of the masses" is both an end and a means for the Communists. The "United Front" idea serves them as a pretext to merge already existing organizations into larger units, and to add new organizations corresponding to the spirit and purpose of the United Front. The first step usually is the creation of a single national trade union organization out of unions that in most cases have different political colorations. In the process of unification, which is accomplished under Communist prodding, the Communists usually succeed in occupying the few administrative positions that secure control of the entire body. Almost without fail, the Communists have pressed for the creation of new "united" organizations for women, youth, veterans, etc., flanking all of these with a "friends of the Soviet Union" organization. It seems that the mere fact of Communist initiative, plus the absence of natural leaders for such organizations in the traditional setting of the respective countries, enable the Communists to control the new mammoth structures. Communists are excellent organizers. When organizations are started from scratch, at a given signal, rather than growing from below, the Communists can usually count on seizing the reins before others even realize their opportunities.

Another device of organized mass control is the creation of national committees for some purpose recognized by the basic coalition agreements. These can be national committees for seemingly democratic administration, or committees for agrarian reform, or "liberation committees." The pattern is that of the Russian soviets. These organizations, being new and created on order, can easily be taken over by local Communists who in turn are under the discipline of the Communist Party's central leadership. As they mobilize for political action masses of people who previously were passive, the institution of such organization is in itself somewhat of a revolutionary step. "Mass control" also usually includes a militia, armed groups set up on Communist request and thus under Communist management. Sometimes these armed bodies are composed of hoodlums, sometimes of workers, sometimes of peasants. At all times, however, they can be used as instruments of pressure and terror, until Communists establish their dictatorial rule and once again disarm the people.

The need for all these types of new mass organizations is usually established in terms of the basic coalition agreements. These agreements arouse the hope of a new unity, a new national awakening, indeed a new world of peace and harmony. It seems fitting to parallel the harmony among the political leaders with the unity of the masses, and with the mobilization of the masses for the new national goals. Once there is the illusion of a "new spirit," the Communists have very little trouble in persuading their partners of the necessity to embody that spirit in broad popular organizations, and less trouble in getting their own men into the key positions of control.

The Use of Terror

Finally, the "terrorization of the opposition" is not merely a means to eliminate rival parties, but is at the same time a permanent feature of Communist rule and, thus, an end in itself. The Communist goal, according to Stalin, is the "voluntary and conscious submission" of the individual to the Party's leadership. A person who is amenable to Communist ideology can and must be persuaded to submit to the Party for the sake of the Party's ideological ends. A person who cannot thus be persuaded must still be induced to submit "voluntarily and consciously." This can be accomplished only by fear.

The logic of the Communist process of persuasion is a combination of seemingly lofty and idealistic appeals with criticism and denunciation of the individual which goes on until the last remnant of self-respect and personal dignity is destroyed. This method is applied not only in sessions of "criticism and self-criticism," but also in campaigns against politicians whom Communists want to destroy as public authorities. In the name of apparently ideal principles of social justice, patriotic unity, and political harmony, these leaders are publicly accused of selfishness, reactionary ideas, subservience to sinister interests, and complicity with "imperialism." In addition, they are exposed for personal failings, made to appear corrupt, compromised in doubtful sexual relations, caught in shady deals. Political accusation and personal vilification are followed by arrests. "People's courts," one of the first demands Communists usually make upon entering a coalition, can be counted on to move swiftly and vengefully against someone whom the Communist police have skillfully prepared for public trial. It does not take more than three or four such cases before the other opposition leaders get the message and begin to fall in with the Communist design "voluntarily and consciously."

The regime of terror assures the Communists that there will be no successors to those who thus go down. The terror is extended to local bodies and organizations, so that there is the most complete compliance with Communist rule, out of a deep realization of individual helplessness and exposure. A numbing sense of the government's ferocity and irresistible strength reduces individuals under Communist rule to a state of mind where a little apparent appeal to reason goes very far in securing cooperation with the Party.

The Communists never initiate their campaign of terror with the claim that there is danger for their Party alone, but always with the public discovery of "plots" and "conspiracies" against the country, the coalition, and the declared "national policy goals." This enables them to enlist for their purposes the services of courts, magistrates, and officials who on a traditional basis enjoy established authority. Here is one of the most important reasons for the Communists' desire to begin their rule as members of a coalition with traditional parties. They require, however, not merely the partnership of democratic parties, but also an official ban of certain political elements, in the name of the coalition. When a part of the people have been read out of the political community and declared nationally unacceptable, then it is possible to smear others by the trumped-up charge of "association with the people's enemy."

The United Front coalition that begins by setting political limits to the citizen's rights delivers into the hands of Communists the weapon of terror that will ultimately be turned against the members of the coalition itself.

Fatal Illusions about Coalitions

Coalitions are nothing new in the history of Communism. Communists came to power in Russia in company with other revolutionary parties whom they attacked and destroyed as soon as they controlled the public means of power. Since then, coalitions have been used by Communists wherever they have established their rule. In spite of the historical record, the Communists have again and again been able to find partners willing to bestow on the Communists the mantle of a coalition's respectability and official sanction. Underlying the readiness to enter into a coalition with Communists there seem to be (1) the conviction that "agreement with Communists is possible," (2) the illusion that there are "common interests" between Communists and non-Communists, (3) a confusion between "Communist demands" and "Communist ends," (4) the expectation that "Communists can be controlled through coalition governments," and (5) the hope that out of a coalition with Communists there will come "peace, unity, and/or democracy."

The impression that "agreement with Communists is possible" is not always derived from a mistaken notion about Communism. Quite frequently that impression arises because Communists do change their behavior. Previously they were truculent, now they appear conciliatory. From loyalty to the Soviet Union they seem to have moved toward patriotic loyalty, from destructive action in the streets to the give-and-take of parliamentary debate. When such change of conduct is interpreted as a "change of mind," then people are ready for the conclusion that "agreement with Communists is *now* possible," recognizing that up to that time it had not been. Behind the readiness to assume a real change of mind on the part of the Communists there lies the human disposition to believe that every change of someone else's mind is likely to be a change in the direction of one's own. Democratic parties are all too prone to persuade themselves that, when Communists change their minds, it must mean necessarily a move toward democratic ideas. This explains the fact that at every one of the frequent turns of Communist tactics, many elements in democratic countries stood ready to welcome the wayward sons with open arms, never stopping to find out whether the lost son had actually come "home," or had simply embarked on a new tack.

The "illusion of common interests" between Communists and non-Communists stems, by contrast, from a real ignorance of the Communist mentality. It assumes that Communists, like everyone else, have real interests in the present-day world, even though these interests may widely diverge from the ordinary. On this assumption it makes sense to discover, every once in a while, that in a given situation the Communists must embrace goals in which they are as genuinely interested as others. It is extremely difficult for ordinary persons to understand the mentality of a political movement that actually is based on the complete and utter rejection of the present-day world, has put all its eggs into the basket of a visionary future, and thus has no present interest except that of effecting a transition to that future. This is indeed a very strange and, in the most profound sense of the word, irrational attitude. Since Communists so often seem to be pragmatically rational, it is hard to believe that they or anyone else could entertain such notions. Yet they do, and have again and again demonstrated that they decry the very idea of having interests in common with any group, party, or class that pertains to the present-day world and its institutions. Communists often make use of the institutions of the present world, but without any sense of loyalty or obligation except to their own enterprise of increasing their revolutionary power to total intensity and universal extension. The interests of Communists may, therefore, happen to coincide with those of others at certain points, but they can in no sense be called "common interests."

A similar mistake confuses "Communist demands" with "Communist ends." Parties oriented toward a political order in the present world embody their ends in the form of political demands with which they confront the electorate, the government, and other parties. The Communists approach their coalition partner likewise with certain demands. Projecting their own democratic mentality into that of the Communists, the democratic leaders believe that the Communist demands represent also Communist ends. They then hope to conciliate the Communists by meeting them halfway or even more than halfway, seeking to elicit the Communists' good will by proving their own. Communist demands on the political scene of the present-day world, however, never represent their ultimate ends. Communist ends are not limited but total; Communists aspire to nothing less than a complete transformation of human life and even human nature into something which has not been known before.

Insofar as Communists resort to making demands in the political arena, such demands are merely tactical devices.

Marx tells his followers to raise their demands as soon as they are met or are likely to be met, always to push their demands farther than the concession they expect, and to use them for the purpose of upsetting and disturbing the social order by what he calls "the revolution in permanence." Since the establishment of the United Front pattern, the Communists have deviated from Marx's instructions in one respect: they have leaned over backwards in presenting to their coalition partners moderate demands. They have promised loyalty and cooperation, political non-aggression, and abidance by democratic rules. We know from the Communist documents, however, that these moderate demands are as little representative as the impetuous ones which Marx recommended. Thus one cannot hope to satisfy Communists by meeting their demands even 100 percent. Behind every set of Communist demands there are ends that lie beyond all demands and which cannot be represented concretely except as tactical devices in the struggle for limitless power.

The belief that a coalition government can "control Communists" stems from a naïve underestimation of the skill and persistence of totalitarian movements. Not only the democratic partners of Communists fell victims to this fallacy, but also the non-Nazi politicians in Weimar Germany who joined Hitler's government trusting that, they being present, things could not possibly become disastrous. For democrats, coalition government is a form of political being, but for Communists it is a one-way road to power. Therefore no coalition government can hope to tame Communists. It will either be converted into a Communist dictatorship, or it will have to curb the Communists by means other than parliamentary coalition maneuvers.

The hope that "peace, unity, and/or democracy" can be furthered by a coalition with Communists has less to do with ignorance of Communism than with superficial and fallacious thinking about peace, unity, and democracy. Underlying this view is a vague notion that democracy requires the universal inclusion of all kinds of political forces and elements into one system, that unity can be attained without inner agreement on truth and morality, and that peace consists in the mere absence of overt large-scale violence.

Here is an overestimation of methods and processes, and an underestimation of ends and convictions, which are a legacy of the late nineteenth and early twentieth centuries. Communists confront non-Communists in openly declared total and irreconcilable hostility. It is believed that if one succeeds in bringing such hostile elements together in a coalition government, the hostility has been overcome and peace has been established through unity. But this belief is utterly fallacious, because the hostility between Communists and non-Communists has proved to be unconquerable on both sides, and unity has been used for purposes of conquest rather than peace. As far as democracy is concerned, we would do well to remember one rule at least: democratic polity is impossible in the absence of some basic agreement on goals, on political morality, and on the "rules of the game." On all such grounds, binding agreement with Communists is impossible.

Conclusion

Communists have used coalition governments as their chosen vehicle to establish their own totalitarian and exclusive power. It can be said, however, that the principle of coalition is a general Communist mode of operation, of which coalition government is merely a special application. Communists have always sought the company of non-Communists. By themselves, Communists feel deeply insecure because of their chosen self-alienation from the world in which they live. Totalitarian control of the world and all that moves in it is one means by which they seek to overcome this alienation. On the road to this kind of power, however, Communists have required allies, friends, fellow travelers. They have never isolated themselves prior to having all means of power under their control. They have allied and associated themselves with all kinds of social classes and parties. They have associated themselves with the Nazis. They have fought by the side of the Western capitalist powers during a great war. They have sought the endorsement of democrats, peasants, intellectuals, pacifists—all of whom represent views totally unacceptable to Communists.

Communist successes have been possible ultimately only through the cooperation of their future victims. The first counsel of self-protection against Communist totalitarianism is the realization that, with Communists, no common cause or binding agreement is possible—except on their own terms.

COMMUNIST PRE-INSURGENCY TECHNIQUES

by Franklin Mark Osanka

An operations Analyst in the Stanford Research Institute, Mr. Osanka is currently on assignment in Southeast Asia. Previously he was Special Warfare Consultant at the Naval Ordnance Test Station, China Lake, California. A graduate of Northern Illinois University, he attended special warfare schools of the Army, Navy, Air Force, Marine Corps, and U.S.I.A. His many articles in this field have appeared in military and civilian publications. He is editor of Modern Guerrilla Warfare: Fighting Communist Guerrilla Movements, 1941–1961 (*New York: The Free Press of Glencoe, 1962*).

Published originally in the January 1964 issue of the *Australian Army Journal* as "Population Control Techniques of Communist Insurgents: A Sociological Analysis." Copyright 1964, by Franklin Mark Osanka. Reprinted by permission.

It is now generally recognized that guerrillas cannot operate or exist for long without the active support of a small portion of the population and the passive indifference of a large portion of the population. It is also recognized that the guerrillas actually represent only a small segment of the insurgents. The larger segment consists of a covert underground apparatus within the civilian population. In brief, the guerrillas carry out overt actions on the basis of timely intelligence information from the population about the movements of government forces. The population further aids the guerrillas by providing food, shelter, medical care, labor, and recruits. Most importantly, the population under insurgent control denies information to the counterinsurgency forces concerning the hideouts of the guerrillas and the identities of underground apparatus personnel within the population.

The purpose of this paper is to examine some of the control measures employed at the village level by Communist insurgents to ensure population loyalty during the pre-guerrilla and early-guerrilla stages of insurgency. This paper does not pretend to cover all the factors involved nor does it address itself to any specific past or current insurgency. However, it should be noted that it is the author's contention that Chinese Communist-style insurgency is the archetype for most insurgencies in the underdeveloped areas of the world and that insurgency is the principal export item of Red China.

Insurgents' Operational Environment

It is dangerous to generalize about geographic areas, but it is now commonly recognized that most rural areas of the underdeveloped nations manifest certain environmental characteristics which insurgents can exploit in order to achieve their own ends. In many of these rural areas, living conditions are intolerable: illiteracy, disease, hunger, poverty, inadequate housing, a low crude-birth rate, a high early death rate, definite levels of social stratification, and tribal animosities are the rule rather than the exception. The peasants, primarily farmers, are usually a simple people who do not own the land they have worked all their lives and who are frequently exploited by the landowners. They are often mistreated by the representatives of the government that they encounter (e.g., security forces and tax collectors), and as a result are extremely suspicious of all strangers. Probably their greatest desire is to own their own land.

They are politically unsophisticated and their opinions and attitudes are formed on the basis of what they see and hear in their own immediate area rather than being influenced by mass media.[1] Communications from the ruling class (which is traditionally located in the urban areas) is usually poor at best. The ruling powers seldom view the peasants as an important or powerful political threat. Insurgents, and particularly Communist insurgents, take the opposite view.

The Insurgent Organizers

Long before the first insurgency shot is heard, Communist Insurgent Organizers (hereafter mentioned as organizers) infiltrate the sparsely populated regions of the target country. These men are natives of the target country and very often were born in or near the area they have been assigned to control. They speak the local dialect, are of the same ethnic origin, and blend easily into the population.

The organizers have had at least three years of intensive revolutionary training in a Communist country, with heavy emphasis on the political-military doctrine as expressed in the *Selected Works* of Mao Tse-tung.[2] Although the organizers are dogmatic in purpose, they are extremely practical and flexible operationally. They realize that each target area has its own social dynamics and that they must adapt their methods according to the norms, folkways, and mores of the region. They are hard-core Communists who sincerely believe that their creed is just.

They believe, as do their Chinese Communist mentors, that thought determines action. Therefore, if one can control the thoughts of people, one can dictate the actions of the people. Their mission is to establish an effective underground apparatus, and they are prepared to die rather than fail. Their method of area penetration will follow three phases: identification, propagation, organization.

Identification Phase

A team of two organizers enters a village and requests an audience with the village leader. The organizers are very polite and humble men. They say, "We have come to tell you of the things that we have seen. But first, as we can see that it is harvest time, we would like to help you gather in your crops.

We shall have plenty of time to talk later." The organizers labor in the field and continually talk to the villagers. In the evening, the organizers entertain the villagers with folksongs and stories of the wonderful countries they have seen. Countries where "everyone" owns land and all farmers have a good mule and a fine house; where children wear fine clothes and go to fine schools and live a long life; where no one is ever hungry because the people work together for the benefit of all; and where the government's function is to serve the people.

The organizers never mention Communism nor the pending insurgency. Political terminology is avoided; "plain talk" is the vogue. The organizers' songs, folktales, and conversations are always designed to have some meaning to the immediate lives of the villagers. The objectives of the identification phase are to: establish rapport by identifying with the lives of the villagers; determine the basic needs and aspirations of the villagers; discover the weaknesses of the social norms that dictate the accepted reaction to problems; and slowly plant the seeds of rebellion.

Propagation Phase

The propagation process is both destructive and constructive in nature. Destructively, the organizers must aggravate all the existing social ills and raise them to surface, then transfer the cause of the ills to the existing government. Constructively, the organizers must convince the villagers that through cooperation, united action, and loyalty to each other, all social ills can be eliminated and individual aspirations can be realized. Sociologically, the process is one of inducing an awareness of definite in-group/out-group relationships, the in-group being the people and the out-group being the government. The organizers know that stories of the corruptness of the ruling group in the capital city will have little impression on the villagers. In many cases, the villagers do not realize there is a capital city, much less an established government. To establish credibility and meaning to their propaganda theme, that government is the source of all social ills, the organizers most often use the indirect approach.

The organizers' propaganda as transmitted in folktales, songs, and conversations all has the same general theme: "the rich get richer while the poor get poorer." For example, a conversation with a tenant farmer might sound like this: "You have been working this same plot of land for twenty years. Before you, your father worked it and before him, his father worked it. And what, my friend, do you have to show for an accumulated seventy years of sweat and labor? Of the seven children you have created, four died at birth, two never lived to enjoy their second birthday, and one has survived to do what you, your father, and his father have done—sweat and labor so that the landlord can live in comfort in his fine house and watch his healthy children grow up to exploit your son. Is that right? Is that just? The answer, of course, is that it is not just. Did God create some men to live in comfort by the sweat of other men? The answer is no! How then has it occurred that a small minority of men can legally exploit the larger majority of men? The answer is organization. Many years ago, a small group of men discovered that by working together and cooperating with each other, they could enjoy the fruits of the people's labor. Using various devious methods, they acquired all of the land. They knew that in order to rule they would need a permanent police force and an army, otherwise the people would take back the land. So you see, my friend, your landlord is the grandson of one of these men who originally stole the land. He is able to exploit your labors because he has organized a police force and an army in order to suppress the people's ability to acquire what is justly theirs anyway.

"How then can the people attain what is legally and morally theirs? The answer, my friend, is organization. The minority can exploit the majority because they are organized. Does it not follow then that if the people who are the majority organize, they will be stronger than the minority landlords? All over this country, the people are beginning to organize. Men like yourself are preparing to acquire what is justly theirs. These men know that some will die but they say, 'Is it not better to die quickly and honorably for one's rights than to suffer a living slow death at the hands of the exploiters?' "

Perhaps Roucek best sums up the propagation phase when he writes, "At the core of their activities lies the argument that the . . . oppressor has no legal or moral right to exercise power . . . and that the members and leaders of the secret societies are the expression of the 'legal' will of the . . . people. The leaders must generate in their followers a readiness to die and a proclivity for united action."[3]

Organization Phase

Once three villagers have been won over, the organizers can establish the first cell of the underground organization within the village. As more recruits join the organizers, they are sent off to previously established training camps. Here their training is 75 per cent ideological and 25 per cent military. Most of these individuals return to their village and form the nucleus of the underground apparatus, and can serve as a reserve force for the guerrillas. Others receive further military training and later form into small bands which will establish camps in rugged areas near the village. A few receive further ideological training and serve as assistant organizers to penetrate other villages in the area. One or two will be sent to a Communist country for a year and undergo intensified ideological and military training.

The organizers encourage and direct the establishment of a village medical clinic as well as an elementary school. A variety of civic activities are performed by the underground organization. The organizers' purpose here is to enhance village solidarity behind the insurgents. Tactically, the village medical clinic will prove useful once the guerrilla stage of the insurgency is underway. Psychologically, the school provides the organizers an additional opportunity to propagandize the young. If the government troops, in an effort to weaken the insurgents' organization, requisition the medicines of the clinic and outlaw the school, the insurgents have won a psychological victory. The organizers can attribute the government's action to a desire to suppress the people by keeping them ignorant and weak with diseases. The organizers' propaganda theme will be, "The government knows that an educated and healthy people cannot be exploited!"

Insurgency Population Control

The successful completion of the identification, propagation, and organization phases at the village level results in four principal conditions of control. They are: in-group loyalty, insurgent terror tactics, personal commitment, and government terror tactics.

The in-group loyalty condition is the result of acceptance by the majority of the villagers, of the idea that the insurgent activities are just and that the government is unjust. Insurgent terror tactics are directly related to the in-group loyalty condition. Those who aid the enemy are traitors and harmful to the people and, therefore, must be eliminated. The penalty for traitors, while not often quick, is final. Here, the in-group loyalty condition is reinforced by the underground's spy system, which keeps the organizers informed of everything that is happening in the village.

Personal commitment is probably the most effective condition of control. The organizers make every effort to involve, in one way or another, a member of every family. Consequently, families are reluctant to betray the insurgency, thereby directly or indirectly increasing the possibility of prison, and most likely death, for a member of their family. The personal commitment condition is also operating in those individuals who have made large contributions to the insurgency and expect to be rewarded when the insurgents win.

Being unable to locate and annihilate the guerrilla forces, many governments have resorted to terroristic methods in an attempt to secure the support of the population. Government terror tactics such as burning villages, slaughtering innocent people, and generally mistreating the population, are well documented in the annals of guerrilla warfare. It is equally well documented that such tactics tend to reinforce the solidarity of the people behind the insurgents. The Communist insurgents are well aware of the population's reaction to such action, and very often provoke the government into committing drastic actions. Indeed, one noted specialist maintains that, "the greatest contribution of guerrillas and saboteurs lies in catalyzing and intensifying counter-terror which further alienates the government from the local population."[4]

Conclusion

What has been discussed occurs during the pre-violence stage and the early stage of guerrilla action in an insurgency. As the insurgency escalates into countrywide guerrilla warfare, and later regular warfare, new population control conditions are born. These new conditions can be favorable to either the insurgents or counterinsurgents, depending primarily upon the actions and attitudes of the counterinsurgents. If the counterinsurgents react to the widespread guerrilla violence solely with traditional military and police repressive measures, they will simply reinforce the validity of the insurgent propaganda and insure continual population support to the insurgents. If, on the other hand, the counterinsurgents incorporate into their pacification program at the village level the "psychological action," "civic action," and "population security" principles pioneered primarily by the U. S. Army's Civil Affairs and Special Warfare Schools, they will destroy the very foundation on which the insurgency rests. For it is only when the counterinsurgents demonstrate by attitude and action their desire and ability to eliminate the basic social ills and legitimate personal grievances, as well as to protect the people from the insurgents, will the population transfer its loyalty. As the insurgents lose the support of the population, they will be forced to depend solely upon increased terroristic methods of population control and then it is only a matter of time before the insurgents are either eliminated or rendered ineffectual.

When the immediate threat of the insurgency is eliminated, and a positive "nation-building" program is implemented, the country can be on its way to a state of socio-political stability which greatly reduces the possibility of the recurrence of insurgency.

NOTES

1. For an illuminating view of one peasant's outlook see: Pierre Marchant, "A Colombian Peon Tells His Moving Story," *Réalités*, September 1962, pp. 65–68.
2. The five volumes are published in the United States by International Publishers Co., New York, 1954.
3. Joseph S. Roucek, "Sociology of Secret Societies," *The American Journal of Economics and Sociology*, Vol. 19, No. 2, January 1960, p. 164.
4. J. K. Zawodny, "Unconventional Warfare," *American Scholar*, Vol. 31, No. 3, Summer 1962, p. 292.

THE ROLE OF INTELLIGENCE
IN THE COLD WAR

by Allen W. Dulles

> *Mr. Dulles has served the Government in diplomatic
> and intelligence posts since the Administration of
> President Wilson. Beginning in 1916 he served in
> Vienna and Berne, at the Versailles Peace Conference,
> and in Berlin and Constantinople. From 1922 to 1926,
> he was Chief of the Near East Division of the Depart-
> ment of State. During World War II he served with
> the OSS in Switzerland. In November 1961 he retired
> from the Central Intelligence Agency, having served
> as its Director since 1953.*

This article is an adaptation of Chapter 15 of *The Craft of Intel-
ligence* by Allen W. Dulles. Copyright 1963 by Allen W. Dulles.
Reprinted with the permission of the author and Harper & Row,
Publishers, Incorporated.

Shortly before the Bolshevik Revolution of October–November 1917, a nationwide election was held in Russia for delegates to a Constituent Assembly which was to choose the
leaders of a new Russia.

This was the last, possibly the only, free vote the Russians
ever had. Even under the chaotic conditions which prevailed
in the fall of 1917, about thirty-six million votes were cast for
707 Assembly seats. In this vote, the Bolsheviks received only
about a quarter of the total and 175 seats. Unable either to
control or intimidate the Assembly, Lenin dissolved it by brute
force and the use of goon squads. He gloated:

Everything has turned out for the best. The dissolution of the Constituent Assembly means the complete and open repudiation of the democratic idea in favor of the dictatorship concept. This will be a valuable lesson.

Thus the pattern was set for the techniques used in the destruction of freedom in other countries. Lenin showed that a minority backed by illegal force could trample on a majority which relied on democratic methods.

It was some thirty years later before Communism felt strong enough to try these tactics outside of the area Russia had controlled in 1914. Communism was on the march again. The Communists were consolidating their frontiers on the Elbe River deep in Western Europe, and had their occupation forces and their subversive apparatus at work installing Communist regimes in Poland, Hungary, Rumania, and Bulgaria. Shortly thereafter they took over Czechoslovakia and had begun their advance to the China Sea in the Far East.

The Secret Penetration of Free States

A major part of the strategy of the Communists in the cold war today is the secret penetration of free states. The means they use, the target countries they select, and the soft areas in these targets are concealed as long as possible. They exploit secret weaknesses and vulnerabilities of opportunity and, in particular, endeavor to penetrate the military and security forces of the country under clandestine attack.

The subversion campaigns of Communism generally start out using secret techniques and a secret apparatus. It is against them that our intelligence assets must be marshaled and used. Among the tasks assigned to intelligence, this is one that ranks in importance alongside collecting information, counterintelligence, coordinating intelligence, and producing the national estimates.

The whole range of Communist tactics in the cold war is broader than the type of covert action and political subversion such as we have seen in Czechoslovakia and Cuba. It also includes: limited wars and wars by proxy, as in Korea and

North Vietnam; guerrilla wars, as in South Vietnam; civil wars, as in China; the use and abuse of their zones of "temporary" military occupation, as in the Eastern European satellites and North Korea.

The Communists have not always succeeded, and this is due in no small measure to the employment of intelligence assets, not only of our own but also those of our friends and allies, including those of friendly governments under Communist attack. Their stooges took over power in Iran in 1953 and in Guatemala in 1954, and they were driven out. They tried to disrupt the Philippines and Malaya by guerrilla tactics, and they were defeated. They lavished arms deliveries on Egypt, Syria, Iraq, and Indonesia, hoping these states would join the Communist bloc, and so far they have had only a very modest return on these particular investments.

However, they can look with satisfaction on what they have accomplished by subversion in the two decades since the Allied victory over Hitler and the Japanese war lords was assured in 1944. It is wise to remember that the Communist program was well under way by the time of our peace talks with them at Yalta and Potsdam. Then they were thinking not of peace but of how they could use the common victory, and their zones of military occupation, for further Communist conquest.

In the last fifteen years their progress has been considerably slowed down but by no means stopped. Beginning in 1947 they ran into a series of roadblocks: the United States stood firm in Greece, at Berlin and in Korea, and later on a broad front that reached to the Chinese offshore islands and Vietnam; helped by the Marshall Plan and other aid, Europe and Japan staged spectacular economic recoveries; Moscow and Peking have been more and more divided on the tactics to pursue, although they are still together on the basic objective of burying the free world.

The Soviet Blueprint for World Domination

In 1961, the Soviet policy of covert aggression rather than "hot" nuclear war, which had undergone considerable rethinking in the Kremlin after Stalin's demise and the revolution in Hungary, was vigorously restated by Khrushchev under the general heading of "wars of liberation." In his speech of January 6 of that year, Khrushchev outlined Communist power and Soviet tactics:

Our epoch of the triumph of Marxism-Leninism.

Today . . . socialism is working for history, for the basic content of the contemporary historical process constitutes the establishment and consolidation of socialism on an international scale.

The time is not far away when Marxism-Leninism will possess the minds of the majority of the world's population. What has been going on in the world in the forty-three years since the triumph of the October Revolution completely confirms the scientific accuracy and vitality of the Leninist theory of the world socialist revolution.

The colonial system of imperialism verges on complete disintegration, and imperialism is in a state of decline and crisis.

Later on in his speech, Khrushchev cited Cuba as the typical example of an uprising against United States imperialism. He then added:

Can such wars flare up in the future? They can. Can there be such uprisings? There can. But these are wars which are national uprisings. In other words, can conditions be created where a people will lose their patience and rise in arms? They can. What is the attitude of the Marxists toward such uprisings? A most positive one. These uprisings must not be identified with wars among states, with local wars, since in these uprisings the people are fighting for implementation of their right for self-determination, for independent social and national development. These are uprisings against reactionary regimes, against the colonizers. The Communists fully support such just wars and march in the front rank with the peoples waging liberation struggles.

Now Communist parties are functioning in nearly 50

countries of these continents [Asia, Africa, and Latin America]. This has broadened the sphere of influence of the Communist movement, given it a truly worldwide character.

Khrushchev concluded:

Comrades, we live at a splendid time: Communism has become the invincible force of our century.

This then is the credo, the charter as it were, of the Communist blueprint for world domination by worldwide subversion.

U.S. Reactions

This country had been slow to arouse itself to the dangers we face from the tactics of Communism, which Khrushchev so clearly described in 1961. Since Lenin's day this had always been a part of the Communist program. With Khrushchev, it became its major weapon in the foreign field.

In 1947 President Truman proclaimed the doctrine which bears his name and applied it particularly to the then present danger of subversion facing Greece and Turkey. The doctrine, in effect, was that where a government felt that its "free institutions and national integrity" were threatened by Communist subversion and desired American aid, it would be our policy to give it. A decade later, this policy was restated in more precise language with respect to the countries of the Middle East in what became known as the Eisenhower Doctrine.

But these doctrines contained the general proviso that action would be taken if our aid were *sought* by the threatened state. Such was the case in Greece in 1947, and in Lebanon eleven years later. In both instances, our assistance was invited by a friendly government. The Truman and Eisenhower doctrines did not cover, and possibly no officially proclaimed policy could cover, all the intricacies of situations where a country faces imminent Communist takeover and yet sends out no cry for help.

There have been occasions, as in Czechoslovakia, when the blow was sudden. Then there was no time for the democratic Czechs to send us an engraved invitation to help them to meet that blow. We knew that the danger was there, that well over one-third of the Czech Parliament and several members of the Cabinet had Communist leanings, and that the regime was seriously infiltrated, but the free Prague government of the day was overconfident of its own ability to resist. Between daylight and dusk, the Communists took over without firing a shot.

On the other hand, in Iran Mossadegh and in Guatemala Arbenz came to power through the usual processes of government. Neither man at the time disclosed the intention of creating a Communist state. When this purpose became clear, support from outside was given to loyal anti-Communist elements in the respective countries, in the one case, to the Shah's supporters; in the other, to a group of Guatemalan patriots. In each case the danger was successfully met. There again no invitation was extended by the *government* in power for outside help.

During Castro's takeover of Cuba we were not asked by him for help to keep the Communists out; he was the very man who was bringing them in. Such crises show the danger of a slow infiltration by Communists and fellow travelers into a government where the last thing the infiltrators wish is outside intervention to check Communism.

What are we to do about these secret, underground, creeping techniques such as were used to take over Czechoslovakia in 1948 and Cuba in recent years? Because Castro in one of his rambling and incoherent speeches has boasted about early Marxist views, the hindsight specialists are now saying that this should have been recognized years ago and action taken. Exactly what action, they do not specify except for those who advocate open military intervention. But thousands of the ablest Cubans, including political leaders, businessmen, and the military, who worked hard to put Castro in and were risking their lives and futures to do so, did not suspect that they were installing a Communist regime. Today they are in exile or in jail.

The Soviet Apparatus for Subversion

What are the main assets which the Kremlin can marshal for these tasks of subversion? To simplify a complicated subject, this discussion will be confined to the apparatus of the U.S.S.R.

The first element of the Kremlin's nonmilitary apparatus of subversion is the galaxy of worldwide Communist parties. In April 1963, Khrushchev boasted:

> The international Communist movement has become the most influential political force of our epoch. . . . Before World War II Communist parties existed in forty-three countries and counted in their ranks a total of 4,200,000 members. Today, Communist parties number ninety and the total number of their members exceeds 42,000,000.[1]

Most of these ninety parties are outside the Communist bloc but respond to discipline from the parent Party in Moscow; a limited but growing number look to the Chinese Communist Party in Peking. Khrushchev's total numbers include only those who are actually Party members and not the large numbers who vote the Communist ticket—when voting is permitted.

The most numerically powerful Communist parties outside the bloc are in France, Italy, India, and Indonesia; but numerical strength is not always the real test. For the purpose of subversion, the element of an effective hard core of dedicated, disciplined members may be a more important factor than actual Party membership. Wherever there is an organized Communist Party, there is generally a nucleus of dedicated Communists which can become an effective spearhead for subversive action.

Unfortunately, also, the local Communist parties in many countries have been able to establish themselves as the major party of protest against the regime in power. Thus they draw to their ranks, not necessarily as Party members but as fellow travelers, on such issues as nationalism, anticolonialism "reform," and "ban the bomb," a large number of supporters who are really not Communists at all or who know and care little about Marxism and all its theories. At election time the Communist Party apparatus rallies together all these people and many others who are merely seeking a change and naïvely believe that the Communist Party represents their best or sometimes their only vehicle for effecting a change.

Representatives of the Communist parties in the free world regularly attend the Party congresses in Moscow, of which the twenty-second was held in 1961. Here they are received as honored guests and often are given special briefings. At the Twenty-first Party Congress, in 1959, the Communist delegates from Latin-American countries were given special attention. They were gathered together and given secret guidance as to their methods of operation. To mislead the rest of the world and particularly the United States, they were told to play down Marxism and Communism and their relations with Moscow, and to build their ranks by appealing to nationalism and using anti-American slogans. All this was not lost on Castro.

The Kremlin has always been willing, within bounds, to permit local Communist parties to take positions which differ from the official Moscow line. Sometimes this has been done by prearrangement. On the other hand, the Kremlin has always had to cope with tendencies toward autonomy in other Communist parties. In recent years, as the Sino-Soviet schism has broadened, it has been increasingly difficult for the Kremlin to control the positions of all the other parties that were once subservient to it.

The tasks assigned by Moscow to Communist parties in free world countries, and to the other elements of the Communist apparatus, are tailored to the estimated capabilities of the particular parties or "fronts," to the "softness" of the countries where they operate, and to the general program of the Kremlin, i.e., the order of precedence for eventual takeover set by Moscow. For example, the objectives assigned to the Party in the U.S.A. are relatively modest. They are told to stress propaganda against armaments in general and nuclear tests in particular; against American policy in Latin America; against NATO and our other alliances and our overseas bases.

In England it is much the same; "ban the bomb" is a chosen rallying theme. Such pacifist appeals are used to disguise real Soviet intentions and to soften the defenses of the Western world. In the spring of 1963 the "ban the bomb" movement achieved a level of unusual insidiousness through the publicity which gave away the location of certain classified government centers prepared for emergency use in case of nuclear attack.

In countries where Communism has better prospects and more power, the horizon of objectives and tasks is raised. In France and Italy, the Communist Party and its allies poll a vote which generally represents between 20 and 30 per cent of the voters and, to the dismay of many who mistakenly believed that economic recovery alone would eliminate or at least weaken Communism, the Communists gained over a million votes in the Italian general elections of 1963. There and in Indonesia, Japan, and in several countries of this hemisphere, as well as in Asia, the Communist parties take more aggressive positions. So far, in Africa, both north and south of the Sahara, Moscow's activities, both direct and through the local Communist parties, have been misconceived and ill-concealed.

Communist Front Organizations

A series of Communist front organizations supplement the work of the local parties and are used as tools for reaching specialized objectives. For example, through the World Federation of Trade Unions and its multiple branches, the Communists control the strongest labor organizations in many countries of the world—France, Italy, and Indonesia in particular—and are able to manipulate significantly the unions in Japan, in many countries of this hemisphere, and in certain countries of Africa and Southeast Asia, where trade unions are in their infancy. In the area of labor relations, the Party makes particular use of its ability to exploit popular local issues. Sometimes even where they do not actually control a union, well-organized and activist Communist minorities in unions can provide vocal and riotous leadership for mass demonstrations, and force a hesitant majority to engage in strikes and walkouts not openly attributable to any Communist initiative. Such activity at crucial times may paralyze the economy of an entire country.

Other Communist front organizations include the World Peace Congress, various youth organizations, women's organizations, and organizations of specific professions. These they try to surround with a degree of respectability and to lure into membership the unsuspecting and the gullible, particularly on their "peace" and "ban the bomb" issues.

At various intervals the Soviets at great expense to themselves have held "Youth Congresses," to which the youth of the world have been invited. Initially these meetings were held behind the Iron Curtain—Moscow, East Berlin, and Prague—but in recent years the Soviet managers of these affairs have become bolder. The last two meetings were held in Vienna and then in Helsinki. However, the climate of opinion was so unfavorable in those capitals that the Communists are now reconsidering whether to repeat the experiment.

Moscow's directing hand can help to guide and manipulate all these diverse assets of the Communist "presence" in a particular country through the State Security Service (KGB) personnel located in Soviet embassies and trade missions. The KGB, in addition to its regular intelligence function, can direct the activities of the local *"apparat"* set up in country X to promote a subversive program; they can act as Moscow's paymaster for the operations of the local Party and fronts and will keep Moscow advised of progress.

Infiltration of Target Governments

Wherever possible Soviet tacticians will maneuver Communists or their sympathizers into key government positions and attempt to penetrate the target country's military and security structure with the idea of eventually taking them over. In the Allied Control Commissions which were set up in most of the Eastern European countries at the end of World War II the Soviet contingents consisted largely of intelligence personnel. While the British and American representatives were trying to create some semblance of order and liberty and to restore the public utilities and the economy, their Soviet "colleagues" were spending their time contacting reliable native Communists, organizing the conspiracies which were shortly to emerge as "united fronts" dominated by Communists, and laying the groundwork for an efficient political police under KGB tutelage.

Operating in newly developed countries, the Communist movement endeavors to present itself as the protector of the liberated peoples against their former colonial overlords. In support of these activities, promising young men and women from the target areas are invited to Moscow for education and indoctrination in the expectation that they may become the future Communist leaders in their homelands. Also they bring to the bloc for training in intelligence and subversion individuals of a different type who on their return will help to direct the local Communist Party apparatus.

The Scope of Soviet Propaganda

As a part of the *apparat,* Moscow also vigorously uses all the instrumentalities of its propaganda machine. In one year, the Soviets, according to the Soviet Ministry of Culture's report, published and circulated approximately thirty million copies of books in various foreign languages. This literature is widely and cheaply distributed through local bookstores, made available in reading rooms and in their information and so-called cultural centers. In many countries throughout the world, they control newspapers and have penetrated and subsidized a large number of press outlets of various kinds which do not present themselves openly as Communist.

With some of the most powerful transmitting stations in the world, they beam their messages to practically every major area of the world. They step up their propaganda to the particular target areas which they consider to be the most vulnerable, and adjust it as their policy dictates. An organization known as the All Union Society for Cultural Relations Abroad, which poses as an independent organization but is strictly controlled by the Communist Party of the Soviet Union, endeavors to establish cultural ties with foreign countries, supply Soviet films, and arrange programs to be given by Soviet artists.

The foreign news agency of the Soviet Union, well known as Tass, a state-controlled enterprise, has offices in more than thirty major cities of the free world. It adjusts its "news" to meet Soviet objectives in the recipient country. All these instruments of propaganda are part and parcel of what is called the *"agitprop."*

What the U.S. Can Do

Such is the apparatus of subversion we face today in the cold war which the Communists have forced upon us. To meet this threat we will need to mobilize our assets and apply them vigorously at the points of greatest danger and in time— before a takeover, that is, before a new Communist regime becomes firmly installed. History so far has indicated that once the Communist security services and the other elements of the *apparat* get their grip on a country, there are no more free elections, no right of protest.

We have assets against this threat. First there is our declared foreign policy, for which the State Department under the President has the burden of responsibility. Second, by our defense posture we can convince the free world that we and our Allies are both strong enough and ready enough to meet the Soviet military challenge, and that we can protect, and are willing to protect, the free countries of the world, by force if need be; and that meanwhile we will aid them to build up their security against subversion. If the free countries feel that we are militarily weak or unready to act, they are not likely to stand firm against Communism.

The third asset is what our intelligence service must help to provide: (1) It must give our own government timely information as to the countries which the Communists have put high on their schedule for subversive attack; (2) it must penetrate the vital elements of their subversive apparatus as it begins to attack target countries and must provide our government with an analysis of the techniques in use and with information on the persons being subverted or infiltrated into local government; (3) it must, wherever possible, help to build up the local defenses against penetration by keeping target countries aware of the nature and extent of their peril and by assisting their internal security service wherever this can best be done, or possibly only be done, on a covert basis.

Many of the countries most seriously threatened do not have internal police or security services adequate to the task of obtaining timely warning of the peril of Communist subversion. For this they often need help and they can only get it from a country like the United States, which has the resources and techniques to aid them. Many regimes in the countries whose security is threatened welcome this help and over the years have profited greatly from it. On the other hand, in some cases, especially in Latin America, a dictator has later taken over an internal security service previously trained to combat Communism and has diverted it into a kind of Gestapo to hunt down his local political opponents. This happened in Cuba under Batista.

Too often a threatened country feels that it can go it alone and sometimes too late awakens to the danger or comes quickly under the effective control of those who are promoting a Communist takeover. In these situations, there is no easy answer if no resistance is made and no call for help is sent out as the Communist apparatus slowly crushes out freedom. Often the apparatus uses its access to democratic processes, the ballot box and a parliamentary system, to infiltrate with what are called "popular front" governments. Then the mask falls away, the non-Communist participants in the coalition are eliminated, and a Communist dictatorship has hold of the land and the secret police take over. Then it is too late indeed for protective action. Czechoslovakia is an example of this pattern.

Wherever we can, we must help to shore up both the will to resist and confidence in the ability to resist. By now we have had a good many years of experience in combating Communism. We know its techniques, we know a good many of the actual "operators" who run these attempts at takeover. Whenever we are given the opportunity to help, we should assist in building up the ability of threatened countries and do it long before the Communist penetration drives a country to the point of no return.

Fortunately for the free world, because of the nature of the subversive activities in which the disparate Communist parties are engaged and the large numbers of untrained personnel involved, it is difficult for them to maintain adequate security and secrecy. It is revealing no secret to state that a very large number of the Communist parties and front organizations throughout the world have been penetrated. Dramatic information has already been published in regard to the effective work of the FBI in its penetration and neutralization of the Communist Party of the United States and its various appendages.

Obviously it is somewhat more difficult for us to ferret out Communist activities in other parts of the free world. But many Communist plots to subvert friendly governments have been discovered and thwarted. Local publicity in the early stages of planned *Putsch,* pinpointing the plotters, tying them in to Moscow or Peking, has proved effective. This has been particularly useful in dealing with the bogus "front," "youth," and "peace" organizations of the Communists and their highly advertised meetings and congresses. Here a free press is also a great asset.

Vulnerabilities of Communist Subversion

Formidable as is the Communist subversive apparatus, it is vulnerable to exposure and to vigorous attack. Furthermore, the Communists are in no position to push their program of takeover simultaneously in all quarters of the globe. They must pick and choose the areas which hold out the greatest promise to them. Meanwhile on our side there is much to be done, and a good deal is being done to shore up weaker countries and to keep them beyond the reach of the Communist grip. Certainly we must not limit ourselves to maintaining a defensive position and solely to reacting to Communist aggression. There have been instances where we have taken the initiative, where we have turned back the Communists, and there should be more. Apart from their problems at home and among themselves, many of their well-laid schemes to penetrate free countries have failed. After many frustrations in central Africa, the Soviets appear to be regrouping and rethinking their prospects. Their large investment in the Middle East and North Africa has been a bitter disappointment. In some areas of the world they have found that lack of experience and ineptitude on the part of their envoys and agents, their parties and front organizations, have led to disaster. Their ignominious flight from the Congo in the early 1960's is a chapter in their history to put beside their earlier retreat from Albania.

Furthermore, the indigenous Communist parties are often torn between local, nationalistic issues and the over-all policies of Communism. It is hard for them to shift as fast as Moscow does. One day they must bow down to a Stalin; then Khrushchev tells them that Stalin is a bloodstained tyrant who betrayed the "ideals" of the Communist Revolution. They preach Moscow's peaceful intentions and then have to explain the brutal crushing of the Hungarian patriots, just as earlier, in 1939, their strong appeal as an anti-Nazi force was dissipated overnight by Moscow's alliance with Hitler to destroy Poland.

As long as Khrushchev or his successors use their subversive assets to promote "wars of liberation"—which means to them any overt or covert action calculated to bring down a non-Communist regime—the West should be prepared to meet the threat. Where the tactic takes the form of open, hot, or guerrilla warfare as in Korea, Vietnam, or Malaya, the West, on its side, can provide assistance openly in one fashion or another. But Western intelligence must play its role early in the struggle while subversive action in preparation is still in the plotting and organizational stage. To act, one must have the intelligence about the plot and the plotters and have ready the technical means, overt and covert, to meet it.

Of course, all actions of this nature undertaken by intelligence in this country must be coordinated at the level of policymaking, and any action by an intelligence service must be within the framework of our own national objectives.

The Choices We Must Make

This country and our allies have a choice. We can either organize to meet the Communist program of subversion and vigorously oppose it as it insinuates itself into the governments and free institutions of countries unable to meet the danger alone, or we can supinely stand aside and say this is the affair of each imperiled country to deal with itself. We cannot guarantee success in every case. In Cuba, in North Vietnam, and elsewhere, there have been failures; in many cases, many more than is publicly realized, there have been successes, some of major significance. But it may be premature to advertise these cases or the resources used.

Where Communism has achieved control of the governmental apparatus of a country, as it had, for a time, in Iran and Guatemala and as it still has in Cuba, the European satellite countries, and in North Vietnam and North Korea, should we as a country shy away from the responsibility of continuing efforts to right the situation and to restore freedom of choice to the people? Are we worried that the charge be made that we too, like Khrushchev, have our own policy of "wars of liberation"?

In answer to these two questions it should be pointed out that this issue, one important for our survival, has been forced upon us by Soviet action. In applying the rule of force instead of law in international conduct, the Communists have left us little choice except to take counteraction of some nature to meet their aggressive moves, whenever our vital interests are involved. Merely to appeal to their better nature and to invoke the rules of international law is of little use. We cannot safely stand by and permit the Communists to take over the free world, by their "salami tactics," slice by slice. Furthermore, we cannot safely take the view that once the Communists have "liberated" a piece of territory, this is then forever beyond the reach of corrective action.

If the people of a particular country, of their own free will, by popular vote or referendum, should adopt a Communist form of government, that might present a different situation. So far this just has never happened.

In the conduct of foreign relations it must be recognized there are limits to the power of any nation. A country's enlightened self-interest, with all the facts taken into consideration, must guide its actions rather than any abstract principles, sound as they may be. No country could undertake as a matter of national policy to guarantee freedom to all the peoples of the world now under the dictatorship of Communism or any kind of dictatorship.

On the other hand, we cannot safely limit our reponse to the Communist strategy of takeover solely to those cases where we are invited in by a government still in power, or even to instances where a threatened country has first exhausted its own, possibly meager, resources in the "good fight" against Communism.

We ourselves must determine when, where, and how to act, hopefully with the support of other leading free world countries who may be in a position to help, keeping in mind the requirements of our own national security.

As we reach our decisions and chart our courses of action in meeting Communist secret aggression, the intelligence services with their special techniques have an important role to play, new to this generation perhaps but nonetheless highly important to the success of the enterprise.

NOTE

1. New York *Times*, April 22, 1963.

PART FOUR

ALTERNATE STRATEGIES:
THE CONTINUING DEBATE

INTRODUCTION

The Soviet Union does not want to go to war with anyone. We
do not need anyone's territories, anyone's wealth. How could
we covet anyone's wealth, considering that the Soviet Union
possesses vast natural resources, a highly developed industry, wonderful cadres of scientists, engineers, technicians,
workers, and agriculturalists?

> N. S. Khrushchev (August 6, 1961)

When Apostolov reeled off the standard list of Soviet successes and said that our industrial production had increased
thirty-three times in forty years as against three times in the
United States, and that this proved the rightness of our ideas,
the Frenchman observed: "I had a friend at college—that was
also forty years ago. He had an income of a million francs a
year, while I had only ten thousand. Since then my income
has gone up thirty times, and his only three—yes, *monsieur,*
only three. . . . That's statistics for you, Monsieur Apostolov.
May I say in the words of the Russian proverb that figures are
like the shafts of a cart—they point whichever way you turn
them. Very remarkable these Russian proverbs. . . ."

> Valeriy Tarsis, *The Bluebottle* (1963)

Enlightenment was the slogan of Czarism in Europe during
the eighteenth century as was the National Liberation in the
nineteenth. There was no land-grab, no outrage, no repres-

sion on the part of Czarism which was not carried out under the pretext of enlightenment, of liberalism, of the liberation of nations. Russian diplomacy alone was allowed to be legitimist and revolutionary, conservative and liberal, orthodox and enlightened in the same breath. One can understand the contempt with which a Russian diplomat looks down on the "educated" West.

Friedrich Engels

The one fact that most impressed us in the U.S.S.R. was the extent to which the Nation is committed to education as a means of national advancement. In the organization of a planned society in the Soviet Union, education is regarded as one of the chief resources and techniques for achieving social, economic, cultural, and scientific objectives in the national interest. Tremendous responsibilities are therefore placed on Soviet schools, and comprehensive support is provided for them by all segments and agencies of Soviet society.

"Soviet Commitment to Education," Report of the First Official U. S. Education Mission to the U.S.S.R., U. S. Department of Health, Education, and Welfare, Bulletin 1959 No. 16

STRATEGIC GOALS IN SOVIET POLICY

by Robert D. Crane

Mr. Crane is a Research Principal of the Center for Strategic Studies, Georgetown University, and Chairman of its Study Program on Arms Control. As an intelligence analyst he specialized for several years on Soviet and Chinese political and military affairs. After receiving an LL.B. from Harvard Law School in 1959 he contributed articles to various professional journals on the role of the military and legal strategy in Soviet foreign policy, including the article "Soviet Attitude toward International Space Law," The American Journal of International Law, July 1962. His most recent publication, "Basic Strategies for Arms Control in the Post-Nuclear Age," appears in the symposium Détente: Cold War Strategies in Transition, *Robert D. Crane and Eleanor L. Dulles, eds. (New York: Frederick A. Praeger, 1964).*

This selection is adapted from the author's year-end summary of Soviet military writings, which appeared under the title "Strategic Goals in Soviet Policy: Possible Implications of Khrushchev's December Plenum Speech," in the report *Soviet Materials on Military Strategy: Inventory and Analysis for 1963*, edited by Wlodzimierz Onacewicz and Robert Dickson Crane, The Center for Strategic Studies, Georgetown University, Washington, D.C., January 1964.

President Johnson's first major foreign policy decision of 1964 was to devote this year to a "peace-probe" offensive against the Soviet leaders. His determination to improve the tenor of international relations was echoed by Premier Khrushchev, who indicated in his New Year remarks that if the world's leaders would do their "utmost" so that "the baton of the peace relay race could be passed and carried forward . . . then the coming year of 1964 can undoubtedly become a year of decisive change for the better in the entire international situation."

The Soviet leader revealed the extent of his commitment to a "new look" in international affairs at the concluding plenary session of the Central Committee of the Communist Party of the Soviet Union on December 13, 1963. In this speech, he announced his intention to lower the numerical strength of the Soviet armed forces, to reduce the military budget for 1964, and to invest forty-two billion rubles during the period 1964–70 to develop the chemical industry as an essential measure for the modernization of Soviet industry and agriculture.

In the field of international relations and military strategy, Premier Khrushchev stressed the Soviet desire to reduce international tensions in order to: (a) slow down the arms race, (b) promote further steps toward disarmament, and (c) help, as he put it, "the sensible forces in the United States . . . rebuff the aggressive militaristic circles." In the context of international developments during the last half of 1963, these pronouncements of the Soviet leader serve to reinforce the many indications that the Soviet leadership, both political and military, has reached a working consensus on the need to support a policy of détente as a strategic course of action.

Why have the Soviet leaders adopted this new policy? If this is indeed the new Soviet strategy, what do Soviet strategists hope to gain from détente? For the Soviet strategists, a period of détente may serve to support at least three different goals, all seemingly contradictory, but none necessarily incompatible with the others.

The first goal may be the sublimation of the military competition between Communism and capitalism into an economic and political competition designed to secure victory over the United States without the necessity of using or even threatening to use modern weapons. A period of détente would permit the Soviets to concentrate their limited resources to build up their economic and political power both at home and abroad in order to support the "historical inevitability" of the triumph of the socialist system.

The second goal may be the attainment of strategic military equality between the Soviet Union and the United States. A period of détente might serve to slow down the military buildup in the West so that the Soviet Union could catch up with less strain on its economy. Furthermore, détente might make possible a policy of finite deterrence sufficient to protect the Soviet Union from direct attack in the event of unexpected Western opposition to Soviet expansionist moves.

The third goal may be to attain decisive Soviet strategic superiority over the United States by a "technological end run" in the development of advanced and futuristic weapons. If the Soviets could "leapfrog" the United States through quantum jumps in weapons development they might be able to reduce their expected damages from a general nuclear war to acceptable levels, and thereby make more rational a bolder foreign policy. A period of détente might change such a goal from the visionary to the possible by creating or stimulating pressures in the United States against expensive weapons research for which there can be no guarantee of an eventual payoff. Détente might also reduce the pressure for wasteful and expensive development of prototypes and interim weapons systems in the Soviet Union and might provide the Soviets with the freedom to concentrate their limited personnel and material resources on the development of a broad base of basic research to permit more rational and rapid development of advanced weapons at a later date.

Whereas economic growth and strategic stability may be correlative objectives during the present decade, the objective of strategic supremacy could be realistic only within a longer time frame. Nevertheless, détente during the mid-1960's could contribute to all three of these goals, keeping the options open and postponing until the latter part of the decade any difficult commitment until it became apparent which is the optimum course.

The Goal of Economic Growth

The necessity for increased emphasis on the goal of economic growth has resulted from the steadily declining rate of growth which the Soviet economy experienced during the half decade from 1958 to 1963. This decline occurred in part because the rate of growth during the earlier part of the postwar period was artificially high. A major portion of this high growth rate was caused by the effects of the postwar recovery and later by the effects of the improved economic management and environmental reforms instituted by the post-Stalin leadership. By 1959 the maximum benefit from these two causes of the earlier high growth rate had ended. The other cause for the declining rate of Soviet economic growth during the past half-decade has been the shift of scientific and economic resources into the armaments industry. This burden on the Soviet economy began to have disruptive effects when Khrushchev tried to support not only an accelerated advanced weapons program but also to maintain large ground forces.

The seriousness of this disruptive effect can be seen in the fact that explicit Soviet defense outlays rose 44 per cent, from 9.3 billion rubles in 1960 to 13.4 billion in 1962, whereas investment in fixed capital during this same two-year period decreased by half in annual rate of growth, from 8 to 4 per cent. The impact on the Soviet economy is indicated by the fact that the growth rate of the Soviet gross national product (GNP) declined from an average of 8 per cent during the period 1955–58 to 4.5 per cent during the period 1959–62.[1] The agricultural picture was even worse. After 1958 the growth of agricultural output hardly kept up with the increase in population. Soviet agriculture produces, for a population 20 per cent larger than the American, only 60 per cent of what U.S. agriculture produces, using a labor force six times as large and with actually larger investments. Until the Soviet planners priced the poor population out of the market through some 30 per cent price hikes in 1962, the queues were for meat; now the people are lining up for bread.

The true seriousness of these economic failures for Soviet

long-range planning is revealed by projecting Soviet and U.S. growth rates into the future and comparing the result. In 1963, according to U.S. intelligence estimates, the ratio of Soviet to U.S. GNP had dropped to about 45:100. In mid-December 1963 the Department of State announced that during 1962 and 1963 "the Soviet GNP . . . has been growing but little more than 2 per cent per annum."[2] In order to give the Soviet Union the benefit of the doubt, we shall assume that the Soviets can boost the annual rate of growth of their GNP to 5 per cent[3] and that the annual U.S. growth rate will average only 4 per cent, which is below that of every major industrial nation in the Western world, including the United States. At these rates of growth, the GNP of the United States would increase from $585 billion in 1963 to $770 billion in 1970, and the Soviet GNP would rise from $267 billion in 1963 to $376 billion in 1970. The absolute gap between the two economies would grow from $318 billion in 1963 to $394 billion in 1970. The gap in favor of the United States would be one and a half times greater than the entire present Soviet GNP.

It is in view of such a prospect that Premier Khrushchev announced plans in his December Plenum speech to almost double the level of capital investment in the Soviet Union during the period 1964–70. He expressed the hope that this investment not only would be recouped but would result in a great gain. In the field of chemistry, Premier Khrushchev announced that from a forty-two billion ruble total investment he expected to obtain a fifty-seven billion ruble income, and that the fifteen billion ruble difference could be channeled into welfare benefits for the people and into higher wages and lower prices. He emphasized that the success of his great program with its benefits for the people would depend on an increase in labor productivity, but added the exhortation that: "Comrades, we have never been afraid of work."

Premier Khrushchev concluded his speech with the assertion that:

> We have everything. We must only organize the work well and then we will really rise to a level and achieve

heights that our country has never seen before. Our Communist society will insure the creation of material and spiritual assets which will become even more attractive for the peoples of all countries of the world, including the peoples of the most developed capitalist countries. . . . The time is not far off when the Soviet people will overtake the United States in per capita production and will become the first country in the world in economic development.

Premier Khrushchev might have recalled the prophecy of V. V. Kuibyshev, Chairman of the State Planning Commission in 1932 before the Seventeenth Party Conference that:

In 1937 . . . as far as the level of consumption is concerned, the Soviet Union will be the most advanced country in the world, so that all the toilers can see with their own eyes what the working class can achieve in creating socialism.

If Premier Khrushchev's claims are not to suffer the same fate as Mr. Kuibyshev's thirty years earlier, he must recognize that he cannot concurrently support a significant rise in consumption levels, a meaningful rate of economic growth, meaningful progress in advanced weapons research and development, and a large military establishment based on conventional weapons and massive manpower. It appears from Premier Khrushchev's December Plenum speech that, at a minimum, he opted not to sacrifice Soviet economic growth.

The Goal of Equal Strategic Power

The second goal of the Soviet planners may be the attainment of strategic power equal to that of the Western world in order to maintain or increase the political utility of Soviet strategic nuclear *weapons* and at the same time to assure that no nation can rationally resort to the military use or even the grave risk of strategic nuclear *war* as an instrument of policy.

The cheapest and quickest way to promote the equalization of strategic power between the Soviet Union and the Western world during the period 1964–70 would be to persuade the Western nations that further increases in their military power, whether for general or limited nuclear war, are unnecessary. Premier Khrushchev's preferred method has been to conclude limited arms control measures, especially the nuclear test ban and the agreement of intention to exclude weapons of mass destruction in space. The third major step in this process was revealed in Premier Khrushchev's December Plenum speech, when he advocated limited disarmament through tacit understanding by matching the proposed American cuts in defense appropriations with a proposal for roughly equal cuts in his own defense budget. By such a policy of interlocking unilateral arms control measures to reduce the overt arms race, the Soviet leader would hope to avoid the necessity of increasing his investment in present as distinct from future (post-1970) strategic capabilities during the seven years of his program for the modernization of Soviet industry.

Although the limited goal of strategic stability might constrain the foreign policy of an expansionist power, this would not prevent the Soviets from actively supporting the expansion of Communist influence, perhaps even in areas of vital interest to the United States such as Europe. This would be particularly true if by equal strategic power the Soviets were to gain a measure of functional deterrent superiority.

The timing of the Soviet Premier's announcement shortly before crucial meetings of the leaders of NATO countries suggests that a principal aim was to influence future NATO policy by undermining both those in Europe (and the United States) who advocate the creation of an independent European nuclear force with contributions from West Germany, and those in the United States (and Europe) who advocate large European conventional forces and the creation of a North Atlantic strategic deterrence system, particularly an interim system of high cost and limited service life such as the Multilateral Force. This, in turn, supposedly would support the growth of U.S.-Soviet bilateralism in world affairs, the growth of polycentrism within the Atlantic alliance, the withdrawal of American troops from Europe, and the decline of American influence in the Western world. These occurrences would help neutralize the existing strategic superiority of the United States over the Soviet Union and would increase the power of the declining Soviet ground forces as a psychological instrument to hold Western Europe hostage and thereby to inhibit any American response to Soviet expansionist policies elsewhere in the world.

In pursuing the goal of equal strategic power the Soviets may follow both a "carrot" approach to Western policymakers designed to slow down their weapons programs and stall their efforts toward closer military cooperation, and also a policy of occasional limited threats designed to give greater realism to the Soviet policy of détente, to promote the concept of nuclear stalemate by demonstrating both to the West and to any doubting Thomases at home that the deterrent power and resolve of the Soviet Union have not decreased, and to probe, perhaps sometimes incidentally, for opportunities to exploit any weaknesses in Western policy. These considerations may explain Premier Khrushchev's deliberate provocation of the Autobahn crises in October 1963 and his strong reaction to Secretary McNamara's November speech which deprecated the Soviet conventional counterbalance to Western nuclear missile superiority. A few weeks later in his December Plenum speech Premier Khrushchev followed this up with a carrot-like approach by suggesting that if the NATO countries believe the Warsaw Pact conventional forces are really inferior to their own they should reduce their own forces to the level of the forces of the Warsaw Pact.

The application of the carrot and stick approach in other areas of the world calls for Soviet support of (1) "liberation movements" to transfer underdeveloped areas from the sphere of influence of the Western industrial states into the sphere of influence of the Soviet Union; (2) "respect for the national sovereignty of all countries," as Premier Khrushchev phrased it in his December Plenum speech, which is aimed at the termination of U.S. "occupation" and "aggression" in Korea, Vietnam, Taiwan, Guantanamo, and any areas, including the Panama Canal Zone, where the Soviets think they can usefully appeal to the principle of "territorial integrity"; (3) "peaceful settlement of disputes," "negotiated solutions," and "neutralization," accompanied by warnings that Western failure to abide by these principles might undermine or destroy the entire structure of détente.[4]

The Goal of Strategic Supremacy

The third possible goal of Premier Khrushchev's policy of détente may be to provide a breathing spell while he diverts resources from present weapons production into advanced research and development to provide advanced weapons technology. Concomitantly he can hope to modernize and expand Soviet industry to provide a broad and flexible economic base for the production of advanced weapons, particularly space-based systems, during a post-détente period. Premier Khrushchev's grand design to lessen international tensions and his plans to rejuvenate his economic system would constitute little more than a holding operation so that he could concentrate on the creation of future strategic supremacy.

For such a goal to be rational the Soviets must have: (1) substantial doubt about the prospects of implementing their offensive foreign policies, including ultimate victory over the United States, through non-nuclear conflict techniques; (2) a rather high degree of optimism about the prospects of politically decisive weapons breakthroughs, particularly in the area of strategic defense, so that the necessarily great expenditures of money on basic military research and development would be justified; (3) an optimistic view that during détente the strategic thinking, awareness, and preparedness of the United States might permit the Soviet Union to "leapfrog" the United States in the development of advanced weapons and perhaps eventually also in their production and deployment.

The failure of the Soviets to achieve significant successes in promoting the growth of forces friendly to the Communists throughout the world may suggest to Soviet planners that the prospect for Communist victory through "peaceful coexistence," unsupported by strategic superiority, have not greatly improved in recent years. Despite what the Soviets may consider to be the beginning of a new "flow" period in Communist global expansion during 1964, exclusive reliance on non-nuclear conflict techniques is for Soviet strategists at best a gamble. The alternatives are either to abandon their goal of total global victory, at least *de facto,* or to supplement their revolutionary efforts with military force and with sufficient strategic power to neutralize American opposition. The evidence is not sufficient to conclude that the Soviet leaders have abandoned their basic Marxist-Leninist aims of total victory.

The second requirement for a Soviet goal of strategic supremacy is an optimistic view of the prospects for weapons breakthroughs. Premier Khrushchev's views on this subject were indicated indirectly in his December Plenum speech by his statements on the value of modern weapons and on the value of basic research and development. The value of advanced weapons was acknowledged in his statement that the determining factor in the strategic balance no longer is the size of the armed forces, the number of "bayonets and sabers," but the quality of the weapons. The Soviet Premier's highly favorable attitude toward research and development, which is basic to the creation of an environment for weapons breakthroughs, was indicated by his statement that:

> In questions of new scientific achievements, new technology, new materials, it is necessary to show a high feeling of interest and sympathy. It sometimes happens that the scientist has no blueprint, but [one must ask] is there a rational seed in what he proposes? Is there a good idea? If you feel that there are prospects, you must create conditions enabling the scientist to turn his scientific design and calculations into reality . . .

In his December Plenum speech Premier Khrushchev was indirectly reiterating his basic philosophy of quantum jumps in weaponry first put forth in his speech of January 15, 1960, which has served as a guideline for much of subsequent Soviet military thinking. In this speech he announced that:

> The armament we have is formidable. The armament under development is more perfect and more formidable.

The armament which is being created and which is to be found in the folders of the scientists and designers is truly unbelievable.

One area of advanced weapons technology emphasized by the Soviets is that of electromagnetic warfare (ECP). The recent Soviet book *Military Strategy,* for example, states: "The question of war in the ether [electronic warfare] has been sharply posed by the fact that electronic equipment has been widely introduced into the armed forces and is used extensively in all areas of military activity. . . . One of the main missions of such [electronic] warfare is to disrupt the command and control of personnel and weapons by active radio interference and destruction of the enemy's most important electronic systems and installations. This involves destruction or jamming of the electronic fuses of bombs and missiles by electronic radiation; interception of radio signals and generation of interference in the electronic equipment for aerial reconnaissance, navigation, bombing, and in-flight missile guidance . . ."[5] The Soviets often emphasize the effect of high-yield blasts, either in the atmosphere or in space, on both land-based missile systems and Polaris submarines. The Soviets place equally great emphasis on neutron-flux weapons, because a neutron bomb not only could destroy the circuitry of ICBM's passing through space but, as the above-quoted Soviet statement indicates, could detrigger their warheads.[6]

Recent Soviet writings also emphasize the potential of various futuristic systems which require much further improvement both in the weapons themselves and in the booster power necessary to inject these weapons into space. These futuristic systems discussed by the Soviets are based on jets of plasma heated millions of degrees into the "fourth state" of matter, radio-directed ionized gas or "ball-lightning," and the direction of nuclear and solar energy by laser and other means. This latter area of weapons technology is a favorite of Premier Khrushchev, who keeps a laser-scarred piece of steel on his desk to remind himself and his visitors of the potential of what he considers to be Soviet superiority in advanced military technology.

The Soviets stress the potential of space weapons. Whereas American strategists emphasize their possible use as a defensive means to degrade the opponent's strategic capabilities, the Soviets emphasize the value of space weapons for offensive use in general and limited war, and, according to the recent Soviet book *Military Strategy,* even for tactical use in local war. One of the principal advantages of offensive space weapons would be in the reduction of "reaction" time from initiation of a strike to impact on target, which could give both psychological and perhaps eventually also military advantages. For the more conventional types of space bombing, Soviet advances in maneuverability and in deorbiting thrust could reduce the response time from deployment orbit to surface impact from the present interval of five minutes to as little as one hundred seconds. If and when the Soviets perfect the advanced radiation weapons mentioned in their strategic and scientific writings, the near elimination of reaction time and the increases in accuracy and destructive yield of Soviet space weapons would provide important military advantages and might destroy any mutual counterforce stalemate for many purposes even more effectively than would the perfection of active defense measures. During an era when the psychological value of resolve might surpass the military value of strategic power, increasingly important might be also various spacebased environmental countervalue weapons, including weapons for biological warfare and high-megatonnage or even gigatonnage nuclear weapons. These high-yield weapons, according to Soviet writings, could serve not only to disable or destroy communications, nuclear submarines, and other counterforce targets, but could destroy the resolve of an opponent by producing terror blasts in near space or by burning the crops over large areas of a continent to weaken the opponent's ability to recuperate.

Two days before the signing of the partial nuclear test ban treaty in August, Premier Khrushchev indicated that he had tried to get across at least some of these points to the technologically and perhaps strategically more backward Chinese Communists when he stated on August 3, 1963 that:

> The Soviet Government has already called the attention of the Government of the People's Republic of China to the simple truth that life does not stand still, that science and technology are developing rapidly, and that something which was unacceptable yesterday may turn out to be useful and even very useful today [referring to the nuclear test ban, which had the effect of prohibiting U.S. repetition of the advanced testing which the Soviets had recently completed].

In his statement of August 21, 1963, Premier Khrushchev repeated this statement and seemed to warn that Mao Tse-tung and his entourage should keep quiet until they understood better the elements of modern Soviet strategy:

> Of course, we cannot now divulge such things, for example, as the concrete results of the nuclear weapons tests we carried out in 1961–1962, the data on the calibers of the nuclear warheads in our arsenal, the destination of the specific nuclear combat devices of which the Soviet Union has plenty, where these means are deployed, and so forth. That would be against the security interests of the Soviet Union and of all socialist states, including the security interests of the People's Republic of China.[7]

The third requirement for a rational Soviet goal of strategic weapons supremacy would be the belief among Soviet leaders that during détente the development of U.S. military planning might permit a *fait accompli* by the Soviet Union which could put the Soviets an entire generation or two ahead of the United States in weapons development. It has probably become only too clear to the Soviets that the United States overreacts to any Soviet attempt to capitalize politically, either through prestige or blackmail, on the successes of Soviet military research and development. This has been true particularly in the field of space and missiles. If the past is a guide to the future, the Soviets therefore can achieve meaningful strategic superiority perhaps only by advocating a policy of arms constraints and self-denial based on tacit understandings, false assumptions, and sufficient secrecy to permit Soviet evasion in the critical areas of weapons development.

The ability of the Soviet Union to build up a formidable weapons arsenal in complete secrecy is greater than newspaper accounts of the Samos program and the "Penkovsky spy case" might suggest. Although budgetary analysis is helpful in identifying the expensive programs necessary to develop modern weapons, reliable analysis of the Soviet military R & D budget is impeded, for example, by the distribution of what are in fact defense expenditures among non-defense categories in the Soviet budget, such as the categories of "social-cultural measures" and the general residual category "other" (which alone has accounted for up to 10 per cent of the total Soviet budget), and by the higher purchasing power of the ruble in capital intensive sectors of the economy caused by hidden subsidies extended through an arbitrary pricing system. The margin between the overt and covert Soviet military budget may range higher than 100 per cent.[8] In critical areas of the economy Soviet budgetary obfuscation through arbitrary accounting and pricing may make it impossible to identify by budgetary analysis more than 20 per cent of Soviet expenditures. This is particularly true in the area of research and development for futuristic (post-1975) weapons, which according to inconclusive indications is funded at a level three times that in the United States.

If the Soviets have adopted the building-block method for military program management by advancing technology on a broad front and concentrating on the lower levels of the weapons pyramid, Soviet budgetary obfuscation would make it very difficult for the United States to obtain meaningful intelligence indications on their progress until the Soviets had completed their basic research, selected the optimum weapons, and started to test and evaluate them.

The Soviet economy could support such a program of research and development and at the same time could prepare the industrial foundation to capitalize on whatever weapons breakthroughs might result. In his definitions of the new Soviet chemical program, the Soviet leader made it clear that he contemplated a program broad enough to support not only fertilizers and plastics for consumer industries, but rocket fuels and whatever might be required by the military sector. He indicated this in his December Plenum speech by stating: "it is quite clear that the program planned for the development of the chemical industry will be implemented without detrimental effect on the consolidation of the defense of the country or on the growth of other branches of the national economy." The 1964 budget for science, which is always closely related to Soviet military programs, was, in fact, even increased by five hundred million rubles. Moreover, it is significant that the proposed reduction in the Soviet military budget for 1964, if indeed there is to be such a reduction, is only six hundred million rubles, which could be taken from elements of the ground forces without at all interfering with the maintenance or even with the acceleration of military research and development. It should be recalled also that, although the growth rate of the Soviet GNP has fallen below that of the United States, the Soviets have maintained a high rate of industrial expansion, particularly in areas vital to their military effort.

Conclusion

Soviet strategic goals are still in a state of flux. Until Soviet leaders make final decisions on long-range foreign policy, Premier Khrushchev may engage in concurrent programs to achieve economic growth, strategic equality, and strategic supremacy. By pursuing these goals concurrently, he may hope to keep his options open until a final decision is reached on the optimum course for the Soviet Union.

Alternatively, he may regard these goals as possible phases or incremental steps in a single strategy, whereby further economic growth would serve as a step toward the attainment of strategic parity, and strategic parity would serve as a necessary step toward strategic supremacy.

Which of these alternatives will dominate in Soviet strategic planning and which of the goals will ultimately win out will depend, first of all, on the skill with which the leaders of the

United States can demonstrate their resolve to maintain U.S. weapons supremacy, especially in advanced strategic weapons, and their determination to use these weapons if, but only if, forced to by the aggressive policies of the Soviet Union. The greatest problem for American policymakers during a period of détente will not be how to continue the momentum toward disarmament but how to optimize our defenses. This problem was best summarized by Roswell L. Gilpatric, Deputy Secretary of Defense, at the Annual UPI Editors and Publishers Conference on October 19, 1963, as follows:

> For the moment, our power base is in good shape. But inevitably, over the years, there will be new periods of readjustment and reshaping of our defenses. Neither technology nor the world situation will ever remain static. . . . So it behooves us, regardless of the immediate climate in the international scene, to maintain the forward thrust of U.S. military technology, to remain sensitive to shifts in the power equation and not to count on a status quo which we know is not going to last. . . .
>
> How well we are able to meet [these] defense problems will depend heavily on the attitude of the press and the public which it serves. . . . It is relatively easy to develop understanding and support in a period of expanding defense effort against the background of rising international tension. Now there is at least a possibility that both those trends will be reversed. Yet the defense issues we will be facing in the next several years, whether or not they prove to be less dramatic than those in times of crisis, remain of the highest importance. Our effectiveness in dealing with these relatively "quiet" challenges is going to play a large role in determining whether we are going to be successful in the coming years in really advancing the cause of a just peace, or whether we are to accomplish nothing more than to set the stage for a renewed, and perhaps even more dangerous, period of crisis.[9]

The future development of Soviet strategic goals will depend not only on the clear demonstration by the United States and its allies that a Soviet attempt at nuclear blackmail can never be successful, but also on the measures we are willing to take to prove that Communism cannot win by non-military means. The statesmen and peoples of the leading countries in the West must show patience and determination in the military containment of Communism; they must concentrate their primary energies, however, on improving the educational and living standards of the peoples of the world and on promoting political and economic systems which are both free and socially responsible. Only by such a dual approach can we remove the incentives for Communist aggression and give the Russian Government time and opportunity to adopt strategic goals which are more compatible with our own. Only by increasing both the military and non-military strength of the free world can we prevent the ultimate victory of a closed society and assure the victory of justice and peace for all men and nations.

NOTES

1. Morris Bornstein, "The Role of Economic Growth," in *National Security: Political, Military, and Economic Strategies in the Decade Ahead* (New York: Frederick A. Praeger, 1963), David M. Abshire and Richard V. Allen, eds.; also Warren G. Nutter, "The Effects of Economic Growth on Sino-Soviet Strategy," ibid., p. 154.

2. Department of State Special Information Note, Number 28, December 13, 1963, p. 2. On January 8, 1964, the New York *Times* reported that "the Soviet Union's economic growth in the last two years has been less than 2.5 per cent annually."—Edwin L. Dale, "Sharp Slowdown in Soviet Growth Reported by C.I.A."

3. Projection of the Soviet annual growth rate during the next five years at 5 per cent is based on CIA estimates of the continuing impact of factors which contributed to the decline of Soviet annual economic growth during 1962 and 1963. This projection assumes a considerable recovery in agricultural growth rate. See also Stanley H. Cohen, "Annual Economic Indicators for the USSR," Statistical Supplement to Dimensions of Soviet Economic Power, Joint Economic Committee, 88th Congress, 2nd Session, February 1964.

4. Premier Khrushchev's policy for the conduct of détente in Asia, Africa, and Latin America was indicated in one of his most important pronouncements on December 21, 1963, entitled "The

National Liberation Movement in the Present Period." This "declaration" served as the ideological basis for his twenty-one-page circular letter of December 31, 1963, on territorial non-aggression, which many analysts consider to be more important than his announced strategy of "general and complete disarmament" as an instrument to suppress the defensive power of the United States.

5. *Soviet Military Strategy,* translated and with Analytical Introduction and annotations by Herbert S. Dinerstein, Leon Gouré, and Thomas W. Wolfe (Englewood Cliffs, N.J.: Prentice-Hall, 1963), pp. 337–38.

6. The question of Soviet potential and goals in futuristic weaponry has been discussed in several recent articles, including those in the symposium entitled "Our Gamble in Space" in *The Atlantic,* August 1963 and in the symposium entitled "Does Russia's Space Program Pose a Threat to Our National Security?" in *The Air Force and Space Digest,* November 1963. This whole question has been examined at length in numerous Congressional hearings. See U. S. Congress, Senate, Committee on Foreign Relations, *Hearings, Nuclear Test Ban Treaty,* 88th Cong., 1st Sess., 1963, particularly pages 242–46, 303, 377, 387, 423, 451, and 863 on various estimates of Soviet potential and goals in advanced weapons. Also U. S. Congress, Senate, Committee on Foreign Relations, *Report, Nuclear Test Ban Treaty,* 88th Cong., 1st Sess., September 3, 1963, pp. 11–16. The relative status of nuclear weapons programs in the U.S.S.R. and the United States and the history and trends of the Soviet programs are discussed in U. S. Congress, Senate, Preparedness Investigating Subcommittee, Committee on Armed Services, *Interim Report, Military Implications of the Proposed Limited Nuclear Test Ban Treaty,* 88th Cong., 1st Sess., September 1963. See especially U. S. Congress, Senate, Preparedness Investigating Subcommittee, Committee on Armed Services, transcript of *Hearings, Nuclear Test Ban Treaties,* 88th Cong., 1st Sess., May–September 1963, to be published.

7. Indications have been reported that the effects of a one megaton blast in space could disrupt the circuitry of unhardened space devices within a minimum radius of 100 miles, that the Soviets used a one megaton blast in space as an experiment to disable their anti-ballistic missile electronic system in October 1962, and that they used the same technique in October 1962 to disable a space device of the United States. Edward W. O'Brien, "U.S. Satellite Crippled in Space by Russian Nuclear Test Blast," *St. Louis Globe-Democrat,* July 30, 1963.

8. See Timothy Sosnovy, "The Soviet Military Budget," *Foreign Affairs,* April 1964. See also J. G. Godaire, "The Claim of the Soviet Military Establishment," in *Dimensions of Soviet Eco-*

nomic Power, Joint Economic Committee, 87th Congress, 2nd Session, December 1962.

9. Roswell L. Gilpatric, "The New Phase in Our National Defense," *Air Force Information Policy Letter,* Supplement No. 125, November 1963. See also Robert D. Crane, "The Cuban Crisis: A Strategic Analysis of American and Soviet Policy," *Orbis, A Quarterly Journal of World Affairs,* Winter 1963, and "Basic Strategies for Arms Control in the Post-Nuclear Age," ibid., Summer 1964.

HOW STRONG, HOW WEAK
IS THE SOVIET UNION

by Robert Strausz-Hupé

Dr. Strausz-Hupé is recognized as one of the leading writers in the field of geopolitics. Born in Vienna, a banker by profession before he turned to teaching and writing, he is the Director of the Foreign Policy Research Institute of the University of Pennsylvania. He has been a consultant to the United Nations Secretariat, the United States Government, and the NATO Parliamentarians' Conference, and has lectured widely in this country and abroad. He has published many books dealing with geopolitical and strategic problems and has contributed articles to numerous magazines and journals. He is the Editor of Orbis, A Quarterly Journal of World Affairs *published by the Foreign Policy Research Institute, and co-author of* Protracted Conflict, A Forward Strategy for America, *and* Building the Atlantic World.

This selection originally appeared in the Philadelphia *Inquirer* on April 5, 1964 and is reprinted by permission.

An organism is said to be vulnerable insofar as it is liable to attack by an injurious agent. Although weakness and vulnerability are not synonyms, we deduce vulnerability from ascertainable weakness. Yet, a potential vulnerability remains potential—nothing more—as long as it is not exploited by the appropriate action. Thus, a state derives small comfort from the ascertainable weaknesses of another hostile state if it does not know how to take advantage of this condition. In other words, a state, though weak, might not be vulnerable to its opponents who, for a variety of reasons, will not or cannot attack through the open breach. One can be weak and still quite comfortable. It takes two for turning weakness into vulnerability.

For more than five hundred years, the Byzantine Empire suffered from a number of diseases, each of which should have killed it off within, let us say, one or two generations. Groaning under the weight of a vast parasitical bureaucracy, riven by religious strife, led by a long line of demented despots, demoralized by the luxury of the few and the poverty of the many, circled by warlike peoples avid for loot, the Byzantine Empire stood up longer than any other empire of the Christian era. The Byzantines, perfectly aware of their vulnerability, made good use of their shrinking assets—and the vulnerabilities of their opponents. Brilliant diplomacy, efficiency in psychological warfare, the best propaganda machine before the era of mass communications, a judicious blend of savage cruelty and shameless appeasement, a head start in the military-technological race, namely the Greek Fire, these were the weapons with which the Byzantines compensated for their vulnerabilities and fought their foes, superior in forces and slow in wit. It is not a mere coincidence that the Soviet Union, together with its vulnerabilities and its remedial practices, resembles so closely the Byzantine Empire. Russia has never disclaimed the heritage of Eastern Rome.

Some Weaknesses of Russian-Based Communism

Although neither the Soviet state nor Communist ideology are coextensive with the country called Russia, both Soviet state and Communist ideology have established their principal base upon Russian soil. Some of the weaknesses of Russian-based Communism are those of Russia. Four-fifths of Russia's land surface is located north of the northernmost limits of the territory of the United States with the exclusion of Alaska. Climatic and soil conditions make it much more difficult for Russia to feed a growing population than for the United States. Even allowing for Soviet mismanagement of

the agricultural sector of the national economy, the short-
fall of Soviet agricultural production has been caused, at least
in part, by environmental conditions which do not confront
the United States and most of Europe. For many years Soviet agronomists and even the Soviet rulers have been aware
of the ecological problems peculiar to Soviet agriculture.
Various schemes for expanding Russia's cultivable land and
shifting population to new land have been tried. No doubt,
the willful diversion of capital investment from agriculture to
the military-industrial complex has aggravated the chronic
crisis of Russian agriculture. But, in fairness to Khrushchev,
not all the dietary woes of the Russian people should be
ascribed to Soviet economic policy. Moreover, Khrushchev's
well-publicized admission that all is not well in Soviet agriculture and his pledge to increase capital investment in agriculture might be intended as much to assure the West of the
pacific preoccupations of the Communist regime as to mollify
the Russian consumer. Such a deep finesse would be in the
best tradition of Byzantine diplomacy.

Another weakness of contemporary Russia is rooted in
geography. The enormous size of Russia's territory, three
times as large as that of the United States, is fraught with
unique problems of transport by sea and land. A series of
Tsarist and Soviet military disasters in this century can be
traced, in part, to a rickety railroad system and an even more
sketchy system of highways. Khrushchev knows full well
that the stringencies of urban food supply are as much
due to an inadequate system of distribution—i.e., rail and
highway transport and storage—as to poor yields per acre.
Transportation was the Achilles heel of Tsarist Russia; after
nearly fifty years, Russia under the Communists has not succeeded in curing a weakness which has hampered economic
growth and diminished the mobility of military power.

Tsarism has handed on to the Communists another generic
weakness of Russia. In the course of his history, the Great
Russian has subjected to his rule many races. He has incurred
the abiding hatred of nearly all of them. The Communists
have failed to liquidate this historical bequest. They have
continued the Tsarist program of Russification. They have

tried to submerge such Central Asian subject peoples as the Kazakhs, the Kalmyks, and the Uzbecks in the massive settlement of colons from European Russia. Khrushchev, first as the lieutenant of Stalin and then as Premier, has tried his hand at solving the problem of the Ukrainian minority. It is estimated that his ministrations cost over one-half million Ukrainians their lives. The Soviet troops stationed along the Baltic coast are charged as much with cowing the smoldering resistance of the Estonians, Latvians, and Lithuanians as with the defense of Mother Russia against an invasion across the Baltic Sea. In these countries the recruitment of select natives into the Communist Party has not always furthered their assimilation to Soviet Russian culture. Moscow has found it necessary to purge repeatedly the local governments and the Communist hierarchies of several member states of the Soviet Union.

The Communists have built on the historic weaknesses of Russia the contradictions of their political system and the inefficiencies of their economic management. From its birth, Marxist Socialism has been afflicted by its founder's mistaken assumptions about the nature of man. Marxist ideas have penetrated into the public policy of many Western countries. Yet, practical experience and progress in social science have brought a considerable re-evaluation and revision of Marxist doctrine. Although collectivist experiments are being carried out in many places, they deviate considerably from Marxist orthodoxy. In the Soviet Union, the body of Marxist thought has been kneaded and rekneaded by the sacrilegious hands of Lenin and his successors. In lieu of the dictatorship of the proletariat, Lenin established, under the slogan of democratic centralism, the dictatorship of a priestly class of professional revolutionaries. Lenin postponed indefinitely the advent of the classless society.

A Despotic Bureaucracy Topped by an Autocracy

The Soviet hierarchs have yoked their subject peoples with a despotic bureaucracy topped by autocracy. Of course, an autocracy does not devote its best energy to solving the problem of genuine popular representation. It is not unreasonable, however, to expect it to develop some sort of procedure which will assure the smooth succession to highest office. The fact is that, after forty-seven years, Communist rule has worked out only two methods of succession: co-option and murder. Again, a weakness need not necessarily become a vulnerability.

Again and again, the opponents of the Soviet Union have watched with uncomprehending amazement the paralysis and the turmoil which invariably follow upon the demise of one autocrat and precede the rise of another autocrat. Shocked by these dreadful goings-on, they did nothing. Yet, at no time were the Soviets more vulnerable to Western initiatives than after the death of Stalin. Certainly, the West could have taken safely the offensive in many a debated ground, such as, for example, Berlin, Korea, and Southeast Asia, without fear of prompt and forceful Soviet counteraction. In any case, the West would have been well advised to test cautiously the mettle of Soviet leadership convulsed by the internecine struggle. Stalin's death seems to have come to the West's propaganda strategists as a complete surprise: they did not even have a considered plan for exposing the scandalous disarray in the Kremlin to the world's public opinion.

There is good reason to assume that the Communists have still to find a solution to the problem of legitimate succession. The chances are fair that Mr. Khrushchev's demise will be attended by the same tumult which ensued upon the disappearance of his predecessors. The chances are even better that the Communists need not fear being discommoded by Western activities designed to gain advantage from another struggle for the crown in the Kremlin.

Often Repeated Promises of an Improved Economy

Many years ago, an English peeress in the odor of progressive leanings said: "We all are Socialists now." Indeed, Marxist philosophy, the materialist approach to politics and ethics, has rubbed off on non-Marxist thought. A good many professed liberals and conservatives view Communism as an economic system and insist upon judging the goodness or badness of Communism by its economic performance. If this were the proper criterion of Communism then all would be well with the Soviet Union as long as the living standards of the average Soviet citizen would be rising as rapidly as in capitalist countries such as, for example, the United States or Britain or Germany. It is not surprising that those who hold this view center their attention upon the growth rates of the Soviet gross national product and seek to ascertain the strengths and weaknesses of the Soviet state from such economic indices as per capita income, wage rates, and the purchasing power of the ruble. This kind of economics-minded analysis of Soviet realities has, at various times, suggested conclusions about Soviet capabilities and intentions which, after a while, invariably have proved wrong.

In the 1920's, some of the most celebrated Western experts on Soviet affairs, noting the terrible state of Soviet agriculture, the collapse of the Soviet transportation system and the misery of the Russian people in general, predicted the demise, within a few months, of the Communist regime. The regime stood and strengthened its hold on the Russian peoples. When the five-year plans hit their stride and Soviet propaganda flooded the universe with tales of overfulfilled quotas in industry and joyous harvests on the collective farm, the celebrated Western experts changed their tune. The Soviet Union was about to catch up with the sluggish capitalistic economy. Even the Stalinist purges were not allowed to mar the image of the Soviet people marching forward under the banner of socialist planning toward prosperity, free from exploitation and inequality.

After World War II, Stalin, so many Western experts thought, would have to labor hard for many years to rebuild his war-devastated country and hence could not venture upon costly, non-economic undertakings such as, for instance, modernizing the Red Army and producing atomic bombs. Stalin starved, as he had always done, the average Soviet consumer. He ruthlessly drove, as he had always done, the average Soviet worker. He modernized the Red Army and produced atomic bombs.

During the late 1950's, another set of celebrated experts, awed by the Sputnik, estimated the growth rate of the Soviet economy at anywhere from 6 to 10 per cent per annum, and predicted that, in a matter of a few years, the productivity of the Soviet Union would catch up with, or even overtake, that of the United States.

For good measure, some eminent experts versed in military matters discovered that the Soviets had taken the lead in the military technological race. By 1960, they had—at least in their expert pronouncements—opened, not to be outdone by the economists, the "missile gap."[1] While the Soviet economy was breathing down the neck of the American economy, Soviet military power was drawing abreast with, if not over-taking, American military power.

In 1963, the Soviet Union passed one of its periodic agri-cultural crises. The paternal Soviet state sharply increased the price of bread and butter. Premier Khrushchev, acknowledging the shortfalls of Soviet agriculture, announced himself in fa-vor of diverting a larger share of future socialist investment into the construction of fertilizer plants. The Soviet budget for 1964 envisaged the moderate decrease of military ex-penditures. Again, the West's hardy Sovietologists delved into enigmatic statistics and revised their previous estimates. Soviet productivity, far from catching up with American productiv-ity, was now falling behind the U.S. annual rate of growth.[2] Confronted by the need for increased investment in the con-sumer goods sector of the national economy and mindful of his people's clamor for the better things of life, Premier Khru-shchev now craved a genuine détente with the West.

Changes in the Communist World

All throughout the Communist world great changes were in the making. Premier Khrushchev, although he could be ex-pected to retain control of the Presidium and defeat the mach-inations of the Stalinist opposition, had to yield to his people's longing for peace and plenty and to the demands of the satel-lite states, notably Poland and Rumania, for greater freedom from Soviet economic controls. On the horizon gleamed the vision of a "mellow," "more liberal" Soviet society. Incidentally, the "missile gap" of 1960 closed miraculously in 1963. The United States was now ahead by about three to one, a wondrous feat considering the fact that the lead time in missile production is about seven years.

The Communists, even if they wanted to transform Soviet society and give the peoples under their rule a semblance of representative government, could not do so—except at the price of collective self-immolation. Nowhere have they come to power by gaining a clear electoral majority. The chances are that free elections in Russia would topple the Soviet regime. Certainly, the Communist regimes in Eastern Europe could not survive by one minute free, direct, and secret election. Not even the most eccentric member of Communist polycentrism, Yugoslavia, has lifted the Communist Party's absolute control over the press or abolished the secret police or introduced into its legal system the notion of *habeas corpus*. In all Communist states, the state is the sole employer, and the state and Party—Siamese twins—determine who shall work, at what, and where and for what wages. The Communist Party represents a small minority of the population. It is the absolute power of this small minority over the very life of every man, woman, and child under its domination which is the most abominable and forever incurable disease of the Communist system. Indeed, this disease is the principal cause of the chronic malfunction of the Soviet economy and of all national economies under Communist control. No more grievous and ludicrous error can be made than to attribute the political conditions in the Soviet Union to the woes of the Soviet economy, and to expect the Soviet political system to mellow in the warmth of rising average standards of living. The Communist political system inhibits the fair distribution of the fruits of the people's labor and orderly economic progress. To ensure fair distribution and orderly economic progress, the Communists would have to introduce a market economy, divest themselves of their absolute controls—and thus commit political hara-kiri. As good Communists, they will not betray the basic tenets of their faith; as ordinary men, they can restrain themselves from committing suicide.

No amount of purging and planning can cure the ills of the Soviet economy. The Soviets read voraciously foreign professional literature. They are familiar with the methods of industrial management and cost accountancy developed in the United States. They know all about programing and automating industrial production, and their agronomists are no slouches. Since the malfunction of the Soviet economy derives from non-economic causes, namely the rottenness of the political system, the Soviet economists, clever as they are, cannot remedy the situation.

Stresses and Strains within the Communist Bloc

Thus far, the Communists have dealt with the chronic and unstable domestic crisis by exporting it into world politics. They have channeled internal pressures into foreign conquest. The West, insofar as it has succeeded in thwarting Communist expansionism and bottling up the Communists in the malodorous pit of their own contradictions, has aggravated the stresses and strains within the Communist bloc. Thus, for example, NATO's successful defense of Europe has heightened the tensions within both the Soviet Union and the Soviet bloc. America's successful defense of the Formosa straits, the offshore islands, and South Korea has pushed back the Red Chinese onto the Soviets. The worst that can befall the Communists is being kept at home and having to live with one another.

Among the most characteristic features of Communist dynamics are rythmic economic crises and rythmic political purges. These two kinds of convulsions are closely related to one another. Whenever the system breaks down, as every so often it must, the Communists sacrifice an appropriate number of scapegoats upon the altar of their theory. Thus, they propitiate the wrathful spirits of Marx, Engels, and Lenin and, incidentally, the resentment of their long-suffering helots. Every so often, the Soviet economy falters and flops. The sequence is always the same: The Communists race the machine in order to accelerate their power drive. The machine heats up. Then it slows down. It needs extensive repairs. A period of relaxation is indicated. The Communists are passing through such a period now. In a period such as this, they switch gear. Now, the wheels of overt aggressiveness—nuclear blackmail and armed subversion—are turning slowly. The wheels of psychological warfare—progaganda, infiltration, and non-violent subversion—are running faster.

Communist Mastery at Psychological Strategy

Mastery at psychological strategy has brought the Communists to power. It has gained them domination over more than one billion people. It has matched the superior material resources of the Western democracies. It now threatens to divide the Western alliance. An ingenuous psychological maneuver, so it seems, is now about to wrest success abroad from the jaws of domestic failure. The Communists, out of breath from their own exertions, seek to persuade the West to stop racing for military technological superiority and to permit them to catch their breath. The Communist economies badly need a reviving infusion from abroad. The "prudent members of the bourgeoisie," to use Khrushchev's coy phrase, are expected to supply it.[3] They have always done so before. Chances are they will do so again. The scheme, though remarkable for its insolence, has been executed so often with the same result, namely another hard Communist push against the free world, that by now, even the most witless among the "prudent members of the bourgeoisie" should be able to decipher it. Such is the psychological finesse of the Communists that some of the West's leading statesmen and opinion leaders look at this hoary ploy as if they had never seen it before. One Western delegation after the other troops to Moscow and confers earnestly with the Communist bosses on how the West can best help them shore up their rule. As always, the easiest mark for Communist psychological conditioning is the West's sophisticated intellectual. Sophisticated people consider themselves more immune to psychological manipulation than their more simpleminded fellow men. They are loath to concede that they, too, have been had. Not less successful have been the Communists' periodic overtures to that citadel of Western capitalism, Big Business. In a pinch, the Communists have always been able to count on the assistance of some hardheaded businessmen, eager for export markets, as well as on the sophisticated Western intellectual impatient of the imperfections of his own society—and international reality.

The Myth about "Opening Up" Communist Society

It has been argued in defense of the various commodity agreements concluded in 1963 between Western governments and the Soviet Union that Western imports will "open up" Soviet society. Presumably, the Soviets and the Communist governments of Eastern Europe, charmed by Western goods and salesmen, will obligingly raise the Iron Curtain and let the fresh breezes of freedom waft across the lands. No one has as yet explained satisfactorily why the contemplation of an American bushel of wheat, or an English plastics factory or a West German steel mill erected upon Russian soil should stir the average Soviet citizen to admire the supplier's political institutions. The average Soviet citizen, if he knows and thinks about such matters at all, is likely to be impressed by the cleverness of his rulers who have managed to procure these commodities on easy credit terms. In brief, advantageous trade with the West strengthens the position of the rulers, i.e., the Communist Party.

If Western imports could "open up" Communist society, then the Soviet Union should by now be about as "open" as, let us say, Austria or Switzerland or, at least, as partially "open" as India. In the interwar period, socialist construction in the Soviet Union would have been impossible without plentiful foreign imports ranging from foodstuffs to heavy industrial equipment. Even more massive Western imports helped the Soviets to win the war against Germany. Lend-Lease provided the Soviets not only with arms but also with whole industrial plants, a merchant fleet, and a large number of automotive vehicles. Thus the United States ceased Stalin's labors of postwar reconstruction. After the war, Western private business, notably British, supplied the Soviets with all kinds of highly sophisticated tools which, only by a stretch of the imagination, could be designated as non-strategic. If these and other trading ventures have "mellowed" Communist rule or lessened Communist aggressiveness throughout the world, then these beneficial effects have not been visible to the naked eye.

The Soviets' Greatest Vulnerability

The appalling and incurable weakness of the Soviet economy should constitute the greatest vulnerability of the Soviet Union. The fact that economic weakness has never seriously threatened the rule of the Communist Party in Russia or hampered Communist expansion abroad is largely due to the intellectual and moral confusion of the very people whom Premier Khrushchev proposed to bury. There has been no dearth of Western experts who have argued, in and out of season, that the Soviets cannot be brought to fall by an economic blockade. The fact is that this strategy has never been tried. The Western experts argue that an economic blockade, though it might be successful in stunting Soviet economic growth, would provoke the Soviets into awesome political and military retaliation. The fact is that, throughout the last forty-seven years, no one has been able to provoke the Soviets into starting a fight as long as they thought that the odds were against them. Of course, the Western allies, in order to exploit the economic vulnerability of the Soviet Union, would have to agree upon one common strategy of economic warfare and restrain their individual eagerness for profitable trade with the Soviets. They will do neither as long as they mistake the nature and purpose of Communism and keep on negotiating for the impossible compromise between despotism and freedom.

The West's Greatest Weakness

The single greatest weakness of the Western Alliance resides in its failure to coordinate the political and economic policies of its individual members with its military strategy.

One would suppose that the NATO allies, wiser by fifteen years of experience in collective military defense, would have come to understand the interrelationship of war and economics. Unfortunately, they have not only not understood this connection but have also pursued separate political and economic policies which run counter to the purpose of the alliance. The Soviets *have* noted this basic weakness of the Western alliance. The Soviets *have* exploited this weakness and thus turned it into a Western vulnerability. It is difficult to see how the West can exploit the many and manifest weaknesses of the Communist system until it has cured its own fundamental weakness, namely, lack of understanding and purpose. "Physician, heal thyself!"

NOTES

1. On December 16, 1959, Secretary of Defense Thomas S. Gates asserted that the United States had "present nuclear superiority" over the Soviet Union both in weapons and means of delivery. On January 28, 1960, Senator Stuart Symington, replying to Mr. Gates, declared that the "missile gap was greater than 3 to 1 in favor of the Russians and was still growing." Senator Richard B. Russell, too, refused to be assured by Mr. Gates's statement. "I can't accept," Senator Russell said, "that there is no missile gap. I think there is."
2. On January 6, 1964, the Central Intelligence Agency released a report hailed by the press as an "exhaustive analysis" of the Soviet Union's economic growth. The Agency concluded that, in the two years ending in 1963, the Soviet growth rate had dropped to 2.5 per cent annually, well under the rate of the United States, estimated variously at from 3.7 to 5 per cent.
3. In an address, on December 9, 1963, to the Central Committee, Premier Khrushchev conceded that the Soviet Union would have to seek much of the equipment and know-how for the new chemical complex in the West. He said: "We shall place orders with those who want to make an honest profit, provided there are credits, because this has become the norm of economic relations."

SHIFTS IN SOVIET STRATEGIC
THOUGHT

by Thomas W. Wolfe

A longtime student of Soviet affairs, Colonel Wolfe, U.S.A.F. (Ret.), is a member of the Social Science Department of The RAND Corporation, Santa Monica, California. He received his M.A. degree from Columbia University and his Ph.D. degree from Georgetown University. He is also a graduate of the Russian Institute of Columbia University. Colonel Wolfe served as U. S. Air Attaché in Moscow from 1956 to 1958. He is one of the American editors of Marshal Sokolovskii's Soviet Military Strategy.

This selection appeared in the April 1964 issue of *Foreign Affairs* and is reprinted by permission. Copyright 1964, by the Council on Foreign Relations, Inc., New York.

The great predicament of the modern world was summed up by the late President Kennedy in one of his last public remarks: "The family of man can survive differences of race and religion . . . it can accept differences in ideology, politics, economics. But it cannot survive, in the form in which we know it, a nuclear war." Widespread appreciation of this fact accounts in part for the growing significance of the strategic dialogue between the United States and the Soviet Union, particularly insofar as it represents a means by which the two great nuclear powers may seek to clarify the complexities and mitigate the dangers of their strategic relationship in the nuclear-missile age.

The two sides are not, of course, speaking just to one another or wholly in the interest of better understanding. Each is seeking to advance its policy interests, to enhance its posture of deterrence, to obtain political advantage from its military power or prevent the other from doing so, to impress the authority of its position upon allies and onlookers, and so on. There is at the same time a perceptible desire on both sides to promote better, or at least more precise, communications with respect to military policy, strategy, and corollary problems. This in itself may be a small start toward a more fruitful and intelligent strategic discourse between East and West, with the participants talking past each other less and to each other more.

Soviet Strategy *by Marshal Sokolovskii*

The most notable new expression of Soviet strategic thinking is a revised and slightly expanded edition of the book *Military Strategy,* written by a collective team of Soviet military experts headed by Marshal V. D. Sokolovskii. The original edition, published in mid-1962, was described in the Soviet Union as the first comprehensive work on military strategy to appear there in more than three decades. It attracted a good deal of attention abroad, so much so, indeed, that it was brought out in English translation by two different American publishers, not to mention versions in several other languages.[1]

The revised Sokolovskii edition appeared in the Soviet Union in November 1963. The interval of fifteen months between editions was unusually short for such a work. This, plus obvious Soviet awareness of Western interest in the original volume, suggests that the Soviets regard the book as an important vehicle of external as well as internal communication on strategic problems of the nuclear age. Another noteworthy Soviet contribution to the discussion of strategy was a direct riposte to U.S. commentary on the first Sokolovskii edition, published recently in the Soviet newspaper *Red Star* (November 2, 1963) over the signatures of four of the Sokolovskii authors. Like a number of other recent expressions of Soviet strategic thinking, this article gave evidence of Russian sensitivity to Western interpretations of Soviet military policy and posture, and contained "corrective messages" on such questions as escalation of local conflicts, Soviet second-strike capability, and the pre-emptive strike.

A Trying Period for Soviet Leaders

The last year and a half has been a critical and trying period for the leaders of the Soviet Union. They have been confronted by serious internal difficulties in agriculture and the economy; the dispute with Communist China has worsened, calling into question Soviet leadership of the world Communist movement; and the after-effects of the Cuban missile confrontation with the United States have underscored the failure of this effort to redress the strategic imbalance between the United States and the Soviet Union. These difficulties have sharpened the problems facing the Soviet leadership in the strategic field, including the central problem of the allocation of resources between competing economic and defense requirements. The developments of this period also have left their imprint on Soviet strategic thought, which shows an awareness of the need to adjust policy to changes in the character of the strategic environment.

There is first an insistent effort to enhance the credibility of the Soviet deterrent posture in Western eyes, coupled with an attempt to disabuse the United States of any idea that it can count on a successful first strike or draw political advantage from its strategic position vis-à-vis the Soviet Union. The methods employed to put this dual point across range from doctrinaire play upon the theme that Soviet military strength and readiness to employ it should be taken seriously by the West to fairly close-knit technical arguments to demonstrate the certainty of the Soviet ability to deliver a retaliatory nuclear strike.

One finds an example of the first type of warning in the preface to the revised Sokolovskii book, where the authors state that the Communist countries do not wish to ". . . leave the enemy with any illusions that they are unprepared to rebuff him." Citing a pamphlet by Marshal Malinovskii, the

Soviet Minister of Defense, to the effect that in Soviet eyes the best means of defense is not an attack, but rather "a warning to the enemy about our strength and readiness to destroy him at the first attempt to carry out an act of aggression," the Sokolovskii authors then observe: "That is why, rather than hiding our views on the nature and means of waging a future war, we have revealed them in the book, 'Military Strategy'."[2]

A more precise argument seeking to establish that the Soviet Union is now militarily in a sound position to carry out a retaliatory second strike can be found in an article by I. Glagolev and V. Larionov in the November 1963 issue of *International Affairs*. The authors assert that "foreign military analysts" have erroneously concluded that ". . . Soviet nuclear rocket weapons are highly vulnerable and are designed for a first and not a counterstrike."[3] The authors then make a series of points designed to refute this impression.

First, they argue that Soviet measures to disperse, harden, conceal, and otherwise reduce the vulnerability of their strategic forces mean that an enemy "cannot hope to knock out all these counterstrike means simultaneously." Next, they contend that modern warning techniques make it possible for the defender to avoid being taken by surprise, and that even missiles "can be detected in the first section of their flight path"—which, by the way, represents a rather novel claim for very early detection of missile launchings. A third point advanced to buttress their argument is that the attacker would be limited to a relatively small initial strike with missiles if he wishes to achieve "a measure of even relative surprise." The article discounts U.S. bomber forces as a factor in an initial attack on the grounds that they ". . . would hardly produce any element of surprise, in the modern sense." This tendency to re-evaluate the factor of surprise is to be noted also in the revised Sokolovskii volume, which, while charging that the United States is still actively studying ways to achieve "maximum surprise," suggests at the same time that changing conditions may now be reducing U.S. confidence in the feasibility of conducting a surprise attack.[4]

Rather interestingly, the Glagolev-Larionov article does

not specifically spell out the problem of target location as one of the factors that would have a significant bearing on the success of a U.S. attack. By contrast, in a new discussion of U.S. counterforce strategy in the second edition of the Sokolovskii book, the problem of locating targets receives great emphasis. In fact, this problem emerges from the Sokolovskii authors' analysis as one of the principal reasons for increasing doubt as to the political and military effectiveness of a counterforce strategy: ". . . the political value of a counterforce strategy may be depreciating even more rapidly than its military value, because it becomes increasingly difficult for the representatives of the military command to convince the political leadership of the absolute reliability of their plans and calculations, based on fragmentary intelligence data on enemy targets."[5]

The new treatment of U.S. "counterforce" or "city-sparing" strategy in the revised Sokolovskii work furnishes another example, incidentally, of the tendency to present a more detailed and objectively argued analysis than has been customary in Soviet military discourse. The authors review the evolution of this strategy and examine various basic requirements which they say must be met in order for it to be "realistic and practical."[6] The resulting analysis indicates that the authors have at least done their homework on the subject, even though their argument is cast in terms designed to support Soviet charges of aggressive U.S. plans and to fortify claims of an invulnerable Soviet retaliatory posture.

The Main Element of Soviet Military Power

In connection with efforts to reinforce the credibility of the Soviet deterrent posture, a notable feature of current Soviet military discourse is the increasing emphasis placed on the strategic missile forces as the main element of Soviet military power. This reflects not only a serious endeavor to adapt the doctrine and structure of the Soviet military establishment to a new technological environment, but also a desire to exploit them for political and psychological purposes.

Today, the strategic missile forces bear a special cachet in

Soviet discussion. They are frequently described as "the mighty shield standing in the way of the imperialist aggressors,"[7] and the "special care" which the Presidium of the Central Committee and Khrushchev personally have bestowed on their development is often mentioned. Besides being pictured as the guarantor of Soviet security, these forces also are credited with being a major tool of Soviet foreign policy. Thus, for example, the Glagolev-Larionov article ascribes a string of diplomatic victories to the Soviet missile forces, observing that the Soviet Union has "used its nuclear rocket might to shield Socialist Cuba, to avert aggression against the Chinese People's Republic, and to safeguard the independence and freedom of Egypt, Syria and Iraq."

Some treatment of the missile forces in the Soviet press in the fall of 1963 dwelt on the superior virtues of missile personnel in a fashion which may have been meant to pave the way psychologically for further reductions in the traditional branches of the Soviet armed forces—a move which Khrushchev later (in December) indicated he intended. An article in *Red Star* (November 6), for example, seemed to be aimed at spinning a mystique around Soviet rocket personnel. Remarking that a strategic rocketeer may not be distinguishable outwardly from an officer in any other branch of the Soviet armed forces, the author went on to say: "But if you knew that here before you stands a lieutenant or a colonel of strategic rockets—then, word of honor, you would doff your cap in his presence."

A further feature of Soviet discourse today is a consistently negative attitude toward concepts of the controlled use of strategic weapons and restraints designed to limit damage if a major war should occur. The treatment of U.S. counterforce strategy in the new Sokolovskii edition exemplifies Soviet resistance to what the authors describe as "some sort of suggestion to the Soviet Union on 'rules' for the conduct of nuclear war."[8] Arguing that this strategy is founded on "illusory" American hopes of saving the capitalist system by conducting a "so-called 'controlled' nuclear war," the authors point to what they regard as obstacles to such a strategy. First, how "convince" others of the need to adhere to "new rules" of sparing cities when "most military targets are located in or near cities?" Second, if these rules are to be followed, the United States and its European allies should start to remove all their military installations from cities. However, this is not only unrealistic, but as noted in the Western press, if such a move were carried out, ". . . the U.S.S.R. would draw the conclusion that the United States was preparing to attack."

Throughout Soviet military writing there is insistence that only measures to avert war are a permissible subject of discussion, which of course ignores the question of trying to place limits on the level of violence in case a war unwanted by either side should begin through accident or miscalculation. Nevertheless, the Glagolev-Larionov article displays a notably defensive attitude on this question when taking note of Western comment that "the Soviet strategic concept is rigid and does not set any limits to the use of nuclear weapons in the event of war." The article then goes on to argue, however, that the Soviet refusal to entertain agreements which would have the effect of "legalizing" nuclear war is actually more humanitarian than the position of Western advocates of measures to limit destruction.

On the question of the likelihood of war, current Soviet views remain ambiguous. The general line, consonant with efforts to cultivate an atmosphere of détente in East-West relations, is that the danger of war has abated somewhat, thanks largely to respect in the "imperialist camp" for Soviet military might. The new Sokolovskii volume reflects a divided mind on this matter. On the same page, for example, it offers a slightly more optimistic judgment on the likelihood of war in the current period, but continues to stress the danger of Western attack on the Soviet Union, "despite the growing influence of factors ensuring the preservation of peace."[9] In general, Soviet military spokesmen seem more inclined than the political leaders to emphasize that the danger of war is ever-present. Although "official" views are generally foreboding, the impromptu remarks of political leaders are sometimes more relaxed, as when Khrushchev suggested in the spring of 1962 that threats of war from both sides had the effect of canceling each other out and stabilizing things, which, as he put it, ". . . is why we consider the situation to be good."[10]

Local and Limited Wars

The subject of limited war customarily has received much less attention in Soviet military literature than has general nuclear war. By insisting that general war will be violent and global in character, and by rejecting the idea of limitations on its scope and destructiveness once it has begun, the Soviets may have hoped to strengthen deterrence by emphasizing an unqualified Soviet nuclear response. Similarly, on the danger of small wars, the Soviets' unvarying stress on the great danger of escalation has reflected a rather high degree of doctrinal rigidity.

Today, however, there are some signs that the Soviet position on local and limited wars is undergoing change. A good deal of inconsistency characterizes Soviet treatment of the subject, and no unified doctrine of limited war applying to Soviet forces has emerged. Nevertheless, more attention is being given to the possibility of local wars, and there seems to be some effort, particularly in military journals, to treat the subject of escalation in a less arbitrary way. These tendencies, which were evident to a small degree in the first Sokolovskii volume, are still more apparent in the new edition and in other current Soviet commentary.

The most interesting evidence of an effort to redefine the Soviet doctrinal position on limited war and escalation is to be found in the November 1963 *Red Star* article by four of the Sokolovskii authors, who went to rather unusual lengths to make the point that Soviet doctrine does not preach the "inevitable" escalation of limited wars into general war. Taking issue with the U.S. editors of their book, they said they had merely warned that local wars "can grow into a world war," and they charged that the U.S. editors had deliberately ignored an important proviso linking escalation with the participation of the nuclear powers in local conflicts. In point of fact, this charge amounted to setting up a straw man, for the U.S. editors in question had quoted in full from the pertinent passage in the Sokolovskii volume, which stated: "One must emphasize that the present international system and the present state of military technology will cause any armed conflict to develop, inevitably, into a general war if the nuclear powers are drawn into it."[11]

The Sokolovskii authors then resorted in their *Red Star* article to the curious step of misquoting themselves in order to reinforce the point they were interested in making. In citing the above passage from their book, they quietly omitted the key word, "inevitably." This particular omission, along with general denial of the inevitability of escalation, represents a notable shift in the usual Soviet argument. The Russians may hope thereby to reduce their vulnerability to Chinese charges that a hard line on escalation immobilizes support of national liberation movements, and at the same time to deter the West from feeling that it has greater freedom to act because of hypersensitive Soviet concern about escalation. It is of some interest, incidentally, that it has been the Soviet military who have recently placed the greatest emphasis on vigorous Soviet support of national liberation struggles.

Related to the apparent Soviet desire to convey an image of greater flexibility in supporting local conflicts is a new suggestion that in the case of certain third-power conflicts the Soviet Union might try to avoid expanding the conflict by withholding attacks against the United States in return for U.S. abstention. This "message" emerges somewhat tentatively from the November *Red Star* article by the Sokolovskii authors. Commenting on a statement by the U.S. editors of their book to the effect that Soviet doctrine seems to imply a retaliatory strike against the United States in the event of Western action against a Soviet bloc member, the Sokolovskii authors denied that this was a valid interpretation of the Soviet position. In their book, the Soviet authors said, they were dealing simply with the case of "an attack by imperialist forces" on a socialist country, and "the United States was not mentioned." Only if the United States were "to carry out such an attack itself" would the Soviet Union be impelled to deliver a retaliatory blow, "in which case the United States would have been the aggressor."

This circumlocution appears to be more than an effort to avoid the implication that there are circumstances under which the Soviet Union might strike first. Rather, the Soviet authors seem to be trying to convey the thought that there are some situations where the Soviet Union may be anxious to dampen the possibilities of automatic escalation, by distinguishing between the United States and third powers in the event of local conflict. That the Soviets are thinking specifically of Central Europe is suggested by Khrushchev's references to the high escalation potential of a local clash between countries in the heart of Europe,[12] and by statements elsewhere that West Germany might start a local war against East Germany on its own initiative.[13]

Despite what seems to be a general Soviet desire to be reassuring to the United States, the Soviet position on pre-emption remains, perhaps intentionally, ambivalent. Thus, for example, while the Sokolovskii authors went to some pains in their *Red Star* article to disclaim that statements of Soviet readiness to frustrate and break up an enemy attack are meant to imply pre-emption, the revised edition of their book still adheres to a formula that calls for ". . . breaking up the opponent's aggressive plans by dealing him in good time a crushing blow."[14] The Glagolev-Larionov excursus also contains a statement suggesting that the Soviet Union may contemplate a strategy approximating that of pre-emption, in fact if not in name. Speaking in a context where the Soviet Union represents the defensive side, the article states: "The first rockets and bombers of the side on the defensive would take off *even before the aggressor's first rockets, to say nothing of his bombers, reached their targets.*" (Italics in the original.) If this description is to be taken at face value, a fine line indeed exists between the Soviet conception of a pre-emptive and a retaliatory strike.[15] At the very least the passage seems meant to convey the notion that Soviet response to warning of a strategic attack would be instant and automatic, without waiting for incontrovertible evidence that an attack actually had been launched at Soviet targets.

The Balance of Military Power

Much of the East-West strategic dialogue to date has centered on the question whether the balance of military power in the world favors one side or the other. Today, the Soviet voice seems to reflect growing uncertainty whether the Soviet Union's best interest lies in asserting military superiority over the West, at the risk of stimulating more vigorous Western defense efforts, or in settling for the notion of a second-best position. The predominant note in Soviet discourse up to now clearly has favored a doctrine calling for military superiority over the West. Khrushchev himself more than once made plain that the policy of peaceful coexistence rests in essence on the premise that the Soviet bloc countries, as he put it, "have a rapidly growing economy and surpass the imperialist camp in armaments and armed forces."[16] A typical expression of Soviet commitment to a policy of military superiority was the statement made in the spring of 1963 by Marshal Andrei Grechko, Soviet First Deputy Minister of Defense, and commander of the Warsaw Pact forces: "The Communist Party and the Soviet government base their military policy on the fact that as long as disarmament has not been implemented, the armed forces of the socialist commonwealth must always be superior to those of the imperialists."[17]

On the other hand, it is recognized that there are liabilities in professing a policy of military superiority, for if the Soviet military posture is made to look excessively formidable, the result may well be simply to spur the West to greater efforts, leaving the Soviet Union relatively worse off than before. For a country whose resources already seem strained by the high cost of arms competition, this is a serious consideration, and a principal reason for cultivating an atmosphere of détente. A revealing sign of Soviet wavering on the question of military superiority appeared recently in an article by the same Marshal Grechko, who some six months before had spoken categorically for a policy of military superiority. Grechko took note of Western military preparations, singling out remarks by Secretary of Defense Robert McNamara at the NATO Council meeting in December on "the number of American long-range missiles and the number of bombers on air alert." Western preparations, Grechko said, were meant "to attain military superiority over the Soviet Union." Instead of responding with the customary assertion that Soviet forces are superior to those of the West, Grechko adopted a notably restrained tone. The Soviet Union, he said, "has sufficient means to restrain any aggressor, no matter what kind of nuclear power he may possess." Further, said Grechko, the Soviet Union is not "in the least interested in an armaments race," but merely intends to maintain its defense "at the level necessary to assure peace."[18]

At bottom, Soviet policy on the question of military superiority is complicated by many factors. Not only is the Soviet Union at a relative disadvantage in resources, but, as experience shows, it has managed to live for a considerable period in a position of strategic inferiority to its major adversary without being subjected to the "imperialist attack" so often predicted. The underlying issue hinges intimately on what the limits of military power in the nuclear age are understood to be. Can the use of military power, or the threat of its use, enable one side to alter the political situation to its advantage, or is the feasible limit merely to prevent the other side from attempting to do so? Putting it another way, has war or the threat of war lost its meaning as an instrument of policy? Interestingly enough, an internal discussion has developed in the Soviet Union during the past year, and has carried over into the polemics with the Chinese, over the continuing validity of the Leninist thesis on war as a continuation of politics by violent means.[19] This is more than a matter of splitting doctrinal hairs.

If on the one hand there is still a prospect that war can be won—or lost—in a meaningful sense, then it might seem worth the effort to strive for a war-winning strategy and military forces commensurate to this task. But if on the other hand there should no longer seem to be anything to choose between victor and vanquished in a nuclear war, then the course to take might look quite different. So far as Soviet military policy is concerned, a second-best solution might be readily rationalized as the best solution. That is to say, the

Soviet leadership might settle indefinitely for a strategy of deterrence and Soviet forces at a level sufficient to maintain credibility but still clearly inferior to those of the adversary. Perhaps it is safe to say that neither the Soviet political nor military leaders have yet made up their minds on this issue, if indeed they have posed it in this way at all. However, life itself, as Khrushchev sometimes puts it, may now be making a place for the matter on the agenda.

It would be premature in the extreme to suggest that the Soviet image of the West, as projected in the strategic dialogue, now mirrors reality with reasonable fidelity. Soviet perception of the West is still filtered through ideological and parochial suspicions that produce a woefully distorted picture, particularly of Western motives and intentions. At the same time, the picture of the West that emerges from recent Soviet strategic discourse is beginning in some respects to take on more objective dimensions, notably in treating the United States as a strong but withal responsible adversary. This in itself can be regarded as a small advance.

NOTES

1. The two U.S. versions of the first Sokolovskii edition were: *Military Strategy: Soviet Doctrine and Concepts,* published by Frederick A. Praeger, New York, 1963, with an Introduction by Raymond L. Garthoff; and *Soviet Military Strategy,* published by Prentice-Hall, Englewood Cliffs, N.J., 1963, with an Analytical Introduction and annotations by Herbert S. Dinerstein, Leon Gouré, and Thomas W. Wolfe of the RAND Corporation.

2. Marshal V. D. Sokolovskii, *et al., Voennaia Strategiia (Military Strategy),* second edition, Voenizdat Ministerstva Oborony S.S.S.R., Moscow, 1963, p. 3 and 4. Hereafter referred to as *Military Strategy,* 2nd ed. The pamphlet referred to here was by Marshal R. Y. Malinovskii, *Bditel'no stoyat na strazhe mira* (Vigilantly Stand Guard over the Peace), Voenizdat Ministerstva Oborony S.S.S.R., Moscow, 1962, p. 25. Malinovskii had alluded on previous occasions to the value of "warning the enemy." See, for example, his article in *Kommunist,* No. 7, May 1962, p. 15.

3. The authorship of this article represents an interesting combination. Glagolev is a Soviet specialist on international relations and disarmament affairs who has been active in promoting

the informal discussion of disarmament questions with various American scientists and government officials. Colonel Larionov, a Soviet military expert and a prolific writer on strategic affairs, is one of the authors of the Sokolovskii work. The collaboration of these two men marks a departure from customary Soviet practice, suggesting that the particular competence of a military specialist like Larionov was deemed desirable to reinforce the policy arguments of the *International Affairs* article.

4. *Military Strategy*, 2nd ed., p. 90.
5. Ibid., p. 87.
6. Ibid., p. 85–86. These requirements, as discussed by the Sokolovskii authors, include: (1) reliable reconnaissance; (2) large numbers of missiles of great accuracy, reliability, and readiness, "since there are considerably more military targets than cities"; (3) reliable systems of command and control, warning and communications; (4) careful coordination of missile strikes and other military operations; (5) surprise.
7. *Red Star*, November 19, 1963.
8. *Military Strategy*, 2nd ed., p. 85.
9. Op. cit., p. 232.
10. Remarks by Khrushchev in Maritsa, Bulgaria, on May 15, 1962, broadcast on that date by the Sofia domestic radio, but not circulated in the Soviet Union.
11. *Military Strategy*, 2nd ed., p. 44.
12. *Pravda*, January 4, 1964.
13. *Military Strategy*, 2nd ed., p. 362.
14. Ibid., p. 260.
15. There are large practical differences between a pre-emptive strike—which by definition would be intended to break up or blunt an enemy attack that had already been set in motion—and a retaliatory or second-strike, which would be mounted only after having absorbed the full force of the enemy's initial blow. Soviet rhetoric customarily claims the practical results to be expected from a pre-emptive strike, while disclaiming at the same time that the Soviet Union would ever contemplate any course but a retaliatory strike. Ambiguity as to where the Soviets really stand on this question is the result.
16. *Pravda*, February 28, 1963.
17. *Izvestia*, May 9, 1963.
18. *Red Star*, December 22, 1963.
19. Soviet discussion of this question may be found in the following articles: Boris Dimitryev, "Brass Hats, Peking and Clausewitz," *Izvestia*, September 24, 1963; Colonel P. Trifonenkov, "War and Politics," *Red Star*, October 30, 1963; Marshal S. Biryuzov, "Policy and Nuclear Arms," *Izvestia*, December 11, 1963. See also *Military Strategy*, 2nd ed., pp. 25, 216.

SOVIET EDUCATION FOR SCIENTIFIC
AND TECHNICAL SUPREMACY

by Nicholas DeWitt

Dr. DeWitt is Associate Professor of Economics and Government in the College of Arts and Sciences, Indiana University; Director of the Carnegie Project—"International Survey of Educational Development and Planning." He was formerly a Director of the Non-Western Studies Project for the State of Indiana and, as a Research Associate of the Russian Research Center, Harvard University, author of Education and Professional Employment in the USSR, *National Science Foundation, 1961.*

This selection is adapted from an address, "Soviet Science Education, The Status of Teaching Sciences in the United States and the U.S.S.R.," presented at the Institute for Soviet and East European Studies, John Carroll University, Cleveland, Ohio, September 20, 1963.

Throughout the world today fundamental changes are taking place in the assessment of conditions under which social and economic development is achieved. The traditional approach to the problem of economic growth, which assigned well-nigh an exclusive role to the accumulation of material wealth as a precondition to industrial development, is giving way to new trends in economic thinking. It is increasingly being stressed that economic development and social change are conditioned by investment in human capital. Recognizing that education is the main tool in the development of the human resources required to augment the strategic capability of a nation, Soviet planners over the last few decades have been busily engaged in the buildup of high-level professional manpower, particularly specialists in science and technology needed for their industrial expansion.

The Soviet Commitment to Functional Education

In the last few years, the new phrase "Soviet commitment to education" has become popular. But much of the fancy talk about the Communist commitment to education comes dangerously close to missing the really important point: what we must ask ourselves is the basic question—*commitment to what kind of education?* The answer is disarmingly simple: first, last, and always, the Soviet commitment to education is a commitment to scientific education, to technological education, to an education which will enable Soviet citizens to perform specialized functional tasks to the best of their ability in their expanding industrial society.

The Russians orient their educational effort so as to maximize the returns from it for the advancement of their political, military, and economic objectives. The Communists do not believe in education for education's sake. They do not believe in education for the individual's sake. The Russians do not want any part of liberal or general humanistic education. They don't want any generalists at all—they want only specialists. Their main objective is to offer *functional* education so as to train, to mold, to develop the skills, the professions, and the specialists required by their long-run development programs, who are capable of performing the tasks of running the industrial and bureaucratic machinery of the Communist state. And in order to accomplish this, the Russians *have been,* they *are,* and they *will be* training an army of scientists and technologists. The integration of education into over-all economic planning in the Soviet Union has caused a pronounced shift toward functional education as the dominant criterion as to the extent, type, and quality of education which the government offers and which qualified and selected individuals may receive.

Education in the U.S. and U.S.S.R.: Basic Differences

In contrast, Western nations—the United States in particular —have followed a much broader approach in education. Here, the individual determines what kind of education and how much of it he will seek, be it in response to the demands of the economy or to a variety of consumptionist aspirations—diversified cultural, social, and self-enlightenment needs and aspirations. As a result of these differences in the basic educational objectives in the two nations, the U.S. system of education has emerged as the more diversified one, accommodating substantially larger numbers of people than the more specialized and still highly selective educational system of the U.S.S.R.

The educational systems in the Soviet Union and in the United States can be compared in quantitative terms in relationship to respective age groups of the population. Elementary education and junior secondary education are nearly universal in the U.S.S.R., as well as in the United States. It is on the senior secondary and higher levels that the major differences between the Soviet and American educational efforts are evident. In the United States about 90 per cent of the secondary school-age population are actually enrolled in schools. In the U.S.S.R. only about one-half of the respective levels are found in educational establishments. If we were to consider only the regular upper secondary grades (8–10) of Soviet schools, then about one-third of the appropriate age group is in attendance. While in the United States about one-fourth of the college-age population is actually enrolled in institutions of higher learning on a full-time basis, the corresponding proportion in the Soviet Union is only 6 per cent. In the Soviet case, however, if part-time education enrollments are considered, the rates of attendance would obviously increase (to about 12 per cent). In short, Soviet education is much more selective than is the case in the United States.

Although professing the aims of general and well-rounded education, the Soviet educational system in reality is uniquely geared to the training of specialized manpower. By means of mass persuasion, by means of coercion if necessary, and by means of bold incentives, the Soviet state makes every effort to channel the best and largest share of available talent into professional occupations and into engineering and scientific professions in particular. This is clearly evident when we compare the professional manpower situation and current training trends in the Soviet Union and the United States.

Educational Trends in the U.S.S.R.

The historical trends in the production of higher education graduates, the main source of high-level manpower, may be summarized as follows: At the professional level, the Soviet Union produced during the thirty-five years from 1926–60 some 4.5 million graduates of higher educational institutions, or about 40 per cent less than were trained in colleges and universities in the United States during the same period (total 7.7 million). In spite of this, the Soviet Union graduated 1.8 times as many engineers as did the United States (U.S.S.R.– 1,200,000; United States–700,000). There were 2.4 times as many agricultural field graduates in the Soviet Union as in the United States (U.S.S.R.–440,000; United States–180,- 000). While in all health fields put together the number of Soviet and American graduates was about the same, in medicine alone, 2.4 times as many "physicians" (460,000) were graduated in the U.S.S.R. than medical doctors (190,000) in the United States. The U.S. trained about 800,000 graduates with science majors, while Soviet university and pedagogical institutes graduated 480,000 science majors and science teachers.

While the Soviet training of specialists in engineering, medical, and agricultural occupations proceeded rapidly, the number of higher education graduates trained in other fields was relatively small. In all other fields, United States colleges and universities trained 5,800,000, or almost three times as many as did Soviet higher educational establishments (1,900,000). In the social science fields the Soviet Union trained only about one-tenth as many persons as were trained in these fields in the United States. In the humanities, liberal arts, and other miscellaneous fields, Soviet higher education trained but a small fraction of the number of persons trained in these fields in American colleges and universities.

At the present time, the Soviet Union produces annually:

116,000 engineering graduates, three times more than we train; 30,000 physicians, about five times more than we train; 31,000 agricultural specialists, about one-third more than we train. But it produces only 143,000 pedagogical, humanities, and social field graduates, or half as many as we train in the socio-economic and humanities fields. For teachers, alone, the numbers are about the same.

The scorecard looks unfavorable, no matter how many reservations one has about the validity of such numerical comparisons. It is all the more disheartening because during the last ten years there has not been a single study in the United States or in Western Europe which could challenge the proposition that in *qualitative* terms, Soviet science and engineering education is not inferior to that in the West. Soviet faults are many and complaints about shortcomings are monotonous; but the basic proposition of qualitative comparability (and at times superiority of Soviet science and technical education) remains in force.

Two Central Problems

It is obvious that the Soviet success in training such large numbers of specialists on the professional level depends, to a large degree, upon secondary school training. Soviet education today is in a state of flux. During the decade of the 1950's, two central problems arose. The first related to the educational policy of the Soviet regime, and the second to current demographic—labor force—trends in the Soviet Union. The educational policy problems are basically as follows. First, it was not until recently that the goal of universal secondary education has even begun to be approached. As late as 1952, less than 10 per cent of seventeen-year-olds were able to complete the entire ten-year program of Soviet primary and secondary schooling. Either because of personal circumstances or the stringent academic requirements, some 90 per cent of the youngsters fell by the wayside. But by 1956 there were close to 1.5 million secondary school graduates. In relation to the corresponding age group, the rate of completion of the ten-year school increased from less than 10 to 35 per cent.

Admission quotas in higher education, however, did not expand appreciably in the intervening period, and consequently the *majority* of recent ten-year-school graduates found themselves outside the walls of institutions of higher learning. Meanwhile, although there have been some revisions in the primary and secondary school curriculum, among which the introduction of manual training and workshop activities are to be particularly noted, the program of skilled training and vocational preparation has *not* made much headway. As a result, in the course of the last few years the problem has reared up with full force as to what should be the next step to prepare secondary school graduates for *practical* occupations—or simply employment—immediately upon graduation.

The second problem was that the Second World War not only made for tremendous physical devastation within the Soviet Union but also played havoc with the Soviet population. In 1959 the Soviet population was 208 million, while twenty years earlier, just before the outbreak of the war, it was already 192 million. Had it not been for the war, the Soviet population would be thirty or forty million more than it actually is today. Also, the birth rate declined drastically during the war, and it is only natural to expect that the heavy losses in population were reflected in the school enrollment. While in the fall of 1948 in the elementary grades (1–4) of Soviet schools there were some twenty-four million youngsters, by 1953 their number had been cut in half, to only twelve million. This staggering decline occurred in the course of five years. Recovery since 1953 has been very slow, and in 1958 there were still only eighteen million pupils in the elementary grades. The obvious implication is that the prime age groups for new additions to the labor force, as well as for those who are to serve in the armed forces or to continue their training in Soviet institutions of higher learning, are now considerably reduced. The year 1963 marks indeed the low point in number of eighteen-year-olds. The Soviet Union in 1963 had only two million eighteen-year-olds, instead of the normal five million in this age group. This deficit will continue to be felt throughout the 1960's.

Educational Reform

These two forces are considered to be the most influential in triggering Khrushchev's "Educational Reform," begun in 1958 and scheduled for completion in 1963. No doubt political factors also had a role, but economic considerations predominated. For several years Western observers were quite puzzled by what the future would hold for Soviet education. Now we have enough evidence to state conclusively that the reform will not diminish, but will in effect *intensify* not only functional, but particularly the scientific and technical orientation of Soviet schooling.

As far as general education and the social sciences and humanities are concerned, the ax did fall. The new educational reform provides for reorganization of the Soviet complete primary-secondary school from ten to eleven years. The first eight years will be universally available and compulsory. After completion of the eight-year school, most youths at age fifteen or sixteen will be integrated into productive activity in the labor force, and their schooling may be continued on a *part-time* basis only. The three upper secondary school grades, 9–11, are called "general polytechnical school with production training," and these grades are more selective than were grades 8–10 in 1956. Instead of the 50 per cent age group they accommodate only one-third. The scientific and technical content is intensified in these three upper grades, as well as through the general school structure itself, as revealed by a brief comparison of the ten-year and the new eleven-year curriculum, with allocations of instructions approximately as follows:

	1956 Curriculum 10-year		1963 Curriculum 11-year	
	Instr. Hours	%	Instr. Hours	%
General subjects (language, literature, humanities, and social sciences)	4700	44	4900	38
Scientific subjects (sciences and mathematics)	3300	31	3700	29
Applied activities and vocational skill subjects	2800	25	4200	33
TOTAL	10,800	100	12,800	100

In sum the bulk of these additional two thousand hours of instruction are to be allocated to vocational subjects, workshop, and industrial practice. The sciences gained four hundred instruction hours, and the addition to the humanities was only two hundred hours. But what this redistribution overlooks is that the "polytechnical subjects" are exclusively science- and technology-oriented. Over one-third of polytechnical instruction is in technology-applied science, and two-thirds will be industrial arts and skill subjects. In other words, although the instruction is to be applied in nature, it will be closely tied in with regular science and mathematics instruction. In essence, sciences gained well over eleven thousand instruction hours.

Science Education: "The Light and Hope of Humanity"

In examining Soviet science education, there is an additional consideration. In the Soviet Union, with education calculated to serve political ends, a central dilemma has always been the inculcation of objective knowledge—and I emphasize "objective" knowledge—without jeopardizing ideological and purely subjective political aims. In order to cope with this problem, one must understand that Communist education in general, and Soviet-type education in particular, has been made *functional*, that is, practical, applied, and specialized.

Among academic subjects, both on the secondary and higher education levels, only the sciences and mathematics are relatively free from political bias. Languages, literature, history, geography, and other social science and humanity courses are invariably slanted politically—the superiority of the Communist system over any other. Distortion is built directly into course contents.

While this is usually not the case with the sciences, they also are used deliberately to serve political indoctrination goals. In themselves, science instruction subjects may not be biased, but the course contents are used to serve ideological aims. In Soviet practice this is achieved by linking science education with an atheistic upbringing.

Soviet ideology is based on the categorical assumption that science and religion are not only irreconcilable, but mutually antagonistic. The fundamental philosophical tenet of Communist doctrine is the so-called "dialectical materialism," which is in effect a crude mechanistic materialism of nature and social evolution. Any expression of religious belief or sentiment (despite proclamation of the so-called "neutrality" of the Soviet state toward church) is viewed by the regime with contempt, which is carried over into educational practice. Without exception, all types of science education in the Soviet schools are used quite deliberately as a vehicle for atheistic indoctrination. In the last two years or so, because of an officially acknowledged upsurge of religiosity, there has been a marked increase in anti-religious propaganda in the Soviet schools. Science is represented as light and hope for humanity; religion, as darkness and the source of human misery and social evil. Khrushchev himself heralded the new assault on religion. "Our public education," he said, "our popularization of science, our study of the laws of the universe should leave no room for faith in God." Soviet youngsters are repeatedly told today that the Russian space probes prove there is no heaven.

As already mentioned, the Soviet "high school" of the 1960's is called "general polytechnical school with production training." As the wording suggests, the polytechnical-vocational component of education has now come to the fore. The curriculum remains standard as far as academic subjects are concerned. The major change is that some vocational and skill training subjects have been added on top of the academic courses.

With this reorientation of Soviet schooling, a cardinal problem remains: how to achieve labor-oriented schooling for the masses without sacrificing altogether the essential academic preparation of the relatively small number of persons required by the socio-economic plan to be trained for advanced professional tasks. The solution consists in superimposing on the standard general education curriculum a localized system of supplemental labor training shaped in accordance with local economic needs and the availability of skilled training outlets. In essence, these measures open up the path for introducing in the U.S.S.R. diversified and comprehensive secondary schooling such as exists in many other countries of the world. The purely academic "high school" in Russia is dead, and this too poses a problem.

It seems fair to say that the vocationalization of the Soviet secondary school is bound to have some negative effects upon the quality of academic instruction. The Russians are fully aware of this. Although the Soviet authorities claim that labor preparation of youth provides a very harmonious complement to academic schooling, there are already many reports in the Soviet press that such harmony is far from reality.

In mathematics and sciences, the situation has not been so bad. In the first place, there were actual gains in the curricular load and the content of science courses. In the second place, the new programs have been organized in such a way that the new polytechnical undertakings are very often oriented toward technology and applied science, and some educators (aside from political talk that this is such a healthy thing) insist that there may be some benefits from the polytechnical programs to the science-mathematics part of the academic curriculum. But the humanities, in terms of curricular emphasis and course content, have suffered most, and there is now a wide outcry among Soviet educators that preparation in languages and literature has been undermined and now should be strengthened again. Although their voices are loud, so far they have not been able to reverse the trend.

Conclusions

The Soviet school reforms are really an attempt to revamp, to change the school system from above so as to make it more responsive to pressing national needs—skilled manpower and specialized technical education. It is a drastic educational venture in this sense, for it proceeds from above; but it is also a dramatic enterprise, the basic assumption being that the state—the central planning board—knows the basis for deciding and determining what education individuals ought to have.

Individual choices and preferences are not even considered, and the age-old issue of education—what kind and for what purpose—has been explicitly resolved not in favor of the individual, but in favor of the Soviet state.

It is in this context that we must talk about the changing role of education in a modern society. We must recognize for a fact that the Soviet educational system succeeds indeed in developing the human mind to a high degree of competence in many areas, especially those vital to the technological effort of the nation and its power potential in the world. But, at the same time, the Soviet type of schooling deprives the individual of his potential to exercise *independent* and creative thought in the sphere of social values. Applied technical training, now added to the Russian secondary curriculum, certainly furthers technical competence; but it apparently adds precious little to the cultural, ethical, or social values which are cherished so much in our own educational effort.

Soviet science and education *do* serve the state, the military, political and power objectives. But in pursuing these objectives, they often fulfill their self-purposiveness and thus get full benefit and full credit. We often fail to grasp this in trying to understand the Soviet effort. Today the Soviet Union is in a new phase in its economic evolution, the essence of which is that more hands doing physical labor have to be replaced as rapidly as possible by machines and higher quality of technical skills. The army of scientists, engineers, and technologists which the Soviet Union has trained in recent years and will continue to train is to be deployed to achieve this task. In order to succeed in this, what the Soviet Union apparently needs most of all today is higher quality in the laboring and technical skills. And Soviet education, as in the past, is being called upon to perform a specific, functional task in developing these skills. This is the essence of Premier Khrushchev's educational reform. I hope we will never have to resort to veering our educational philosophy so that it serves the state rather than the individual; but in order to avoid such a course, we will have to begin to do much more for the betterment of our own education. For education can be no better than the society it serves.

PEACE IN OUR TIME?

by Hans J. Morgenthau

> *Dr. Morgenthau received degrees from the Universities
> of Munich and Frankfort. From 1949–51 he was a
> consultant to the State Department, and is at present
> consultant to the Departments of Defense and State.
> Dr. Morgenthau has been visiting professor at numer-
> ous institutions, including Harvard, Yale, Columbia,
> and the Princeton Institute for Advanced Study, and
> is currently Albert A. Michelson Distinguished Service
> Professor of Political Science and Modern History at
> the University of Chicago and Director of the Center
> for the Study of American Foreign and Military Policy
> at Chicago. He is the author of numerous articles and
> books, including* Politics Among Nations, *3rd ed.
> (New York: Alfred A. Knopf, 1960).*

This selection originally appeared in the March 1964 issue of
Commentary. Copyright 1964 by the American Jewish Committee.
Reprinted by permission.

That the cold war should come to an end is indeed a rational
wish shared by the overwhelming majority of people on both
sides of the Iron Curtain. This wish is particularly strong
among us whose instincts still long for the normalcy of isolation from the risks and liabilities of world politics and who
find ourselves engaged in a contest for the world only (so we
like to think) through the ill will of the enemy. If the Russians would only change, if they would only liberalize their
domestic affairs and be less harsh in the conduct of their

foreign policy (so the reasoning goes), we could "normalize" our relations with the Communist bloc, disarm, and live happily ever after. Thus we continuously search for the swallow which will make a summer, and whenever we feel a little less cold than we did yesterday we imagine a "thaw" in the cold war.

The emotions from which such expectations spring are honorable and generous, but they are politically blind, and pernicious if translated into action. And it makes no difference whether they manifest themselves as euphoric statements by high government officials, as involuted theories about polycentrism by former diplomats, as indiscriminate trading with the enemy by businessmen, or as the longing of the man in the street for peace and quiet and lower taxes.

The Lesson of Neville Chamberlain Unlearned

Paradoxically enough, these manifestations of a decent aspiration for peace are actually a threat to peace; for they are a source of weakness in judgment and action, and hence they encourage and strengthen the enemy. Of decent emotion engendering futile and self-defeating policies, Neville Chamberlain has become the historic symbol. We pride ourselves on having learned the lessons of Chamberlain's appeasement. But in truth we have only learned half the lesson. On the one hand, equating negotiations with appeasement, we have shied away from negotiated settlements even when there was a chance for them, as in 1953 after Stalin's death. On the other hand, we have yielded to pressure where the enemy was strong, or gave the appearance of being so—e.g., Hungary in 1956 and Cuba in 1962—and we have foregone the opportunity of offering inducements and exerting pressure when the enemy was weak, as he is at present. We have, moreover, been unable to shed the illusion that civilized social intercourse among nations whose interests clash is somehow conducive to peace, and that the cold war could easily be ended if the antagonists would only treat each other in a more friendly and reasonable fashion. These attitudes and the policies springing from them have not brought peace but only a

fleeting illusion of peace, for they leave the conflicts of interest from which the cold war arose and on which it has fed
exactly as they found them.

The Myth of "Relaxation of Tensions"

The next to the latest euphoric interval occurred in 1959
in the aftermath of Mr. Khrushchev's visit to the United
States; its symbol was "the spirit of Camp David." At that
time I assumed in this magazine [*Commentary*][1] the thankless task of contrasting the illusory character of that "relaxation of tensions" with the inescapable realities of the cold
war. Today we are living in another such interval, and the
thankless task must be performed again. It is, indeed, even
more urgent today than it was in 1959, because then our illusion was primarily intellectual and had no great political
consequences, whereas today that same illusion is reflected
in policies advantageous to the enemy. Responsible people
are even talking about "replacing" the cold war with the war
against poverty, as though the cold war had already come to
an end.

Origin and Nature of the Cold War

In order to see our present condition in its true perspective,
it is necessary to remind ourselves again of the origin and
the nature of the cold war. The cold war arose in the aftermath of the Second World War from a conflict of interests,
operating on two different levels, between the Western world
and the Soviet Union. On the level of traditional power
politics, that conflict has centered upon the control of Europe
and, in particular, Germany. On the level of competing phi-
losophies and social and political systems, the issue is the
control of the world. The substance of these two great issues
has remained constant for almost two decades. Only their
modalities have been transformed, in that all-out nuclear
war has been ruled out as a rational instrument of national
policy and the struggle for the world is being waged primarily
through political and economic competition and through

what Mr. Khrushchev calls "wars of national liberation." Has anything happened to affect this picture in any material way?

The Substance and Modalities of the Cold War

Secretary of State Dean Rusk, in his press conference of January 2, 1964, answered that question by enumerating five changes which in his view have contributed to the improvement of relations between the United States and the Soviet Union: the establishment of a "hot line" teletype link between Washington and Moscow; the limited nuclear test-ban treaty; the United Nations resolution prohibiting weapons of mass destruction in orbit; negotiations for wheat purchases between the Soviet Union and the United States; the suspension by the Soviet Union of its jamming of the Voice of America. It is hardly necessary to demonstrate in detail that the Secretary of State has, by implication, given a negative answer to our question. None of these five changes has any bearing upon the substance of the cold war, while only one of them bears upon its modalities, and in a way that is detrimental to the interests of the United States.

The "hot line" facilitates communications between Washington and Moscow, but obviously the all-important question as to the kind of communications to be transmitted is not answered one way or the other by the installation of this politically neutral device. The limited test-ban treaty transforms into a temporary multilateral obligation the technological necessity, which had previously been observed by the nuclear powers unilaterally, to stop testing for a considerable period of time after the completion of a series of tests. The United Nations resolution prohibiting weapons of mass destruction in orbit is a recommendation which the United States and the Soviet Union have been able to accept because they are at present incapable of doing what the recommendation asks them not to do (though both nations are engaged in research exploring the usefulness of outer space for purposes of war). The sale of wheat—as we shall see in greater detail in a moment—helps the Soviet Union to wage the cold war, but does nothing to liquidate it. Finally, the decision to cease jamming is a peripheral measure which may be due to any number of technical or political reasons but does not affect the substance of the cold war.

The Soviet Union Faces a Triple Crisis

While the issues over which the cold war started, then, still divide the United States and the Soviet Union today, three interrelated changes have occurred in recent years which add up to a drastic deterioration of the position of the Soviet Union: the conflict with China, the weakening of control over its allies, and an economic crisis of the first order.

The issue dividing the Soviet Union and China is in the short run the leadership of world Communism; in the long run it is the same issue that currently divides the United States and the Soviet Union: who shall inherit the earth? On the one hand, the Soviet Union has been able to stifle the economic development of China by severing economic relations. On the other hand, in the dispute as to who is the true exponent of Marxism-Leninism, the Chinese—both objectively and in the eyes of many Communists, especially outside the developed industrial nations—have had the better of the argument. Indeed, Khrushchev and Togliatti are today defending the positions which Bernstein and Kautsky held fifty years ago, while Mao Tse-tung and Chou En-lai are advancing the arguments which Lenin and Trotsky formulated then.

This conflict between the Soviet Union and China has weakened the control of the Soviet Union over its allies, for it provides the allies with an alternative to the Soviet connection. And while only Albania has openly defied the Soviet Union and taken the side of China, by being able to do so with impunity it has set an example for the other allies of the Soviet Union. Thus Cuba has refused to sign the test-ban treaty; Rumania has defied the Soviet Union in its plans for a division of economic labor within the Communist bloc which would have inhibited Rumanian industrial development; and Poland has, however cautiously, tried to play the Chinese off against the Russians in order to gain a greater measure of national independence.

Finally, and most importantly, the crisis of agricultural production, endemic in all Communist countries, has become acute in the Soviet Union. The Soviet economic system has proved incapable of providing "guns and butter" plus consumer goods at the same time, and is in consequence undergoing a drastic reallocation of resources. This economic crisis is bound to impose severe limitations upon the Soviet Union's ability to keep pace with the United States in the armaments race and to make political use of its economic resources through the instruments of foreign aid and trade.

One does not need to be an expert in foreign policy in order to notice that this triple crisis in which the Soviet Union finds itself today opens up new and unprecedented opportunities for Western initiative. Common sense will tell us that, given the relativity of power, the weakness of our enemy is a source of strength for us—provided we know how to use that weakness to further our own interests. This is not the place to spell out these opportunities; nor is it possible for the outsider to analyze such opportunities in detail. It is sufficient for the purposes of this discussion to state the general principle which ought to guide our policies, and to judge the policies we are actually pursuing in the light of that principle.

There is only one lesson nations will readily learn, and that is the lesson of necessity. This is particularly true of a nation like the Soviet Union, which combines the traditional objectives of a great imperial power with the worldwide aspirations of the leader of a revolutionary movement. Nations will stop when they realize that to advance entails risks greater than the benefits to be expected, and they will retreat when they realize that the advantages to be gained from retreat outweigh those to be expected from standing pat. The art of diplomacy consists in presenting the enemy with inducements in the form of advantages and liabilities, for doing what one wants him to do.

The Folly of the Commercial Approach

Applying this principle to the present stage of the cold war, one would think that the West is in an excellent bargaining position vis-à-vis the Soviet Union. It has for sale what the Soviet Union desperately needs—agricultural products and industrial machinery—and it could use that need as a diplomatic lever to gain concessions concerning the Soviet Union's control over Eastern Europe and, more particularly, East Germany, the Western presence in Berlin, the Soviet military presence in Cuba, its subversive activities throughout the world (especially through the instrumentality of Cuba), and disarmament. As I wrote in the New York *Times* Magazine on September 20, 1959:

> Yet it is exactly because trade between the United States and the Soviet Union poses an issue which is not primarily economic but political that it would be affected by a political agreement. An American concession in the form of increased trade might be a proper price for a Russian guarantee of the status quo in Berlin, especially since it could be enlarged, decreased, or cancelled altogether, as circumstances might require. Foreign trade is by its very nature a most flexible instrument of foreign policy and can be a most potent one, provided one side has a much greater interest in trading than the other. The use of foreign trade in the Russian manner—that is, as a political instrument rather than in an economic context—offers the United States a bargaining power of which it has not even begun to take advantage.[2]

"Idiotic" is not too strong a term to characterize the Western response to these opportunities—"idiotic" meaning, according to Webster, "foolish; senseless." For we have welcomed the present crisis in the Communist camp as an opportunity for trade, and we are willing to sell the Communist nations everything they ask for from wheat through buses and airplanes to whole petrochemical plants.

In order to understand the folly of this commercial approach to issues of high policy, it is first necessary to point to the obsolescence of the traditional distinction between strategic and non-strategic trade. The total war Communism has been waging against the West since Lenin accounts for that obsolescence. Ideally, foreign trade is carried on by private enterprise for the purpose of private gain. Actually, however, governments have time and again endeavored to use foreign trade as an instrument of national policy. "Dollar Diplomacy" is a case in point.

The leaders of the Soviet Union have consistently laid the greatest stress upon the expansion of foreign trade. They have evoked memories of Cobden and Bright, the leaders of the Manchester liberals of a century ago, as well as our own former Secretary of State Cordell Hull, with their emphasis on what foreign trade can do for private profits and international peace. They have consistently shown a particular interest in whole industrial plants rather than manufactured goods. But the Russian leaders are not Manchester liberals. They have wanted foreign trade not for the commercial purposes our businessmen want it for, but in order to gain the political strength necessary to achieve the universal triumph of Communism. As Lenin put it: "We welcomed Genoa [the International Economic Conference at Genoa in April 1922], we understood perfectly well, and did not conceal it that we were going there as merchants because trade with capitalistic countries is absolutely essential for us (so long as they have not yet collapsed)." Khrushchev was even more explicit when he said in 1957: "We declare war upon you . . . in the peaceful field of peaceful production. We are relentless in this, and it will prove the superiority of our system." And in 1952 Stalin also voiced his confidence in the profit motive of Western businessmen as an instrument through which the Soviet Union would be made strong enough for its final triumph.

Soviet Alternatives

It is against this background of consistent Soviet attitudes and policies with regard to foreign trade and the accentuation of these attitudes and policies owing to the present critical weakness of the Soviet Union that one must judge the Russians' current lack of aggressiveness and our response to it. The supremacy of the Soviet Union in the Communist camp is seriously threatened by Chinese competition, and in order to counter this threat the Soviet Union must be able to demonstrate to the world Communist movement that its policies are more likely to have beneficial results than those advocated by China. Thus the Soviet Union must be able to point at least to a semblance of successes in its dealings with the Western world. The partial test-ban treaty, enormously oversold by Soviet propaganda, has been important for the Soviet Union primarily as such an argument against Chinese competition.

The Soviet Union is compelled by the dynamics of that competition to search for other successes, real or apparent. It might find one in the placing of stationary ground observers on both sides of the Iron Curtain in order to prevent a conventional surprise attack. Such an arrangement would be innocuous because those observers could observe nothing that ordinary intelligence could not detect more completely and reliably, and it would also be meaningless since no government in its senses could seriously consider a conventional surprise attack in the center of Europe. It is exactly for these reasons that such an agreement has a better chance of being concluded than others that have been discussed.

As long as the Soviet Union can hope to follow up the test-ban treaty with other agreements, it will persist in its present non-aggressive attitude. If, however, this hope should fail, the Russians would then be compelled by the very same dynamics of their competition with China to compete with the latter in revolutionary militancy. For if the Soviet Union can no longer demonstrate that its policies—in contrast to the Chinese—strengthen Communism without increasing the risks of war, it must at least show that its revolutionary militancy is second to none.

Yet this alternative is unlikely to be of much avail to the Soviet Union. For China can counter by pointing to the advantages it is reaping in spite, or by virtue of, its militancy. Do not Western businessmen compete with each other for the privilege of trading with China, just as they do with the Soviet Union? And if Chinese militancy has not opened the door to the uncommitted nations, the United Nations, and general international respectability, it certainly has done nothing to close it.

Conflicting Views of Trade

I am not arguing here against Western trade with Communist nations per se. I am only arguing in favor of the proposition that foreign trade has a different meaning for Communist nations than it has for us. Trade with Communist nations is a political act which has political consequences. It is folly to trade, or for that matter to refuse to trade, with Communist nations without concern for these political consequences. There is no reason to object to our selling a Communist country goods it needs in exchange for goods we need. There is no reason to object to trading with Communist countries like Yugoslavia, if such trade promises political results favorable to our interests. But it is folly, comparable to that of selling scrap iron to Japan in the thirties, to stabilize the Castro regime by trading with a Cuba that is today the most important training center for Communist subversion throughout the world and to equip the Soviet Union and China with whole industrial plants and transportation systems which will then be used as weapons in the political, military, and economic offensives of Communism against the West.

That folly is compounded in the case of trade with China. The Soviet Union terminated its economic relations with China, especially in the form of aid, at the beginning of the sixties because it did not find it in its interest to supply the economic foundations for the power of a hostile China. An industrially developed China, whose population might then approach a billion, would be the most powerful nation on earth, more powerful than either the Soviet Union or the United States. It is extremely doubtful that China, in view of the numbers and poverty of its population, could find within her own borders the resources for such industrial development if she is not supplied with capital and goods from abroad. She would then remain for the foreseeable future a weak and fragile giant, a threat to her immediate neighbors but not to the two superpowers.

The Soviet Union has understood this prospect and has left China to her own economic devices. Yet with that blind and self-destructive folly which is the quality of men and nations whom fate has doomed, Western governments and businessmen are rushing into the gap left by the Russian withdrawal, replacing the Soviet Union as a source of capital and goods for China. But is China less hostile, and will she be less dangerous to the West if and when she has become an advanced industrial nation, than she is, and will be, to the Soviet Union? Obviously, the West has at least as good reason as the Soviet Union to fear a powerful China. If it is in the interest of the Soviet Union not to help China become a modern industrial nation, it is by the very same token in the interest of the West.

Yet while the Soviet Union knows its interest and acts upon it, the West does not know it and, insofar as it does, is unable to act upon it. Marx said that the capitalists would be their own gravediggers. Western businessmen, so staunchly anti-Communist when it costs nothing, except perhaps freedom of speech for others, seem bent upon proving that Marx was right.

NOTES

1. "Khrushchev's New Cold War Strategy." November 1959.
2. Copyright 1959 by the New York Times Company. Reprinted by permission.

PART FIVE

THE ROLE OF THE MILITARY

INTRODUCTION

But no; you cannot, men of Athens, you cannot have done wrongly when you accepted the risks of war for the redemption and the liberties of mankind; I swear it by our forefathers who bore the brunt of warfare at Marathon, who stood in array of battle at Plataea, who fought the sea-fights at Salamis and Artemisium, and by all the brave men who repose in our public sepulchers, buried there by a country that accounted them all to be alike worthy of the same honor—all, I say, Aeschines, not the successful and victorious alone. So justice bids: for by all the duty of brave men was accomplished: their fortune was such as Heaven severally allotted to them.

Demosthenes, "On the Crown" (330 B.C.)

There are those, some deeply devoted to the cause of peace, who would swerve away from any line of effort that is cast in a military mold. But unfortunately no program will suffice unless it provides men with a sense of security as against the menace of those who exalt ways of violence and practice the use of terror.

Senator John Foster Dulles, July 12, 1949

But it is one thing to engage in academic discussions, ignoring the lessons of Berlin and Korea, and another thing to negotiate directly with unyielding Muscovites, grasping for every advantage no matter how minute, supported by a military establishment of the first magnitude. Americans have learned, not without cost, that aggressive tactics may be suspended at times by negotiation, but that basic Communist policy is never abandoned. Until that system deteriorates or collapses, the United States can deal with it only at arm's length from positions of strength. And strength does not consist solely of industrial and agricultural wealth and vast quantities of military equipment. Our opponents must understand that there is also a capacity and determination to use our resources whenever American security is threatened.

Robert Murphy, *Diplomat Among Warriors* (1964).

MILITARY-CIVILIAN PARTNERSHIP
IN EDUCATING TO THE
COMMUNIST THREAT

by Dwight D. Eisenhower

> *General Eisenhower has served his country with dis-*
> *tinction throughout his life—in the military, in educa-*
> *tion, and from 1953 to 1961 as the thirty-fourth Presi-*
> *dent of the United States. Since 1961 he has served as*
> *an adviser to government officials both in this country*
> *and abroad. In 1963 General Eisenhower's* The White
> House Years: Mandate for Change, 1953–1956 *was*
> *published.*

This selection consists of the text of a letter former President
Eisenhower wrote on January 15, 1962 to Senator John Stennis,
Chairman of the Special Subcommittee, Senate Armed Services
Committee, United States Senate. The title and subheadings used
here were not a part of the original letter, but have been added by
the editors. Printed by permission.

I am complimented by your invitation to comment on various
matters of current interest to your subcommittee. Because
I have had no occasion to examine these issues in detail since
leaving the Presidency, I shall direct my remarks to basic
considerations rather than to the specifics of pending issues.
This statement, therefore, will deal in general terms with the
public need for information on the Communist threat; extremism; the military role in providing information on communism; slurs on the military; and censorship.

Need for Non-Partisan Education
on the Nature of the Communist Threat

I am sure that all of us would deplore any move which would restrict public access to reliable information on the deadliness, implacability, totality, and cunning of the Communist assault on freedom. We should not trouble ourselves over the possibility of overinforming the public. Rather we should be watchful of any tendency to withhold releasable information. Those of us who over the years have had to deal directly with the Communist leaders and system believe—unanimously, I think—that the more our people can be brought to comprehend the all-encompassing nature of the threat, the stronger will be our own determination to preserve freedom at home, and the greater will be our national willingness to sacrifice to advance freedom throughout the world. Telling the stark truth about communism is the best way to make our own citizenry and other peoples appreciate the blessings of liberty. We should encourage all individuals who are well informed on Communist tactics and strategy to expound freely and often on this subject. We should concentrate on assuring ourselves that the public has ready access to the best available information, rather than expending too much energy on deciding which persons or groups should fill this need.

One phase of this matter concerns me deeply—as it has for many years. I refer to the tendency to impugn motives when matters of this kind enter the public arena. Because the public is, rightly, troubled by the Communist menace, the subject tends to excite fear and suspicion and is susceptible always of being exploited for political or other purposes. Thus, extremism finds a fertile soil. And as charge begets counter-charge, unless the nation's leaders move with wisdom and restraint the fanatics of both the right and left so belabor each other as almost to monopolize the issue, leading the nation to preoccupy itself with the evils of extremists instead of the evils of communism. Facts are forgotten in the extravagance of mutual accusation. Extremism always distorts—what we need is hard fact, calmly presented and digested, so that we may act with prudence and some wisdom in defending ourselves. Incidentally, I have noted that the fanatic thrives on publicity; he withers when ignored.

Next, I take up the matter which, so you indicate to me, engages your particular interest—the appropriate military role in helping to inform the non-military in respect to the tactics, strategy, and concepts of communism.

The Appropriate Military Role in Helping to Inform the Non-Military in Respect to the Tactics, Strategy, and Concepts of Communism

First, I mention in passing that I endorse without qualification the doctrine of military subordination to civil authority. The Armed Services are not policy-making bodies. Their function is faithfully to execute the policy decisions of the properly constituted agencies of civil government. It is equally true, however, that, in this modern day, the need of civil government for the counsel and advice of military personnel in devising of policies grows more acute.

I subscribe also to the position expressed to your subcommittee last fall by the Secretary of Defense, that military involvement in the providing of information concerning Communist potential aggression—indeed its involvement in all matters—must be clearly non-partisan, directed to subjects related to the defense of America, and in harmony with approved national policies.

This is, of course, easily said. But difficulties are inescapable when one attempts to decide what type of statement or gathering is partisan and what isn't—what, conceivably, in these times is unrelated to the nation's strength and safety—and what, precisely, national policy really is. Such determinations are necessarily, in good measure, subjective. I suspect that many active duty personnel could conclude from such broad guidelines that virtually any utterance before a non-military group might be construed as a violation of instructions of higher authority; hence, the course of prudence would be to say nothing at all.

It is, of course, not the function of the military services to ferret out the details of attempted Communist subversion in our nation. This is the task of the Federal Bureau of Investigation, under Mr. J. Edgar Hoover. However, by virtue of its vital mission to defend our country, its long professional experience with Communist tactics and its highly developed educational system, our military is singularly well trained to provide to the public, as well as to the members of the Armed Forces, the implications of the extreme threat of Communist imperialism.

The Singular Qualifications of Senior Officers

Incidentally, Mr. Chairman, if your committee should glance over the curriculums of the National War College and, indeed, of all the service war colleges, you will find, I believe, that the aims, objectives, and methods of communism and its aggressive threats to our system are probed more intensively and more pragmatically in these institutions than in virtually any civilian university in the nation. This has long been true. The Armed Forces Industrial College, for instance, began conducting very fruitful national security seminars on matters of this kind as long ago as 1948. I believe these seminars are still in progress. The result is that senior officers in the Armed Forces are qualified to develop among their units the necessary understanding concerning potential aggressors, and their purposes and tactics.

The National War College Seminar for Reserve Officers

As an example of this kind of education: In the summer of 1959, the Joint Chiefs of Staff authorized a two-week strategy seminar of 210 selected reservists. The War College Seminar presented 55 top experts as lecturers. This "faculty" was strictly bipartisan—including former Secretary of State Dean Acheson and other prominent Democrats, as well as Republicans. Some of the speakers were openly critical of various policies and programs of my Administration. But I thought it unwise to suppress or inhibit such discussions since I believe that the American people have a right and a need to know the alternate ways of meeting the Communist challenge. As an indication of the caliber of students, three "alumni" of the first seminar are now U. S. Senators. Others were college presidents, deans, editors, publishers, Congressmen, Governors, lawyers, college and high school teachers, and businessmen. I believe that all concerned found the discussions highly provocative and useful, and that there is value in such efforts for the nation as a whole.

The Lesson of Korea

The need for anti-Communist education in the Armed Forces is self-evident. Your committee recalls, I am sure, our sad experiences in Korea a decade ago, in respect to the conduct of some of our captured Americans. This gave rise to improved troop information programs designed to strengthen troop appreciation of the fundamentals of our own and the Soviet system.

Military and Non-Military Strategy Closely Related

I need not remind your committee, especially, that in these times military considerations and economic, political, and ideological considerations are interrelated to such a degree as to make an arbitrary dividing line between the military and the non-military increasingly unrealistic—a truth, indeed, which gave rise fifteen years ago to the establishment by law of the National Security Council. Here, in the nation's topmost planning group, the military, through the Secretary of Defense (and, by invitation, the Chairman and/or members of the Joint Chiefs of Staff) directly advise in the development of America's master policies. These advisers, and their supporting staffs, are an asset of incalculable value to this nation, and policies governing their usefulness and employment should leave a great deal of latitude to the judgment and responsibility of these men.

Informing the Public: The Rule of Reason

As to informing the public at large, I have heard statements to the effect that the use of the military in this effort stems from a National Security Council directive of 1958. This, I believe, is in error. It is true that during my Presidency great pains were taken to coordinate the efforts of the military services in its preparations for countering hostile moves against the external threat, on the one hand, and those of the Federal Bureau of Investigation concerned in combating internal Communist subversion on the other. But, to the best of my recollection, there is no national security document specifically directing military involvement in the internal problem, and unless material has been taken out of context, or general language interpreted very loosely, I think there is no basis for these assertions involving the National Security Council. Nevertheless, both procedures—the troop education programs and the general educational program— seem to me as desirable for our country now as they did just a few years back. Each supplements and supports the other—Defense personnel takes the lead in the first, civilian agencies do so in the second.

Naturally, when civilians or soldiers undertake programs of this kind, within or outside the Government, the process cannot be expected to work perfectly at all times and at all places. Faulty techniques, error of judgment, impulsive statements, occasional excesses—these are bound to occur. As always in cases of inescapable overlappings of responsibility, the heads of affected agencies must apply judgment—a rule of reason. Such responsible heads can expect to receive the full cooperation of the military leadership in seeing to it that policies are obeyed and flaws are corrected.

Communism Profits from Rigid Restrictions on U.S. Military

Accordingly, should departmental instructions be so phrased as unduly to prohibit desirable military participation in these educational efforts respecting the Communist menace,

I suggest that your committee recommend their restudy with a view to appropriate revision. The Reds are well aware of the integrity, patriotic motives, and high qualifications of our military. I suspect they would be delighted if we should prevent such people from spreading the truth about Communist imperialism.

Absurdity of Charges that American Military Is Extremist or Politically Partisan

Pertaining at least indirectly to this subject, I have heard of accusations alleging that military education is so narrow as to make service personnel incapable of grasping the whole complex of dangers confronting our country. It is hinted that the entire officer corps has become politically infected, and prone to be disloyal to the Commander in Chief. I, for one, want to be on record as expressing my indestructible faith and pride in our Armed Services—even though their loyalty, patriotism, and breadth of understanding need no defense from me or anyone else.

The entire nation, including the Armed Services, insists that in our free system military influence must be kept within proper constitutional, legal, and administrative bounds. Moreover, as mentioned in my final address as President, we must watchfully mind the military-industrial complex, for it tends to generate powerful economic and political pressures beyond the anticipations even of the participants themselves. But these are matters of proportion and sensible national leadership, requiring the same kind of continuing oversight and perspective that other major power groupings in our society, including business, labor, and government itself, require in the interest of keeping our system flexible, balanced, and free. In a half century of national service, I have yet to meet the American military officer who viewed himself as a budding Napoleon, or even a Rasputin, and I suggest it is worthy of note that in recent world history the three major dictators—Hitler, Mussolini, and Stalin—came from civil life. This fact does not warrant a general indictment of civilian motivation any more than one or two military extremists might warrant the absurdity that all the military harbors political designs dangerous to our constitutional form of government.

No Iron Curtain for American Military

I believe, therefore, that your committee will render valuable service by rejecting the recent spate of attacks upon the competence and loyalty of the military and by disapproving any effort to thrust them, so to speak, behind an American iron curtain, ordered to stand mutely by as hostile forces tirelessly strive to undermine every aspect of American life. I say, let our informed military speak, always under properly established policies and the general—not petty—supervision of their civilian superiors. Should they, here or there, speak or act partisanly, imprudently, or in contravention of national policies, then hold them directly accountable, for it is a function of command to keep military personnel properly respectful of the obligations of the uniform. At all events, I am certain of this: Give military leaders a lucid explanation of the nation's policies, and they will, with rare and easily controllable exceptions, loyally perform.

Voluntary Cooperation Better than Censorship

Generally in the same connection, I question the desirability of requiring the topmost Government officials, whether military or civilian, to submit their proposed public statements for what amounts to censorship of content—as distinguished from security matters—prior to their utterance. I am aware, in saying this, that procedures in my own and in the Administration of my predecessor may have functioned in this way. But in thoughtful reassessment of this procedure, I incline to the view that when responsible and respected officials feel compelled to submit to censorship, we are smothering the concept of personal responsibility under a practice of heavy-handed and unjustified staff supervision.

Responsible officials, when in doubt, will voluntarily "coordinate" proposed public statements within their own and sister departments so as to protect the nation, their services, and themselves, but such voluntary coordination is some distance from censorship. I would hope that all who study this problem objectively will see the virtues of such a "co-operative" system as opposed to censorship, except, of course, where security is involved. I have always believed—as I now do—that good faith and close understanding among the important officials of great human organizations are far more important to success than are any number of arbitrary regulations and pedantic instructions. This is really the meaning of this letter.

So viewing the problems before your subcommittee, I wish you and your colleagues well in your endeavor to maintain balance and good sense in respect to the matters receiving your current consideration.

THE CHALLENGE TO MILITARY PROFESSIONALISM

by Robert N. Ginsburgh

Colonel Ginsburgh, U.S.A.F., graduated from the U. S. Military Academy in 1944, and received his M.A. degree in 1948 and his Ph.D. degree in 1949 from Harvard University. He has served in the offices of the Secretary and of the Chief of Staff of the Air Force and in both Europe and the Far East. Colonel Ginsburgh has been an Assistant Professor of Social Science at West Point, an Air Force Research Fellow at the Council on Foreign Relations, and is now a member of the Policy Planning Council, Department of State.

This selection appeared in the January 1964 issue of *Foreign Affairs* and is reprinted by permission. Copyright 1964, by the Council on Foreign Relations, Inc., New York.

The mounting tension in civil-military relations within our Government is made up of many factors—especially, perhaps, the tightening of civilian control and the postwar changes in the nature of war and of the military profession itself. The conflicts are reported almost daily by the Pentagon press corps, and the frustrations of the military are made evident in the writings of Generals Gavin, Ridgway, Taylor, Medaris, White, and Admiral Anderson. It is not that these men question the principle of civilian control. Nor is the struggle simply a contest for power. What the military are principally reacting to is the implicit challenge to their professionalism.

Undoubtedly, there exist certain elements of a power strug-

gle for the control of defense policy. A succession of Secretaries of Defense have discovered that it is no easy job to
exercise control over officers accustomed to lead and command. The very fact that Mr. McNamara has sought to exercise a greater degree of direction than has any of his predecessors is certainly one cause of the conflict. Yet this fact
alone is not sufficient to explain the extent of present tensions
in civil-military relationships in Washington.

Although the American military have not always been submissive to the civilian controllers, they have never seriously
challenged the right or the tradition of civil control. They
have recognized that the ultimate decision-maker must balance military recommendations against other considerations.
It is not too difficult for a military man to accept an adverse
decision based on nonmilitary considerations. It becomes extremely difficult, however, for him to reconcile himself to an
adverse decision by his civilian superior based on military
considerations. This strikes at the very *raison d'être* of the
military man. It challenges his military professionalism.

The maintenance of a high degree of military professionalism is essential to the preservation of our nation's security
without sacrifice of basic American values. The challenge to
military professionalism is reflected in each of what Samuel
P. Huntington calls the essential characteristics of a profession: corporateness, responsibility, and—especially—expertise.

The Military's Sense of Corporateness

A sense of corporateness is especially strong in the military profession. Like other professions the military has its
community of interests, common experiences and common
values which bind the profession together. But two additional
factors make the corporateness of the military especially
strong. First, the military man can pursue his profession
only within his own national military establishment. Although he may transfer some of his expertise to other areas
of endeavor, he cannot continue as an active member of
the military profession outside the national military establishment. Second, the sharing of common danger, inherent in

the profession, provides a unifying bond—and one which grows stronger as the danger becomes more immediate.

Prior to World War II there was a third factor which contributed greatly to the military's sense of corporateness—its isolation. Geographically, politically, and philosophically the military profession lived its own life in a military society set apart from American society. A fundamental challenge to military corporateness today stems from the fact that the military are no longer isolated from the mainstream of American life. There still exist isolated military bases and long tours outside the United States on ship or shore, but the military have become intermingled with civilian society both within their local communities and in the nation.

It is undoubtedly desirable that the military be closely identified with the society they have sworn to defend. But in the intermingling process, many military officers have become less willing to sacrifice personal convenience and have become more concerned with the adequacy of military pay than when they were living on military stations isolated from the impact of the more attractive wages and hours of work of the civilian community.

These two factors—personal inconvenience and pay—combined with the policy which permits early retirement have caused many military men to think of their profession as just a job rather than as a lifetime career. At an early date many military men start planning for their second careers; in fact, many dedicated military professionals have felt that they could simultaneously have greater impact on military policy and receive greater personal rewards by leaving the military profession to work for industry, the "think factories," or even for the Defense Department in a civilian capacity.

Finally, the administrative fusion of the military services in the Department of Defense has not been accompanied by a fusion of their corporate loyalties, which remain attached to the individual services. More than that, emphasis on specialization has tended to splinter the sense of corporateness within the services so that Naval officers think of themselves as black shoe or brown shoe, while Air Force officers may classify themselves as SAC types or TAC types.

The Erosion of Authority

As compared to the interwar years, the responsibility of the military has clearly increased, but their authority has been progressively eroded. As a result of the expansion of the unified command concept, the authority of the Service Chief as an individual has been supplanted by the corporate authority of the Joint Chiefs, while the authority of the Chiefs of Staff has been reduced through the creation of the elaborate superstructure for defense policy-making in Washington. At the same time the important responsibilities of the Joint Chiefs of Staff have not lessened, and exist whether or not they can agree on the actions to implement them. Their authority to act, however, depends on their reaching agreement.

A further challenge to the responsibility of the military is inherent in our form of government. Because of the separation of powers between the Executive and Congress, the individual public servant may justifiably be confused as to where his responsibility lies. This is especially true for the military. As a result of the increased importance of military affairs in our national life, questions of defense policy have been added to the political issues in the continuing power struggle between the executive and legislative branches. Congress took pains specifically to grant to the Chiefs of the military services the right to appeal to Congress—a right which President Eisenhower once described as "legalized insubordination." There remains, too, in the military profession a sense of responsibility to the people and to the Constitution which transcends the more immediate responsibility to Congress and the Administration. When beset by frustration, the military man tends to satisfy his need for a feeling of responsibility by turning to this ultimate loyalty.

Finally, the concept of responsibility is also challenged when the expertise of the military profession is put in question. When the political decision-maker asks for and accepts the opinion of an expert, he can hold him responsible for the adequacy of such advice. When he refuses to accept his advice because he challenges his qualifications, he can no longer expect to hold the expert responsible. Certainly the expert's sense of responsibility also suffers as a result.

Military Expertise

The challenge to military expertise is the most important aspect of the challenge to military professionalism, because expertise is, after all, the very basis of any profession.

Military expertise encompasses strategy, tactics, and administration. Generally speaking, military expertise in tactics and administration has not been seriously challenged. The reason for this, according to Bernard Brodie, is that: "There is no doubt that tactics and administration are the areas in which the soldier is most completely professional. The handling of battles by land, sea, or air, the maneuvering of large forces, the leadership of man in the face of honor and death, and the development and administration of the organizations that affect these purposes are clearly not jobs for amateurs." In the area of strategy, however, Brodie asserts as a "basic fact" that "the soldier has been handed a problem that extends far beyond the expertise of his own profession."[1] In similar vein Joseph Kraft argues that "the professional soldiers—not through any fault of their own, but on the contrary in consequence of their virtues—are ill-fitted for high-level strategic thought."[2] This is indeed ironic when we consider that originally the word "strategy," derived from the Greek *strategos,* meant simply the art of generalship.

Even before World War I, however, wars were usually considered too important to be left to the generals—unless the commanding general was also chief of state. Since World War II, the political leaders have become more concerned than ever before with the problems of war, strategy, and military affairs in general. War is no longer a question merely of victory or defeat on the field of battle. With the advent of nuclear weapons and strategic delivery systems, we have reached the stage where peacetime preparedness is likely to determine the outcome of a major nuclear war. Thus not only war but also peacetime defense becomes too serious a matter to be left to the generals.

At the same time that technology has forced political leaders to concern themselves with military affairs, it has operated to make the military man less of an expert. The development of new weapons has always been of great importance in the history of warfare. In earlier times, however, the military professional was able to assimilate the military impact over a period of years or even generations, and if he was not necessarily the creator of the new technology, he was almost invariably its exploiter. Today, however, technological developments come so thick and fast that it becomes difficult to keep abreast of their existence, much less assimilate their impact on military problems. Furthermore, the professional has a much smaller role in the creation of new weapons because their complexity requires the specialized services of the scientist and engineer, and their magnitude generally requires that they be produced by industry rather than government.

The Scientist, Engineer, and Industrialist

Thus in the continuing technological race for new and better weapons, the scientist, the engineer, and the industrialist become partners with the military man; and he becomes dependent on them in the pursuit of his profession. By no means silent partners, they may be in a position to insist successfully that a particular project of great interest to the military is impractical. It may, in fact, be impractical, but it may also be that the scientist or engineer for one reason or another personally thinks it undesirable. In any ensuing dispute the military man frequently finds himself at a disadvantage. The scientist probably has more technical knowledge of the subject; and if, as is probable, the dispute involves new weapons requiring new military techniques, the military man will have little experience on which to rely. Furthermore, to the extent that warfare has advanced toward the push-button stage, there is increased emphasis on peacetime pre-planning at the expense of decision-making and military judgment during the heat of battle—the peculiar province of the military professional. Thus, the nuclear scientist can say that he knows more about nuclear physics than the military and that, after all, the military man hasn't had any actual experience in waging nuclear war, in which there isn't much need for military judgment anyway.

It is not only the natural scientists and engineers who cast doubt on the expertise of the military; it is also the political scientists and those whom David Lilienthal calls "the methodologists."[3] The military services had of course used the techniques of operations analysis during World War II, and subsequently their application was expanded within the military services to include the determination of desirable characteristics and uses of new weapons and the development of new tactical and strategic concepts. The services also created a variety of nongovernmental think factories. Thus, we find the RAND Corporation working primarily with the Air Force, the Research Analysis Corporation with the Army, the Operations Evaluation Group at M.I.T. with the Navy, and the Institute for Defense Analyses with the Joint Chiefs of Staff and Defense Department. In addition, there are some 350 other nonprofit corporations, some 300 college research centers, and 1400 industrial companies, as well as various private foundations and scientific advisory committees—all involved in some degree in the business of thinking about military problems.

Unquestionably, these think factories have performed a valuable service to the military professional in his search to adapt technology to military problems. But on occasion they have further complicated this search, and they have undoubtedly challenged his professional expertise.

Here once again, the professional military man frequently finds himself at a disadvantage in comparison with a member or "graduate" of the think factories. First, the very independence of a think factory tends to lend its findings greater prestige than if the same conclusions were reached by the government agency which employed it. This independence also gives the think factory the opportunity to approach other agencies in an attempt to persuade the government as to the correctness of its findings. Similarly, the individual "academic strategist" who has graduated from a think factory may move back and forth among other think factories, universities, and government. If his ideas on military strategy and policy are not well received by one organization, he may be more successful through one of the other avenues.

The strategist in uniform, on the other hand, finds himself constrained both by the hierarchy of the strategic planning organization and the military discipline of subordination to higher authority, which make it more difficult to take issue with accepted policy. Nor can he publicize his views through magazines or books as easily as the lay strategist can. Writing for publication is an important element of the academic rather than of the military profession, and the academician is much more likely to be granted time and financial support for his research. Even when the military man combines both the opportunity and inclination to write for publication he finds himself more severely constrained by rules of military security and government policy review. These circumstances partly explain why most of the influential books and articles on military policy and strategy published since World War II have been written not by professional military men but by civilian academic strategists, many of whom have been associated with the think factories. But the cause lies also in the failure of the military colleges to "stand on the frontiers of knowledge."[4]

Thus, since the end of World War II there has gradually developed an increasing number of civilian experts on military policy. This growing body of academic or lay strategists is being used more and more to challenge the views of the professional military man. In fact, Joseph Kraft maintains that "the Academic Strategists emerge as a key factor in the maintenance of civilian control over the Armed Services. . . . Their generalizations provide civilian officials with a useful yardstick for judging rival service claims, and for keeping the whole defense establishment in line with the nation's strategic goals." On the other hand, he notes that "without the Academic Strategists, the basic decisions about how defense monies were spent would be thrust upon the professional soldiers."[5]

The Growing Influence of the Lay Strategist

The growing influence of the lay strategist has been accentuated and accelerated by the so-called "Whiz Kids" who were brought to the Pentagon by the Kennedy Administration and who personify the new civilian experts. Unquestionably a brilliant and gifted group, they nevertheless—in Stewart Alsop's words—"display occasionally the intellectual arrogance that is the chief failing of the overintelligent."[6] At its extreme, this results in the assertion that there is no longer any need in nuclear warfare for military judgment because the outcome of nuclear campaigns can be predetermined by precise mathematical computations. In many ways this is reminiscent of the eighteenth-century "scientific" approach to strategy based upon a system of complicated and carefully calculated geometrical movements and angles of attack. Since the occupation of key geographical points was designed to make victory almost mechanical, it might make actual fighting unnecessary.

The proliferation of lay strategists has been accompanied by an expansion of civilian influence and a decrease in military influence in the councils of government having to do with national security policy. Thus there is no military representation on our highest military policy-making body, the National Security Council. Although the Joint Chiefs of Staff are designated as advisers to the N.S.C., they are also advisers to and subordinate to the Secretary of Defense, who is the principal adviser to the President in all matters relating to defense. And as a matter of practice the Joint Chiefs—other than the Chairman—are rarely invited to attend meetings of the National Security Council. Furthermore, between the military Service Chiefs and the civilian Secretaries, there have grown up new ranks and hosts of individuals—mostly civilian—without any corresponding decentralization of authority; in fact, taking full advantage of modern communications and computer techniques, the decision-making authority has become more centralized. As a result, the military professional faces many more roadblocks—more people who can say no and fewer who can say yes.

The invasion of the area of military strategy and policy by the lay strategist has been facilitated by the military professionals' sallies forth into nonmilitary areas—in pursuit of what Huntington calls the theory of political-military fusion. "This theory started from the undeniable fact that military policy and political policy were much more closely interrelated in the postwar world than they had been previously. It went on, however, to assert that it had become impossible to maintain the distinction between political and military functions at the highest level of government."[7]

One aspect of this theory was that military leaders were expected to incorporate political, economic, and social factors into their thinking. This gave rise to situations in which the Joint Chiefs of Staff defended the importance of political considerations while the State Department was concerned with military arguments. The fusionist theory also gave impetus to the heavy emphasis in the senior war colleges on nonmilitary subjects. Most recently, it has stimulated professional and popular interest in problems of cold war and counterinsurgency which require successful fusion of a wide variety of military and nonmilitary techniques.

A second result of the fusionist theory was the heavy demand for military leaders to undertake nonmilitary responsibilities. Because of their wartime popularity, prestige, and experience, professional military men were called upon to fill influential positions in politics, in industry, and in government. Some of the governmental positions required the exercise of military as well as political functions, but others were filled by military men not because of the relevance of their experience, but because of their prestige or general executive ability and the comparative lack of experienced and available civilians immediately after World War II. Once the military professionals had breached the wall between military and nonmilitary affairs the route was widened into a two-way street, so that the military professional found himself challenged both on his own ground and on nonmilitary grounds as well. Meanwhile, the application of the fusionist theory forbade him to retire from the non-military field to his former sanctuary.

In addition to political-military fusion, World War II set the stage for the fusion of the military profession itself—a fusion, however, which has not been completed. The Unification Act, born of World War II experiences pointing up the need for coordinated military actions on land, sea, and air, established a coalition of the military services rather than a fusion. The military profession has not yet successfully met the challenge posed by even this much change. It requires the development of broad-gauged military professionals who can speak with authority on a full spectrum of military matters rather than a collection of individual experts in air, land, and sea warfare. The more specialized expertise is still needed, but the military profession must also develop the generalists who can fuse together the particular competence of the specialists. This does not necessarily mean that the specialists themselves or their organizations must be integrated into a single service but that their individual points of view must be fused into a more broadly professional military expertise.

The singular failure of the military profession to meet this challenge has provided the lay strategist the occasion to invade the area of military affairs. In fact, the conflicts within the military profession have made it imperative for the civilian to step in to reach decisions. To avoid making purely arbitrary decisions, the informed expertise of the lay strategist has, with justification, been relied upon. In fairness to the military profession, however, we should note that the failure to develop professional generalists has been abetted by some civilians who have not wished to see the military services develop a common profession—who felt that a policy of divide-and-conquer was the surest way to maintain civilian control.

The extent of the conquest is, I think, aptly illustrated by the following commentary by Huntington on the influence of the military professional on military policy between 1945 and 1960: "It is not surprising that military leaders played a key role in implementing policy and that they seldom actually made important decisions on policy. Perhaps more striking is the relatively unimportant role which they played in proposing changes in policy. In no case did military leaders initiate major new policies and in no case did they effectively prevent changes in old ones."[8]

The Development of Greater Expertise

Huntington's analysis of military professionalism leads him to conclude that "the requisite for military security is a shift in basic American values from liberalism to conservatism. Only an environment which is sympathetically conservative will permit American military leaders to combine the political power which society thrusts upon them with the military professionalism without which society cannot endure."[9] Another proposed solution is to divide the problems of national security into total war and limited war, with specialists for each. The limited war specialists would retain the traditional "heroic" characteristics of the old military profession. Huntington, in effect, would solve the fundamental problem by changing the environment which creates it. The other approach would solve the problem by dividing it in two, by ignoring the more fundamental half, and by turning the clock back to solve the other.

Either response would, of course, help to resolve the frustrations caused by the current challenge to the military profession. But the first seems to be an extreme solution unless it is the only way to preserve our nation's security; and the second does not really solve the problem.

To meet satisfactorily the challenge to its professionalism, the military must first of all become more professionally expert. Under today's conditions the military profession can meet this requirement only by developing an expertise which transcends that of the individual service. The military profession must develop strategy, tactics, and techniques which can deal with the entire spectrum of organized conflict from total war to guerrilla war, in all its media—land, sea, air, and space.

The development of an all-around military expertise would

be aided by greater mobility of personnel among the services. This should be something more than the occasional opportunity to transfer from one service to another. More intensive use should be made of the existing exchange programs, with particular emphasis on areas of military management, especially at higher staff levels—rather than trying to make a single individual into a submariner, an infantryman, a pilot, a ship's captain, and a missile expert.

The development of greater expertise will not be enough in itself, unless it can be effectively communicated to the political decision-maker. This will require a flexibility in adapting to changing political administrations and the ability to explain military concepts in the particular language of each administration. It will also require a special skill in mastering the techniques of the think factories in order to evaluate the efforts of its own thinkers and to compete successfully with the independent lay strategists.

If the desired professional military expertise is ever to be achieved, the military school system—especially the senior military colleges—will have to assume a key role. The average military man probably devotes a larger proportion of his career to formal schooling than any other professional. If the military schools are to fulfill their function adequately, the best of them must encourage original thought, research, and publication comparable to that of our leading universities. In the course of study the military aspects of national strategy should be emphasized anew with the objective of developing new strategic concepts and doctrines. Politics and economics need not be ignored, but the curriculum should focus on military subjects. The courses should also develop a general knowledge of contemporary military technology and a competency in the techniques of operational research.

A prerequisite for the re-creation of military expertise is the abandonment of the fusionist theory whereby military and nonmilitary factors are so entwined that a separate expertise in the military aspects of national security is simply impossible. Obviously there is an intimate interrelationship between military and nonmilitary factors; but there is a difference, and we need to re-establish the concept that the problems of national security can, in fact, be broken into various aspects even though they interact on each other. The statesman needs sound military advice; the military professional needs firm policy guidance. Each must, of course, understand the problems of the other. The military man should be aware of the political, economic, social, and other factors which affect national security, but it is not his business to evaluate them. He should limit himself to a consideration of the military aspects which are within his area of competence. The civilian authorities, both executive and legislative, should assist him in exercising self-restraint by not requiring his comments on nonmilitary matters. Similarly, the statesman who is concerned with a political problem must recognize that it may have important military implications but he should refrain from making military analyses. He should use the results of the analysis of the military expert as one of the factors bearing on his total problem.

The separation of a national security problem into its various aspects does not mean that the military man and the statesman should work independently of each other. A military analysis may well depend on the particular political, economic, or psychological assumptions which are made. The establishment of these assumptions should be the task of the statesman. The military man can contribute by pointing out how various ranges of assumptions may materially affect the military estimate.

Solutions to the Problem

A traditionally military—and perhaps also American—response to most problems is to reorganize. While this predilection should not lead us to expect too much, it is apparent that certain organizational changes in the Department of Defense would help the military to exercise their expertise and make them more responsive and more responsible to civilian control.

First of all, the organization and procedures of the Joint Chiefs of Staff need to be streamlined so that they can act more quickly and be more responsive to the Secretary of

Defense. The host of special committees, councils, assistants, and groups should be realigned to report through staff directors with increased stature and authority. The Joint Staff should exercise effective direction over the various defense agencies. It would be highly desirable for the Chiefs to use the Joint Staff as their primary advisers and to give the Joint Staff officers increased stature and authority in their relations with the Service staffs. Finally, the Joint Staff should be given greater authority to act on certain operational matters within established policy. This would make it possible for the Chiefs to fulfill their responsibilities without having personally to consider and agree on all matters for which they are responsible.

A second major effort should be to improve the working relationships between the J.C.S. and the staff of the Secretary of Defense. These staffs ought to be cooperating rather than independent and competing staffs, and some realignment of functions is desirable to achieve that end. Serious consideration should be given to opening up the "closed system" of the J.C.S., whereby lateral communication is prohibited and access to its studies is only by way of the Secretary of Defense. If this system could be altered, perhaps the J.C.S. would fill the proposed position of Assistant Secretary of Defense for Plans and Operations with some of its existing functions and personnel distributed to the various existing offices of Assistant Secretaries of Defense.

A third measure would involve organizing to encourage self-criticism on the part of the military profession itself. The military professional must be able to produce new ideas and concepts if he is to compete with the lay strategist. It is perhaps too much to expect that the military, with its emphasis on discipline and the chain of command, can ever achieve the same degree of academic freedom enjoyed by the lay strategist. It should be possible, however, to encourage more original military thinking without sacrificing the traditions of obedience to higher authority. One possibility, for example, would be the creation of small groups charged with long-range planning and new conceptual thinking and made directly responsible to the military service chiefs. This system would make it possible for a new idea to be aired at the highest levels without having to follow the tortuous path of military command which tends to reject concepts not in accord with previously approved policy.

Taken together, these measures would respond to the challenges to the responsibility as well as the expertise of the military. Its sense of corporateness could also be strengthened by measures to re-create the prestige and attractiveness of a military career—without, however, trying to return the military to its prewar state of isolation. Especially effective would be the resurrection of the traditional fringe benefits of the military. Similar personnel policies within and among the individual services would also contribute. This does not require uniformity in personnel matters, ignoring differences in requirements and problems, but it does mean the elimination of conflicting policies based on historical differences which are no longer relevant.

A fundamental obstacle to achieving the various responses which have been outlined is likely to be the continuing fear of military power and the traditional anti-military bias of the liberal ethic. To the extent, however, that the suggestions made here are nonpolitical and encourage professional expertise and responsibility, they should, in fact, lead to more effective civilian control. If civilian control seems reasonably well assured, perhaps military professionalism could be acceptable without necessarily substituting the conservative for the liberal ethic. Surely the United States is strong enough to allow Americans to choose their political philosophy—whether liberal or conservative—on grounds other than national security alone.

NOTES

1. Bernard Brodie, *Strategy in the Missile Age*, (Princeton, N.J.: Princeton University Press, 1959), pp. 15–16 and 9–10.
2. Joseph Kraft, "The War Thinkers," *Esquire*, September 1962, p. 148.
3. The New York *Times* Magazine, September 29, 1963, p. 23.
4. John W. Masland and Laurence I. Radway, *Soldiers and Schol-*

ars, (Princeton, N.J.: Princeton University Press, 1957), pp. 436, 509.

5. Kraft, op. cit., p. 149.

6. Stewart Alsop, "Master of the Pentagon," *The Saturday Evening Post,* August 5, 1961, p. 46.

7. Samuel P. Huntington, *The Soldier and the State,* (Cambridge, Mass.: Harvard University Press, 1957), p. 351.

8. Samuel P. Huntington, *The Common Defense,* (New York: Columbia University Press, 1961), p. 114.

9. Huntington, *The Soldier and the State,* p. 464.

SECURITY IS TOO IMPORTANT
TO BE LEFT TO COMPUTERS

by Colonel Francis X. Kane, U.S.A.F.

*Colonel Kane is Chief of Space and Ballistic Missile
Planning of the Air Force Systems Command. He
received his B.S. in 1943 from the U. S. Military
Academy at West Point, and his M.A. and Ph.D. from
Georgetown University. He has served as U.S.A.F.
Operational Planner during the Korean War; as As-
sistant Air Attaché, American Embassy, Paris; and
as Special Assistant to Chief of Air Force Research
and Development, Headquarters, U.S.A.F. Colonel
Kane participated in establishing the Mutual Defense
Assistance Program.*

This article appeared in the April 1964 issue of *Fortune*. Reprinted
by permission.

*The Battle of Chancellorsville, fought for five days in May,
1863, is one of the best-known textbook examples of the
value of initiative, skill, and daring in military command.
Had there been computers in Richmond and Washington
in Civil War days, things might have gone differently. In
the Confederate capital, Jefferson Davis might have taken
one look at the results of the computerized gaming of
the impending advance of 130,000 Federal troops on Chancellorsville and sent the following message to General Lee:*

*"The probability of a successful defense against General
Hooker's federal forces is less than 50 percent. Addition-
ally, we run the risk of your forces being annihilated. We*

reach these conclusions because the plan you propose cannot be quantitized in sufficient detail. There are too many
qualitative unknowns and uncertainties that can be turned
to our advantage only by Federal mistakes and accidents.
Therefore we have decided to abandon the defense of
Richmond and withdraw the government to Raleigh. You
are directed to prepare a covering operation. Communicate
your plan to me as soon as possible."

In Washington, President Lincoln might have studied
the output of his computers in the same situation, and
prepared this directive for General Hooker:

"Repeated simulation of your plan for the attack on
Richmond shows that we have an extremely high probability of defeating and even annihilating Lee's forces. This
probability is so high as to be almost a certainty. You are
therefore directed to execute your plan as soon as possible
after receiving this message."

History tells us that Lee, with forces less than half
the size of Hooker's, seized the initiative, made a succession of decisions born of genius, capitalized on Hooker's
mistakes in judgment, and inflicted a smashing defeat on
the Federal forces. He thus opened the way for the Confederate invasion of the North.

Can the results of computerized war be so wrong? The
question has special relevance since much of the current
planning for the present and future security of the U.S. rests
on computerized solutions. The answer is that we simply do
not know because we have no experience in comparing the
currently accepted theory of predicting wars by computer
with the actual practice of executing plans. But I believe that
today's planning is inadequate because of its almost complete
dependence on scientific methodology, which cannot reckon
with those acts of will that have always determined the conduct of wars.

So long as the security planner uses science and its methodology, however modern, as the foundation for his plans,
he will be limited in knowing how to act by the bounds that

science cannot pass in dealing with human affairs. The planner must look beyond the static systems involved in mathematics and computerized logic; he must look beyond science if he is to carry out his basic responsibility. The more he depends on "closed" systems the less able will he be to cope with dynamic, mobile worlds brought into being and constantly changed by desires and actions of creative individuals. In sum, at the dawn of the space age the security planner's knowledge of his own problems is still at the stage of plane geometry. If he continues down his present, narrowing intellectual path, he may well become divorced from the real world, and as a consequence we may be unable to cope with the new situations that will come from our dynamic environment.

The crux of our problem is that the philosopher has been forgotten in the planner's evaluation of human activity. Forgotten with him is the overriding importance of individual acts of will, intuition, and genius. In today's planning the use of a tool—the computer—dictates that we depend on masses of data of repeated events as one of our fundamental techniques. We are ignoring individual experience more and more and depending on mass experience instead. To find a way of breaking out of these existing bounds, I propose a new approach, which I have termed "meta-planning" (from the Greek "beyond," as in "metaphysics"). Fundamentally, it seeks to bring the whole of experience and of the human personality to bear on planning, as will presently be explained.

We have not had a new idea in planning methodology for over a decade and a half. Since the Air Force began to use computers, we have done little but refine the resulting methodology. In the interim the technical explosion in weapons has made our planning problems both more complex and more dynamic. Meanwhile, the lengthening time required to develop new weapons and the ever-mounting costs in dollars and skilled personnel have caused decision-makers to press for more and more certainty in the forecasts of the planners. Perhaps the most important reason for urgency is that the Soviet Union has now embarked on applying com-

puters to planning. Marxism, Leninism, dialectical materialism in general are proving inadequate in solving Soviet
problems. The Communist attraction to doctrinaire solutions
may lead to a more modern pseudo-science. If this should
be true, the Russians may lose touch with reality, and we
may face new dangers. Our planning considerations then will
be confronted with still another new complexity. Significantly,
we have an advantage in coping with this development. We
are not bound intellectually by doctrinaire considerations; we
are free to speculate and innovate as demanded by the circumstances.

In advancing this critique, I am fully aware of the role of
the scientist in developing our weapon systems and in contributing to our security and well-being, and I am not dis-
paraging cybernetics. These and other uses of computers have
been among the major advances of the postwar era. However, it has been observed quite aptly that no program of
breeding horses, however scientific, would ever have produced
the internal-combustion engine. Similarly, we could say that
no program of applying science to human affairs will give us
the intellectual advances we need today. Meta-planning is a
new field of endeavor that cannot be bound by past methodology and techniques. It must explore new fields of thought
and initiate new intellectual achievements.

The Marriage of Theory and Machine

At the close of World War II, two events occurred in quick
succession that determined our postwar planning pattern. The
first of these was the investigation by the Air Force of the use
of the early computers for military planning. The second was
the discovery and application to planning of the theory of
games, developed by Von Neumann and Morgenstern; this
proved attractive because it showed the possibility of applying
laws of statistics and probabilities.

The marriage of theory and machine led to a basic planning assumption that it is possible to create mathematical
models of future wars that permit us to arrive at conclusions
about strategy, tactics, and force composition. This assumption

depends on the propositions that: human action can be expressed in mathematical form; qualitative action (such as a strategy or tactic) can be expressed quantitatively; and a calculus of warfare is possible. It also led to a second assumption that events in the military world are related on the basis of cause and effect.

All of this has taken place by force of circumstance, almost by accident. Because of the planner's naïveté, he has a body of principles selected almost at random, the choice often having been made without any attempt to analyze either the foundations of individual principles or the interrelationships of principles. However, these concepts, though unrecognized, have, in fact, shaped the course of methodology and imposed the limits on our processes.

In order to construct models and manipulate them mathematically, we need masses of data on repeated events. This necessitates the discarding of data on individual events that do not fit into the mass. Such "unique" events lie principally in the field of decisions that have occurred only once in history—e.g., the Japanese decision to attack Pearl Harbor, the U.S. decision to defend South Korea, the Soviet decision to put missiles into Communist Cuba. These individual acts of will cannot be handled by scientific methodology.

"How Many Nuclear Wars Have You Fought?"

This scientific technique is being imposed on planning at a time when a theory of another kind has found acceptance in intellectual circles—namely, that a discontinuity has occurred in human affairs because of the influence of nuclear aerospace power in the hands of two superpowers. As a direct result, much of past experience has been discarded as being unrelated. This fact is indicated by the question alleged to have been asked in the Pentagon of an Air Force general: "How many nuclear wars have you fought, General?" In practice, this means restricting our modelmaking to *situations of the moment*. It means that a once-useful body of knowledge and doctrine has no place in today's scheme of things. These observations are not an implied plea to re-create the past; they are an indication of the unproved theories on which our planning is based today. Even we firm believers in manned space operations know we cannot afford to divorce ourselves arbitrarily from past experience.

These two trends, the restriction of intellectual foundations and the elimination of past experience, are producing a backward movement for which we find no counterpart in contemporary human events. Our problem is pressing. We must make intellectual progress and find new routes to reality. The point of departure for such progress is to look carefully at the differences between the goals of planning and science.

Planning is a form of human action, that is to say, purposeful action. The realm of the planner is human events in the real world. The realm of the scientist, on the other hand, is what Max Planck, the originator of the quantum theory, calls "physical events." Both the planner and the scientist are concerned with forecasting future events in the real world, but the events are of two different types. Human actions, in the planner's world, are "purposeful," a word foreign to the physical sciences. Forecasting the future is not an end in itself. The planner seeks ways of translating acts of will, the choice of ends and goals, into practical courses of action. He seeks to do more than know what is going to happen; he seeks to *control* what will happen, to ensure that the future state of events will be the one he desires.

The military planner lives in the future, and he knows that an interaction of wills, both his own and the enemy's, produces a dynamic situation, characterized by constant change. All military men sense instinctively that "you cannot step into the same river even once." We live in a world of political change and of uncertainty, the former the result of the conflict of wills, and the latter the product of deliberate action by the enemy.

Even though the military man believes this, the national security planner currently does not make it the basis for his methodology. He uses a static, quantitative methodology. He has adopted computers and mathematical techniques because he finds them "useful" in facing a variety of problems.

Weapon systems are compared; battles are analyzed; warfare systems are evaluated.

Yet in creating his images of the future, what kinds of experiences is the planner using and comparing? For some weapon systems he has at hand large masses of data. For example, the accuracy of bomber crews has been recorded over months and years of exercises, practice, and alerts. For others, such as the presumed accuracy of a Soviet orbital bombardment system, he has none. In any case, *all the numerical values used in simulation by computers are assumed values*. In order to apply the experience of bomber crews to future warfare conditions, the planner must make some allowance for the differences between the known exercises and the unknown conditions over enemy territory during all-out hostilities. Also, we need only point out that we have no knowledge at all of men dropping bombs from orbit. Yet the planner *accepts* his assumptions as being a reflection of the real world. Moreover, he uses some assumptions without recognizing that they are such.

This is a small matter, he would say, because the end result of these simulations, based on factors, is probability values. The great attraction of the application of computers to war gaming is that by using large masses of data the planner can apply the laws of statistics and probabilities to his problem.

Here is a principle that must be examined for its validity in military planning. As far as we are concerned, there are two points of importance. First, probability values are derived from masses of data on repetitive events, and they apply only to such events. Second, if the planner attempts to apply probability values to a single event, and most important, to a "unique" event, he makes a judgment. There is no quantitative defense of such judgments, and we have great difficulty in trying to put numerical values on these events. The defense of the judgment of the probability values chosen can come only from individual experience. But how to use experience and whose experience to use?

The Role of Intuition

The world of the planner is in truth the world of volition, of purpose, of goals, of ends. Because it results from creativity, it is the world of the individual, the particular. It is the world of the dynamic, of flux and change. It is the world of uncertainty. As we look at volition and creativity in general, we must come to grips with intuition. We have to be careful about introducing the word "intuition" in this discussion. Scientists get highly emotional about it, so perhaps it would be better to invent a new term, "not charged with the debris of man's past experience," as John Dewey has described the need. For our purposes, the word means those aspects of human activity that lie beyond science, beyond the static, beyond the general, beyond the limits of reason.

That these limits exist and form some of the boundaries of today's planning is a critical point in constructing metaplanning. Pure rationality is one of these boundaries. Reason is held in the vise of experience. Its premises are drawn from experience and its conclusions are limited by the experience on which reason is based. An example points up this fact. It was the desire to fly that gave man the airplane. Rationality, especially as used by the skeptic, proved the following: manned flight was technically unfeasible; it had no worth competing with existing modes of transportation, especially the train; it had no strategic value and defense dollars would be better spent elsewhere. Nearly all discoveries and inventions could be shown to be rationally impossible before they were made. But these facts are so well known as to be boring, except that we never seem to learn that it is desire, perseverance, patience, and accident which transform potentialities into realities. The realm of new experience comes not from rational extrapolation of the present but from the intuition that produces events new in kind.

Perhaps more basic to the problem is the resistance that would come to using philosophy in planning. The corporate president or commander who has only recently gathered support for the use of computers and programers will look askance at taking on an untried and unproved solution to his planning problems. We can anticipate the reaction to the proposal that he hire a Chief Philosopher. Today's military planner fails to heed what certain scientists and philosophers of science say about imagination and creativity. The great French mathematician, Poincaré, said, in a seemingly Gallic hyperbole: "A machine can take hold of the bare fact, but the soul of the fact will always escape it."

If, as Poincaré says, it is vain to attempt to replace the mathematician's free initiative by a mechanical process of any kind, it is equally vain, the intuitionist says, to replace philosophy with what is the sum of mechanical processes, science. We will leave the arguments about values and virtues, superiority of one form of knowledge over the other, to those who worry about such matters. The meta-planner must adopt the principle that without individual choice, judgment, creativity, we would not have invention, discovery, or application in science or elsewhere in life. We derive the conclusion that, as practical individuals looking for ways of improving the planning process, we should examine an alternative route to our basic objective, which is to forecast reality so as to control it.

In accord with this pragmatic approach, we turn to philosophy. Here we define philosophy as the body of theories, tools, and techniques that permits us to know the state of reality and to apply that knowledge to today's problems. In effect, it is a second road to reality, and it leads to that part of reality which is inaccessible to science—the dynamic world of flux and uncertainty.

The planner who grasps the importance of change can understand Henri Bergson's concept of the philosopher and the role of intuition. He has so immersed himself in the flux of the world around him that he knows intuitively the meaning of the constant change and grasps the sense of the direction in which that change is going. The significance of intuitionism for the planner is that it emphasizes the central role played by man, by the individual, in an evolving reality. *To give life to military planning, we must reinterpret the element of volition in military affairs.*

We have a point of departure for this effort in one of the principles of planning. The importance of the mission (objectives, goals, tasks) is emphasized in military affairs, operations, and plans. The plans of subordinate and collateral units are integrated by a hierarchy of mission objectives. Application of this principle produces unity of action, up to a point. That point is when we cannot cope with the unknown, the unforeseen that come from the creative action of the enemy. We may guess at the enemy's plans, but it is he who carries them out. His actions, as the experience of all wars can testify, usually introduce substantial changes in our plans.

The Key Role of Decision-making

As we attempt to find practical ways of coping with uncertainty, of improving the planning process, we must recognize that we will always be unable to solve part of the problem. Discovery of new ways of doing things, of new relationships, is, by its very nature, not subject to logic or to knowledge *a priori*. Discovery nearly always comes by chance. Similarly, the appearance on the scene of history of the man of genius or of the decisive individual with the power to act cannot be forecast. The genius himself cannot foresee the content of his innovations or the time when he will make them. In all of our efforts, we must keep in mind that some events will occur "by chance," i.e., be inaccessible to our methodology of forecasting.

The planner must launch a concerted effort to understand the creative process, especially the key role of decision-making. The decision to pursue a course of action is vital to any impact on the real world. An effort to understand creativity is under way in individual, isolated studies. These need to be unified and focused on the planning process.

An important aspect of this phase is to investigate the birth, death, and rebirth of the ideas that motivate and guide decision-makers. For example, was it possible to forecast the current vogue of the renaissance of gunpowder technology, which determines so much of our present military posture? When will the concept of technological supremacy, which once was the foundation of our military strength, become completely extinct as a factor in military affairs?

As another phase, the planner must investigate the role of the assumption in planning. The relationships between the abstractions and reality must be more clearly defined. No matter how many models he creates of a future reality, the planner will not be able to produce any sounder plans until he can relate those models to the real world by the correct assumptions. This is a new field of activity that is unique to the military planner, dependent as he now is on "closed systems" for his deliberations.

A Search for Insights

An aspect of forecasting the future which needs more investigation is that of model-making. The models that the planner constructs need not be restricted to statistical, quantitative analyses. Models of social situations can lead to insights, to empathy, to understanding of the relationships within a segment of society. Such empathetic models are qualitative in nature. They comprise an understanding of the history, of the psychology, of the aims and aspirations of the individuals within a group. Models of this sort can lead to insights into the behavior of potential enemies and their future decisions.

Still another phase must be an understanding of how to apply past experience to present and future circumstances. Concurrent with the understanding must come a reversal in the present attitude, which rejects past military experience. A reinterpretation of military doctrine is an essential element of this step. While such a reinterpretation is occurring continually, it must be formalized and made authoritative. Another element of this step must be an investigation of the human, continuing features of war, as opposed to the material, transitory features.

Here there is a parallel with the past interweaving of science and philosophy. All metaphysics become outdated because of their physics: that of St. Thomas (and Aristotle) because Aristotle's physics became obsolete, that of Descartes because of Cartesian mechanics, that of Kant because of Newtonian physics. Similarly, military doctrine becomes outdated as weapon technology changes. Nevertheless, arguments about the ephemera should not destroy acceptance of what is permanent. The permanent aspects come from the human elements of warfare.

A fourth phase is an examination of the question that we can have knowledge *a priori* of the possibilities of the future. This question has been the subject of debate among philosophers. Those who rule out precognition do so on the basis of experience. We cannot explain it scientifically and we cannot visualize any mechanism by which to foresee coming events. However, the knowledge, the certainty of the planner is not judged in absolute terms, but in relative terms, i.e., relative to the certainty of the enemy. It follows that the closer the planner approaches perfection, the more certain he will be that he possesses the edge on the enemy.

If certainty is unattainable, it is also unnecessary. The observation applies especially to current requirements that the results of the research and development process be certified before the process is begun. As military affairs go now, schedules, results, and costs must be forecast before a new project is approved; quantitative measurements are the principal criteria of progress in R. and D. Clearly, by any philosophical standard and by the primary practical standards, this goal is unattainable. In practice, the need for forecasting with certainty is a barrier against constructive action.

Calling All Philosophers

When we come to the next phase, we approach the heart of the problem of creating meta-planning. That phase consists in attracting and motivating the individuals who can find roads to reality other than science. Here, primarily, I mean philosophers. If we are to bring the whole of human experience, the whole of the human personality, to bear on the problem of planning, we must depend on individuals to enlarge our perspective and the scope of our effort. We must also generate understanding of the need for ultrascientific knowledge to be utilitarian, to be devoted to the problems that weigh on us so heavily today. If the philosopher continues to remain detached, meta-planning will fail. If he becomes immersed in our dynamic reality, he will contribute to the effort of the military planner. This is one aspect of meta-planning that will require time. It may take a decade, as it did for computerized planning to become a part of our accepted practices. Fortuitous circumstances, chance, could reduce that lead time.

The cornerstone of meta-planning, of course, is to find acceptance of the concept and its applications. This can come only through demonstrating how to solve the problems of defense today. Success is the only road to acceptance. Yet there is no preordained reason why man should be less successful in dealing with those aspects of his internal and external existence that lie beyond science than he is in applying science within its own realm. The fact that those who should be tackling this part of the problem have not been successful is partly because they have not tried.

The solution lies in large measure beyond the realm of the planner, for the situation is a reflection of society, of values, and of attitudes. Yet we clearly need unity of effort on common problems. And the construction of meta-planning is a way of starting to generate that unity.

Meta-planning will be characterized by greater awareness of the foundations of knowledge and sources of ignorance. The meta-planner will understand more fully the unpredictable nature of the creative process. He will have greater acceptance of his intuition for foreseeing the direction and nature of the future.

Finally, having said this, we must recognize that these general conclusions are the sum of meta-planning today. The content of meta-planning and its influence on the future depend on the effort of the planner to find new principles, on the success of the philosopher in providing them, and on their combined endeavor to construct a unified and consistent methodology that will be the foundation of planning and the key to human action. Meta-planning, if successful, will return man to the center of affairs and make volition, not statistics, the source of decisions.

The views and opinions expressed in this essay are those of the author. They have not been verified or indorsed by the U. S. Air Force or the Department of Defense.

PART SIX

WHAT FORWARD STRATEGY FOR AMERICA?

INTRODUCTION

In developing the military might of our armed forces and raising their military preparedness, we must vigilantly follow the intrigues of the imperialists and study all their habits. And if they still impose a war upon us, let the imperialist gentlemen then blame themselves. Soviet armed forces will crash down upon them with their entire all-crushing might; it will be the last war, one in which the imperialists and their whole system of capitalism will be buried once and for all.

> Marshal Rodion Malinovsky,
> (February 22, 1963)

Better men throughout the land means men who cherish liberty, who enjoy it themselves and respect it in others. Of such men, the democrats of the spirit, we can never have enough. Unless tens of millions of Americans are determined to be free themselves and to support other men in freedom, democracy is doomed to disorder and sorrow. The price of liberty, today as through all history, is self-reliance and self-discipline. Nothing has happened in this revolutionary age to relieve each of us of the prime responsibility for the state of his own freedom. Rather, the shift from independence toward power within the equation of personal liberty, and from untrammeled individualism toward a sense of community in the public philosophy, makes the practice of self-discipline more essential than ever before.

Clinton Rossiter, "The Democratic Process" in *Goals for Americans,* The Report of the President's Commission on National Goals, 1960

The lesson of the two wars has been learned: The unleashing of violence settles nothing. Europe would be the victim of a hyperbolic war, whatever its issue. We have not concealed this antinomy of means and end. The object of the West is and must be to win the limited war in order not to have to wage the total one. But the West will not succeed unless it is animated by an inflexible resolution, unless it believes in itself and in its mission of liberty.

Raymond Aron,
The Century of Total War (1954)

When Marxism started over one hundred years ago, Marx had to invent a social theory. He presented unproven theories as supremely desirable and at the same time discredited existing theories and practices. Western society, in the meantime, has improved on precisely those things on which Communism has defaulted, namely, the humanities, greater freedoms, and living standards. A countermovement may thus draw inspiration from the effective contrasting of the two. Nor does the new countermovement need to base itself on unproved theories. On the contrary, it can take the best accomplishments of the West, adjust them to Russian conditions as of now, and proceed from there. It can thus, if ably supported from the West, proceed at a twentieth-century pace to effect great changes behind the Iron Curtain, and do so in our lifetime. In fact, if a new catastrophe, such as a world war, is to be avoided or its consequences minimized, this must be done. Dialectically, the theory and practice of Western freedom and standards of living would thus become the counterthesis to that of the Kremlin; the Communist Party expropriators thus would be in turn expropriated.

William R. Kintner and Joseph Z. Kornfeder,
The New Frontier of War (1962)

WHY WE TREAT DIFFERENT
COMMUNIST COUNTRIES DIFFERENTLY

by Dean Rusk

> *Secretary of State since 1961, Mr. Rusk has served in*
> *that Department in several capacities since 1946. From*
> *1952 to 1961 he was President of the Rockefeller*
> *Foundation. Mr. Rusk graduated from Davidson Col-*
> *lege and later, as a Rhodes Scholar, received his M.A.*
> *degree from St. John's College, Oxford University. He*
> *served in the U. S. Army from 1940 to 1946.*

An abridged version of an address given by Secretary Rusk to the
Full Citizenship and World Affairs Conference of the International
Union of Electrical, Radio and Machine Workers, Washington,
D.C., February 25, 1964.

Today there is a central question which rightfully looms large
in the concern of the American people about foreign affairs.
What is the policy of this Government toward international
Communism?

At the present time, as throughout the postwar period,
there are some who, for political or other reasons, deliberately
sow confusion about our real intentions. Also, both at home
and abroad, puzzlement may arise on more legitimate grounds.

We are asked how we can object to other free countries
selling goods to Cuba when we are willing to sell wheat to
the Soviet Union. We are asked why we refuse to recognize
the Peking regime when we recognize the Soviet Union. We
are asked why we have treated Yugoslavia and Poland somewhat differently from other Communist states in Eastern Europe. We are asked why we enter into cultural exchange

agreements, or a test ban treaty, with a government whose leader has continued to boast that he will "bury" us.

If the Communists, as a group, have as their aim the destruction of our way of life, how is it that we can treat one Communist country differently from another? And why do we enter into an agreement or understanding with a Communist government over one matter, while accepting the hard necessity of continued hostility and conflict over other matters?

Communist Designs

Before answering those questions, let me make one point clear. We, in this Administration, and in this country, are under no illusions as to the designs of the Communists against us and the entire free world. No one needs to tell us that the Communist menace is deadly serious, that the Communists seek their goals through varied means, that deception is a standard element in their tactics, that they move easily from the direct attack to the indirect, or to combinations of the two.

To know what the Communists are up to, and to understand their varied techniques, is a major order of business with us in the State Department and other branches of the Government. It is an order of business we do not neglect.

We are fully aware that Moscow, as well as Peking, remains committed to the Communist world revolution. Chairman Khrushchev tells us bluntly that coexistence cannot extend to the ideological sphere, that between him and us there will be continued competition and conflict. We hope this will not always be so. But as long as Mr. Khrushchev says it is and acts accordingly, we must believe him and act accordingly ourselves.

Our First Objective

The first objective of our policy toward the Communist states must be, and is, to play our part in checking Communist imperialism. This Administration will vigorously oppose the expansion of the Communist domain—whoever the Communists in question may be—by force or the threat of force, whether directly or indirectly applied.

To that end we maintain a nuclear deterrent of almost unimaginable power. To that end we have increased our conventional military forces and made them more mobile—and have encouraged and assisted other free nations on the front lines of the free world to strengthen their conventional forces.

Given the catastrophe that a nuclear engagement would be for the entire world, we do not intend to fall into a position where we may have to choose instantly between a nuclear reaction and the loss of one or another outpost of freedom. We are resolved to maintain, and to persuade other free world nations to maintain, the capability to repel partial or limited attacks.

We have also improved our capacity to deal with guerrilla warfare and are helping our allies and friends who are subject to that type of aggression.

In Southeast Asia, and to a lesser extent in certain areas of Latin America, indirect aggression is not just a threat but an immediate danger, involving both daily loss of life and danger to vital free world positions. This type of assault was beaten in Greece, the Philippines, and Malaya. With resolution and continuing endeavor by the peoples beset by these tactics, and with help from us and other free nations, those earlier victories can be repeated elsewhere.

The free world must prevent the Communists from extending their sway through force, whether through frontal assault, piecemeal territorial grabs, or infiltration of men and arms across frontiers. We will continue to do our part to make aggression not only unprofitable to the Communists but increasingly costly and dangerous to them.

Working for Peaceful Progress

We also combat Communist imperialism by helping the developing countries to modernize their economies and to overcome the social and political problems which breed discontent. In addition we do what we can to help settle disputes within the free world—disputes on which the Communists try to capitalize.

We are not defenders of a sterile status quo. We do not oppose peaceful changes. We favor economic, social, and political progress for all peoples, including our own. And we believe that every nation has a right to choose and modify its own institutions.

We provide economic and technical assistance to developing nations and take part in peace-making and peace-keeping within the free world because we want to build a decent, peaceful world order. At the same time these activities are important methods of preventing the Communists from extending their domain.

Nobody knows that better than the Communists themselves. That is why their favorite slogan is: "Yanks, go home." Why any good American would wish to further that central Communist objective is beyond my comprehension. Yet that would be the effect of retreating from our international commitments, of turning our back on dangers and disputes at distant points, and of gutting our foreign aid program and other means of strengthening and defending the free world. Until the Communists themselves change, the most elementary security considerations demand that we remain ever alert to the dangers their very outlook on life raises for us and for others committed to freedom.

Trying to Reduce the Risk of War

But our policy does not end there. In the longer run we want the Communists to come to see that their aggressive hostility toward the free world is not only costly and dangerous but also futile. Meanwhile, we want to reduce as much as we can the chance that the hostility they have created between them and us may lead to a great war. Thus we search patiently for agreements and understandings to settle or blunt dangerous disputes between them and us and to bring armaments under control.

The Soviets appear to recognize that there is a common interest in preventing a mutually destructive thermonuclear exchange. We have managed to reach a few limited agreements with them. These do not yet constitute a détente. We hope for further agreements or understandings. But in the field of disarmament there are severe limits to the progress that can be made without reliable inspection and verification of arms retained. And on many vital political issues Moscow's views and the West's remain far apart. Nevertheless, we shall pursue unceasingly our earnest quest for mutually acceptable steps toward a more reliable peace.

But it is not enough to "contain" Communism and to try to negotiate specific agreements to reduce the danger of a great war. The conflict between the Communists and the free world is as fundamental as any conflict can be. Their proclaimed objectives and our conception of a decent world order just do not and cannot fit together.

Our View of Communism

We view Communism as a system incapable of satisfying basic human needs, as a system which will ultimately be totally discredited in the minds of men everywhere. We believe that the peoples who have been brought under Communist rule aspire to a better life—one of peace, economic opportunity, and a chance to pursue happiness. This, indeed, has always been so. But in recent years an important new trend has been perceptible. Some of the Communist governments have become responsive, in varying degrees, if not directly to the aspirations of their subjects, at least to kindred aspirations of their own. The Communist world is no longer a single flock of sheep following blindly behind one leader.

The Soviet Union and Communist China are engaged in a deep and comprehensive quarrel involving ideology—how best to promote the Communist world revolution—a struggle for influence in other countries and other Communist parties, conflicting national interests, and personal rivalries. The dispute between Moscow and Peking has spread through the world Communist movement and, in many countries, has divided the local parties.

The Chinese Communists have demanded that the Russians

risk their national interests, and even their national survival, to promote the world revolution, as that cause is defined by Peking. The rulers of the Soviet Union have rejected this doctrine. They appear to have begun to realize that there is an irresolvable contradiction between the demands to promote world Communism by force and the needs and interests of the Soviet state and people.

The smaller Communist countries of Eastern Europe have increasingly, although in varying degree, asserted their own policies. We have always considered it unnatural for the diverse peoples of Eastern Europe, with their own talents and proud traditions, to be submerged in a monolithic bloc. We have wanted these peoples, while living in friendship with their Russian and other neighbors, to develop in accordance with their own national aspirations and genius. And they seem to feel a strong nostalgia for their traditional ties with the West. Most of them are increasing their trade and other contacts with Western Europe and, to some extent, with us.

Economic Shortcomings of Communism

Throughout the Communist world the economic shortcomings of Communism are vividly manifest. Failures in food production have become endemic. In Communist China the standard of living is even lower than it was before the calamitous collapse of the "great leap forward." The Soviet rate of growth has dropped below that of the United States and Western Europe and far below that of Japan. The actual increase in income, both national and per capita, in the last twelve years was less in the Soviet Union than in the United States. The fact that Communism is economically inefficient has become increasingly plain to most of the peoples of the world.

Since 1948 we have used export controls to keep strategic commodities from the Soviet Union and its European satellites. Since 1950 we have maintained a total embargo on trade with Communist China and North Korea; and somewhat later this embargo was extended to North Vietnam. In October 1960 we embargoed exports to Cuba, excepting foods and medicines.

All these actions were taken and have been maintained for what seem to us to be very good reasons. In controlling exports of strategic goods to Soviet bloc countries we consult and coordinate with fourteen other free world industrial countries through a Coordinating Committee known as COCOM. We have never embargoed or opposed the sale of foodstuffs to Soviet-bloc countries. Thus, our sales of wheat to the Soviet Union involved no change in basic policy. And from a traditional Yankee trading viewpoint, we are not unhappy about swapping surplus foodstuffs for gold and hard currency which help to balance our international payments.

Our capacity to influence events and trends within the Communist world is very limited. But it is our policy to do what we can to encourage evolution in the Communist world toward national independence and open societies. We favor more contacts between the peoples behind the Iron Curtain and our own peoples. We should like to see more Soviet citizens visit the United States. We would be glad to join in cooperative enterprises to further mankind's progress against disease, poverty, and ignorance. We applaud the interest of the Soviet leadership in improving the lot of the Soviet people.

Thus our policy toward international Communism has three objectives:

1. To prevent the Communists from extending their domain and to make it increasingly costly, dangerous, and futile for them to try to do so;
2. To achieve agreements or understandings which reduce the danger of a devastating war;
3. To encourage evolution within the Communist world toward national independence, peaceful cooperation, and open societies.

Policy toward Various Communist States

We believe that we can best promote these objectives by adjusting our policies to the differing behaviors of different Communist states—or to the changing behavior of the same state.

When Yugoslavia challenged Stalin's centralized control of Communist affairs in 1948, we gave that country military and economic assistance. Yugoslavia not only defied Stalin but stopped supporting the guerrilla aggression against Greece, reached an agreement with Italy on Trieste, and increased its economic, political, and cultural ties with the West. It is not a member of the Warsaw Pact. As a nonaligned state, it has gained influence among the uncommitted nations of the world. Sometimes it agrees with the Soviet Union on particular points of foreign policy, sometimes not. In brief, Yugoslavia is an independent state. Its success in defending its independence made other peoples in Eastern Europe wonder why they could not do likewise. And not least important from our viewpoint, Yugoslavia is not shipping arms to be used against a democratic government in Venezuela and is not trying to destroy non-Communist governments in South Vietnam and Laos.

For some years we have treated Poland somewhat differently from other Soviet bloc states. A good deal of the national autonomy and domestic liberalization which the Poles won in 1956 persists. Most of Polish agriculture remains in private hands; religion is strong; Poland has developed a broad range of relations and exchanges with the West. Poland has historic ties with the West. And its people are the close blood relatives of many citizens of the United States. We apologize to none for our efforts to help the brave people of Poland to preserve their national identity and their own aspirations.

At one time we felt compelled to break diplomatic relations with Bulgaria. Since the ruthless suppression of the Hungarian national revolution in 1956, we have been represented in Budapest not by a regular envoy but by a Chargé.

We have never had diplomatic relations with Communist Albania, the most blatantly Stalinist state in Europe.

Thus, for good reasons, we have treated various Soviet bloc states differently and the same state differently at different times. And we shall continue to differentiate our policy according to the conduct of the various Communist states.

Recently Rumania has asserted a more independent attitude and has expanded its trade and other contacts with the West.

It has taken steps to improve its relations with the United States. We are responding accordingly.

Hungary has turned to a more permissive policy of national conciliation. We of course welcome any tendencies promising to ease the lot of the Hungarian people. We will do what we can to encourage them.

In Czechoslovakia and Bulgaria there are some signs of movement away from earlier and harsher policies. We are watching these developments with close attention.

The Threat of Communist China

When we consider Southeast Asia, we see a quite different situation. There, two nations—Laos and South Vietnam—are the targets of subversion and aggression directed and heavily supported by Communist North Vietnam, with the backing of Peking. These aggressions violate specifically the Geneva agreements of 1954 on Indochina and the Geneva accords of 1962 on Laos. It is vitally important to the security not only of Southeast Asia but of the entire free world that these aggressions shall not succeed. Our nation is committed to the support of Vietnamese freedom, and we shall continue to honor that commitment. The forces we have in South Vietnam to assist and support the Republic of South Vietnam are evidence of our commitment. And, as President Johnson said: ". . . those engaged in external direction and supply" of the assault against the lives and liberty of the people of South Vietnam "would do well to be reminded and to remember that this type of aggression is a deeply dangerous game."

We have special and very grave concerns about Communist China. And here let me clear away a myth. We do not ignore the Chinese Communist regime. We know it exists. We talk with it regularly through our respective ambassadors to Warsaw. There have been 119 of these talks. And what the Peking regime itself says to us is among the reasons why we continue to have very grave concerns about it.

Peking continues to insist upon the surrender of Formosa as the *sine qua non* of any improvement whatever in relations with the United States. We are loyal to our commitments to the Government of the Republic of China, and we will not abandon the twelve million people of Free China on Taiwan to Communist tyranny.

Peking incites and actively supports the aggression in Southeast Asia in violation of the Geneva agreements of 1954 and the Geneva accords of 1962. Peking attacked India and occupies a position from which it continues to threaten the subcontinent of South Asia. Peking is attempting to extend its tactics of terror and subversion into Africa and Latin America. In other words, Peking flouts the first condition for peace: Leave your neighbors alone. And we in the United States have not forgotten Peking's aggressive intervention in Korea—an act for which it stands condemned by the United Nations.

The American people cherished their close and cordial ties with the people of the Chinese mainland. They look forward to the time when it will be possible to renew this historic friendship. As I said in Tokyo: "When mainland China has a government which is prepared to renounce force, to make peace, and to honor international responsibilities, it will find us responsive."

Meanwhile we shall resolutely oppose aggression. We believe that all free nations should, in their own elementary self-interest, take care not to do anything that would encourage Communist militancy.

Insofar as the dispute between Peking and Moscow involves the question of militancy in prosecuting the Communist revolution, we would of course prefer realism about the dangers and potential consequences of aggression in the nuclear age.

The Castro Regime in Cuba

On our doorstep another Communist regime incites and supports subversion, terror, and guerrilla warfare against its Caribbean neighbors. More than two years ago, the Organization of American States unanimously declared this regime to be incompatible with the inter-American system. The OAS has taken various steps to isolate Castro's Cuba and to curb its capacity to do harm. It is now considering further steps.

There will be no retreat from our policy toward the Castro regime in Cuba as long as it continues to threaten the security and stability of other nations in this hemisphere. Moreover, we regard this regime as temporary. With the other nations of this hemisphere, we expect the Cuban people to regain their freedom and rejoin the inter-American system.

Recently a large quantity of arms was shipped into Venezuela to be used in an effort to overthrow the freely elected government of that country. The OAS has conclusive evidence that those arms came from Cuba. Consequently it is considering further steps to protect the free nations of this hemisphere from subversion and aggression, indirect as well as direct, based on Cuba.

The free nations who sell to Cuba goods and equipment important to the Cuban economy are interfering with the efforts of the free nations of this hemisphere to curb this danger. In the missile crisis of 1962 it was evident that what happened in Cuba could directly affect the security of the entire free world. That is still so.

Our Goal Remains Constant

The world is changing. And as it changes, we shall adjust particular policies. But our great goal remains constant. It is to build a decent world order—the kind set forth in the opening paragraphs of the Charter of the United Nations. Our major policies for moving toward that goal have produced favorable results. The free world has its problems—and we are drawn into most of them because of our power and commitment to the defense and promotion of freedom. But I prefer our problems to those of the Communist world.

The most powerful force at work in the world is the force which we have been identified with since our very birth as a nation, which we have nurtured and fought for over the generations: the ideas of freedom, of government with the consent of the governed, of the rights of man, of the rule of law, of individual human dignity. These ideas have gripped the minds of men in all parts of the world. They constitute the great, enduring revolutionary movement in human affairs.

So let us have the good sense to persevere in our threefold policy toward the Communist states, taking care always: to make resort to force or threat of force costly and futile; to search for agreements and understandings leading to a more stable peace; and to promote the trends within the Communist world which lead away from imperialism, away from dictatorships—and toward independence and open societies with freely chosen governments, with which we can live in enduring friendship.

EXPLOITING COMMUNIST VULNERABILITIES

by Richard L. Walker

> Dr. Walker is Director of the Institute of International Studies and Head of the Department of International Relations, University of South Carolina. A graduate of Drew University, he received his M.A. degree on Far Eastern and Russian Studies and his Ph.D. degree in International Relations from Yale University. He has taught at Yale, Taiwan National University, the University of Washington, and the National War College; and has frequently lectured in Japan, Hong Kong, Singapore, and Australia. He is the author of several books, including The Continuing Struggle: Communist China and the Free World (1958).

This selection is based on an address Dr. Walker gave in 1963 to the Fifth Annual National Strategy Seminars at Town Hall, New York City.

Observers have frequently pointed up critical aspects of the struggle between the free world and the Communist powers by analogies with various sports and games. Some, for example, noting that the Western countries carry on few activities beyond the Iron Curtain while the Communists conduct major operations this side of the barrier, have likened the struggle to a football game in which the rules deny the home team the right to penetrate beyond the fifty-yard line and thus consign its role exclusively to defense. In this situation a scoreless draw is the best that can be hoped for, and the defenses have to be perfect. Again, world politics in the cold war is sometimes likened to a chess match in which skill requires strategy and detailed advance planning.

Another useful comparison is with fencing. A standard work on that sport notes that it "cannot be excelled as a developer of trigger-speed movement, adaptation to the opponent, and of greater reliance upon skillful deception than upon brute strength . . ." It goes on to point out that the essence of sword-play is strategy, placing a premium upon "intelligence of conception and accuracy of execution."[1] One school of fencing (the Italian) stresses an aggressive style with emphasis on the lunge, the beat, and the thrust; another (the French) emphasizes defense against the aggressive lunge and a rapid *riposte* for scoring against the opponent when he is extended, possibly off balance, and his weak points exposed. No matter which approach is followed, certain points are quite obvious: it is impossible to win simply by parrying the thrusts of the opponent; it is necessary to penetrate the opponent's defenses; and this means finding his weaknesses, exploiting them, and doing so in a calculated and sustained manner.

Swordsmanship also requires that the participant be alertly on guard at all times, for the opponent is also probing for his weak points. Thus, for example, it is necessary to be sure that the type of *riposte* selected will not make him vulnerable for the opponent's *remise* if the riposte is parried. It is necessary therefore to feel out and know the opponent in order to develop a winning strategy. For such a strategy the art of the feint—misleading the opponent, throwing him off balance or disrupting his plans—is essential. But no feint is of real value unless it is followed up in a calculated manner, and this means it must be part of a coordinated strategy designed to win the contest.

The analogy is only too obvious. The United States as free world leader is engaged in the most crucial fencing match in history. The opponent is determined to penetrate our defenses with an aggressive strategy, to do us in, and to bury us. Although our style is essentially defensive, obviously we cannot win without a willingness to riposte, and this means penetrating the defenses of our opponent. It would be naïve to expect that by some stroke of good luck the opponent will give up his attack or that perhaps by accident he will wound himself. Obviously we must win, and this means that (1) we be in top condition physically and mentally; (2) we study and know the opponent; (3) we find his vulnerabilities; and (4) we devise and develop a sustained strategy for exploiting them. In order to win this match, a key feint which we must learn to employ is political and psychological warfare, but no feint is of real value unless it is linked with an over-all strategy and carefully coordinated. Coordination is usually regarded as the final mark of the master fencer, for it means an accurate control of all movements in terms of distance, timing, calculation, and a decision linked to an over-all strategy.

The Nature of the Opponent

There can be little doubt that our Communist opponents are ruthless and dangerous. Khrushchev and Mao Tse-tung belong to the age of Hitler and Stalin. They are representatives of modern totalitarianism in its fullest development. Since the start of the cold war, every State of the Union message by American Presidents has stressed the dangerous nature of the contest in which we are engaged and the formidable threat we face. On January 9, 1952, for instance, President Truman stated, "We are moving through a perilous time. Faced with a terrible threat of aggression, our Nation has embarked upon a great effort to help establish the kind of world in which peace shall be secure." Exactly six years later, President Eisenhower noted, "The threat to our safety, and to the hope of a peaceful world can be simply stated. It is Communist imperialism." He went on to point out, "what makes the Soviet threat unique in history is its all-inclusiveness. Every human activity is pressed into service as a weapon of expansion. Trade, economic development, military power, arts, science, education, the whole world of ideas—all are harnessed to the same chariot of expansion. The Soviets are, in short, waging total cold war." President Kennedy spoke of an "hour of national peril and national opportunity" and warned, "The outcome is by no means certain. The answers are by no means clear."

The conflict in the world today is symbolized by Stalin's dictum *kto-kovo* or "who-whom." By this he meant "who destroys whom." Today Khrushchev phrases it in terms of "who buries whom" and disagrees with Mao Tse-tung over the most effective method by which interment can be accomplished as soon as possible, but there is no disagreement as regards the basic conflict with the democracies of the West or the desirability of destroying the values for which the free world stands. Khrushchev is a self-proclaimed Leninist and follows belief that "Until the final issue is decided, the state of awful war will continue."

For the struggle which they have posited, the Communist leaders have developed a strategic perspective which enables them to exploit calculated periods of tension and relaxation in order to move toward a victory about which they are supremely self-confident. Concessions or moves toward temporary "peaceful coexistence" are viewed within a framework of strategy and tactics. Here, too, Khrushchev follows Lenin, who stated, "Concessions do not mean peace with capitalism, but war on a new plane."

Within their strategic perspective and for the expected period of protracted conflict with the United States and its allies, the Communists have fashioned a formidable organizational weapon for waging cold war, and it is proving especially effective in the "in-between world." The key to the effectiveness of the Communist synthesis of propaganda, espionage, subversion, economic penetration, front organizations, military assistance, international groupings, cultural diplomacy, etc. is strategic unity and coordination. Thus if the U.S.S.R. is involved in a trade deal with Western Europe, it is pursued and calculated in terms of over-all strategy and has been closely coordinated with other aims of Soviet policy.

Our awareness of this coordination and the over-all strategy of our Communist opponents—as well as a testament of our own problems—can be easily illustrated. At the time of the Congo crisis in 1961, for example, there was a general belief in the West that the problem of internal order and security in that troubled area would prove well-nigh insurmountable for the United Nations. Yet there was general agreement that the Soviets or Chinese Communists should not be allowed to move in. Presumably there was an expectation that they would bring order and success because of a superior organizational ability. Much of the same attitude can be found in other reactions to activities of the Communist powers. Leaders in the West, for example, frequently express worry about the many students from the countries of the in-between world who go to the Soviet Union or Communist China for higher education. Yet the hundreds of thousands of such students in free countries are seldom viewed as offering the West opportunities in the struggle with the Communist powers.

The effectiveness of Communist coordination around the world can be seen in the massive left-wing demonstrations in support of Communist policies. At the time of the Cuban missile crisis in October 1962, millions of demonstrators in countries near and far were called out to protest against "American imperialism." But, we may ask, where were the demonstrations of protest against the Soviet breaking of the atomic test moratorium in the fall of 1961? Who marched in great parades to protest the execution of Imre Nagy, or the rape of Tibet?

The extent to which even minor matters are coordinated to support Soviet or Chinese Communist strategic design is illustrated by the handling within their areas of control of foreign news media. As a result of a television program, "The Plot to Kill Stalin," shown in the United States on September 25, 1958, CBS correspondents were ousted from Moscow. The anxiety of the network to re-establish its competitive position in the Soviet capital was probably reflected in its initial decision in January 1961 to cancel a projected program, "The Spy Next Door." (It was eventually shown.) A subsequent expulsion of NBC from Moscow was likely to make that network more sensitive about its programing in the future.

There can be no doubt that the Communists have a formidable organizational and strategic design posed for use against the outside world. They are determined through totalitarian control to block any effective influence or action by the

Western powers in their areas of control while they seek to take advantage of pluralism in the West for their own aggressive thrusts.

Our Own Condition

Against such a formidable opponent we tend sometimes to become defeatist and to underestimate not only the achievements of our own civilization but also our own ability for an effective riposte against a Communist thrust. The strength and influence of the United States and the example it has set for the world are of profound significance. In 1964, with one-sixteenth of the earth's surface and one-seventeenth of the earth's people, the United States had an estimated gross national product of $625 billion, produced over 30 per cent of the world's goods and services, and consumed more than a third of the world's energy. Among people everywhere, it is the United States which is the model and the goal. We are copied all around the world, and our influence is large. Even Khrushchev's much-heralded twenty-year plan, which was little more than a propagandistic promise of pie-in-the-sky, offered no more than the pie which is already on American tables.

United States leadership in the field of international relations has also been strong. As Secretary of State Rusk has pointed out, it is hard to find anywhere in the annals of mankind a match for our peace-making efforts and the constructive employment of our power. Our world involvement includes more than fourscore countries receiving our military and economic assistance, more than twoscore in mutual security arrangements with us, our armed forces protecting ourselves and our allies around the globe, and American goods setting standards in every land: such achievements are difficult indeed for the Communist countries to match. And behind all this is military strength with weapons in good order.

There are numerous difficulties which have attended America's new world involvement. Many of these difficulties are directly related to our democratic form of government. During the cold war, as one crisis quiets down, we are apt to forget the over-all continuing conflict. More than a century and a quarter ago, that famous French observer of the American scene, Alexis de Tocqueville, wrote:

> Democracy appears to me better adapted for the conduct of society in times of peace, or for a sudden effort of remarkable vigor than for the prolonged endurance of the great storms that beset the political existence of nations. The reason for this is very evident; enthusiasm prompts men to expose themselves to dangers and privations; but without reflection they will not support them long. There is more calculation even in the impulses of bravery than is generally supposed; and although the first efforts are made by passion alone, perseverance is maintained only by a distinct view of what one is fighting for. A portion of what is dear to us is hazarded in order to save the remainder.
>
> But it is this clear perception of the future, founded upon judgment and experience, that is frequently wanting in democracies. The people are more apt to feel than to reason; and if their sufferings are great, it is to be feared that the still greater sufferings attendant upon defeat will be forgotten.[2]

Then, too, there are problems related to enabling a pluralistic society to bring to bear all of its resources within the total framework required by the cold war. Again, timing of budgeting cycles and election campaigns frequently preclude sustained effort. Nevertheless, it has been only too evident that the United States is capable of making a far more sustained effort and bringing far more of its power to bear than it has in the past.

Communist Weaknesses

But the Communist powers have their weaknesses, and these must be taken into account. An important point to be made, however—and it cannot be emphasized too strongly—is that weaknesses in the Sino-Soviet camp are not necessarily vulnerabilities. A weakness does not become a vulnerability until an opponent has shown a capacity as well as a willingness to exploit it. In the case of our duel with the Communist powers, this means moving past their defenses causing them to drop their guard, diverting their stratagems and requiring them to expend energies in a wasteful manner.

It is useful, though, to call attention to some obvious Communist weaknesses which offer opportunity for exploitation:

1. As Bertram D. Wolfe has pointed out, Communist despotism is in itself a weakness. Performance has not begun to measure up to promise.[3] Valuable resources and energies are channeled in preserving the despotic rule of the few. The contrast between claim and reality is symbolized by the Iron Curtain and by the Berlin Wall. It is borne out by Communist necessity to rewrite history and their attempts to remake facts.

2. Communist colonialism is another major weakness. In an age when the imperial powers of Europe have given independence to their colonies, the Soviet and Chinese Communist empires stand in marked and anachronistic contrast. Nationalism and national differences plague the Communist camp. As President Kennedy pointed out in his State of the Union message in 1963, "the forces of diversity are at work within the Communist camp, despite all the iron discipline and regimentation and all the iron dogmatisms of ideology. . . . This disarray of the Communist empire has been heightened by two other formidable forces. One is the historic force of nationalism and the yearning of all men to be free." Thus, the free world continues to have many allies within the areas of Communist control.

3. The other force to which President Kennedy referred constitutes yet another major weakness within the Communist camp: the gross inefficiency of the economy. Communist rulers everywhere have been singularly unsuccessful in agriculture. As President Kennedy pointed out, "a police state cannot command the grain to grow." Both mainland China and the U.S.S.R. have been in the embarrassing position of having to import large quantities of foodstuffs from abroad. Communist regimes have also failed to develop meaningful pricing systems or adequate methods for resource allocation. In many instances the Communists have been able to escape

their own inefficiencies because they have turned to the very "bourgeois" methods they denounce.

4. The bureaucracy of a system which attempts to manage all aspects of human life is also a weakness. Under Communist totalitarianism, an individual must fill out multiple-copy forms for such activities as visiting a friend in a neighboring town or even for minor purchases, forms which can be both irritating and inefficient. It should be noted that this weakness is a constant matter of concern to the Communists themselves.

5. The Sino-Soviet dispute has highlighted major weaknesses within the framework of an important Communist alliance. Two great nations have been finding that the constraints of conformity have led to friction and disagreements over such items as: (a) the approach to war, (b) leadership of the underdeveloped countries, (c) internal interference in each other's areas of control, (d) strained economic and trade relations, and (e) disagreements and personal antagonisms among the top leaders themselves.

6. Another weakness has been the performance and frequently the behavior of the Soviets and the Chinese Communists abroad. The "ugly Russian" and the "ugly Chinese" have in many areas been attempting to replace the American, who appears to be not so ugly after all. In many underdeveloped areas, Soviet representatives have been charged by local regimes with drunkenness, exclusiveness, haughtiness, sexual promiscuity, and such crimes as smuggling. The quality of Communist products has left much to be desired. For example, a Soviet-built road sank into a swamp in Indonesia after first heavy use, and Soviet jeeps in Egypt were found to have faulty steering. Again, a Czech-built plant in Afghanistan yielded such poor quality cement that it could not be used for an airstrip which the Soviets had agreed to build. Both the Chinese Communists and the Soviets have been long on promise and very short and slow on delivery. Internal pressures have forced curtailment in Communist-bloc economic assistance in the 1960's, with many projects incomplete or called off.

7. One more weakness deserves some mention—the growing

demands and expectations of the masses under Communist control. In our concern about the "revolution of rising expectations" we have often failed to note that this same force is operative on the other side of the Iron Curtain. Growing demands in the Communist camp are a good illustration of a weakness which could become a vulnerability. Given the limits of the Soviet economy, for example, a stepped-up program of military preparedness in the West could force the Soviets to take away even more butter for guns, and, in that event, growing consumer demand becomes a real vulnerability. On the other hand, if by challenge and example the Soviet government is pressured into making more consumer goods available to its people, this too becomes a vulnerability because it detracts from some of the effort which would otherwise be channeled into world revolution and Soviet thrusts against individual countries in the free world.

Our Experiences to Date

How has the United States fared to date in attempting to transform the many Soviet weaknesses into vulnerabilities? What has been our strategy in this great global duel? There has been a general tendency to assume that the United States is doing nothing, that our propaganda is ineffective, and that the Soviets do not have to respond to our initiative. This is simply not so.

American citizens frequently do not hear about United States propaganda activities and successes abroad because by law the United States Information Agency is precluded from disseminating information inside the United States. But our propaganda has caused no small amount of concern and embarrassment in Communist capitals. There are many actions which, though usually not part of a coordinated plan for defeating the opponent, nevertheless put him at a disadvantage and force him into unintended fields of activity. Whatever the United States does, the Communist rulers in Peking and Moscow notice and follow closely. American activities in the field of foreign aid probably provided a major reason why the Soviets decided to enter into that field, and surely the amount of Soviet aid to India has been one of the factors underlying the Sino-Soviet dispute.

In general, however, United States efforts to turn Soviet weaknesses into vulnerabilities and to bring about the changes which would make Soviet policies less of a threat have been piecemeal, uncoordinated, and unrelated to an over-all strategy. The United States has had many successes, such as capitalizing on the Khrushchev "secret speech" revealing Stalin's crimes, the American exhibition in Moscow, or activities at the last two World Youth Festivals. But, while these have been good feints, they have hardly been useful ones. They were not part of a strategic plan nor was there adequate follow-up.

It is useful to examine in somewhat more detail two examples of successful initiative action on the part of the United States which put pressure on our Soviet opponents and kept them off balance, at least for a while.

1. On December 8, 1953, President Eisenhower made his now-famous "Atoms for Peace" speech before the United Nations. The following day *Pravda* rejected the plan, without giving any indication of serious consideration or even informing the Russian people what it was all about. Within a few days, world pressures and the activity of our Information Service were obviously troubling Moscow and by December 12, the Russian people were being told that the American proposal would get close attention. Nine days later, on December 21, Moscow Radio finally broadcast several hundred words of direct quotation from the Eisenhower speech. On December 26, the Soviets announced the postponement of a scheduled Foreign Ministers' Conference. They were obviously still disturbed about how to answer this new "imperialist scheme." On January 6, 1954, Moscow indicated that it would be willing to start procedural discussions on the Atoms for Peace plan. The United States continued to push the issue. The Soviets eventually bypassed the proposal by an attempt to link it to an all-out, but naturally uninspected, ban on nuclear weapons.

2. On July 21, 1955, President Eisenhower made his famous "Open Skies" proposal at Geneva. Moscow was some-

what more prompt on this occasion in broadcasting the text and along with it the Soviet explanation of this "deceitful scheme," which was rejected out of hand. But by August 5 enough pressure had been built up that Bulganin was obliged to note that the U.S.S.R. was seriously studying the proposal and that its rejection was misunderstood around the world. Moscow's eventual answer on August 13 was a diversionary announcement of a proposed Soviet troop cut of more than half a million men.

There are some very instructive points which emerge from the above two examples. In the first place, these were clearly cases of imaginative initiative on the part of the United States. Second, in both cases the Soviet hierarchy seemed hard-pressed to develop answers which would be convincing, both to their own people and to the outside world. Third, and certainly very important, for almost a month the Soviets launched no cold war initiative action of their own. Fourth, Moscow's behavior indicated that the Iron Curtain could not keep out such important news. Eventually, the controlled Communist press and radio gave the full text of each Eisenhower speech.

Unfortunately, we had no new initiative prepared and, although we did keep pushing our opponents on both occasions, we did not seem to possess the facilities for backup which the Soviets themselves would have employed. We did not, for example, have the massive organized demonstrations to support our proposals. Such demonstrations would have caused even greater concern in Moscow. Though these two initiatives were in many respects successful as isolated and individual schemes, their effectiveness against the Communist cold war organization could only be minimal.

In part, our piecemeal approach has resulted from organizational difficulty in the United States Government. In 1963, for example, we had sixteen separate departments and agencies with direct major concern in foreign affairs and another twenty with somewhat lesser concern. They have frequently worked at cross-purposes and there is as yet no method for concerting their many talents and functions as a part of a strategy. Many agencies have grown up precisely because of the Communist cold war challenge, yet they have not been given the organizational unity which they know their Communist enemies possess.

In an attempt to remedy the chronic absence of strategic utilization of our resources, President Truman established the Psychological Strategy Board on August 7, 1950. Unfortunately, jealousies and bickerings among key agencies concerned with foreign affairs were never ironed out, nor was the Psychological Strategy Board ever given adequate power. In an effort once again to tackle the problem, President Eisenhower replaced the Psychological Strategy Board with the Operation Coordinating Board but it, too, lacked the power and prestige and has now been eliminated. Thus, in 1964 there is no agency or division of the United States Government capable of long-range coordination and strategic planning. We are still unable to utilize our own many strengths, to turn Soviet weaknesses into vulnerabilities or to develop plans to win the cold war struggle.

Almost two decades of conflict with Communist totalitarianism have at least made clear some basic conclusions for our strategy in the future. First, it is now obvious that the free world has far more access to the Soviet and Chinese Communist communications networks than is normally supposed. When high American officials speak, Communists listen, and usually answer. Increasing travel, worldwide radio networks, and the spread of television offer ever greater means of penetrating the curtain of totalitarian communications control. The Communist official who works out an answer to a proposal of the United States or one of its allies frequently feels enjoined to convince his fellow members of the apparatus of his brilliance and therefore internal and external information is not nearly as well separated under the Communists as we might suppose. Under Khrushchev, the Soviets have become increasingly sensitive to outside pressure on issues which Stalin would have shrugged off with contemptuous indifference.

A second conclusion is that we cannot win in the type of struggle which we call the cold war without a toughly directed coordination of effort within the framework of a long-range strategy and with the power to back it up. Third, given its economic power and influence around the world, the United States has a capacity for far more initiative in political and psychological operations than we have generally assumed. Our Communist opponents cannot ignore our major actions and words. Finally, if given the realities of Communist totalitarianism—hunger, schism, the Wall, police terror, and economic failure—we are unable to develop a political warfare strategy which can convert Communist weaknesses into vulnerabilities, break through their defenses, score against them on their own ground, and effect fundamental changes in their ideology, then perhaps we deserve the burial which their leaders promise us.

Developing a Winning Strategy

Americans have been prone to believe that strategy is confined to the field of military activity. But it is now time to recognize that a broad strategy—political, economic, and psychological, as well as military—is an essential requirement if we are to prevail against the spectrum of cold war activities employed by our Communist opponents. In order to develop a strategy for exploiting Communist vulnerabilities, there are at least four pressing and immediate needs.

1. Obviously, the first need is coordination of effort. The United States requires a new and reinvigorated Psychological Strategy Board, with powers and influence to match its important functions. Too long, government agencies have worked at cross-purposes, both at home and abroad, and we have been denied the unity of effort, the timing of actions, and the follow-up activities for our desperate fencing match with our Communist opponent.

2. The United States needs a highly trained group of political and psychological warfare strategists to staff a reconstituted Psychological Strategy Board. As Franklin A. Lindsay has pointed out:

> Specifically, we require a system of training—both for our own personnel and for those we are aiding—com-

parable to that for an army officer, a physician or an engineer. A national institute or staff college comparable to those of the Army, Air Force and Navy is needed to provide a center for training of United States and possibly foreign personnel and for elaborating strategic concepts of unconventional warfare and developing practical and effective tactics to meet the operational problems we now face in many parts of the world. . . .

The Communists have allowed themselves lead times of as much as 10 to 20 years in training revolutionary leaders. One can only hope that the free world yet has time to build the political leadership, both abroad and at home, to meet their threat successfully.[4]

3. A third requirement is the development within the United States of program planning and contingency planning. For example, concerted efforts and alternate policies involving all relevant government agencies are required for such events as the death of Khrushchev or Mao Tse-tung. Americans tend to shy away from concepts of planning, and yet their most successful industries prepare planned expansion and coordination years in advance. To quote Mr. Lindsay again, "Program planning is not a strait jacket that commits us to a particular course of action, no matter what new circumstances arise, but a means of increasing our freedom of action and our ability to grasp the initiative in the long, cold war."[5]

4. A final need is the will to win this great cold war match in which we are involved. Only a will to win, to penetrate the enemy's defenses, to cause him embarrassment, to cause him to misdirect his resources, to carry on long-range political and psychological operations can create the conditions in which our view of the world, focused on human freedom, can prevail. The free world is engaged in a contest *which it has to win,* but our fragmented efforts to date do not bespeak a strategy for winning. Our few feints have been only that and there has been little pursuit.

What would be the type of activity which a coordinated and long-range strategy for exploiting Communist vulnerabilities would involve? There could be, for example, a consistent and sustained effort of exposure of poor Communist performance. This could be coordinated with allied leaders in such a way as to breathe some new life and cooperation into our alliance system. Given the fact that the United States President, the French President, and the British Prime Minister have to be answered when they make important formal statements, our President could, for instance, make a well-publicized statement on Soviet promises and performance in the field of agriculture. A few days later, the British Prime Minister could call a conference on how to help Khrushchev deliver on his promises of food to the Russian people. This could be followed at an appropriate interval by a statement from the French President, referring to the former two developments and suggesting that perhaps the Soviet Premier would like to come to a conference to discuss food rather than atomic weapons. The French President could, like his allies, wonder aloud just how scientific Communism is, in view of poor performance in China and the U.S.S.R.

In addition to such campaigns of exposure, a long-range strategy would also develop programs of challenge which might push our Communist opponents into unintended fields of activity. The Western powers, for example, pointing to the fact that Mongolia, with only a million people, has been under Communist control for more than four decades with limited progress could challenge the Communists to prove the supposed superiority of their system by developing a standard of living there to match the standard of living in a small country of like population in the free world, which we would then support. The Communists could be challenged to a ten-year competition to be judged by representatives from leading neutralist countries. They would obviously be unwilling to permit the type of scrutiny from the outside which could determine basic starting points and rates of progress in the two competing experimental countries.

Other fields for long-range strategic exploitation of Communist vulnerabilities include passive resistance. It is worth recalling that in 1961, longshoremen in Odessa went on a protest slowdown over loading butter for Cuba when none was available at home. Organization would also be involved.

Communists, as has been indicated above, are sensitive about organized demonstrations. A willingness to embark on a strategy for exploiting Communist vulnerabilities could lead to organized demonstrations in the free world in favor of, for instance, Tibetan freedom and access to Tibet by the outside world. Again, a strategic perspective would enable programs for keeping alive the issue of Communist colonialism and for making allied efforts to exploit the revelations that have come in the wake of the Sino-Soviet dispute. Communist bureaucracy can also be overloaded, in part as a result of the fact that top Communist officials do indeed have to answer our initiative, and all the more so, if they come as a part of an allied plan.

There are no simple blueprints or magic formulae for the cold war struggle, but to date there has been little indication of our willingness to think and plan in strategic terms. Like the fencer, the free world requires diligent training and a knowledge of the opponent. But it is necessary that we understand clearly that our opponent is not vulnerable until we penetrate his defenses which have been opened up by our political warfare feints and until our riposte has been able to carry through because we have the physical strength, the mental agility, and the coordination required for this greatest bout in history. The time for coordinating our agencies and efforts, for personnel, for political warfare, for the adoption of a strategic perspective, and for the acceptance of a will to win by exploiting Communist vulnerabilities is now.

NOTES

1. Julio Martinez Castello, *The Theory and Practice of Fencing* (New York: Charles Scribner's Sons, 1933), p. 14.
2. Alexis de Tocqueville, *Democracy in America* (New York: Alfred A. Knopf, 1948), Volume I, pp. 228–29.
3. See Bertram D. Wolfe, "Communist Vulnerabilities," in Walter F. Hahn and John C. Neff, eds., *American Strategy for the Nuclear Age* (Garden City, N.Y.: Doubleday Anchor Books, 1960), pp. 89–102. Mr. Wolfe's points are summarized and in addition much more helpful material dealing with the problems of psychological operations against the Communist powers is

added in Robert Strausz-Hupé, *et al.*, *A Forward Strategy for America* (New York: Harper & Row, 1961), Chapter 8, "Psychological Operations," pp. 253–85.

4. Franklin A. Lindsay, "Unconventional Warfare." *Foreign Affairs,* January 1962.

5. Franklin A. Lindsay, "Program Planning: The Missing Element." *Foreign Affairs,* January 1961.

THE COLD WAR OF WORDS

by John Richardson, Jr.

Since 1961 Mr. Richardson has been President and a member of the Board of Directors of the Free Europe Committee. A native of Boston, he is a graduate of Harvard College and Harvard Law School. He has served as Treasurer and President of the International Rescue Committee and between 1956 and 1960 he initiated various private efforts, first to help the free-dom fighters in Hungary, and later to organize and carry out the distribution of several million dollars worth of medicines in Poland in association with CARE. The Free Europe Committee is a private, non-profit organization which includes Radio Free Europe and other divisions engaged in international programs of information, research, publishing, and East-Central European émigré affairs.

This selection is based on an address given by the author to New York State publishers at Albany on January 30, 1963. Reprinted by permission.

The clearest statements on Communist objectives and tactics are made by the Communists themselves. When Khrushchev said some years ago, "The day the Communists abandon their drive to liberate the world will be the day the shrimp has learned to whistle on the mountain top," he meant it. He meant that the takeover of the world was a basic, inflexible Communist objective. This objective remains unchanged.

Thus, in "The Materialistic Conception of the Freedom of

the Press," an article which recently appeared in the quarterly publication *Novinarsky Sbornik* (*Newspaper Almanac*) of the Journalistic Research Institute of Prague, the Communist press lords reveal—more clearly than any Western analyst can—how cynically, but purposefully, the Communists strive to make words and ideas serve their ends. The article also illuminates a key principle which guides and inspires Communist Party activists the world over: the highest "moral" value is assigned to *any* action which strengthens the Party dictatorship. Everything is secondary to power—which means, among other things, controlling the hearts and minds of people. It is a religion of expediency in which might—physical and psychological might—makes right.

Following a discussion on some problems of "censorship," the Czechoslovak article referred to above continues:

> The difficulty lies in the fact that it is not always easy to distinguish a contest of ideas in one's own ranks—within scientific socialism and communism—from the struggle between proletarian and bourgeois ideologies. That is to say, the dividing line between the classes, as well as that between truth and falsehood is . . . uncertain and invisible, inasmuch as it is always flexible. What was a lie yesterday can be the truth today, and vice versa. What served the bourgeoisie yesterday can serve the proletariat today . . .

How well this thinking echoes the nightmarish vision of Communism depicted by George Orwell in his novel, *1984*. Here is a leading Communist speaking in *1984*—a book that appeared to many to be a highly exaggerated version of the ultimate Communist state:

> There is need for an unwearying moment-to-moment flexibility in the treatment of facts. The key word here is black-white. It has two mutually contradictory meanings. Applied to an opponent, it means the habit of impudently claiming that black is white, in contradiction to the plain facts. Applied to a Party member, it means a loyal willingness to say that black is white when Party discipline demands it. But it means also the ability to *believe* that black

is white, and more, to *know* that black is white, *and to forget that one has ever believed to the contrary*. This demands a continuous alteration of the past. . . . And since the Party is in full control of the records, and in equally full control of the minds of its members, *the past is whatever the Party chooses to make it.*

In other words: "What was a lie yesterday can be the truth today and vice versa." We must never forget for a moment—because this is a key reason for many of the victories the Communists have won—that they *do* have what Orwell's Communist called: "the ability to *believe* that black is white, and more, to *know* that black is white, *and to forget that one has ever believed to the contrary.*"

Of course, censorship in a Communist country—whether it is manifested by absolute control of the internal communications media, the banning of publications from the outside, or the jamming of Western broadcasts—is also a defensive weapon. No Communist state can survive freedom of expression. The Communists candidly admit this. The Czechoslovak journal already cited defines censorship as "a means of defense against bourgeois ideas and their spreading under conditions when these ideas, under certain circumstances, become a social danger, because there still exist in our society individuals who could turn these ideas, however temporarily, into a force aiding a reversal of the political and social order."

So as to leave no room for doubt in the minds of its readers —the publishers, editors, and journalists in Czechoslovakia— the article goes on to say: "Only highly naïve people could get the idea that the Communists, who had not hesitated a single moment before prohibiting the bourgeois newspapers, would cavil about whether or not to prevent the penetration of counterrevolutionary bourgeois ideology into the pages of the legally existing press. . . . In politics and in the sphere of ideology, the Communists are *not* adherents of free competition!"

The Communist Compulsion to Control Thinking

This, then, is the prevailing Communist fear: competition in the realm of ideas. And hence their compulsion to control the thinking as well as the actions of the people living under their domination. But it doesn't work.

True, Communism has physically conquered one-third of the world but, generally speaking, it has *not* conquered people. Communism has in particular not succeeded in controlling the yearnings and aspirations of youngsters subject to relentless indoctrination and punishment. The role played by the young people in the 1956 Hungarian Revolution was clear evidence of this Communist failure—and since then, the stubborn and frequently successful efforts of youngsters behind the Iron Curtain to defy their rulers and share various Western habits . . . rock 'n' roll, to name just one widely publicized manifestation of Western civilization that has penetrated the Iron Curtain.

Furthermore, within the Communist empire itself, a spectacular ideological dispute and deeply divisive power struggle has come to the surface for all to see. The monolith—if, indeed, one ever truly existed—has cracked. It is true, as the late President Kennedy pointed out, that "a dispute over how best to bury the free world is no grounds for rejoicing." Nevertheless, new opportunities do exist for America and the free world: opportunities that must be pursued with skill and determination if we are to protect our own societies, advance the cause of freedom, and reduce the awful risks of thermonuclear war.

Opportunities for the West

These opportunities are of fundamental, and not merely of tactical or provisional importance, when they both reflect and are conditioned by genuine national and popular interests. Thus, the Communist-ruled peoples of East-Central Europe, through their continued resistance to Communist tyranny as well as to Soviet Russian hegemony, are in my opinion transforming Communist factional infighting into a process which quite possibly will ultimately lead to the disintegration of Communist political power. To make their peaceful pressures effective, these peoples must be fully and accurately informed, both as to the real situation in the world and as to developments within their own countries. This is the task of Radio Free Europe—the broadcasting arm of the Free Europe Committee, a private American organization which is one of the most significant non-violent offensive weapons available to the West today in what is still a cold war against Communist imperialism.

Here, it may be worth recalling a like history. Following World War II, in complete violation of all their solemn international commitments, the U.S.S.R.—true to the Marxist-Leninist principle that might makes right—occupied the ancient states of East-Central Europe with their troops. They imposed Communist dictatorships on these proud and independent and religious peoples, ignoring the protests of the rest of the civilized world.

Since then, utilizing total control of all productive enterprise, all communications media, all educational institutions, and the whole awesome array of pressure and terror weapons available to a modern police state, these Communist regimes have sought to mold one hundred million people—from the Baltic States in the north, to Albania in the south—to conform to Moscow specifications. But they have failed. They have failed because the people, in spite of all pressures and terrors, have never given in, have never given up hope, have never ceased to resist in every way open to them. The free world has not done what these patriotic peoples once hoped we would do: that is, risk a war by attempting to intervene with force against their Soviet rulers. And the free world today does not do what these people still pray for—the exertion of maximum political, moral, diplomatic, and economic leverage to weaken Communist control and Soviet influence in East-Central Europe.

In spite of these disappointments, in spite of all the pressures to conform—if only to give a better chance to their children in the society they must make their lives in—these people are still overwhelmingly anti-Communist, anti-Soviet, pro-European, pro-American, and pro-democratic.

A major factor in these attitudes is that these peoples have not in fact been forgotten by the free world: we—especially in America—have continued to try to communicate with them through many channels; they know that we have not abandoned their struggle to regain both their individual liberties and national independence.

Radio Free Europe

The single most important channel of communication between the West and these subjugated peoples for many years has been Radio Free Europe. In volumes of programing in the languages of its broadcasting area, for example, RFE leads all other Western stations combined.

For eighteen hours every day to Poland, Hungary, and Czechoslovakia, and seven hours daily to Bulgaria and Rumania, Radio Free Europe is on the air with sufficient power, and over sufficient frequencies, to reach the great majority of the eighty million people in these five countries. Well over half the families in this area have short-wave radios which can and do receive our broadcasts.

Over Radio Free Europe they hear—first and foremost—ten minutes of straight news every hour on the hour. This particular segment of programing is, so to speak, our "front page," which we constantly bring up-to-date as the broadcasting day progresses. It includes information not only of the "outside" world, but also hard news of developments *inside* the Communist orbit and our listeners' own countries. Radio Free Europe's Central Newsroom in Munich receives a daily average inflow of 1,100,000 words. This includes information from the West (primarily from wire services, our own news bureaus and correspondents, refugees and travelers from behind the Iron Curtain) plus our own monitoring of some fifty Communist orbit radio stations and news agencies. It does *not* include much of the information that our expert analysts read in hundreds of Communist newspapers and other publications.

Our listeners also hear, usually following the newscasts, political commentary and news analysis. These programs would be the equivalent of what our own newspapers carry in the way of political columns, background analysis, and interpretation, and editorial page comment. These programs help our listeners to put into clear and sensible perspective their own position in the ebb and flow of world developments. Radio Free Europe has special daily programs, too, consisting entirely of summaries and excerpts of articles and editorials from the Western press—especially from leading West European and U.S. newspapers. In this way, we specifically bring a free press behind the Iron Curtain.

Our daily schedule is rounded out with on-the-spot coverage of major Western events, drama, music, sports, religious broadcasts, educational and cultural programs, and special programing for the various segments of our listening population: workers, farmers, professionals, women, children, intellectuals, and even the Communists themselves.

To indicate the volume and intensity of programing we are geared to on a single topic, I would like to cite the Cuban missile crisis as an example:

On Monday night, October 22, 1962, Radio Free Europe stayed on the air after midnight (Central European Time) to bring its listeners President Kennedy's historic "quarantine" address. The following day, October 23, our transmitters broadcast the full text of the speech (in translation, as always) from two to five times to each of our five target countries. In the week that followed, 160 hours of programing were devoted to the subject of the Cuban situation alone. The reason? To be certain that the people of East-Central Europe—people subject to a relentless barrage of distorted propaganda from Communist communications media—would know the truth and the whole truth about a situation not only of the highest international urgency, but also one of possibly grave importance *to them* personally.

Radio Free Europe's programs are written and broadcast by East Europeans chosen for their professional skills and democratic convictions. These exiles are highly motivated people with a highly sophisticated understanding of Communism, both theoretical and in practical terms of strategy and tactics. As a voice speaking back to his enslaved countrymen, over an American-sponsored station, the exile conveys an authority and conviction that has made Radio Free Europe a unique instrument in the world of mass communication.

Our five broadcasting divisions located in Munich—one for each target country—gain knowledge of developments and activities behind the Iron Curtain from comprehensive monitoring of Communist radio stations and reading of hundreds of Communist publications, including the daily newspapers. They also have the benefit of one of the finest research facilities concerning East Europe anywhere in the world. Listenership, and the moods and attitudes of the East European peoples, are objectively evaluated on the basis of thousands of interviews every year with refugees and travelers from behind the Iron Curtain.

Policy, top leadership, and ultimate control of the broadcasts are in the hands of American management, with the Radio Free Europe Director in Munich reporting to the President of the Free Europe Committee in New York. He is responsible to the Committee's Board of Directors, which still includes many of the distinguished private citizens who had the unique energy and foresight to launch this enterprise in 1949.

The Impact of RFE Broadcasts

What do the Communists think of our broadcasts? If one judged devotion by meticulous attention paid to every word broadcast, one would indeed conclude that the Communists are profoundly devoted to Radio Free Europe. Such a conclusion can be supported by citing, for example, the reactions to RFE broadcasts in Czechoslovakia—the reactions there being similar to those in all other East European countries.

Western broadcasts in Czechoslovakia are fully and systematically monitored by a branch of CETEKA (the official Czechoslovak news agency) under the supervision of the Ministry of Interior. A daily news bulletin, issued to a limited number of leading regime functionaries, includes information on the Czech and Slovak broadcasts of foreign stations. A much smaller number of "subscribers," about thirty, receives a special appendix on the more "delicate" broadcasts on developments in the Soviet Union and its satellite countries. These "subscribers" include members of the Politburo, some leading Communist Party secretaries, chiefs of certain ministerial departments, a few chief editors, and some members of the government considered to be absolutely "reliable."

The listening to Radio Free Europe broadcasts forms the most important part of the Czechoslovak monitoring service. Orders in respect to this monitoring come from either the Communist Party Secretariat or the Ministry of Interior. Occasionally the Office of the President or the Premier will issue a monitoring order regarding the inclusion or exclusion of a particular monitoring report on the situation within Czechoslovakia.

The rule regarding Radio Free Europe broadcasts is to monitor as completely as possible *all* broadcasts and to note the quality of the reception. Full texts of RFE broadcasts are in particular demand by the Department of Interior, which sometimes demands tape recordings of the programs. (This monitoring service, by the way, has no connection with the Czechoslovak jamming service, which is under direct control of the Interior Ministry. Jamming personnel wear military garb and are considered to be members of the armed forces.)

The effect of RFE and other Western programs on the population of Czechoslovakia is the subject of independent research conducted by the Propaganda Department of the Communist Party Secretariat, and the political Counter-Propaganda Department of the Interior Ministry. Through the local Party apparatus, the Party determines the degree to which foreign stations are heard; the structure of the audience; and which stations, programs, and commentators are most popular. The results are analyzed by a special section of the Propaganda Department.

Much more detailed research is carried out by the Interior Ministry's political Counter-Propaganda Department, which reports its conclusions to the Communist Party Secretariat, with recommendations for counter-propaganda measures. The Secretariat finally issues directives to press, radio, and television officials on how to fight the influence of Western broadcasts.

On one point, at least, Communist findings on listenership are in agreement with the vast research we ourselves have done on the subject: The people want to hear facts, full and objective information, and thoughtful commentary. They also want to think for themselves, and are sick and tired of Communist propagandists trying to think for them. RFE's advantage over regime media in this respect is clear: The Communists *cannot* tell the facts without digging their own graves. RFE *can*, and effectively—ideological grave-digging is one of the reasons it is in business.

Radio Free Europe has another great advantage: It is able from the outside to reach the people behind the Iron Curtain with fast-breaking news before it is published or broadcast by the Communist media. One reason for this anomalous situation was described in the following way by the chief London correspondent of CETEKA after he defected in London:

No newspaper in Czechoslovakia ever publishes any important home or foreign news on its own. They are always waiting for CETEKA. Why should they burn their fingers? The horror of committing a "political error" hangs constantly over the worried heads of Communist journalists in Czechoslovakia, and whoever can shift the responsibility to someone else always does so gladly. The reporter or rewriter shifts the responsibility to the sub-editor; he passes the buck to the editor, and so on up to the Party secretary in charge of the propaganda department or even —and this is by no means as rare as one might think—up to the Prime Minister himself. A system in which the news must be politically "cooked" and approved at many stages is inevitably cumbersome, and causes long delays. In the atmosphere reigning in a Communist news agency, the speed and efficiency characteristic of the work of Western news agencies are inconceivable.

Communist Attacks against RFE

The meticulous attention the Communists pay to Radio Free Europe's broadcasts leaves no doubt that they deeply respect and fear our influence, our ability to break their internal monopoly of communications. Because they cannot successfully jam out our programs, they resort to a massive smear campaign through their own press, magazines, radio and television stations, books and films. This continuous propaganda against the Free Europe Committee has its inspiration in Moscow, but is developed in impressive variety throughout Eastern Europe.

In the ideological organ of the Bulgarian Communist Party *Nove Vreme* (*New Times*), for example, there recently appeared an attack bearing the byline of Mitko Grigorov, Secretary of the Central Committee of the Bulgarian Communist Party, also an important member of the Politburo. A few sentences from this article reveal—through the usual welter of verbiage—the Communist failure to keep the influence of Western media from the people:

> Bourgeois propaganda penetrates into our country through all kinds of channels. . . . The imperialistic bourgeoisie possesses enormous, well-organized and experienced propaganda apparatus, with powerful means for influencing not only the capitalistic world *but also for the penetration of the socialist countries.* . . . In their ideological expansion, the imperialists zealously direct their efforts against our country. Particular zeal is displayed by the imperialistic stations Radio Free Europe, BBC, the Voice of America and others, which spit out vicious slanders and interminably speak out against our Fatherland. Great activity is conducted by the Free Europe Committee, which possesses five large radio stations and 29 transmitters. . . .

These illustrations of the influence of Western media in captive East Europe should not suggest that one be scornful of the Communist propaganda effort. On the contrary, it should be clearly stated that the international Communist movement conducts a propaganda operation—both internally and to the outside world—that is monumental compared to Western efforts.

At the beginning of 1963, Radio Free Europe completed a definitive report on "Communist Foreign Radio Services" —a survey including the activities of Communist radio programs that are transmitted *abroad*, not internally. The report includes only *voice* programs of propaganda content, and it covers thirteen Communist-ruled countries: Russia, the East European regimes, Red China, North Vietnam, North Korea, and Cuba.

The radio stations of these thirteen Communist regimes transmit more than four thousand hours of radio programing abroad every week in sixty-three languages. Leaving nothing to chance, the broadcast languages include even Esperanto. No corner of any continent is left unreached. The Soviet Union leads with some thirteen hundred weekly hours of radio propaganda directed abroad. Red China comes second, with almost seven hundred hours weekly, followed by East Germany and—surprisingly—with little Cuba in fourth place. Czechoslovakia and Poland tie for fifth-place honors and are followed by Rumania, Bulgaria, and Hungary.

The total increase of all Communist foreign radio transmissions, between April 1962 and January 1963, amounts to almost seven hundred hours weekly, or 21 per cent, with a good deal of this expanded effort directed to the people of Africa.

Benefits to the West

One cannot doubt the high priority given by the international Communist movement to the matter of conquering the minds of men everywhere. The dissemination of ideas —if I may dignify Communist dogma with that respectable word—is a key element in Communism's goal of ultimate world conquest. It was the realization of this fact that in 1949 led to the formation of the Free Europe Committee, with its focus on East Europe. Its founders understood not only the priority of America's moral commitment to the once-free peoples in this area; they also realized that *if* these captive peoples refused genuine cooperation with the Soviet Union, and with the regime rulers in their own lands, these benefits to the United States and its Western allies would follow:

1. Moscow could *not* count on the staggering economic, military, and psychological support of East-Central Europe to tip the world power balance to the Soviet side.
2. Moscow would have to tie up hundreds of thousands of Russian troops, just to assure civil obedience.
3. Moscow would always have to reckon with unforeseeable, but clearly unpleasant, disruption to its line of communications in the event of hostilities in Europe—whether around Berlin, or anywhere else.
4. Moscow would have to face, behind the Iron Curtain, on the doorstep of the Soviet Union, peoples bound to produce heretical ideas, gravitations toward disunity, pressures for diversity and change.
5. Moscow would not have a quiet and stable bridgehead from where she might effectively expand her power—through political, psychological, and military operations —into Western Europe, imperiling the entire Atlantic Community.

All of this has happened, justifying both the wisdom of the founders of RFE and every cent contributed by the American public to RFE over the years. Even now, the quickening pace of West European unity and vitality (despite some problems), combined with the conflicts apparent throughout the world Communist movement, offer Radio Free Europe its greatest challenge and greatest opportunity. RFE is informing our listeners about both Western strength and basic unity, and about the divisions in the Communist world. De-Stalinization, revisionism, agricultural disasters, deviationism, youth problems, the Sino-Soviet split—these are a few of the words which suggest some of the problems on the other side. We are saying that not we, but they, represent an anachronism in the twentieth century; that the cause of liberty, of individual free choice, of individual dignity and responsibility, of the open society, is the winning cause. We are saying that nationalism and national diversity, once thought to be a free world problem, has turned into what is now realized to be a free world strength, and a probably fatal Communist world weakness.

Conclusions

We do not overstate this case. We acknowledge the divisions in the free world, and we do not suggest that the road ahead is either safe, easy, or short. But we are convinced, and we regard it as extremely important that our listeners —both Communist and anti-Communist—be convinced, that the tide has indeed begun to turn in world affairs. We expect that the opportunists as well as the very few believing Marxist-Leninists in Eastern Europe will soon begin to doubt very seriously whether the Communist wave is, after all, really the the wave of the future. In a society ruled by an inherently unpopular totalitarian party, committed to world victory, such doubts can lead eventually to disintegration in East Europe.

We must continue to bring effective political, cultural, moral, and psychological assistance to the people behind the Iron Curtain. These peoples know that Soviet and other Communist leaders are no supermen. They know that Communist ideas and practices of government, economy, and social organization are contrary to every basic principle which civilized man has painfully developed and learned to cherish. But they know that without continued support from the West, especially the United States, their determination to be free and independent peoples again will wither away.

History will indeed judge this generation harshly if we in the West do not make the required effort to meet the challenge of Communist imperialism, especially in those areas where this imperialism has violated legal, political, and moral commitments which we have solemnly pledged to uphold —precisely the same areas where this imperialism is most vulnerable.

If we in the United States carry out our responsibilities with vigor, initiative, courage, and conviction, there can be no doubt that this world, now half-slave and half-free, will free itself from tyranny, will become one world, a free world, under the rule of law. No lesser achievement can provide any solid assurance against total thermonuclear disaster. No greater, more noble, or more challenging opportunity has ever faced America.

PLANNING IN FOREIGN AFFAIRS:
THE MISSING ELEMENT

by Franklin A. Lindsay

Mr. Lindsay is a graduate of Stanford University as well as its Graduate School of Business, and of the Graduate School in Economics of Harvard University. As an Army officer during World War II, he served in Iran and later as Chief of the U. S. Military Mission to Yugoslavia. He has served the Government as a civilian in many capacities including an assignment, in 1954, as Consultant to the second Hoover Commission (on operations of the National Security Council), and since 1960 has been a member of the U. S. Advisory Group to the NATO Parliamentarians' Conference. Mr. Lindsay is President and a Director of Itek Corporation, Lexington, Massachusetts.

It is now generally accepted that in the last fifteen years the conduct of our foreign affairs has undergone a fundamental revolution. The United States has progressed from an era in which foreign policy was executed only through negotiations between an ambassador and a foreign minister to an era in which the broadest and most active contacts are maintained at all levels within a foreign country. In many areas of the world, we are actually helping to build new nations from the ground up.

Before World War II, our concern with foreign affairs

was much more limited. The active issues of policy requiring foresighted planning were confined almost entirely to tariff and disarmament negotiations and these occasional activities could be handled by a small corps of professional diplomats, aided by a few professional soldiers. All that was required was: first, broad policy decisions on the positions to be taken; second, diplomatic negotiations with other interested powers; and possibly third, treaty ratifications if negotiations were successful. This was the totality of foreign affairs. Even Sir Harold Nicolson, in his classic book *Diplomacy*, written in 1939, treated diplomacy as the sole means available to a nation for the peacetime execution of foreign policy.

In today's world, the tools for carrying out policy have multiplied. In addition to diplomacy, they include information and propaganda; economic aid; technical assistance; scientific discovery and development; educational and cultural activities; monetary, trade, and tariff controls; foreign military assistance, and the maintenance of military power in being. Under these circumstances, the conduct of foreign policy becomes incredibly more complex. Today sixteen separate departments and agencies of government have a major concern with foreign affairs and twenty more have a somewhat lesser concern. Each of these organizations conducts its own programs, either directly or indirectly in contact with foreign governments and peoples. Each competes for limited resources of money, facilities, and skilled manpower.

The need to coordinate these many activities has been seen since the end of World War II, and many proposals have been made to cope with it. But they have not dealt with a related problem which may be even more responsible for the many shortcomings now generally recognized in our foreign policy. The second weakness is the inadequacy of planning, or perhaps more precisely of program planning, at all levels of government.

Program Planning

Program planning is the process by which policy objectives are translated into action programs of the scope, mag-

PEACE AND WAR IN THE MODERN AGE

nitude and timing required for their realization. Because to-day's policies require massive applications of manpower, money, and facilities—and because it takes time to bring these assets into being—we must increasingly *anticipate* the needs posed by our objectives. It takes years to train a public information officer capable of working effectively in, say, Southeast Asia, to bring into being a new investment bank capable of wisely directing the flow of capital investment, to build a competent corps of public administrators in a newly developing country, or to create a limited-war military force capable of moving at a moment's notice by air to a distant point of danger. We are doing this job inadequately today because we are not anticipating sufficiently our needs for these instruments of policy execution. Hence our foreign policy often must be "reactive" simply because we have not created in advance the assets needed to take the initiative.

In the fall of 1960, for example, the Government asked for outside assistance in recruiting from private life no less than fifteen financial advisers for fifteen new countries, mostly in Africa. The sudden requirement was the result of a failure to foresee this need and to train a corps of financial advisers who were competent to deal both with the technical and with the political problems of underdeveloped nations. The jobs had been open for several months, and at that time there had been no success in filling them. When a likely candidate is found who is reasonably competent professionally, he undoubtedly will be shipped off to Africa immediately. But he almost certainly will not have had any special training in the economics, politics, or social structure of the country to which he is assigned. And this lack of background will hamper his effectiveness as a financial adviser, as well as his ability to help prepare the country to mature politically within the free world.

This is not an isolated case of lack of planning. None of the principal agencies of government concerned with foreign affairs foresaw the emergence of new independent states in Africa even to the extent of starting special training programs for their own career personnel. As a result, posts in Africa are either entirely unmanned or filled by officers hastily reassigned from other areas of the world, and by new recruits fresh out of college.

Examples of Inadequate Planning and Research

In the field of disarmament the record of the last fifteen years is largely of one makeshift improvisation after another. In April 1958, for example, the President proposed to the Soviets that a conference of technicians be convened to consider the problems of preventing surprise attack. On September 15 the Soviets accepted the proposal and asked that the conference begin on November 10. As of the date of Soviet acceptance, almost no preparations had been made, and it was not until October 2, when William C. Foster was appointed chairman, that work began on the preparation of policy positions. Groups were hastily assembled, both from within and outside government, to work for the remaining month before the conference. At the end of the conference, which reached no agreement, Mr. Foster reported to the Senate, "I doubt that we have up to this time really given the intense study of the kinds of measures which will make the [prevention of surprise attack] possible . . . I think that with hard work and deep thought and putting together competent people to work on this, not on a part-time basis but on a full-time basis, something very valuable could be accomplished."

Again in 1959 the same thing happened. In January, the United States proposed that a group of qualified scientists be convened to study the technical possibilities of detecting underground tests. The Russians delayed for nearly a year and then announced that they were ready to meet immediately. A scientific team under Dr. James Fisk, President of the Bell Laboratories, was assembled and departed almost immediately for Geneva. Most of the preparations were carried out in Geneva concurrently with the negotiations. At this conference, agreement was reached that it would be possible to detect underground explosions above five kilotons with 160–170 seismic stations located throughout the world. Only later did we discover that perhaps ten times this number of stations would be required to achieve a reasonable probability of detection. This predicament was the result of inadequate planning and of inadequate research to back it up. Had an agreement been reached on the basis of the technical report, we could have found ourselves in the position of having either to live with an inadequate agreement or to suffer the political and propaganda consequences of abrogating the treaty.

Why the Lack of Program Planning?

The lack of program planning in the foreign field probably can be laid to two underlying causes: (1) skepticism about the value of planning—owing at least partly to a misconception of its role—on the part of many career Foreign Service officers; and (2) the inevitable operational orientation of most of the top foreign policy officials.

The essential unpredictability of the future is often used as the principal argument for not planning. A Foreign Service career officer, when asked why the State Department did not put more emphasis on planning, replied, "How can you plan foreign policy when no one can possibly know what Castro is going to do two years, or even two days, from now?"

This of course is a distortion of the purpose of planning. The purpose is not to prepare rigid programs that will apply only if predictions about future events have been accurate to the point of clairvoyance. Rather, the purpose is to prepare broad, flexible programs with room for maneuvering as events take shape. One need not have been able to predict the revolt of the *Force Publique* in the Congo to foresee that there would be serious political instability and that political officers would be needed who were thoroughly acquainted with the forces at work there and who had, by their personal knowledge and acquaintanceship, covered all reasonable political bets, including both those who did and those who did not attain power.

Perhaps the skepticism with which some in the State Department regard planning stems from the career officer's traditional concept of diplomatic negotiation as the sharp cutting edge of foreign policy. Success as a diplomat is the ultimate in career success and usually is rewarded with assignment to the highest posts in the service. Diplomacy is an art that should by no means be depreciated, and we shall have great need for this skill over the years ahead, no matter how well we plan. But skill in diplomacy depends on an approach to problems that is quite different from that of a good planner. The diplomat must be able to make the best of day-to-day developments over which he has little or no control. The planner, in contrast, must try to anticipate future situations by building capabilities in advance to meet them.

A second reason for the lack of planning is that agency and departmental chiefs are forced by circumstance to devote practically all of their energies to operating problems. This is because the operating problems are the hot issues that demand immediate attention. They are played up in the press and are the subject of Congressional inquiries. They are the subject of urgent messages from foreign governments demanding immediate telegraphic replies. They are the latest bombshells of Khrushchev and Mao that require immediate attention. Planning, in contrast, has no day-to-day deadlines. Nor does planning bring immediate rewards. No one will know until years later whether or not a given plan has been adequate.

The Need for Greater Institutionalization

Even if there were no pressures of operating problems, the incentive to plan far in advance would be weak. The creation of the modern tools of foreign policy—whether they be technical systems for the verification of arms-control agreements or a corps of professionals skilled in nation building —often requires years of planning and preparation. A particular administration in Washington is thus dependent almost entirely on the assets that have been created by previous administrations and must make the best of it when these assets are inadequate to do the jobs at hand. Equally, the effort of any administration to plan and build new instruments of national power is a form of investment that will pay most of its dividends in subsequent administrations. For this reason the planning processes require greater institutionalization to ensure that future interests are not neglected by those who may never themselves enjoy the fruits of their planning.

Whatever the underlying causes of the lack of planning may be, however, the immediate cause is an inadequate organization for planning, both in the National Security Council and in the various departments having foreign policy interests. It is true that "planning bodies" exist. The N.S.C. has a Planning Board, and the State Department has since 1950 had its own Policy Planning Staff, now headed by an Assistant Secretary reporting directly to the Secretary of State. Under the N.S.C. there is also the Operations Coordinating Board, which is charged with coordinating the operational planning of the responsible agencies in their execution of N.S.C. policies.[1]

The titles of these three organizations suggest that the planning function is adequately recognized, in both the White House and the State Department. Unfortunately titles are often misleading, and that is true here. The Planning Staff of the N.S.C. plans only in the sense that it prepares the groundwork of the N.S.C. It is composed of the deputies of the N.S.C. representatives, and its function is to steer first drafts of national security policy statements through the shoals of interdepartmental interests. It is thus no more concerned with actual program planning than is its parent body, whose function is to establish national policies. These policies are, of necessity, broad and general statements of the problems confronting us, and of our objectives in coping with them. Moreover, the N.S.C. is more concerned with short-range than with long-range problems.

A hypothetical N.S.C. policy dealing with an underdeveloped country in which we are strongly interested might read something like this: "It shall be the policy of the United States to assist Country X in establishing a stable and effective government capable of maintaining public support, of progressing in a sustained and orderly manner with economic and social development, and of avoiding the extremes of Communism or right-wing dictatorship. The United States should be prepared to assist in improving public administration, in fostering economic development, and in upgrading general education."

Before approving a policy of this sort, the Council should be provided with a reasonably accurate estimate of the magnitude of the program that must be undertaken, the time required, and the costs involved if the proposed policy is to have a reasonable chance of success. For without such an estimate, the Council cannot properly weigh the costs and urgency of implementing this program against the costs and urgency of implementing other programs in other areas.

Admittedly, many of the N.S.C. policy papers do carry financial appendices that purport to be the price tags of the policies advocated. But these projections usually are not backed up by specific plans and hence do not accurately reflect the actual costs of the program if it were carried through in the magnitude needed to achieve the stated objective. More often these financial projections are based on last year's budget, increased or lowered by 5 or 10 per cent, depending on the shift in the urgency of the problem. This lack of adequate plans for arriving at the real cost of any individual program affects our total foreign policy. For without such information, the Executive Branch and the Congress cannot make informed decisions on the total amount of resources that should be allocated to foreign policy objectives, or on the division of these resources among competing programs.

The real decisions controlling the size and direction of foreign programs—and therefore many of the real decisions on basic policy—are made instead as a part of the annual budget process. In theory, the budget is expected to reflect and implement national security policies. In practice, these are so broadly drawn that a correspondingly broad range of alternative budgets can be accommodated. Because of the lack of adequate plans to implement these policies—and thereby to define more closely the dollar costs—the budgets can often be jiggered substantially in support of any one program at the expense of others. The result is that the budget sets the real scope of a program, and the plans—such as they are—are then made to fit that budget.

the advantages of the Soviet system to the underdeveloped countries.

The Communists have demonstrated their ability to foresee future problems and opportunities and to plan well in advance to meet them. They have, for example, operated university-type training schools for potential political leaders of virtually all the uncommitted countries. In 1945, when they reinstituted these political academies, they did not know when Africa—or Southeast Asia—would be ready for a stepped-up program of political action. But they went ahead with comprehensive training programs with confidence that they would find the opportunity, sooner or later, to throw their trained cadres into the conflict.

An Illustration of Planning Needed

To illustrate the type of planning needed, let us look again at the hypothetical N.S.C. policy for Country X, which called for assistance "in establishing a stable and effective government . . . in improving public administration, in fostering economic development, and in upgrading general education." In developing a government-wide program plan to carry out that policy, the following sequence of steps might be taken.

1. Preparation of a preliminary estimate of what will be needed to establish a stable and effective non-Communist government. This estimate must first identify those key needs that must be met if our policy objective is to be realized. In this example, the key needs might be a corps of public administrators, a police and public security force, public information media, and a program for economic growth. This estimate would include such things as numbers and types of skilled administrators needed; the investment requirements for economic growth; the needs for public information through books, magazines, radio, newspapers; the requirements for technicians and skilled workers; and the police forces needed to maintain order. Planning should then concentrate only on these key elements for "success" and should not be encumbered with nonessentials.

As a result of experience gained by American advisory groups who have served in underdeveloped countries, such as that to Pakistan headed by Professor Edward Mason of Harvard, we now have the resources in the United States to enable us to make reasonably accurate estimates of the initial critical needs in building a new nation.

2. An estimate of the degree to which these essential requirements can be met from the resources already available within the country. This would include personnel trained by the former government, European technicians and administrators likely to remain, and the graduates of technical and professional schools within the country and abroad.

3. An estimate of the remaining needs that must be met by the West if the minimum objectives are to have a reasonable chance of success. A part of these needs may be met by other nations, by the World Bank, and possibly by the United Nations. The remaining critical needs will have to be provided by the United States.

4. At this point a preliminary estimate of costs and time required will provide a test of the feasibility of achieving the N.S.C. policy objective. If it appears that requirements are substantially beyond our capabilities in the light of our resources and of other competing requirements, two alternatives are open: to shift resources from other programs or to cut back our policy objectives. If the latter is decided, an important function will have been served by putting ourselves on notice that actual or implied commitments to foreign governments beyond our limited resources must not be made.

5. A next step is the development by the responsible departments and agencies of more detailed but still long-term plans. For example, the need for public administrators in the African countries may be so great that a major program must be established to create new institutes of public administration in Africa in addition to bringing increased numbers of Africans to the United States and Western Europe for further training. If a country has only fifteen or twenty college graduates, as is actually the case in some of the new African republics, it will not be enough to spend a few thousand dollars—as we are, in some cases, doing now—to send an

expert in public administration to the country or to bring a half dozen people to the United States for a limited period of training. While such a program might meet the letter of an N.S.C. policy, it would not contribute very much to the solution of the problem. Similarly, the need for public information media may be so urgent—and the dangers of Communist infiltration and control so great—that the U.S.I.A. would be called upon to develop a program by which the Africans can be helped to set up locally owned radio stations, a news agency, one or more book publishing houses, and a series of newspapers.

The special importance of the planning process is that it provides an estimate of the magnitude of a problem early enough to do something about it. If instead we wait until the problem is breaking around our heads, it may be too late.

6. At this point planning should be tied integrally with the budget-making process. This will require a shift from the annual budget to longer-range commitments of funds. The approval of the policy program by the N.S.C. and the approval of the budget to be submitted to Congress must be part of a single, consistent process. The present practice of preparing budgets only incidentally related to policy decisions clearly leads to breakdowns in the execution of policy.

7. Continuing central guidance and coordination of planning will be needed to be sure that the programs will be mutually supporting, and in the aggregate will give the best chance of success while making the minimum drain on scarce resources. Revision, modification, and extension of plans will be a continuing process as new situations unfold and as we learn from initial successes and failures. Finally, at each step of the way we must work in close association with our allies, especially in those areas where they have important interests.

As the cold war develops during the 1960's, we must be increasingly prepared to seize opportunities as they occur. This means that we must think through in advance both the types of opportunities that might reasonably be expected and the actions we will have to take if we are not to let them slip by unexploited. By so doing we can create in advance assets that will be available when needed. For example, revolts such as those in East Germany and Hungary may occur in the next decade. If we fail to anticipate the different ways that events might unfold and to evaluate both the risks and opportunities of any action we might take, we will not know what preparations must be made in advance. If no preparations are made, there probably will be little or no freedom of decision at the moment the event occurs. As was the case in 1956, we shall have foregone the opportunity to exploit the break because we have not prepared for it. If, instead, we have made reasonably adequate contingency plans and have the necessary assets on hand, such as trained manpower, food, communications, medicines, air transport, and weapons, we shall be free to decide at the time whether and to what degree we should intervene.

Summary

Obviously we cannot make plans for every conceivable contingency. Judgment must be used in identifying those possibilities that contain the greatest opportunities and dangers. Equally we cannot create assets to meet every contingency, but it is often possible to create assets that can be used in a variety of ways. A final question is, how shall comprehensive planning be organized? To this decision, the following criteria should be applied:

1. Centralized over-all direction and supervision of planning, to ensure completeness, balance, and timeliness.

2. Decentralization of detailed planning, to ensure that plans are grounded in reality.

3. Full-time attention to planning by a small but highly competent group.

4. Accurate estimates of costs as plans are made, to provide adequate bases for budget decisions.

5. Follow-up and review, to ensure that plans are in fact carried out.

Clearly, to meet these criteria, a central planning staff will be needed. Its functions will be to provide continuing leadership within the Government in the field of planning, to prepare over-all plans, to allocate responsibility for more detailed plans to departments and agencies, to review the adequacy of their plans, and to see that approved plans are carried out. In all the operating departments and agencies, it should have small counterparts reporting directly to their agency heads but having day-to-day working contacts with responsible line officers, as well as with the central planning staff.

Many pieces of such a program already exist. What is lacking is central coordination and direction, and a philosophy to make it work. Through improved planning, we can significantly increase the probabilities that our foreign policies will be successful and that the vast resources we are now committing to these policies will be effectively used. Without it, there will be lost opportunities, half-effective programs, and waste of resources. Program planning is not a strait jacket that commits us to a particular course of action, no matter what new circumstances arise, but a means of increasing our freedom of action and our ability to grasp the initiative in the long, cold war.

NOTE

1. The Operations Coordinating Board was established by Executive Order 10483, of September 2, 1953, 18 Fed. Reg. 5379, issued by President Dwight D. Eisenhower. Amendments of that Order were effected by Executive Order 10598, of February 28, 1955, 20 Fed. Reg. 1237, and Executive Order 10610, of May 9, 1955, 20 Fed. Reg. 3179, also issued by President Eisenhower. In 1957, Executive Order 10483, as amended, was superseded by Executive Order 10700, of February 25, 1957, 22 Fed. Reg. 1111, issued by President Eisenhower, providing for "a continuation of the Operations Coordinating Board."

In a White House press release dated February 19, 1961, President John F. Kennedy announced the issuance of an Executive Order abolishing the Operations Coordinating Board. (Executive Order 10920, dated February 18, 1961, 26 Fed. Reg. 1463.) He said the Board was used in the last Administration "for work which we now plan to do in other ways" and that its abolition was part of his program for "strengthening the responsibility" of the individual Government departments. (New York *Times,* February 20, 1961, page 14, col. 3). Editors.

PUBLIC OPINION, THE PRIVATE SECTOR AND NATIONAL DEFENSE

by Frank R. Barnett

Can democracy, which cherishes dissent and encourages diversity, compete with totalitarian dogma in an ideological struggle in which repetition, simplicity of theme, and professionalism in propaganda techniques are not irrelevant to changes in the minds of men? Can men who cherish peace even comprehend the goals and ambitions of those for whom revolution, violence, and the future good of mankind are synonymous? These are questions which pose themselves in any discussion of public opinion and citizen action in relation to national defense.

Professor Toynbee, in recording the demise of many civilizations, talks of "challenge and response." There are at least two reasons why America has failed, thus far, to meet the challenge to her survival with an adequate response. First, we do not admit, as a government or as a people, that we are "at war" with a conspiratorial elite which has perverted every form of human activity to the cause of conflict. Hence, we have no grand strategy and no sustained tactics, either for offensive or defensive action. We tend to treat the siege of Berlin, the capture of Cuba, and the guerrilla wars in Southeast Asia as isolated incidents which only temporarily interrupt the world's "normal state of peace." We fail to perceive that to the Communist every armistice is merely a cloak for unconventional warfare.

Second, although the Soviets have developed nonmilitary combat to an exact science, we have neglected to perfect any comparable cold war weapons system. Thus, between the military hardware of the Pentagon and the orthodox diplomacy of the Department of State, the Communists continue to drive their irregular spearheads tipped with propaganda, psychological warfare, strikes, student riots, precinct politics, blackmail, insurrections, and *coups d'état*. The current Soviet leaders, despite images of "moderation," have by no means dismantled the formal academies in which agents are trained for sabotage, subversion, street fighting, and the manipulation of mob opinion. There are few Americans who can compete on the psycho-social squares of the cold war chessboard with the professional graduates of those Iron Curtain institutes for nonmilitary or political warfare.

Political Warfare Defined

What precisely is political warfare? Various clichés, such as the "contest of ideas," are often mistakenly used as if they were interchangeable with political warfare. Some diplomats seem to believe that the term means nothing more than trade fairs or the exchange of tourists with Iron Curtain countries. Political warfare is a sustained effort by a government or political group to seize, preserve, or extend power against a defined ideological enemy, through all acts short of a shooting war by regular military forces, but not excluding the *threat* of such a war.

Political warfare, in short, is "warfare"—not public relations. As practiced by the Communists, it is one part persuasion, two parts deception, and four parts coercion and blackmail. It embraces diverse forms of violence. The aim of political warfare is not to "promote mutual understanding" between differing points of view: it is to discredit, displace, and neutralize an opponent; to destroy a competing ideology; and to make one's own values prevail.

It is a grave error to regard political warfare as a magic weapon that can be divorced from military capability. Political warfare interacts with the other components of power, such as economic growth and space technology. Actually, there is much evidence to suggest that a primary object of Soviet *political* warfare is to degrade U.S. military strength, unravel the NATO alliance, and—through "peace charades" —stultify our weapons development while the Kremlin gains more lead time for Soviet science.

Other Forms of Nonmilitary Warfare

An important component of nonmilitary warfare is ideology. Pragmatic Americans are often impatient of metaphysicians who talk about dialectics. Ideology is something so alien to our culture pattern that we prefer to explain the behavior of Soviet leaders in terms of more familiar phenomena such as "peasant manners," or a deprived childhood, or the Russian heritage. Nor have we discriminated in favor of Communists in this respect. Fascists, too, have enjoyed the benefits of our unbelief in the power of dogma.

For example, until Allied armies at the end of World War II actually broke into the death camps of Nazi Germany, most people in the West couldn't really believe that a *theory* of race supremacy could lead in practice to the construction of bake ovens for human beings. It didn't seem "plausible." Most of us assumed Hitler was simply the Kaiser all over again.

But Hitler was more than a repetition of the Kaiser. Ideology had been added to the old-fashioned nationalism and had converted aggression from a contest for real estate into a struggle, literally, for the soul and destiny of man. The Nazis took their ideology seriously, and so do the Communists. Failure to understand the ideological grounding of our adversaries has led to a great deal of wishful thinking about Moscow's intentions.

Thus, it is argued in some circles in America today that the cold war may almost be over; that a "moderate" class of new Bolsheviks are trying to lead a Russian middle class away from world revolution toward the rule of law and membership in the racquet club. It is asserted that, since the Kremlin is now introducing "profit and incentive" into the Soviet system, these capitalistic devices will destroy Communism as they mature.

It is maintained, moreover, that the Communist Party

Russia has been forced to train a managerial and technical elite to run an increasingly sophisticated industrial economy, and that these managers and technocrats will exert a "moderating influence" on old Bolshevik ideology and objectives.

Obviously, everyone hopes these expectations may prove to be true; but there are certain grounds for skepticism. Nazi Germany probably had more private capitalism, more profit, more incentives, a larger middle class, more managers, and more technicians per capita than any other country in the world except the United States, Switzerland, and Great Britain. In other words, if a historian looked at Nazi Germany only from the standpoint of management techniques, technical personnel, heavy industry, profit structure, capitalism, banking networks, or literate middle class, he might conclude that Nazi Germany and the United States were far closer together, sociologically and economically, in 1939 than Russia and America could be, even by the year 2000. The crucial difference was that an *ideological* Nazi Germany was governed by a ruthless party elite which brooked no opposition, and that *political* fact made economics, sociology, and middle class morality irrelevant.

Who will take encouragement from the fact that Russia is "introducing profits" into the Soviet system, when the evidence suggests that the largest bonuses go to the most efficient managers of Soviet munitions factories, artful propagandists, and those Soviet scientists who show ingenuity in advanced weapons research? As a matter of fact, Russia has never had as much "socialism" as Great Britain, in terms of equal shares for the working class. The U.S.S.R. is more nearly a system of monopoly state capitalism run by nineteenth-century Russian robber barons. The Soviet system is characterized by extraordinary salaries and privileges for the economic czars, piecework for the proletariat, and conscription for labor.

Moreover, those who believe that Communism is gradually evolving toward peaceful convergence with the United States, in a sort of Fabian, social welfare, world state, evidently forget that Moscow has reintroduced the death penalty for so-called "economic crimes" against the state—a form of state terrorism that disappeared in the Western world over 150 years ago.

Also, in both the Soviet Union and Poland, the Communist Party is reimposing rigid conformity on the intellectuals who have dared raise their voices in what they thought was going to be a permissive atmosphere. We know also from reliable sources that the Communists are spending not less than one hundred million dollars a year on subversion in Latin America alone. Does this sound as if the Soviets are moving toward middle-class morality and a "live-and-let-live" philosophy?

A Lesson from Cuba

There is an aspect of the Cuban coup which illuminates the Communist strategy of nonmilitary warfare. On the theory that "we are waging a battle for men's minds," many Americans urge that we develop a more positive propaganda for our own ideological position. Many Americans would favor that. But what happened in Cuba proves that a contest at the level of pure ideology would be almost irrelevant. Castro and his cohorts seized Cuba by *masking* their Communist beliefs, *not by espousing them*. In Cuba, Communist intellectuals did not create a climate of opinion sympathetic to Marx, and then, inside that climate of opinion, gradually assume power. Not at all. The Communists who boarded the Castro bandwagon carefully concealed their Communist ambitions, so as to enlist the initial support of Cuban middle classes for the Castro revolution.

Castro was helped to power by Cuban businessmen, doctors, publishers, and lawyers fed to the teeth with Batista but wholly opposed to world Communism. It was only *after* Castro had come to power that hidden Communists discredited, isolated, and destroyed their temporary allies in the popular front movement. It was not Marx who persuaded Cuba with ideas; it was Lenin who captured Cuba with proxy fighting and nonmilitary warfare.

The Question of Public Opinion

It is precisely because Communists can be expected to continue "twilight aggression," through psycho-social weaponry aimed in large part at civilian minds and motivations, that the question of public opinion looms so importantly in the equation of national defense. Some observers feel so keenly that we are losing the idea war that they have verged on calling for our own omnipotent Ministry of Propaganda. It is my thesis that the private sector can cope with the problem, provided it will take pains to introduce professionalism into an area too frequently occupied solely by good intentions.

Since some people doubt the need for cold war education, or question the capacity of the private sector to do anything responsible and effective, it is only reasonable to set forth the assumptions on which subsequent recommendations for civic action can be based.

Assumption #1: The Profile of Future Conflict

Despite mounting hostility between Moscow and Peking, struggle between the Communist powers and the free world may last another forty to fifty years. The interoffice memoranda of the Communist world reveal that "peaceful coexistence" is expected to provide new opportunities to expand class war, ideological war, and wars of national liberation.[1] The strategy of the "peace charade" is a time-tested gambit designed by Lenin, not Khrushchev. It was used successfully by Stalin and Mao when they needed a respite to consolidate forces. When Khrushchev talked peace and asked for trade while he subsidized proxy war, thereby both strengthening and safeguarding the Russian heartland, he had only adapted the techniques of Lenin and Stalin to the nuclear age. We can scarcely expect that Khrushchev's protégés, steeped in the ideology of the higher Party schools, will preside over the liquidation of Marxist faith or abandon efficacious Leninist techniques.

Contrary to sentiment in Western capitals, economic gains are not likely to civilize the Communists. The ideological heirs of Marx do not live by bread alone; it is doubtful if the Party elite can be "bought off" with trade or reconditioned by bourgeois gestures of friendship. Certainly not on the eve of triumph! From their point of view, history has already passed its verdict in their favor. Communist leaders have broken the chain of capitalist encirclement. Lenin had no country forty-eight years ago, whereas today Communists have thirteen in hand and ninety-one Parties spread over the globe. They scent victory within the lifetime of the next generation. Their enemies, they feel, are in retreat, "compelled" by Socialist power to sign treaties on Moscow's terms and increasingly coerced by the force of world opinion to accept Soviet definitions of peace, aggression, colonialism, and world law. To Communists our era is not one of détente but of transition to victorious Socialism. This means that U.S. national security in the 1960's and '70's may be in greater jeopardy than it was in the tense days of naked Stalinism.

Assumption #2: Changing Nature of the Threat

Communist power is no longer rooted exclusively in ideology, espionage, and mass peasant armies. The Russian ox-cart economy has planted its banners on the moon. The modern counterparts of Genghis Khan are armed with machine tools, electronics, the hidden persuaders of modern psychiatry, and the maps of outer space. Communists are not only philosopher-thugs, they are also engineers, linguists, and students of cybernetics. They have fashioned new weapons, not only from the laboratory of physics, but also from the arsenal of the behavioral sciences; and they practice guerrilla diplomacy as cunningly as they wage guerrilla warfare and paramilitary precinct politics.

A Bolshevik conflict manager, in short, is the reincarnation of a Cesare Borgia, blind to the treasures of Florence but equipped with computers, the dialectic, mass media, and solid fuel rockets. Such an opponent will not be turned from his designs by the "personality" of a Western statesman, or by rituals celebrating the virtues of free enterprise, or by unilateral disarmament, or slogans that reiterate the benefits to be derived from world peace through world law. This means the American people will have to develop and sustain, over a long period of time, a national will somewhat alien to a pluralistic society which traditionally has wanted as little national purpose as possible in order to make ample room for private and corporate purposes.

Assumption #3: No Stalemate in the Twentieth Century

There can be no such thing as stalemate in the contest between free men and Communist aggressors. Woe betide that great power which, at the most revolutionary moment of history, assumes status quo in alliance systems or stalemate in weapons systems. Since World War II, revolutionary change has become self-renewing, whether in international politics or the internal social structures of nations or research laboratories. Fifty years of "normal" change, as our grandfathers would have defined that term, are now compressed into eighteen months.

Presumably, scientists on both sides of the Iron Curtain are experimenting with lasers, masers, electronic force shields, electromagnetic flux phenomena, and/or other defensive or offensive devices which, by definition, are "inconceivable" to laymen, including many policy-makers and authors of books on strategy who are often oriented more toward political science than technology. One would suppose that the giant computers, the new chemistry, the new metallurgy, and the miniaturization of parts—plus automation, operations research, cybernetics, teaching machines, and so on—will virtually guarantee that new breakthroughs are highly probable in many "unexpected" directions.

It is worth remembering that on at least three dramatic occasions the U.S. was nearly caught off guard in the arena of science: first, when Russia tested the hydrogen bomb five to eight years before most Western scientists thought it possible; second, when the Soviets launched sputnik; third, when they exploded their more than 50-megaton device in 1961—an achievement which may have given them dread insight into methods by which a pre-emptive strike could jam the communications and control systems of their adversaries. If we have underestimated our opponent's capability before, almost to the brink of disaster, it would be prudent to assume that we live in an era of scientific leapfrog where every innovation, instead of being the ultimate discovery, only makes more invention possible. Thus, "Excellence in America's Classrooms" is not a pious slogan but the necessary formula for survival.

Is it not also self-evident that, in the face of continued Soviet refusal to accept meaningful inspection and control of armaments, it would be folly to tempt the totalitarian taste for surprise assault with unilateral U.S. initiatives to de-accelerate the search for military supremacy? Given undiminished ideological convictions in Moscow with regard to "socialist" victory over the decadent bourgeoisie, psychological gambits based on chivalry and the Judaeo-Christian ethic may be misconstrued as weakness and invitations to treachery by the heirs of Ivan the Terrible. Finally, so long as the Soviets maintain the cloak of police state secrecy over their own military research, and gain much access to our industrial techniques and scientific discoveries through open sources and massive espionage, the "knowledge race" is not likely to be symmetrical.

Assumption #4: The Importance of Public Opinion and the Private Sector

In an open society, people get the foreign policy they deserve and the national security they are willing to pay for. The government of a free people can lead. It cannot run counter to the priorities of the electorate. For example, in the 1930's, England wanted above all else "peace in our time." Hence, Englishmen sold machine tools to Hitler and hoped for the best. Not even the eloquent Winston Churchill—out of office—could mobilize his countrymen to attend to the growing menace of Nazi Germany.

The task of private citizens today is to help provide *an educational substitute for Dunkirk and Pearl Harbor*. In the nuclear age, democracies cannot wait for a dictator's surprise assault to alert them to danger. Moreover, since Communists prefer to wage undeclared "twilight war," civilians are as close to the front line as the career military—and being that close to a competent antagonist, they should be familiar with his tactics, strategy, and objectives.

One further fact underlines the need to involve the private citizen in geopolitics, foreign policy, and national defense. In the U.S.S.R. the Communist Party can mobilize the total resources of the Russian empire through *total* government. In America we have a *limited* government in Washington, with powers reserved to the states and people. Washington cannot compete with Moscow on many of the squares of the cold war chessboard which relate to political science, motivation, economic vitality, and ultimate beliefs.

Americans do not want a censored press, a controlled pulpit, regimented school curricula, or a Ministry of Propaganda. But, since limited government cannot match totalitarian government—in ideological and economic warfare, for example—this suggests the need for volunteer action by the powerful private sector: labor unions and corporations, foundations, universities, professional societies, and trade associations. As the private sector becomes professional in the realm of conflict management, Communist nonmilitary warfare techniques can be blunted. There is a clear case, therefore, for sophisticated programs of instruction and orientation in the cold war arena.

The American Bar Association: A Case Study of Action by a Professional Society

On the assumption that free men *can* frustrate Communist goals if they are willing to commit sustained and systematic effort to the protracted conflict, it is encouraging to examine the precedent set by the American Bar Association. In August 1962, in San Francisco, the House of Delegates of the ABA merged two of its special committees into the permanent standing Committee on Education Against Communism. (Appendix, i.) By this act, the ABA underlined the gravity of the Communist threat and recognized the special responsibility of the lawyer to preserve the rule of law from a movement that employs force, violence, deception, and subversion to destroy our Constitution and annul liberty under law. In short, the ABA—by allocating staff time, funds, and the creative energies of outstanding lawyers to the complex challenge of Communism—is testing a method by which the "professionalism" of the private sector can be mobilized for effective action in the cold war. The Committee's program has two objectives:

1. To educate lawyers in the scope and nature of Communist tactics, strategy, and objectives; and
2. To encourage and support schools and colleges in the presentation of adequate instruction in the history, doctrines, objectives, and techniques of Communism, thereby helping to instill a greater appreciation of democracy and freedom under law.

Upon request, the Committee provides speakers and study materials for annual meetings of state, county, or local Bar Associations. In this and other activities, the Committee has enjoyed the active support of past, present and incoming Presidents of the American Bar Association. (Appendix, ii.)

In 1962, the ABA published a twenty-four-page pamphlet entitled "Instruction on Communism and Its Contrast With Liberty Under Law." More than fifteen thousand copies were distributed free to educators, lawyers, and the general public. That pamphlet, prepared at an hour when doubt and controversy still surrounded the question of teaching about Communism, did something to clear the air. It quoted—

PRESIDENT KENNEDY: It is most urgent that the American educational system tackle in earnest the task of teaching American youth to confront the reality of totalitarianism in its toughest, most militant form—which is Communism —with the facts and values of our American heritage.

PRESIDENT EISENHOWER: Competition for men's minds begins when they are students. This is when they must be taught to discern between the American form of government and the Soviet form.

ALLEN W. DULLES: We need, far and wide in this country, more education on the whole history of the Communist movement. . . . We should not be afraid to teach the subject. A history of Communism and all of its works would bear its own indictment of the system. Let the facts speak for themselves.

Now that most Americans have reached consensus on the need to teach about Communism as it contrasts with the values, traditions, and history of freedom, one priority problem is the providing of adequate teaching aids and texts, so that the job can be done properly. But who will teach the teachers? The phrase "Democracy versus Communism" incorporates a great many disciplines: comparative government, comparative economics, comparative ideologies, propaganda analysis, foreign policy, modern Russian and Chinese history, psychological warfare, Maoism, Leninism—to name a few.

Can we expect a social studies teacher, however dedicated, to be articulate in all of those subjects without in-service refresher courses? Almost all educators say "no." The ABA Committee, therefore, has concentrated on helping educators at the college and university level—and through them, high school teachers. It supplies, on request, scholars who consult with a college faculty which plans to organize a teacher seminar but needs advice from someone who has already done the job once. And when a teacher workshop is in need of an outside guest speaker—on, say, Red China or the Soviet economy or Communist espionage—the Committee undertakes to furnish a nationally known expert at its own expense. Thus, in the summer of 1964 the Committee gave assistance to ten universities, from California to the Carolinas, conducting workshops for high school teachers. (Appendix, iii.) At these workshops a total of more than seven hundred teachers received full academic credit for studying Communist ideology, strategy, and tactics.

Since the Committee believes in teaching the essence of

freedom, in contrast to Communism, it also provides, on request, study kits entitled "Sources of Liberty." These booklets were prepared by the American Citizenship Committee of the ABA and published by the American Bar Foundation. They contain, with commentary, reprints of thirty-two documents, including: Magna Carta, 1215; Mayflower Compact, 1620; Abolition of the Star Chamber, 1641; Habeas Corpus Act, 1679; Resolutions of the Stamp Act Congress, 1765; Declaration of Independence, 1776; and The Constitution of the United States, 1778.

In all activities relating to schools and colleges, the ABA is simply using its good offices to help one set of educators transfer experience and expertise to colleagues in the same field. Lawyers are *not* writing a syllabus for the schools. Lawyers are *not* advising professors on what and how to teach. Lawyers *are* providing some modest funds that enable educators to improve their own communications with one another. Moreover, whatever the Committee does is done only upon request. It is not seeking to trespass on any other professional domain.

On the other hand, America's lawyers scarcely need apologize for taking the initiative in helping to preserve freedom. Speaking in San Francisco, in August 1962, Sylvester Smith, then President of the Association, set forth persuasive reasons for his profession's keen interest in the field:

> The first stated objectives of the American Bar Association are most important. They are: "To uphold and defend the Constitution of the United States and maintain our representative form of government." Every lawyer in the United States on being admitted to the bar takes a solemn oath to uphold and defend the Constitution of the United States and the Constitution of his own State or Commonwealth.

In addition to its work with lawyers and educators, this Committee of the ABA produces special studies available to the general public. In the summer of 1964, for example, it published *The New Czars and the Rule of Law,* a symposium of speeches given by lawyers before State Bar Associations on such subjects as Communist terror, guerrilla warfare and intelligence operations, and Soviet attempts to "legalize" these underground activities while, at the same time, seeking to make U.S. counterinsurgency efforts "illegal."

Why focus in such detail on the efforts of one association? Perhaps because they provide a precedent for responsible, "in-house" activity that might be modified as a means by which other associations could participate more systematically in national defense. Suppose, for example, that our book publishers, our radio and TV executives, and our publications professionals were to form an Interprofessional Council, or societies of newspaper editors and publishers were to create *their* own permanent standing committee on better ways to use mass media for national security education. Suppose that bankers, investment bankers, and international trade groups were to set up committees on Soviet economic warfare. Think of the multiplier effect and leverage that might be derived from disciplined activity inside such associations! Already many groups have taken the first step.

Trade and Professional Association Seminars

An efficient way to organize a seminar on national defense and Communist strategy is within the framework of the annual state, regional, or national convention of an association or society. Such a forum has at least two advantages over the general, community-wide seminar so popular in the past. First, no energy or funds need be expended to produce an audience. Members of the association (and their wives) have long planned to attend "their" convention. Key men are not likely to absent themselves at the last minute. Second, something specific can be accomplished since the audience (including officers and directors) can commit the association to a course of action. (In the general community seminar, very few individuals in the audience are empowered to speak for their own groups.)

Thus, for example, on December 7, 1961, the National Association of Manufacturers—in annual congress assembled —set aside the full day for such a seminar. More than fifteen hundred captains of industry listened to discussions on the Total Threat of World Communism, Communist Espionage and Subversion in the U.S., the Question of National Defense, Economic Warfare, Communist Propaganda Techniques, and Businessmen in the Cold War. (Appendix, iv.)

Similarly, the Chamber of Commerce of the United States —at its annual conventions in 1962 and 1963—set aside a half day for lectures and panels on Communism, national defense, and foreign affairs. (Appendix, v.) In addition, the Chamber in 1961 produced a study kit, "Freedom vs. Communism: The Economics of Survival," consisting of a discussion leader's manual, a set of problems and exercises, and a set of eight pamphlets. Thousands of these study kits have been used by local Chambers and affiliated groups as well as by social science teachers across the country. (Appendix, vi.)

Among the many other associations and societies which during the past few years have in increasing numbers included on their convention agendas addresses on Communism and national defense are the Young Presidents Organization, Junior Chambers of Commerce, and the clergy and laymen of the Methodist Church. (Appendix, vii.)

Action Programs

Helping to educate others in national strategy is perhaps the most important long-term job for which citizens can volunteer. But, in the short run, there are targets of opportunity. Some Americans want to go beyond education, to action. The question arises, therefore, what can private citizens do to frustrate Communist subversion in Latin America, or to exploit Communist vulnerabilities behind the Iron Curtain?

Action programs, as opposed to education, require a delicate touch on both brake and throttle, and it is important to know the destination and credentials of one's fellow passengers, since some prefer roadside picnics to sustained and purposeful motoring.

However, there are many responsible organizations whose programs merit the attention of the American people. (A few of these are listed under paragraph viii of the Appendix following this chapter.) One such organization is the American Institute for Free Labor Development. (Appendix, ix.) A tribute to America's genius for achieving consensus, this Institute is supported financially by American business and the AFL-CIO. Its trustees include Peter Grace and George Meany.

AIFLD brings young Latin American labor leaders to this country for a three-month training course during which they begin to understand that "partnership in productivity" and not Marxist class warfare is the path to genuine economic development. They also learn how to cope with Communist efforts at subversion and infiltration. Serafino Romualdi, the labor leader who runs the training course, says: "Throughout the underdeveloped nations in Latin America as elsewhere, the symbol for labor and management is the wolf and the lamb." In contrast, the image promoted by the Institute is that of "a pair of oxen, equally strong, pulling the plow together."

The Institute has trained over twenty-five thousand men in at least seventeen Latin American countries. It has started a workers' credit bank in Peru. It sponsors low-cost housing in Mexico City and co-ops in rural areas where men are now learning they can do things for themselves. In short, the Institute is pioneering in that dimension in which civilians can help to eliminate those conditions which make for successful Communist insurgency.

Propaganda Analysis Is Everybody's Business

There are those who feel that talking about the Communist danger is flogging a dead horse, since everybody is against Communism and abhors Communist propaganda. But many people who deplore Communist propaganda in the *abstract* cannot recognize a *specific* propaganda theme when they hear it. Consider, for example, the following theme which enjoys current popularity in America in many versions and in a surprising number of places:

If we're going to be unemotional and objective, let's admit the cold war is largely our fault. After all, didn't we surround the Soviet Union with military bases? How would we feel if the Russians had maintained military bases in Canada, Mexico, and Bermuda since 1950?

We know how we would feel. We'd resent it! The Russians had missiles in Cuba for perhaps three weeks; and this country nearly succumbed to panic. But the Russian people have had to live with our American missiles surrounding their heartland for more than a decade. No wonder the Russians are belligerent and hostile. No wonder they react against our threatening posture.

If we want to do the fair thing, the just thing, the honorable thing, let's respond to Khrushchev's gesture of friendship in taking his missiles out of Cuba, remove our own missile bases that have so long terrorized the Russian people; and then, in an atmosphere of mutual confidence, our leaders and their leaders can negotiate lasting peace!

No one should infer that people who repeat this theme are, by definition, Communist, pro-Communist, or in any way disloyal. In all probability, they have simply failed to do their homework, preferring to think in clichés picked up at random from unverified sources. Nor can we blame these people too much, except for being mentally lazy. The hallmark of effective propaganda is precisely that it be unrecognized as such. The propagandist has not done his work well unless wholly innocent people transmit his message as their own. One must be careful, therefore, to avoid making the emotional assumption that whoever acts as a megaphone for falsehood must necessarily know the origin of the poison and be a conscious instrument of its dissemination.

What the propagandist has done, in constructing this theme, is to use a technical device known as the "trick of the time machine." The propagandist has rerun history, *inverted* cause and effect, and counted on imperfect memory to blur the sequence of events in the minds of his target audience.

Thus, the propagandist says: "America is largely responsible for all Cold War tensions, because she surrounded the Soviet Union with military bases, bullies the Russian people, and maintains those bases to give jobs to her generals and profits to her munitions makers."

What really happened? In what order? In 1945, at reckless pace, the United States tore apart the greatest war machine the world has ever known. We brought the boys home. We mothballed the fleet. We left the tanks to rust on far islands of the Pacific. Our bomber pilots took off their wings and went to school on the G.I. Bill of Rights. We beat our swords into plowshares and television sets. We stopped making the tools of war and began exporting food and medicine to all of the world —including the Soviet Union—through UNRRA, CARE, and literally scores of relief, refugee and religious organizations.

In 1945 America stood at the pinnacle of world power, armed with the monopoly of the atom. If we had been possessed of the ambition of the Caesars, we could have dominated the world.

Instead of using our monopoly of atomic weapons for conquest, we offered to share our dread secret with all the world, under the Baruch Plan, asking only international inspection and control. We wanted no empire; we asked for no territory from the defeated. Indeed, our military governments in Germany, Italy, and Japan behaved less like military governments than economic development corporations, helping the vanquished rebuild their shattered economies.

And what was Stalin doing while we were allegedly "terrorizing" the Russian people with UNRRA, demobilization, and the Baruch Plan? Stalin kept 4½ million men under arms; and with that vast army blackmailed Western Europe while tearing up the treaties of Yalta, Teheran, and Potsdam. He lured the legitimate government of Poland back from exile in Great Britain, had it murdered, and installed Communist puppets in its stead. He put Hungary, Rumania, Bulgaria, and the Baltic republics in straitjackets of terror.

Stalin subsidized the armies of Mao Tse-tung, who was clubbing free China into the Communist dungeon. He trained the Communist guerrillas that were shortly to penetrate Greece. He threatened Turkey and Iran. He kidnapped German engineers whom he needed to build his rockets, and subverted scientists from Canada, Great Britain, and the United States to give him the secrets he needed to accelerate his development of atomic and hydrogen weapons. He massed the Red

Army on the borders of Czechoslovakia while a Communist fifth column was burying freedom in Prague.

And then, after the Communists had been terrorizing all Europe, butchering whole nations, slandering our leaders, and subsidizing the largest espionage and propaganda network known to human history, *finally,* too late for eight hundred million people, we put up military bases to keep Stalin from seizing another third of the planet by the throat! For that purely defensive and somewhat tardy reaction, we Americans are now supposed to develop an "equal guilt complex" about the origin of the Cold War, apologize for the American affluence (which has made massive foreign aid possible), and suspect our own military of being the "mirror image" of the Red Army.

The battle of propaganda, aimed at undermining U.S. national will and understanding, rages not only in the Socialist press in Europe and teahouses of Asia, but in this country as well. Social science fiction, in novels and films, belabors the motives of American generals and civilian strategists who advocate balanced deterrence while it rationalizes Soviet aggression and dismisses Communist ideology as *our* delusion. The commercial success of this geopolitics of the absurd suggests the need for the private sector to continue in the direction pointed by the American Institute for Free Labor Development, the American Bar Association, and others.

Either we will create for ourselves a healthy climate of opinion based on facts, or we may have American opinion manipulated for us by conflict managers who have learned from Pavlov, Goebbels, and Lenin how to advance their goals through nonmilitary warfare. Indeed, if this country were ever pushed to the wall by Communism, the epitaph on our tombstone might read as follows:

Here lies the only civilization which perished at the peak of its power, with its power unused. Here lies a decent people who wanted love, not empire, and got neither; who tried to trade power for popularity and lost both.

Here lies a nation of advertisers who knew how to change consumer tastes in cigarettes, but were themselves man-lated on all the issues that really mattered to their salvation and survival.

Here died a sort of Lancelot in the Court of Nations who, granting all his grievous flaws, was still somehow the noblest knight of all; except this Lancelot, crippled with an undeserved guilt complex, let his weapons and ideals fall unused, and so condemned all mankind to the Thousand-Year Night of the Russian Bear and the Chinese Dragon.

NOTE

1. Chapter 8 of this book is an abstract from a recent study of the American Bar Association entitled "Peaceful Coexistence: Communist Blueprint for Conquest." This analysis of more than eleven thousand pages of current Communist literature concludes that the cold war may be entering an even more dangerous phase as both Soviet Russia and Red China increase subversion and guerrilla war.

APPENDIX

i. Chairman of the ABA Standing Committee on Education Against Communism is Morris I. Leibman, 208 South La Salle Street, Chicago, Illinois.

ii. ABA Presidents who have supported the Committee: John Satterfield, 1961–62; Sylvester Smith, 1962–63; Walter Craig, 1963–64; Lewis Powell, 1964–65; Edward W. Kuhn, 1965–66; Orison S. Marden, 1966–67.

iii. Appalachian State Teachers College, Boone, North Carolina; Director, Dr. William F. Troutman, Jr.—Arizona State College, Flagstaff, Arizona; Coordinator, Dr. Bernard Eissenstat.—East Carolina College, Greenville, North Carolina; Director, Dr. John M. Howell.—Georgia Southern College, Statesboro, Georgia; Co-Directors, Dr. Jack N. Averitt, Dr. Melvin W. Ecke. —John Carroll University, Cleveland, Ohio; Director, Dr. Michael S. Pap.—Paterson State College, Wayne, New Jersey; Director, Dr. Herbert Lee Ellis.—St. Louis University, St. Louis, Missouri; Co-Directors, Dr. Vincent C. Punzo, Rev. R. J. Henle, S.J.—University of South Carolina, Columbia, South Carolina; Director, Dr. Richard L. Walker.—University of Southern California, Los Angeles, California; Director, Dr. Rodger Swearingen.—Vanderbilt University, Nashville, Tennessee; Director, Dr. Ewing P. Shahan.